INSIDERS' GUIDE® TO

Savannah &
Hilton Head

INSIDERS' GUIDE® TO
Savannah & Hilton Head

NINTH EDITION

GEORGIA R. BYRD
REVISED AND UPDATED BY CHERYL LAUER

Guilford, Connecticut

Globe
Pequot

An imprint of Rowman & Littlefield

Distributed by NATIONAL BOOK NETWORK

Copyright © 2015 by Rowman & Littlefield

Insiders' Guide is a registered trademark of Rowman & Littlefield
Maps: XNR Productions, Inc. © Rowman & Littlefield

British Library Cataloguing in Publication Information Available

Library of Congress Cataloging-in-Publication Data Available

ISBN 978-1-4930-1269-5 (paperback)
ISBN 978-1-4930-1835-2 (e-book)

∞™ The paper used in this publication meets the minimum requirements of American National Standard for Information Sciences—Permanence of Paper for Printed Library Materials, ANSI/NISO Z39.48-1992.

All the information in this guidebook is subject to change. We recommend that you call ahead to obtain current information before traveling.

CONTENTS

ABOUT THE AUTHOR

Georgia R. Byrd, a native of the South, has been writing since her grandparents took her to visit Washington, DC, at the age of 8. It was there that she journaled every stop of a Grey Line Tour in a Reporter's Notebook, which she still has to this day.

Her work with *Savannah Magazine* received more than 50 regional and national awards for editing, graphic design, and art direction. Her articles have appeared in *Atlanta Magazine, Forbes, Southern Living,* and the *Atlanta Journal Constitution.* Her dream of working for *Forbes* magazine came true, and she has since produced advertising supplements, consulted for Forbes TV's travel shows, and worked with yachting companies all over the world promoting yachts in *Forbes.* Her graphic design and marketing skills have included publication work for the Georgia Ports Authority and other Savannah clients. She is also an author and contributor to several tabletop books, including *Megayachts of the World,* published by Edisea, Ltd., and *Romantic Days & Nights in Savannah* (Globe Pequot). She is the coauthor of *The History of Aviation in Savannah* (Savannah Airport Commission) and *Seasons of Savannah,* published by the Savannah College of Art and Design. She has appeared on the Travel Channel, CNN, *Good Morning America,* and the *Today Show* as a travel and yachting consultant.

Georgia is married to advertising photographer Joseph Byrd, and is the mother of Whit, a police officer; and Ammie, a school principal.

ABOUT THE REVISOR

Cheryl Lauer has called Savannah home for more than 30 years and is grateful to live in an area with a beautiful and vibrant historic district, which has become a national architectural showcase, and near the picturesque seaside communities of Tybee Island and Hilton Head, South Carolina. Born and reared in the Pocono Mountain region of Pennsylvania, some days she is still in awe that her home now is surrounded by palm trees.

Cheryl has worked as a reporter in Atlanta and Savannah, retiring from the *Savannah Morning News* after covering news and feature stories mainly from the island communities of Chatham County. She has also written for the *Savannah Magazine* and the Georgia Ports Authority's magazine, *AnchorAge.* She is pleased to return to work on the *Insiders' Guide to Savannah & Hilton Head,* having served as the photography editor in the book's first edition.

Cheryl and her husband, Michael Richter, live on Talahi Island in Chatham County. Their home is about 10 minutes east of the historic district and about 10 minutes to the beach at Tybee. Their son Cason, a home-schooled graduate, attends college in Savannah.

HOW TO USE THIS BOOK

The goal is for this book to be a personal guide that will lead you through Savannah and Hilton Head Island's most popular attractions, restaurants, and accommodations, as well as those special places that only an "insider" could reveal. Before you leave home, purchase a camera bag, backpack, or purse large enough to accommodate this book, as well as your cameras, bug spray, and personal necessities. When you arrive, don your most comfortable walking shoes. Use this *Insiders' Guide* as a constant reference as you explore our city and parts of the South Carolina Lowcountry.

Arranged by subjects, it is recommended that you read this guidebook in full prior to leaving home. Highlight some of your interests and familiarize yourself with the area's history that is a vital part of her present. Rent the film *Midnight in the Garden of Good and Evil,* or better yet, read the best-selling book by John Berendt. You'll be enchanted before you ever step foot here, and your knowledge of the characters and places made famous by authors and screenwriters will be better appreciated. Delve into the history of the city.

The local area is divided into four geographical sections (Historic District, the Islands, Southside/Midtown, and West Chatham) with an explanation of the territory outlined in the Area Overview chapter. The maps are an excellent way to get a good sense of the geographical areas and hence guide you through the city by foot, carriage, trolley, or car. Within the chapters, restaurants, accommodations, attractions, and other points of interest are arranged alphabetically for quick reference. Another good way to find specific topics of interest is by looking in the extensive index in the back of the book. You'll note that the area code for almost every phone number listed is 912 (843 for places in South Carolina). Also look for Insiders' Tips—marked with an **i** that let you in on local secrets.

This edition also reflects highways and roads that are identified by abbreviations. They include: highways, which are denoted by I- for interstate, US for appropriate two-laned (and highways that are not interstates) roads, SR (or an abbreviation of the state) for State Routes or State Highways. And if all else fails, ask a Savannahian for directions if you're lost. This is a city overflowing with hospitality, and you'll find that no one is too busy to help you find your way.

Moving to Savannah or already live here? Be sure to check out the back of the book, where you will find the **Living Here** appendix that offers sections on relocation and real estate, retirement, education and child care, and health care.

Thanks to this guide book, visitors who fly through Savannah going to Hilton Head Island will understand that they are not in Hilton Head when they deplane in Savannah. The hour or so (depending on traffic to the island) drive to Hilton Head Island from the Savannah airport will become much less a trek of boredom as this edition also captures and highlights this popular tourist destination and offers some fun stops along the way. In turn, we have also devoted an entire chapter to Savannah's sister beach, Tybee Island, which is part of Chatham County but very separate and distinct from Savannah, and the neighboring islands.

ACCOMMODATIONS PRICE CODE

Dollar signs indicate the average cost for a one-night stay for two adults, not including taxes, gratuities, or add-on amenities. Many establishments have both high-season and off-season rates, and they define "season" differently, so check current prices, usually posted on the facilities' websites. Most establishments charge $10 to $25 extra for additional guests. Please inquire about additional fees when you call for reservations. Again, remember that reservations are essential.

$................less than $110
$$ ....$110 to $150
$$$ ....$150 to $200
$$$$..............$200 to $250
$$$$$..........more than $250

RESTAURANT PRICE CODE

The price code is based on the cost of an average meal for two, excluding drinks, dessert, or tip.

$.................less than $30
$$ ....$30 to $50
$$$ ....more than $50

WELCOME TO SAVANNAH & HILTON HEAD ISLAND

Savannah is called the Hostess City, and for good reason. Even before the tourism business blossomed in the 1980s, Savannah was greeting visitors through its international port and its role as the largest city in the surrounding rural plain.

Savannah's devotion to historic preservation got started in earnest in the mid-1950s. Without the efforts of a handful of determined society ladies, most of the historic treasures you travel to Savannah to see would not exist, but would be buried under parking lots and urban sprawl. But along with the appreciation of the old is an active slice of the new: a booming container port, the construction of the most advanced corporate jets in the world, a swelling university populace studying everything for art to marine science.

Not all the scenery here is from the hands of humankind, not by a long stretch. Savannah and environs boast acres of beautiful, oxygen-generating saltwater marsh, towering live oak trees, beaches that are nesting grounds for endangered sea turtles and a stretch of ocean that is the breeding ground for the rare right whale.

Called one of America's most beautiful cities, Savannah—the oldest city in Georgia—sits near the mouth of the Savannah River, which forms the boundary between Georgia and South Carolina. Drive across the picturesque Talmadge Bridge over the Savannah River and by the time you're back over dry land, you're in another state.

Thanks for joining us here in what was the final of the original 13 British colonies that eventually made up a unique revolutionary country of its own. We've kept some of the best parts of that country's history—as well as reminders of some of its most painful moments—and we're delighted to share them with you.

AREA OVERVIEW

If you approach Savannah from the west after traveling the monotonous, pine-lined stretch of I-16 from Macon and follow through to the interstate's end in the Hostess City, you'll arrive in the midst of a lavishly beautiful part of the downtown Historic District, where architectural wonders unfold in the form of thick moss-drenched live oaks, townhomes, inns, and private residences.

If you arrive by car across the graceful cable-span bridge called the Talmadge Memorial, which crosses the winding Savannah River and connects South Carolina to Georgia, the city unfurls ahead and below you. Cresting the bridge, 196 feet above the water and looking down and ahead toward your destination, you'll see the city of Savannah. Be careful not to get distracted as you drive, but if you're the passenger, look over to your left. More than likely, you'll see a large yacht or two anchored at the Westin. There could be one or two colorful ferries transporting visitors to and from the Savannah riverfront over to Hutchinson Island, the

Greater Savannah Area

Downtown Savannah

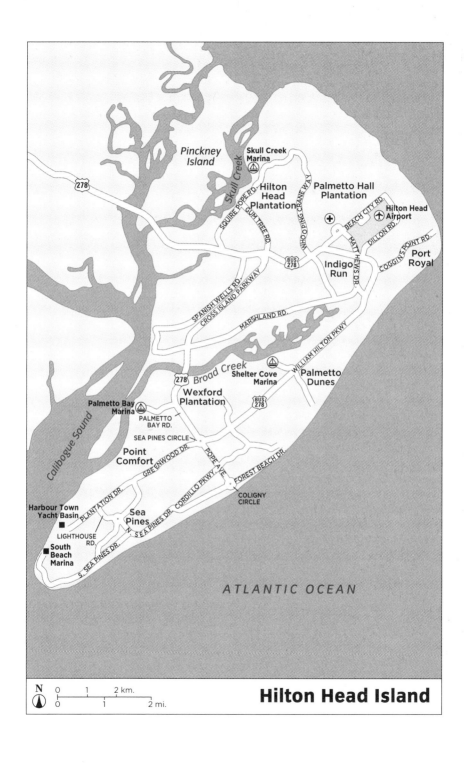

Pinckney
Island

Skull Creek
Marina

278

Squire Pope Rd.

Gum Tree Rd.

Whooping Crane Way

Hilton
Head
Plantation

Palmetto Hall
Plantation

Beach City Rd.

Hilton Head
Airport

Dillon Rd.

Coggins Point Rd.

Port
Royal

BUS 278

Matthews Dr.

Indigo
Run

Spanish Wells Rd.

Cross Island Parkway

MARSHLAND RD.

William Hilton Pkwy

278

Broad Creek

Shelter Cove
Marina

Palmetto
Dunes

Wexford
Plantation

BUS 278

Palmetto Bay
Marina

PALMETTO
BAY RD.

SEA PINES CIRCLE

Caibogue Sound

Point
Comfort

GREENWOOD DR.

POPE AVE.

FOREST BEACH DR.

CORDILLO PKWY

COLIGNY
CIRCLE

Harbour Town
Yacht Basin

PLANTATION DR.

Sea
Pines

SEA PINES DR.

LIGHTHOUSE
RD.

South
Beach
Marina

S. SEA PINES DR.

ATLANTIC OCEAN

N

0   1   2 km.

0   1   2 mi.

Hilton Head Island

home of a pristine Troon-managed 18-hole golf course. Across the river, still looking left as you descend the bridge, you'll see the gold-domed City Hall. It will glisten if the day is sunny, and the view of the Cathedral of St. John the Baptist's twin spires will signal that you are indeed mere minutes from your destination.

Straight ahead is a network of roadways, with some of the thoroughfares leading to the city's south side and to West Chatham County, where many Savannahians live and many more do their shopping in more modern buildings. Finally, there are hints of the tropics and the palm trees and massive oaks that remind you that you are indeed in the Old South.

SAVANNAH STATISTICS

Savannah is the seat of government of Chatham County, and the sixth most populous county in the largest state (in terms of area) east of the Mississippi River. Some 278,434 (*US Census Bureau 2013) people live in Chatham County, with 347,611 residing in the metropolitan statistical area that includes the surrounding bedroom counties. About a quarter of the county's 438 square miles are unincorporated, and there are also seven other municipalities within Chatham's borders: Bloomingdale, Garden City, Port Wentworth, Pooler, Thunderbolt, Vernonburg, and the city of Tybee Island.

Due to the diverse interests and backgrounds that exist here, Savannah's major employers vary from industrial to educational and entrepreneurial. As a port community that dates back to 1733, Savannah's a city that assumes many roles, serving as a harbor, a center of higher education, a tourist destination, a site for industrial plants, a home to the military, and a breeding ground for artists and historic preservationists. Due to its history and aesthetic magnetism, the city is a virtual melting pot. For instance,

take a seat on one of many benches in the squares of the Historic District and you'll most likely observe the mix: international art students hiking to and from class with projects in tow, society matrons chatting with neighbors, a herd of Girl Scouts on foot, corporate executives enjoying bagged lunches, and people like yourself watching people like yourself.

In keeping true to her military and industrial history, Savannah is home to Hunter Army Airfield and nearby (about 50 miles south) Fort Stewart military bases. Combined, the two bases employ more than 42,000 people and generate an annual direct federal expenditure of $1.4 billion dollars. The Georgia Ports Authority's (GPA) Garden City facilities comprise 1,200 acres, North America's largest single-terminal container facility and closing in on becoming its busiest. Gulfstream Aerospace Corporation, home of the world's fastest corporate jets, is headquartered here.

Five industries account for relatively equal shares of employment in the metropolitan Savannah area, further attesting to the area's healthy, diverse industry mix: retail trade, professional and business services, education and health services, leisure and hospitality, and state and local government. Manufacturers continue to account for nearly 9 percent of the area's jobs.

The Savannah area is blessed with a climate classified as semitropical. Average seasonal temperatures are, in degrees Fahrenheit, 51 in winter, 66 in spring, 81 in summer, and 68 in autumn. Remember, though, that averages are pretty useless when it comes to weather: On your typical summer day, the daybreak temp of 72 is rapidly climbing into the 90s, with humidity to match.

Winters are brisk, and rarely is there a morning that provokes a heavy coat. If the day calls for one, more than likely you'll be shedding it by lunchtime so stay close to your hotel or be prepared to tote your jacket as the day warms up.

More accurately, according to the Savannah Area Chamber of Commerce, the city on average experiences 67 days each year when the mercury climbs higher than 90 degrees.

Winters are fairly mild, with the temperature dipping below freezing an average of (ironically) 32 days a year. We seldom see snow, and the descent of even a few flakes is cause for excitement. The average annual rainfall is 49 inches, and Mother Nature delivers some intense downpours now and then, particularly during summer afternoons, so if this is your choice for a visit, heed this warning and bring a stylish pair of rain boots. Because Savannah is in a low-lying area and much of the city's sewer system is antiquated, streets are prone to flooding when tides are high—be careful if you're driving around and get caught in a sudden storm.

Also, check the weather as you venture here between June 1 and November 30, the designated hurricane season. Being on the southeast coast, Savannah occasionally finds itself threatened by hurricanes. In recent years, the city has been spared the destruction caused by major storms. Savannah had close calls from Hurricane Hugo in 1989, Bertha in 1996, and Floyd in 1999, but the last hurricane to hit here was David in 1979, when winds as strong as 90 mph caused widespread power outages that lasted for weeks.

That gives you the big picture. Now let's look more closely at the four areas into which we've divided the county.

HERE'S LOOKING AT YOU, SAVANNAH

Historic District

When mentioning the Historic District, we're actually referring to the area of downtown where there are 22 picturesque squares with restaurants, inns, personal residences, and accommodations. Other neighborhoods may have historic designations of one type or another, but for clarity's sake, our reference is to the classic downtown sector.

Savannah's downtown area is bordered by the Savannah River on the north, East Broad Street on the east, Park Avenue on the south, and Martin Luther King Jr. Boulevard on the west. Downtown is the oldest and most colorful part of the city—James Oglethorpe landed here when he arrived and founded Georgia more than 270 years ago. The 2.5-square-mile Historic District encompasses the 24 city squares Oglethorpe designed in his original plans. (Although his original plans called for 24 squares, there are presently 22 remaining.)

Today those squares still provide an intimate ambience unmatched by any other area of the city. Spend at least a day exploring the squares we like to call "a performance in progress." Like an ongoing film with extraordinary cinematography, they are a constant source of motion with characters changing by the minute. In summer, musicians perform on Johnson Square's monument steps for tourists and employees lunching downtown. On any given day in any given square, couples nestle on benches shaded by live oak trees with enormous branches that are laced with Spanish moss. Horse-drawn carriages click past carrying entire families on holiday and brides and grooms to and from historic churches on the weekends, enhancing the squares' theatrics. The walled gardens of homes surrounding the squares harbor history and a captivating kaleidoscope of intriguing tales and colorful characters.

Apart from the squares, downtown is also the place for fun, Southern eating at its best, and shopping on foot. The city's main thoroughfare, Broughton Street, was once the main shopping district and has captured the interest of locals and tourists with unique and local whimsical boutiques along with its share of chains like Gap and Banana Republic.

Downtown also plays host to festivals, with many of Savannah's major annual events being held along the river, in City Market, and at Forsyth Park, a lush, green playground on Bull Street where a new amphitheater and cafe attract cultural and even more outdoor activities.

Downtown's Johnson Square is called the city's financial district. However, when you actually visit this square, you forget all about money. Situated in the center of several banks is a striking monument to Nathaniel Greene, the Revolutionary War hero. There are fountains at each end that glisten in the afternoon sunlight. The massive branches of the live oaks cover the square like a beautiful web, the Spanish moss dripping like lace on a wedding gown train, and they create a surreal ambience that is characteristic of many other areas of downtown.

Throughout downtown, striking museums such as the Telfair Academy of Arts and Sciences bring a little bit of a European flair to this Southern city. Enhancing the downtown area are a great number of buildings, homes, and inns that have been delicately restored to splendor by their owners.

Literal interpretations of Savannah's cartography might be a bit confusing because names don't always match up to positions. By map, the Historic District is in the northern part of town. That's because Savannah's birthplace was on a bluff on the south bank of the river, causing the heart of the city to be north of everything else. When you're in downtown Savannah, you can't go much farther north and still be in Georgia. Savannah has not grown in that direction, across the north channel of the Savannah River (which is known as the Back River), because what's over there is mostly marshland, and it's also South Carolina.

So when you're downtown on River Street gazing across the south channel of the Savannah River, you're looking at Hutchinson Island, a small part of Georgia that's undergone development to its advantage. Formerly a literal eyesore, the marshland has emerged in the form of a $98 million resort owned by Westin. The resort complex towers above the flat island like a giant sand castle with a lush tropical appeal. Aesthetically, the project has been a great success and makes a splendid accompaniment to the $83.5 million Savannah International Trade and Convention Center (opened there in mid-2000). The Westin resort complex is a 403-room, 16-story hotel that's emblematic of the growth in tourism being experienced by the city.

Because Savannah hasn't been able to expand much to the north, most early development was southward, and much recent growth has been to the east and west.

Islands

Driving eastward on US 80 toward Tybee Island, you'll pass Chatham County's inshore islands. This is where huge residential growth has occurred partly due to the island ambience, proximity to the beach, and distance to downtown. One can live on any one of "the islands" and get to work downtown in about 10 to 15 minutes, depending on the time of day and location of the workplace. Although these islands are not on the Atlantic Ocean, they're separated from the mainland and neighboring islands by salt marsh, rivers, and tidal creeks. The islands in our Islands area are those immediately east of Savannah—Oatland, Talahi, Whitemarsh, and Wilmington—and those southeast of the city—Dutch, Skidaway, and Isle of Hope. Because of its unique qualities and status as a destination for tourists, we have devoted a separate chapter to Tybee Island, which is also east of Savannah.

The residential development of the eastside islands took off in the late 1980s, and Whitemarsh Island (pronounced WHIT-marsh) was the fastest-growing part of the county in 1996, with Wilmington Island not far behind. Growth slowed on Whitemarsh in 1997, with most of the island being built out, but residential development continued on Wilmington, the fastest-growing part of Chatham during 1998. Most of the building on these islands has been residential, although a large shopping center and three schools have been constructed on Whitemarsh in recent years.

Despite the buildup, the eastside islands, particularly Wilmington Island, retain a natural beauty and laid-back quality. Days are lazy and many islanders get around by bike. Spring evenings are filled with laughter and cheering from the crowds at little league baseball and church league softball games that are ongoing on Wilmington Island. It's safe enough to take an evening stroll on any of this island's streets, look up at a sky brilliant with stars, and listen to the back and forth hoots from owls. For the most part, the eastside islands remain quiet havens where folks sit on their docks and watch the marsh turn from gold to green as the seasons change; where oaks festooned with Spanish moss bend over roadways to create cool, verdant tunnels; where you can hop in your car, drive around the corner, and fetch fresh seafood from rustic markets. You can grocery shop in your flip-flops and stand in line at the banks with all your neighbors.

Tiny Thunderbolt, a quaint fishing village, is the jumping-off point before you cross the Wilmington River and hit the Islands Area. This village is also home of Thunderbolt Marine, Inc., a 25-acre site along the Wilmington River where marine skills are utilized to refit megayachts owned by the world's billionaires and registered in exotic parts of the world.

Farther to the south, you'll find the gated residential enclave of Dutch Island; Skidaway Island, site of the Landings, a private community of upscale homes, also gated; and Isle of Hope, distinguished by its quaint cottages, charming Southern homes, and picturesque docks where families enjoy swimming, boating, and fishing. The Landings covers much of Skidaway Island with a gated development of homes, deepwater marinas, golf courses, a fitness center, clubhouses, tennis courts, and more than 40 miles of biking and nature trails.

Isle of Hope is entirely residential except for the marina on Bluff Drive. Bluff Drive is a lovely lane running alongside the Skidaway River, and it's our choice as the Savannah area's most picturesque street. The isle is also the location of Wormsloe Historic Site, the place where one of Georgia's first settlers constructed a colonial estate.

Southside/Midtown

Southside/Midtown is the vast area south of the Historic District. Note that the locals refer to the northern portion of this area as Midtown. Midtown starts in the vicinity of the southern end of Forsyth Park and runs south to DeRenne Avenue, although some folks might say it extends all the way to Oglethorpe Mall. Most of Savannah's Victorian District and all of the Thomas Square Streetcar Historic District are in Midtown. The districts, which are on the National Register of Historic Places, are filled with Victorian-style frame houses.

That distinction also applies to Ardsley Park and Chatham Crescent, two other areas in Midtown. Among the streets of Ardsley Park is one of Savannah's prettiest—oak- and azalea-lined Washington Avenue. At the eastern end of the avenue is Daffin Park, site of a small lake and public tennis courts and athletic fields used by recreation league teams playing baseball, softball, football, and soccer. Historic Grayson Stadium, a classic baseball stadium, stands among the tall pines in the eastern portion of the park.

More Useful Info

Driving laws: Seat belts mandatory for occupants of the front seat of a vehicle and all occupants younger than 18; safety restraining systems required for children younger than 6 years old, but seat belts will suffice for those who are 4 feet 9 inches and taller. Maximum speed limit under normal conditions 55 mph, 70 mph on rural interstates, and 65 mph on urban interstates. Speed limit decreases to 30 mph in business and residential districts. Headlights required between the half hour after sunset and the half hour before sunrise and when raining.

Alcohol laws: Drinking by persons younger than age 21 prohibited. Motorists 21 years and older considered under the influence of intoxicants when 0.08 gram or more by alcohol is present in the blood; for those younger than 21, the limit is 0.02 gram.

The city has an unusually liberal "go cup" policy. Drinking on city streets prohibited except in the area bounded generally by the city limits on the north, West Boundary Street on the west, Jones Street on the south, and East Broad Street on the east. In this area, drinking from cans, bottles, or glasses is prohibited, and paper or plastic cups containing alcoholic beverages must not exceed 16 fluid ounces. Your bartender can keep you posted on the finer points.

Daily newspaper: *Savannah Morning News*

Sales tax: 7 percent (4 percent state, 3 percent local option) on the purchase of all goods and some services except groceries and prescriptions.

Room tax: 6 percent

Information for tourists: Savannah Area Chamber of Commerce/Visit Savannah, 101 E. Bay St., Savannah, GA 31401; (912) 644-6400; savannah visit.com.

You'll find several shopping centers in Midtown, the main library (which has been renovated extensively), and much of Savannah's health-care community. Clustered just north of DeRenne Avenue, between Reynolds Street and the Truman Parkway, are numerous doctors' offices, pharmacies, medical laboratories, and two of the city's hospitals, Memorial University Medical Center and Candler Hospital. Once south of DeRenne, you are in the part of town most locals call the Southside. It's an area of subdivisions, churches, recreational facilities, and commercial development. Savannah's main roadway, Abercorn Street, evolves from a historical setting to the area's primary retail strip where shopping centers, malls, car dealerships, and fast-food restaurants reign. We think of Abercorn south of DeRenne as the Land of a Thousand Curb Cuts. That's an exaggeration, but not much of one. The six-lane thoroughfare is nicked by the myriad entrances and exits to and from business establishments, used-car lots, strip shopping centers, and megastores selling building materials, pet supplies, party goods, books, liquor, and office equipment. Interrupting this cascade of commercialism on Abercorn are the St. Joseph's Hospital campus and the doctors' offices that have sprung up around it and the campus of Armstrong State University. The area we've designated as Southside/Midtown is also home to several other institutions of higher education, including

Savannah State University, Savannah Technical College, and South University.

Outdoor activities abound in the Southside. Just east and southeast of Oglethorpe Mall is Bacon Park, a city- and county-owned recreational complex consisting of softball diamonds, soccer fields, tennis courts, a public golf course, a stadium where high school football teams play, an aquatic center, and a lake surrounded by a walking/jogging track. Nearby is the site of the Chatham County track and field complex inside T. A. Wright Stadium at Savannah State University. Among the features of this world-class facility are an eight-lane track, a dual pole vault runway, a javelin runway, a steeple-chase water jump, and shot put, discus, and hammer-throw circles.

The Southside past Oglethorpe Mall is where suburbia evolved in the 1960s and 1970s, mainly in the sprawling subdivision of Windsor Forest. Residential growth has continued in recent years farther out Abercorn Street at Georgetown, one of the fastest-growing areas in Chatham County during the 1990s. This area extends almost to I-95 and includes a nice and affordable 18-hole Henderson Golf Club, where magnificent live oaks and lush magnolia trees provide a challenging and natural place to enjoy an afternoon.

To the west of the residential and commercial development of the Southside is Hunter Army Airfield, a 5,400-acre military post and site of the Army's longest runway. Hunter and Fort Stewart are the homes of a Ranger battalion, units of the Third Infantry Division (Mechanized), and a Coast Guard air

i Tiny, almost invisible sand gnats appear in spring and fall, and can be successfully repelled with the locals' home remedy of liberal applications of Avon's Skin-So-Soft. If bitten, try not to scratch: the bumps will go away in about an hour if you leave them be.

i Savannahians were thrilled in February 2010, when snow fell in the city and outlying areas. Snow hadn't been seen in the area since December 1989—more than a decade-long gap. That prompted many to sing one of the all-time favorite songs about wintry weather that was written by a onetime resident, James L. Pierpont. He penned the words to "Jingle Bells" and worked as an organist at the Unitarian church in Savannah.

station. The bulk of the division is based an hour away at Fort Stewart, the largest Army installation east of the Mississippi River. With its 11,375-foot runway, Hunter serves as a location from which troops and equipment of the Third can be deployed throughout the world.

One of Chatham's municipalities is in Southside/Midtown: Vernonburg, a settlement of a hundred or so souls who reside on a handful of streets leading to the banks of the Vernon River. South of Vernonburg are the rustic residential communities of Beaulieu and Coffee Bluff.

West Chatham

Once an industrial stronghold surrounded by pine trees, West Chatham has retained that identity but added a residential boom of everything from starter homes to gated mini-mansion enclaves. Near and along I-95, this area is home to industry, i.e., companies that produce paper products, massive structures where sleek corporate jets are built and serviced, and a British company that builds bright yellow backhoe loaders. Home of the county's largest manufacturer, Gulfstream Aerospace Corporation, which employs 10,126 people (per the Savannah Economic Development Authority) and produces corporate jet aircraft, West Chatham is also the site of the headquarters of the

Georgia Ports Authority, which operates two deepwater terminals on the Savannah River. Most of the cargo handled on Savannah's docks is shipped in containers, and the city is one of the busiest container ports in the US. If you don't believe it, settle on a bench along the riverfront and watch the ships bearing containers go in and out.

Many of the people who work at the port and the industries west of Savannah live in West Chatham's four municipalities— Garden City, Port Wentworth, Bloomingdale, and the current king of residential and retail development, Pooler. West Chatham is also the location of Savannah/Hilton Head International Airport.

TRAVEL INSTRUCTIONS & RESOURCES

Once you get here, there are several options to get you around, although the best way is still the oldest way—on foot, or as you might hear it called, "riding shank's mare." If you aren't interested in hoofing it, though, you'll find plenty of taxis, a public bus system, a full array of rental car agencies, even pedicabs, which are kind of a cross between a tricycle and a rickshaw, driven by strong-legged guides.

For the adventurous tourist, Segway of Savannah offers an ecofriendly way to glide through Savannah's Historic District. You won't find elaborate freeway systems with HOV lanes or throngs of harried commuters rushing to catch their five o'clock train. Sorry, Savannah's stage is set to a slower song, and her neighborly disposition makes her a city to be enjoyed at a leisurely pace.

Achieving the Southern way of seizing the day is easy: Take a deep breath and pretend there are no clocks or schedules. To a visitor, it may seem like Savannahians tackle the daily rigors of getting from one place to another in the same way. They are slow to anger and even slower to drive.

On the outskirts of town, suburban sprawl has given us a fairly recent phenomenon—some commuter-hour congestion, especially on I-16 bound for the bedrooms of Effingham County, or on Abercorn Street's southern extremes approaching the Georgetown neighborhood and the entrance to I-95 en route to Richmond Hill's neighborhoods in adjacent Bryan County.

So what happens if your navigation system fails or you're lost? Ask a local. More likely than not, he or she will be happy to get you headed in the right direction. Those of us who live or work in the Historic District are particularly experienced at giving directions.

Directions come with a caution. Although Savannah's aesthetics may lure you out at midnight, remember this: Take all precautions when walking the streets at night.

GETTING HERE

By Air

SAVANNAH/HILTON HEAD INTERNA-TIONAL AIRPORT, 400 Airways Ave.; (912) 964-0514; savannahairport.com. The Savannah/Hilton Head International Airport is about 10 miles north of Savannah. The exit number off I-95 is 104. Delta (800-221-1212; delta.com), and US Airways (800-428-4322; usairways.com) are the largest carriers and also have been with the airport the longest. Other airlines include JetBlue (800-538-2583, jetblue.com), United (800-864-8331; united .com), and American Airlines (800-433-7300; aa.com). Nonstop flights are available via various carriers to Atlanta, Charlotte, Newark, Cincinnati, Houston, Miami, New York (La Guardia), Washington, DC (Dulles), Dallas,

Detroit, Chicago (O'Hare), and Philadelphia. On weekends, Pittsburgh is an additional nonstop destination from here.

The lineup at the airport is prone to change, so stay abreast of flights and airlines via the airport's website. The Airport Commission is on a constant mission to keep the flight selection competitive and cost-effective. It's also easy to confirm flight arrivals and departures because the website stays current.

Not to mislead, the proper name—Savannah/Hilton Head International Airport—is correct, even though there are currently no international flights. (The name was amended to include Hilton Head since about half of the passenger traffic is bound there.)

Rental Cars

Passengers have a choice of several rental-car agencies on the premises, although they tend to change and you should call ahead if it is particularly important to you to deal with a specific car rental agency. Serving Savannah/ Hilton Head International are Alamo (888-826-6893; alamo.com), Avis (800-831-2847; avis .com), Budget (800-527-0700; budget.com), Dollar Rent A Car (866-745-5063; dollar.com), Enterprise (800-736-8222; enterprise.com), Hertz (800-654-3131; hertz.com), National (800-227-7368; nationalcar.com), and Thrifty (800-367-2277; thrifty.com).

Taxi and Shuttle Service

The airport distributes a rate brochure (available either outside near all the cabs or inside near the baggage claim) that gives passengers an idea of what it will cost to take a taxi to local bed-and-breakfasts, hotels, motels, and inns. Maximum rates, set by the Savannah City Council, are $25 to the Historic District, $34 to Hutchinson Island, $53 to Tybee Island, $85 to Hilton Head Island, $60 to Bluffton, South Carolina, $60 to The Landings

on Skidaway Island; and between $33 and $41 to Savannah's Southside. Cabbies are allowed to charge an additional $5 per passenger in Georgia and $10 per passenger after the first two bound for South Carolina.

Taxi service at the airport can be arranged by calling the taxi stand at (912) 964-8016, or by simply showing up at the cab stand curbside, which is clearly marked and impossible to miss. We've never seen the cab stand unattended. Low Country Adventures (800-681-8212) provides airport shuttle service to and from Hilton Head (see our Hilton Head chapter).

Shuttles are a comfortable and efficient alternative to taxis. K Shuttle offers scheduled shuttle service from Savannah/Hilton Head International Airport to Hilton Head. They can be reached by calling (877) 243-2050. The rates are $44 one-way and $79 round-trip. All passengers arriving into the Savannah airport desiring K Shuttle services must have a prearranged reservation.

There is no scheduled provider of limousine service to and from the airport. However, there are several private limousine services in the city, and these are listed later in this chapter. If you are interested in a ride from the airport, always inquire when calling as to whether the company has a permit to serve the airport.

By Train

AMTRAK, 2611 Seaboard Coastline Dr.; (912) 234-2611, (800) 872-7245. The *Silver Meteor* and *Silver Star* take turns coming into Savannah as part of their treks along the Eastern Seaboard. Savannah is in the New York–Miami Amtrak corridor, and travelers have a choice of several departure times each day. Note that there is no train service currently to Atlanta, an omission advocacy groups periodically tackle.

The Amtrak station is about 4 miles from the Historic District. Heading west on I-16, take the Chatham Parkway exit. At the stop sign turn left, then take your first right. The station is open every day 4:30 a.m. to noon and 4:30 p.m. to midnight. Taxicabs are at the station when each train pulls in. Rental cars are not available at the station.

By Bus

GREYHOUND BUS LINES, 610 W. Oglethorpe Ave.; (912) 233-8186; grey hound.com. Savannah is on Greyhound Bus Lines' busiest eastern corridor—the stretch between New York City and Miami. Buses depart the city 23 times a day, 7 days a week, with the most frequent departures, as would be expected, headed north toward New York and south to Miami. There are also westbound options. If you are coming to Savannah on Greyhound, you will disembark at the terminal on the far western reaches of Oglethorpe Avenue, one of the Historic District's main thoroughfares. Head out the front door of the station and walk to your left along Oglethorpe—within a few blocks you will be in the heart of the Historic District. If you arrive at night, use extreme caution when walking, as you would in any city. The bus station's locale used to be on the fringes of the restored Historic District, but revitalization has moved into the area, and you'll find more foot traffic and less gritty surroundings. Taxi service is available at the bus terminal.

By Car

Savannah is reachable by car via two major interstates: I-95 from the north and south and I-16 running east and west. I-95 is the main artery along the Eastern Seaboard, stretching from Maine to the tip of Florida. This interstate is extremely congested in the Savannah area during spring, when snowbirds and spring-breakers are heading south for some winter relief, so drive with caution and expect some delays near the exits. I-16

cuts an east west path across middle Georgia before merging with I-75, which takes you into Atlanta. The following information is a helpful rundown on how to get to the main geographical sections of the city from either of these interstates.

To the Historic District

The best option to get to the Historic District is to use I-16 heading east. There are a couple of clearly marked exits for downtown, but we suggest the one for Liberty Street. Want to swing by the Savannah Visitor Information Center for directions and advice first? As you enter downtown from the interstate, take your first left onto Liberty Street, then your next right onto Martin Luther King Jr. Boulevard (MLK); or take the Louisville Road exit, which is near the end of the interstate and has signs guiding you to the visitor center. You are now essentially a block from the traffic light where the interstate dumped you. The visitor center on the western side of MLK, calling for a tricky left-hand turn into the parking lot. I-95 doesn't go directly into the city, so if you are traveling the north-south route, you'll need to take I-16 (the exit is clearly marked, although it features a wicked curve and tricky dual merge) for the final 10 miles or so.

To the Islands

There are a couple of options to get you to Tybee or the eastern islands of Oatland, Talahi, Whitemarsh, and Wilmington. Take I-16 into the Historic District and get on any northbound street until you reach Bay Street. Continue east on Bay Street, which, in less than a mile, merges with President Street, then becomes President Street Extension. Follow the President Street Extension until it becomes Islands Expressway. In about 3 miles, it will merge with US 80, which is the main route to Tybee and the eastern islands.

A second option to get you to Tybee, along with the eastern and southeastern islands (Dutch and Isle of Hope), involves leaving I-16 at the 37th Street exit. Take 37th Street to Abercorn Street, take a right, then proceed to Victory Drive, where you will turn left (east). To reach Skidaway Island, take a right off Victory onto Waters Avenue. To reach the southeastern islands, look for Skidaway Road off Victory Drive and take a right to get to Dutch Island and Isle of Hope. If you continue east on Victory, it will become US 80, which will take you to the eastern islands and Tybee.

To Southside/Midtown

If you are staying near the Southside, you might want to consider exiting I-95 at SR 204 in the southern reaches of the county, about 20 miles south of the Historic District. SR 204 is also Abercorn Street, the main north-south thoroughfare running throughout the entire city. After exiting, head north. After about 3 miles you will enter the Southside—the city's main commercial district, with strip shopping centers, hotels, car dealerships, and Savannah's malls.

Another option to get to the Southside or Midtown area from downtown is Bay Street: Head east down Bay Street to President Street Extension. Take the ramp to Truman Parkway (south). You may exit right onto DeRenne Avenue, a main east-west thoroughfare, or depending on your destination, continue south on "the Truman" to Eisenhower Drive or Montgomery Crossroads. Each exit (DeRenne, Eisenhower, or Montgomery Crossroads) will eventually cross Abercorn. If you turn left on Abercorn, you'll head south and eventually hit I-95. If you turn right, you'll be driving in the direction of downtown (to the left or right).

To West Chatham

The West Chatham communities of Pooler, Bloomingdale, and Garden City are all accessible from I-16 via various marked exits. From I-95 you can also take the Pooler Parkway, which will connect you to US 80 and take you through Bloomingdale, Pooler, and Garden City.

GETTING AROUND

Once you have made it to Savannah, there are several ways you can navigate within the city—from public transportation to a comfortable pair of shoes. Following are some ideas for getting around and a few things to watch out for while traversing the town.

Sampling Savannah

Historic District

Slip on your most comfortable pair of walking shoes and discover Savannah by foot. Named by *Walking* magazine as "one of the top 10 walking places in America," the title is not only accurate but inviting! To add to the kudos, *USA Weekend Magazine* called Savannah "one of the 10 most beautiful places in America." Savannah's squares are her most adored icons, and there are now 22 of them to explore! Recognized as America's first planned city, General Oglethorpe's design included a series of grids with wide streets connected by shady public squares. These squares served as the town's meeting places. Ellis Square was given a new and contemporary design that reflects the city's progressiveness. There are 13 main north-south streets in the Historic District, stretching from the northernmost point of the city—the Savannah River—south to Forsyth Park. These streets include (listed east to west) East Broad, Houston, Price, Habersham, Lincoln, Abercorn, Drayton, Bull, Whitaker, Barnard, Jefferson, Montgomery, and Martin Luther King Jr. Likewise, there are 23 main east-west streets, starting (for our purposes) at East Broad and ending at Martin

Luther King Jr. (which was formerly known as West Broad). These main east-west roadways include River, Bay, Bryan, Congress, Broughton, State, York, Oglethorpe, Hull, Perry, Liberty, Harris, Charlton, Jones, Taylor, Gordon, Gaston, Huntingdon, Hall, Gwinnett, Bolton, Waldburg, and Park.

If our streets resemble a series of necklaces, then some of them are lucky enough to have pearls in the form of squares. In fact, six of the north-south streets—Montgomery, Barnard, Bull, Abercorn, Habersham, and Houston—have these jewels, making them the most beautiful streets in the Historic District. Bull Street, however, is the most commanding strand. Located in the center of the Historic District and easy to spot because it begins at golden-domed City Hall, Bull Street offers some of the most notable squares in the city, including the one where Forrest Gump waited for his bus and the one where the main plot unfolds in *Midnight in the Garden of Good and Evil.*

It is crucial that you understand how to navigate around the squares while traveling in the Historic District. It's actually quite simple once you understand the basic layout. Imagine heading north or south on one of the six streets with squares. Every couple of blocks you are going to run into one. They're beautiful but they slow you down—not necessarily a bad thing—but local commuters opt for the plainer, straighter Whitaker Street and Drayton Street.

No, the squares aren't your standard traffic circles. There is only one lane, and traffic moves in a counterclockwise direction around a beautiful park filled with trees, benches, and in some instances, a monument or fountain. The traffic moves very slowly, so you have ample time to figure out where you would like to exit. When entering a square, always yield to any car making its way around the square—it has the right-of-way. Once the coast is clear, enter the

square driving to your right. Because we have many visitors (and not a few locals) who don't understand that part about who has the right-of-way on the square, be cautious.

If you don't want to hit any squares, you can take a straight southbound route through the Historic District on either Price Street or Whitaker Street. Both run one way. Drayton Street, a one-way northern thoroughfare, will get you all the way to the Savannah River without being interrupted by squares. These aren't, however, the prettiest routes. Note that you also will run into squares when traveling east to west in the Historic District. The majority of the east-west routes pass by to the north or south of the squares, but a few intersect them. Again, when approaching a square from the east or west, you must yield to any traffic that is already making its way around the square. Once traffic has cleared, you enter the square by traveling to your right or going straight ahead. Liberty and Oglethorpe are the main east-west streets without squares, and they feature broad, tree-lined center medians. Other squareless east-west routes include Jones, Gaston, Broughton (the downtown business district's "main street"), and Bay. All of this sounds complicated. It isn't, as you will see. Yield when entering a square, travel to the right—as is quite obvious—and you'll do fine.

Islands

The eastern islands, including Whitemarsh, Talahi, Oatland, and Wilmington, are directly off US 80, which is also the only route to Tybee Island. It is a fairly wide, four-lane highway taking you through scenic marshlands before narrowing into a two-lane road as you near Tybee. Skidaway Road leads to Dutch Island and the Isle of Hope (but not, oddly enough, without some turns to

Skidaway Island). Waters Avenue is the direct route to Skidaway Island. This well-marked, two-lane road is very busy and congested most times of the day. (Please see our Tybee Island chapter for more information on getting around there.) Pay particular attention to speed limits in school zones and tuck your cell phone away while driving on this road (and all others, for that matter).

Southside/Midtown

Abercorn Street is the main artery running through Savannah's Southside. It begins at the Savannah River in the Historic District, and in its early stretches it is a charming, square-filled route through downtown. It continues south some 20 miles to I-95, picking up additional lanes and additional traffic. All the motels, hotels, shopping centers, car dealerships, and other businesses in the Southside are either right on Abercorn or on a street just off this main drag. The six-lane street is heavily traveled and usually very busy. Try to avoid Abercorn during morning and afternoon rush hours—typically 7:30 to 9 a.m. and 4 to 6 p.m. If you are a road-warrior veteran of a gridlocked metropolis, however, you might find our version of rush hour amusing.

DeRenne Avenue, which becomes I-516 at its western end, is the main Southside east-west route. You will find two of the city's hospitals off DeRenne (one just off, and the other a few blocks north on Waters Avenue), along with gas stations, shopping centers, banks, and several medical offices. This road is also heavily traveled and should be avoided during morning and afternoon rush hours. Since this road serves hospital personnel, rush hour tends to start around 3 p.m. weekdays.

Victory Drive (US 80) is Midtown's main drag. It travels through residential neighborhoods and by shopping centers and Grayson Stadium, home of Savannah's minor-league

baseball team, the Sand Gnats. When traveling east, Victory Drive is the main route to Tybee and the eastern islands.

Eisenhower Drive is another major east-west road that accesses Hunter Army Airfield to the west and Skidaway Road to the east. It parallels DeRenne and Victory.

West Chatham

Bay Street, which runs right in front of City Hall in the Historic District, continues to West Chatham, eventually taking you to Garden City and Port Wentworth. Another route, US 80, runs through the area as well, taking motorists to Bloomingdale, Pooler, and Garden City.

Parking

When Oglethorpe designed the original city plan for Savannah, he didn't leave space for parking cars. He would probably be amused if he could see his city today, some 270 years later. You can find parking, generally, but it is not free, and it is often not as convenient as you would like in the Historic District. We focus our parking information section on that part of town for a couple of reasons: It's the place most tourists want to roam, and it's the main area in the city where you have to pay to park. Venture outside the Historic District to Southside/Midtown, the Islands, or West Chatham, and you shouldn't have any trouble finding ample free parking. (An exception is Tybee Island, which is covered in a separate chapter.)

Despite the high volume of vehicles jostling for places in the Historic District every day, a metered spot or one in a garage or parking lot usually is available. It's the daily downtown worker who finds parking an expensive nightmare, with meters vigilantly patrolled and waiting lists for monthly spaces in the city lots and prime private lots. As a visitor, you might not find a place right next to the square or shop you want to visit, but chances are good you will find one within comfortable walking distance. Utilize one of the modern parking garages to keep you from running back and forth to check the meters. Be advised that it gets more crowded as you get closer to River Street—a main tourist hub overlooking the Savannah River. And remember that no matter how good the parking situation may be the rest of the year, it is going to be tough, if not altogether impossible, to get a spot near downtown on St. Patrick's Day. (See our Annual Events & Festivals chapter for more information on the perils of parking during the city's big fest.)

Parking for the majority of the Historic District (and a little farther south) is metered, costing 30 cents to $1 an hour and more, depending on location. The downtown area is patrolled by vigilant parking enforcers who are out in force 8 a.m. to 5 p.m., Mon through Fri. (Translation: It's free on weekends, provided you don't park anywhere like in front of a fire hydrant.) Leave your meter expired for even a minute or two, and chances are pretty good you are going to get a ticket. Parking meters are serious business in the city of Savannah, so take careful note of the time and carry change. Most merchants are friendly, but some are grouchy about making meter change. Also, messages posted on some meters claim they are checked on Saturday—which is not true.

The city's Parking Services department has gone high-tech downtown, with the installation of two new varieties of meter beyond the traditional put-in-a-coin-and-turn-the-handle versions. One requires parkers to walk to the middle of the block and buy a paper receipt from a machine, then return to the car and put it on the dashboard. Another version requires drivers to note the number of a parking space, walk to a mid-block computer, and feed in coins. If all of this sounds likely to breed confusion,

you're right—it does. On the good side, the newer meters also accept currency and credit cards.

Metered parking is scarcer than ever since security concerns prompted the lifting of curbside parking near federal buildings, so read on to learn about your parking garage options.

You won't find meters along Broughton Street, the main shopping district in the Historic District. This street has undergone a slow transformation and even today, reflects modern, attractive boutiques, as well as some locally owned shops that may need a little TLC. To promote this area, the city allows free two-hour parking along Broughton Street (with a few spaces that allow only 30 minutes of parking). While there are no meters, you can be ticketed for exceeding the time limit—it is monitored.

City Parking Garages

The city operates four modern parking garages, although they are of limited use during weekday business hours because most of the spaces are taken up by contract parkers. The Bryan Street Parking Garage at Bryan and Abercorn Streets is the nicest of the set, and it operates 24/7. The Whitaker Street Garage at Whitaker and Bay Lane is an underground lot. The Robinson Garage is at York and Montgomery Streets. The State Street Parking Garage at State and Abercorn Streets closes at 1 a.m. The same hours apply at the Liberty Street Garage at Liberty and Montgomery Streets. Garage rates are $1 per hour with the exception of the Whitaker Street Garage, which is $2 per hour. Evening, weekend, and special event rates vary.

City Parking

The city operates a few public parking lots as well. Three are on River Street and cost $1 per hour. For easy access to the lots, from Bay Street take the Abercorn, Lincoln, or

Barnard Street ramps to River Street. From the Lincoln ramp, turn left to reach the lots. From the Abercorn or Barnard ramps, turn either way on River Street to reach a city lot. Note that these are small lots; your best bet if visiting River Street is to park at the Bay Street level and walk down or ride the public elevator between City Hall and the Hyatt Regency Savannah.

There are a handful of private parking garages and lots in town. Many cater strictly to local businesses and have lengthy waiting lists to get in.

Visitor Parking Day Passes

Here's a real bargain. To take the hassle out of feeding meters, the city offers a Visitor Parking Day Pass. Get a one-day pass for $7 or a 48-hour version for $12. It allows visitors to park at any meter in the Historic District, at time-controlled lots and parking spaces, in the five city parking garages, or at the city parking lots. The pass, which must be displayed on the driver's-side dash, is not valid in all the areas you would expect—private parking lots, hotel parking garages, sweeping zones, freight zones, bagged meters (meters that are covered to tell you that parking is not allowed temporarily), etc.

You can purchase a day pass or find out more information on parking at the Savannah Visitor Information Center, 301 Martin Luther King Jr. Blvd., or at the offices of City of Savannah Parking Services, 100 E. Bryan St. (912-651-6470). The pass comes with a map showing parking locations. You can pick up a brochure outlining all the parking regulations at these locations, too.

Public Transportation

CHATHAM AREA TRANSIT, 900 E. Gwinnett St.; (912) 233-5767 (TDD); catchacat .org. If you hear someone say they are going to "catch a CAT," they are referring to a ride on Chatham County's public bus system.

CAT offers four free services, most of which are of particular interest to tourists. There's a free CAT shuttle—known as the dot shuttle (the "dot" is deliberately uncapitalized) making its way around the Historic District to some 30 stops, including hotels and prime shopping locations and historic squares. The shuttle bus looks like a well-groomed pseudo-trolley and is wheelchair accessible. Shuttle hours are roughly 7 a.m. to 7 p.m. every day but Sunday, when they start just after 9:30 a.m. and run to about 5 p.m. CAT also operates a passenger ferry to Hutchinson Island, which is also free. Also free is rail-based trolley service along River Street. The fourth free service is a shuttle originating from the city's Liberty Street parking garage, designed to make that new facility on the edge of the business district more appealing to daily downtown workers—but anyone's welcome to ride it.

As far as the regular bus service goes, you can get just about anywhere you want by catching a CAT, including the city's two malls, the Historic District, and the Islands (except Tybee). CAT buses do not, however, go to much of West Chatham. All are wheelchair accessible. There are bicycle racks with a capacity of two bikes on the front of the buses. The website is well designed and informative.

Taxis & Limousines

The best thing to do if you want taxi service in Savannah is to call the cab company directly. In theory, perhaps, you could hail a passing cab, but we've never seen it done—when we want a cab, we telephone and ask for one or go to the cab lineups outside major hotels and the airport. There are several companies in town, typically charging a maximum of $3.50 for the first mile and $1.80 per mile thereafter.

Limousine service is also available from a variety of local companies. Limos typically cost around $65 to $85 per hour, and some of the companies require a two-hour minimum. Advanced reservations are required to ensure prompt service.

Taxi services include Adam Cab Inc. (912-927-7466), Savannah Cab Company (912-236-2424), Yellow Cab (912-236-1133), Checker Cab (912-236-1666), and Ataxicab (912-234-0311).

For limousines, try A & E Luxury Limousine Service (912-354-2982), Low Country Adventures (912-681-8212, 800-845-5582), and First City Limousine (912-484-0455).

Bicycles

You'll find a sporadic series of bike paths on major thoroughfares, but they are designed primarily to assist commuters and are largely fragmentary. Bicycles can be operated legally on public streets, excluding interstates and restricted-access highways. Bike paths or not, be aware that many drivers are unaccustomed to sharing the road with bicycles. While bicycle helmets are not required by law on adult bikers, they're a smart option. Do not ride your bike on sidewalks and stay out of the squares.

CAT, the above-mentioned public transit agency, rents bicycles via facilities in Ellis Square and the CAT Transit Center, 610 W. Oglethorpe Ave., at a base rate of $5 for 24 hours and $20 for a week, plus usage fees on trips exceeding an hour.

Walking

Henry David Thoreau said, "It is a great art to saunter." Although his words were written in 1841, they remain a forging conviction among Savannahians who live in the landmark Historic District. In the afternoons when the sun is at its peak, they'll emerge from their stately homes—dogs in tow—dressed in their most casual attire and practice the art of walking. Trotting through the

squares, they head south to an illustrious setting: Forsyth Park, a magical place that is cast in emerging shadows and flanked by joggers, nannies with children, and an occasional biker who has strayed from the street. Inspired by the grand park fountain that has been pictured in literally thousands of wedding albums, they follow the aura of the artists before their time, seeking a closer look at the fountain sprays that are now illuminated by the setting sun. In short, a walk through this city is a joyous occasion that remains ongoing all year long and is always serenaded by birds and solo street musicians.

A walking tour of the city begins with your favorite shoes. Shy away from those that might bring blisters. Leave your heels in the suitcase. Tie a sweater around your shoulder and focus on the often-uneven sidewalks, scored from years of wear and the settling earth. To help find your way around on foot, we have included a walking tour in the Attractions chapter—and that's a good place to start. Here are some additional tips along with some rules to help make your steps a little surer.

Tread Lightly on Savannah's Squares

You don't have to be in peak athletic shape to see this city's magnificent downtown by foot. Fortunately, the Historic District is only about 2.5 square miles, so it is fairly easy to see the entire area on foot provided you follow our guidelines.

Savannah's squares are a charming blend of splendor and whimsy, order and extravagance, and they entice visitors seeking solitude, romance, and playful adventure. Designed to create compact, cozy interludes for socializing, the squares are framed in quaint boutiques, coffee shops, and rustic eateries, and set amid a background of Southern hospitality. They provide excellent markers for walking tours. These serene

Getting Some Direction in Historic District

Lost in the Historic District? Can't remember where you parked your car or how to get back to your hotel? Look for somebody doling out parking tickets. They can give directions, help point out the nearest bathroom, even use their radios to track down misplaced cars.

Or venture over to **Ellis Square** at Bryan and Barnard Streets. This square was originally designed in 1733 and named in honor of Henry Ellis, the second royal governor. It was here that the "Old City Market" was located, and in its day, it was abuzz with merchants selling their wares. Shooting fountains now adorn the square, and modern benches are plentiful, but most helpful is a computer/touch-screen guide to the city housed in a glass kiosk. It's perfect for getting your bearings!

settings beg for relaxed audiences. There's a story in each and every one. Benches are plentiful, and their beauty unfolds as the days change color and the breezes usher in the aura of nighttime charm.

Crossing Bay Street

Although the Historic District is generally very pedestrian-friendly, one area that isn't is Bay Street. This is the main street running east to west in front of City Hall. Many tourists encounter Bay Street, as it must be crossed to reach River Street, the tourist haven running along the Savannah River. As mentioned in our Bicycles section, Bay Street is a very busy, narrow four-lane road that serves as the main throughway for 18-wheeler traffic trying to make it to other areas in the city. Many visitors think they can beat the traffic on Bay Street, get halfway across, and find themselves stuck in the middle, dangerously close to traffic and unable to safely pass to the other side. After experimenting with several options, the city went with increasing the number of traditional traffic lights to get pedestrians across. Most have a button-activated pedestrian signal: Push it, wait (and wait), then move quite briskly across. A few have audio features designed to serve the blind. So, in short, resist the urge to simply cross this street; go out of your way to cross at the designated pedestrian signals.

Getting to River Street

Savannah is built on a bluff overlooking the river, even though it probably looks flat to you. River Street runs along the Savannah River, which means it's lower than the rest of the city and can present a challenge to pedestrians. One of our favorite city projects—and a favorite improvement to this area—was the 1998 installation of an elevator behind City Hall on Bay Street. The wheelchair-accessible elevator whisks riders down to River Street, avoiding the stairs and the cobblestone streets on its way. The elevator is between City Hall (can't miss that giant gold dome) and the Hyatt Regency Savannah. Part of the elevator project included the installation of a public restroom facility on the River Street level. We've stopped in periodically and have been impressed with its upkeep. There's also a small information station with a friendly question-answerer, a brochure rack, and—most importantly in Savannah's climate—a water fountain. The more adventurous pedestrian might want to skip the elevator and hoof it down the uneven cobblestones to River Street. One option to get to River Street involves treacherous stairs. There are several routes available, although—apart from the elevator—we prefer the wide, easily negotiated set that runs along the east (right-hand when you face the river) side of City Hall. All these stairs are literally hundreds of years old, and many aren't particularly easy to navigate, such as the narrow slate steps curving along a stone wall with an aged metal railing. The steps tend to be beside the ramps that carry traffic to River Street. Be extremely careful, and if you prefer, walk down the ramps that cars use to get to the river.

Although you can avoid the tricky stairs this way, you won't avoid the cobblestone ramps, another potential pedestrian pitfall. The cobblestones, although visually charming, are not as steep as the stairs, but beware when walking on them with any type of heeled shoe. Historians will point out that these are ballast stones used to balance the weight on ships coming in and out of the port, not proper cobblestones. These roads and ramps are uneven and difficult to walk on, even for people with the surest feet and flattest shoes. If you are not above sneaking, you can duck into the elevator at the Savannah Hyatt Regency for a ride down to River Street—but you can't take a ride up without a room key.

Crossing the River

The development of the Savannah International Trade and Convention Center and the Westin Savannah Harbor Resort on Hutchinson Island—an island between Georgia and South Carolina—added some transportation challenges. You can get to Hutchinson Island easily by road, via the Talmadge Bridge. Or try the ferries, which are free. The vessels are named for two historic women—Juliette Gordon Low, the Savannah-born founder of the Girl Scouts, and Susie King Taylor, a former slave who started one of the first schools for African Americans in Savannah.

Savannah Bike Paths

The designated bike paths in the city include the following (although bikes are legal on any surface street):

- West to East Corridor: 52nd Street to Ward Street to LaRoche Avenue to the entrance of Savannah State University
- North to South Corridor: Habersham Street to Stephenson Avenue to Hodgson Memorial Drive to Edgewater Drive to Hillyer Drive to Dyches Drive to Lorwood Drive to Tibet Avenue to Largo Drive to Windsor Road to Science Drive
- McQueen's Island Trail: 6 miles for hiking and biking between Bull River and Fort Pulaski along US 80
- McCorkle Trail: Wilmington Island at Charlie C. Brooks Park, 7001 Johnny Mercer Boulevard

The ferries are designed to look nostalgic and operate at about 20-minute intervals. Unless you are attending an event at the Savannah International Trade and Convention Center or staying at the Westin Savannah Harbor Golf Resort & Spa (or patronizing one of its amenities), you won't really need to use the ferry. We recommend it anyway, especially if you have children in your party. It's fun to see River Street from the vantage point of an arriving sailor, and the sail across the river and back can be completed in about 15 or 20 minutes.

Ferries operate 7 days a week, weather and river conditions permitting, 7 a.m. to midnight. Ferry landings are at River Street behind City Hall, at the Savannah Marriott

Riverfront, and on Hutchinson Island at the convention center.

Quick Driving Tips

Here are a few suggested routes that may save you some time and frustration when getting from a few popular point As to point Bs. Note that all these jaunts are in the 15- to 20-minute range.

i In the city of Savannah you don't have to pay parking meters evenings, Saturday, or Sunday. But enforcement is 7 days a week on Tybee Island.

Historic District to Oglethorpe Mall

Option One: Take Whitaker Street south about 2 miles to Victory Drive. Turn left onto Victory Drive, then right at the second light onto Abercorn Street. The mall is about 4 miles down Abercorn Street. Turn left into Oglethorpe on Mall Boulevard.

Option Two: Take Bay Street east. In less than 1 mile it runs into President Street Extension. From President Street Extension, take Truman Parkway. After a couple of miles, exit to the right on Eisenhower Drive, then turn left onto Abercorn and look for Mall Boulevard after a couple of blocks.

Historic District to Savannah Mall

Take I-16 4 miles west to the Lynes Memorial Parkway exit and go south. After 2.5 miles on the Lynes Parkway, exit at the Southwest Bypass (also known as the Veterans Parkway) and continue 7.5 miles until it ends at SR 204. Turn left onto SR 204, which becomes Abercorn Street, and the mall will be some 3 miles ahead on your left. Or just take one of the options to Oglethorpe Mall and opt to stay on Abercorn instead of turning onto Mall Boulevard; Savannah Mall is only a couple miles farther, on the right.

Historic District to Savannah/Hilton Head International Airport

Take I-16 west to I-95 north. The airport is 14 miles away at exit 104 off I-95.

Historic District to Amtrak Station

Go west on Liberty Street, which turns into Louisville Road after less than a mile. Take a left onto Telfair Road, then a right onto Seaboard Coastline Drive.

HISTORY

Perhaps no other city owes as much to one man as Savannah owes to James Edward Oglethorpe, the English soldier and politician who founded Georgia. Oglethorpe was the mastermind and driving force behind the development of the colony of Georgia, whose first city was Savannah. He selected the site of the city and christened it, giving it the same name as the river that flows beside it. Oglethorpe supervised the first phase of the building of Savannah, and he nurtured the city during its infancy as a town. He defended it in its early years, militarily and financially.

More than that, Oglethorpe bestowed on Savannah a gift that has flourished throughout the decades and centuries since his passing. He designed and laid out the town and, in so doing, created the atmosphere that makes Savannah unique among cities. He left a legacy that has been admired and enjoyed by countless residents and visitors—a treasure that will be the pride of the city for as long as it stands.

OGLETHORPE & HIS IDEA

Oglethorpe was born into a family that had a long history of service to England. After serving in the British army and fighting the Turks as the aide-de-camp of an Austrian prince, Oglethorpe was elected to the lower house of Parliament in 1722 at the age of 25. He developed an interest in the misfortunes of the poor, in particular the plight of debtors who had been thrown into prison by creditors hoping the debtors' friends would secure their release by paying the debts. He worked for prison reform and attempted to find solutions to England's unemployment problems.

Together with John Perceval, another member of Parliament, Oglethorpe hatched the idea of giving people who were out of work a fresh start by transporting them to a new colony in North America that would be located between Spanish Florida and the English colony of South Carolina. Oglethorpe and Perceval petitioned King George II for a charter, which the king signed on April 21, 1732. The deal was not one-sided: The crown was motivated by the prospect of having colonists raise produce and procure raw materials to ship to England, while the colony served as a market for English goods. The idea of having the new colony act as a buffer between the Spanish in Florida and thriving South Carolina was not lost on the royals either. To top it all off, the colony was to be named Georgia in honor of the king.

The colony would be managed by Oglethorpe, Perceval, and 19 other trustees, who would receive no pay and no land for their involvement. There were also rules for the colony: Slavery, lawyers, and "brandies and distilled liquors" (in particular rum) were prohibited, as were Catholics. In time, all would be allowed. Those who took advantage of the free passage to Georgia offered by the trustees agreed to remain in the colony for three years, and each received a town lot for a house and 50 acres to farm. A colonist would not own the acreage and could occupy it only as long as he farmed it properly. Grants of 500 acres were available to people who paid their way to the colony.

The trustees adopted as their motto the Latin phrase *Non sibi sed allis* (Not for themselves but others). It appears on Georgia's original seal, which also bears a rendering of a silkworm crawling across a mulberry leaf; it was hoped that the colony would produce silk in abundance.

BEFORE THE ENGLISH CAME

Although Oglethorpe brought a European-style civilization to this land known as Georgia, he and his little band of settlers were very much the new kids on the block. According to Max E. White, author of *Georgia's Indian Heritage*, human beings had existed in Georgia many centuries before. White states that "the earliest evidence of man's presence in Georgia and the Southeast is in the form of fluted projectile points identical to or very similar to those found west of the Mississippi and dated to about 12,000 years ago." In addition to discovering such rudimentary tools as projectile points, modern man has found other evidence of the native peoples of Georgia—shell middens and ceremonial mounds. The middens are piles of refuse "composed primarily of mussel shells discarded by prehistoric diners." "Many times," says White, "people were buried in these shell heaps and utilitarian objects, such as bone awls, projectile points, etc., were often placed with them." The remnants of shell middens can be seen in the Savannah area at Skidaway Island State Park.

Although Oglethorpe and his Englishmen were the first Europeans to make a go of settling in southeast Georgia, others had visited before them. Spanish explorer Hernando de Soto passed through in 1539–40 during his trek across what became the southeastern US. After de Soto's countrymen established a settlement at St. Augustine, Florida, in 1565, they built Catholic missions and churches on Georgia's sea islands, the last of which was closed in 1702. French explorer Jean Ribault—who started short-lived settlements at what are now Jacksonville, Florida, and Beaufort, South Carolina—sailed along the Georgia coast in 1562.

"Almost all of Georgia was forest-covered when the Europeans first appeared on the scene," says White. The Native Americans living there were, for the most part, members of the Creek and Cherokee nations, "practicing an economy based on agriculture, hunting, fishing, and gathering." Most were Indians belonging to the Creek Confederacy, and one of them—Tomo-chi-chi—would have a significant impact on the survival of Oglethorpe's new colony.

A WHOLE NEW WORLD

Oglethorpe and his fellow trustees recruited 114 colonists comprising 35 families for the first voyage to Georgia and the task of starting a settlement there. Oglethorpe was the only trustee to make the trip. They left Gravesend, England, on November 17, 1732, aboard a 200-ton vessel named the *Anne* and arrived in what is now Charleston, South Carolina, on January 13, 1733. The settlers then made their way south down the South Carolina coast and, after transferring to smaller boats, landed in the new colony on February 1. That was the date of Georgia's founding according to the Julian calendar. When that calendar was abandoned in favor of the Gregorian calendar 19 years later, the date became February 12—the day now celebrated as Georgia Day. Oglethorpe had gone ahead of the colonists several days before their landing and chosen a site for the town of Savannah on a 40-foot-high bluff overlooking the Savannah River—Yamacraw Bluff. In a letter to the trustees explaining his choice of the site for a city, he stated that he "thought it healthy" and wrote, "The last and fullest consideration of the Healthfulness of the place was that an Indian nation, who knew the Nature of the Country, chose it for their Habitation."

The Indians were the 100-odd members of the Yamacraw tribe of the Lower Creek nation, led by an 80-year-old chief named Tomo-chi-chi (meaning "to fly up"). The Yamacraws would prove friendly and helpful to the colonists—providing them with food, interceding with other tribes on their behalf, and aiding them in their struggle against the Spanish. The Yamacraws had come to the coast some eight years before the English, led there by Tomo-chi-chi from what is now west Georgia. Other new neighbors were the Musgroves—Mary, an Indian woman, and her husband John, who was white. The Musgroves ran a nearby trading post called Musgrove Cowpen, and they would serve as interpreters for the Europeans and the Native Americans.

The colonists spent their first night in their new home camped out in an area that is now the site of a small park at Bay and Whitaker Streets. In the following days and weeks, Oglethorpe and Col. William Bull of South Carolina laid out the new city, and the settlers set about clearing the pine woods on the bluff with the help of slaves from the neighboring colony. They also began cultivating a 10-acre plot that would be known as Trustees' Garden. On this parcel, at the current Bay and East Broad Streets, were planted fruit trees and the mulberry trees that were envisioned as the basis of Georgia's silk industry.

Things went well at the outset. By fall 1734, according to a letter from a South Carolina merchant who had visited the town, there were 80 houses and 40 more being built. During Georgia's first decade, the trustees sent more than 2,000 settlers. Other new arrivals brought diversity to the colony. Among them was a boatload of Jews from Portugal who established a Jewish

congregation, Mickve Israel. It was the third founded in North America and continues today as the South's oldest. Another was a group of Germans, the Salzburgers, who settled 21 miles upriver from Savannah in what is now Effingham County. Their community of New Ebenezer prospered, and the house of worship they built in 1769 is the oldest standing church in Georgia.

i One branch of the most heavily traveled road in Colonial America—the Great Indian Warrior/Trading Path—reached to what would become Savannah, all the way from the Great Lakes. A historical marker on Liberty Street near its intersection with Martin Luther King Jr. Boulevard states that the path "passed through here."

Also during the colony's infancy, Savannah became the site of the oldest orphanage in North America with a continuous existence: Bethesda Home for Boys. The orphanage's founders, George Whitefield and James Habersham, came to Georgia in 1738 at the request of two Anglican ministers, the Wesley brothers, Charles and John, the latter of whom preached in Savannah during the mid-1730s and went on to found the Methodist church. Bethesda was situated southeast of the town on the banks of the Moon River, with the foundation of the first building being laid in March 1740. It is still in operation in a related capacity, and visitors are welcome to tour the site, a museum, and a chapel (see our Attractions chapter).

Oglethorpe remained involved with the colony during its first 10 years, and in July 1742, he led a contingent of soldiers and Indian allies in a battle that forever wrested control of the region from the Spanish in Florida. In the Battle of Bloody Marsh, his band of defenders surprised and defeated a numerically superior Spanish invasion force about

Close-up

What Are These Squares All About?

No one knows for sure what inspired Oglethorpe to design Savannah as he did. Whatever Oglethorpe's inspiration, it lives on happily in the form of Savannah's priceless jewels—her squares. Enjoy this brief summary of each:

- **Calhoun Square,** Abercorn and Wayne Streets—This square was named in honor of John C. Calhoun, a South Carolinian considered to be the Old South's greatest spokesman in the US Senate. Designed in 1851, this is the only square where all of the original historic buildings remain.
- **Chatham Square,** Bernard and Wayne Streets—Designed in 1847, this square was named in honor of William Pitt, English prime minister and the earl of Chatham during the period when Georgia was a royal colony.
- **Chippewa Square,** Bernard and Wayne Streets—This square was named for the Battle of Chippewa, an American victory in Canada during the War of 1812. Designed in 1815, the square's center offers a striking bronze statue of the colony's founder, Gen. James Edward Oglethorpe.
- **Columbia Square,** Habersham and President Streets—Named for the female personification of the US. Designed in 1799, this square boasts a fountain from the Wormsloe Plantation, a historic Savannah settlement.
- **Crawford Square,** Houston and McDonough Streets—Named for William Crawford, a Georgia governor and US secretary of the treasury, this square was designed in 1841.
- **Ellis Square,** Bryan and Barnard Streets—Named for Sir Henry Ellis, Georgia's second royal governor, this square lies at the site of Old City Market, a high-traffic zone in days gone by for merchants and townspeople. Restored after bulldozing an unsightly parking garage, this square sits at the hub of present-day City Market and is directly in the center of a revitalized area of downtown.
- **Franklin Square,** Montgomery and St. Julian Streets—This square is named for statesman and inventor Benjamin Franklin, who at one time was an agent for Georgia in London. Once home to the city's water tower, this square is flanked by First African Baptist Church and the west end of City Market.
- **Greene Square,** Houston and President Streets—Named for General Nathanael Greene of Rhode Island, a Revolutionary War hero and short-lived owner of a plantation west of Savannah, this square was designed in 1799. Second African Baptist Church is located here.
- **Johnson Square,** Bull and St. Julian Streets—This square is named for Robert Johnson, the royal governor of South Carolina who aided Oglethorpe in establishing the colony of Georgia.
- **Lafayette Square,** Abercorn and Macon Streets—Named for the Marquis de Lafayette, the Frenchman who was an important ally of the US during the Revolutionary War, this 1873-designed square offers a fountain dedicated by the Colonial Dames of America.

- **Madison Square,** Bull and Macon Streets—James Madison, fourth president of the US, was honored with this square named for him. Designed in 1837, a monument stands of Sgt. William Jasper, who fell during the Siege of Savannah in 1779. The granite marker denotes the southern line of the British defense during the 1779 battle.
- **Monterey Square,** Bull and Wayne Streets—Designed in 1847 and named for the Mexican city captured by US forces during the war with Mexico, the square's monument honors Casmir Pulaski, a Polish nobleman who was mortally wounded while fighting for the Americans during the Siege of Savannah.
- **Oglethorpe Square,** Abercorn and President Streets—Named for James Edward Oglethorpe, founder of Georgia; this is a popular square for outdoor weddings.
- **Orleans Square,** Bernard and McDonough Streets—This square was named for the Battle of New Orleans, an American victory in the War of 1812. Designed in 1815, the fountain in the square was dedicated in 1989 by Savannah's German Society to recognize the contributions of Savannah's early German immigrants.
- **Pulaski Square,** Bernard and Macon Streets—Confederate hero Francis S. Bartow's home stands on this square named for Polish count Casmir Pulaski.
- **Reynolds Square,** Abercorn and St. Julian Streets—This square, perfect for picnics, is one of the most colorful, thanks to beauty of the Olde Pink House and nearby Lucas Theatre. It was designed in 1733 and named for Georgia's first royal governor, John Reynolds. In 1969 the monument was changed as a tribute to John Wesley, the founder of Methodism and the Anglican minister to the colony in 1736.
- **Telfair Square,** Barnard and President Streets—The Telfair family, whose members made important contributions to Georgia in the areas of politics, business, the arts, and philanthropy, is honored in this beautiful square—another popular place for picnics.
- **Troup Square,** Habersham and McDonough Streets—Named for Georgia governor George Michael Troup, who was also a US senator, Troup Square is home to the Unitarian Universalist Church and the McDonough Row Houses. The Armillary Sphere, an astronomical device designed to show the relationship among the celestial circles, stands in the center.
- **Warren Square,** Habersham and St. Julian Streets—Boasting a 1791 design, this square was named for General Joseph Warren, a hero of the Revolutionary War.
- **Washington Square,** Houston and St. Julian Streets—Named for George Washington, first president of the US.
- **Whitefield Square,** Habersham and Wayne Streets—Named for George Whitefield, one of the founders of the Bethesda orphanage, a traditional gazebo sits in the center amid surrounding Victorian architecture.
- **Wright Square,** Bull and President Streets—Named for Sir James Wright, Georgia's third royal governor, Wright Square boasts a rich history as a large boulder marks the grave of Tomo-chi-chi, the Yamacraw chief who welcomed Gen. Oglethorpe and the first colonists.

70 miles south of Savannah at St. Simons Island. The Spanish never attempted another invasion, and a peace treaty between Spain and England was signed in 1748.

i Among Savannah's tributes to **founder James Edward Oglethorpe is a large bronze status of the Englishman in Chippewa Square. The monument is the work of Daniel Chester French, sculptor of the Minuteman statue in Concord, Massachusetts. You'll notice that Oglethorpe faces toward Florida, still guarding his beloved Savannah against an invasion from the south.**

Oglethorpe left Georgia on July 22, 1743, never to return. Even before his departure, Savannah began to decline as the population dwindled due to the hardships of bringing civilization to a wilderness: insects, alligators, extremes in the weather, difficulties in growing crops. The colony remained a trusteeship until 1752, when the trustees, burdened by financial problems and turnover in their ranks, relinquished their charter to the crown a year before it was to expire. As Preston Russell and Barbara Hines wrote in their lyrical *Savannah: A History of Her People Since 1733*, "Non Sibi Sed Allis had fallen on its nose. The dream was long since dead, but Savannah was here to stay."

A ROYAL COMEBACK

Under control of the crown, Georgia's government changed from the benevolent dictatorship of the trustees to a more traditional setup headed by a governor and having an assembly of elected representatives. Under this arrangement, Georgia was upgraded from colony to province, with Savannah serving as the seat of government.

The first Royal Assembly met in Savannah in January 1755, and one of its first acts was to adopt a law allowing slavery. The first of Georgia's three royal governors, John Reynolds, began a 2.5-year tenure in October 1754; he was succeeded by Henry Ellis, who gave way to James Wright in 1760. Wright, who ruled as governor until January 1776, was a godsend for Savannah's struggling economy. "In mere months, Wright led the youngest colony through stages of development that had required years in other colonies," states Edward Chan Sieg in his book *Eden on the Marsh: An Illustrated History of Savannah*. "Wright's administration was geared to accommodate the 'men of substance' who began to pour into Georgia from other colonies and from the plantations of the Indies. Aided by liberal credit policies and cheap labor, they transformed the coastal plains into the great plantations of legend. Wharf facilities and warehouses appeared on the bluff as shipping demands increased almost daily."

The major export was rice, the growing of which had been made possible by the repeal of the ban on slavery. The idea of making Savannah a silk-production center had flopped, apparently due to a combination of mismanagement and the silkworms' problems with the climate. By 1766, Wright was estimating that the province of Georgia was inhabited by as many as 10,000 whites and 7,800 African slaves—up from a total of 3,000 people nine years earlier—and that exports of rice had tripled over a six-year span.

THE GREAT REBELLION

In the mid-1760s, many residents of England's American colonies reacted with outrage to what they deemed unfair taxation of imported items by the mother country. As the following decade unfolded, their dissatisfaction grew to the point that they sought independence from England.

The fervor for freedom took hold somewhat slowly in Savannah, but by mid-1774, it began to show itself in the actions of a group of dissidents called the Liberty Boys. Despite Governor Wright's efforts to stop them, they met several times to protest England's closing of the Boston Harbor as punishment for the Boston Tea Party. In January 1775, Noble Wimberly Jones, a Liberty Boy who had been speaker of the Royal Assembly, convened a meeting of Georgia's First Provincial Congress. Wright dissolved the body, but on July 4 a meeting of a second provincial congress was held, with the 102 delegates electing representatives to the colonies' Second Continental Congress.

In the interim, in May members of the Liberty Boys celebrated the opening shot of the American Revolution by breaking into the city's munitions room, stealing 600 pounds of powder, and shipping it to Boston to be used in the fight against the British. The powder really hit the fan on January 18, 1776, when three British warships showed up off the coast of Savannah. The newly established provincial government placed Wright under house arrest, putting an end to British rule in Savannah for the time being. The governor later slipped away and escaped on an English vessel.

On August 10, Savannahians aching for freedom celebrated the signing of the Declaration of Independence, a document endorsed by three Georgians, George Walton of Savannah and Lyman Hall and Button Gwinnett of nearby St. John's Parish. The new state of Georgia elected Archibald Bulloch as governor and completed a constitution in February 1777. Bulloch died during his first year in office and was replaced by Gwinnett.

Savannah, being in an exposed position on the far southeastern reaches of the new United States, paid for its location on December 29, 1778, when 3,000 British troops commanded by Col. Archibald Campbell routed the city's 700 defenders. The enemy had landed below Savannah two days before

and slipped behind American Gen. Robert Howe and his forces. The British sacked the city, and James Wright returned to take control of Savannah. He and a small redcoat garrison found themselves under siege in September 1779 by a force of Frenchmen, Irishmen, and volunteers from Haiti. They were joined by a contingent of American troops from South Carolina, and on October 9, the overall commander of the allied forces, French count Charles Henri d'Estaing, ordered an attack on a defensive position southwest of the city in an area near the existing Savannah Visitor Information Center. The assault on this position, the Spring Hill redoubt, was, in the words of authors Russell and Hines, "a disaster, the bloodiest single hour in the entire Revolution."

i Downtown's Colonial Park Cemetery is the final resting place of many early settlers, including Button Gwinnett, one of the original signers of the Declaration of Independence.

"Through three valiant advances and the staggering retreat," they wrote, "French and Americans were slaughtered by land and naval artillery from Spring Hill redoubt and from . . . ships in the river." The defenders lost 55 men; the attackers suffered more than 1,000 casualties, including the deaths of 2 men later immortalized in monuments in Savannah's squares—Casmir Pulaski, a Polish count who had brought a group of lancers to the fray, and Sgt. William Jasper, who fell while attempting to save the flag of his South Carolina regiment. Savannah remained in possession of the British until after the climactic Battle of Yorktown. Wright and his compatriots evacuated the city several months after that American victory in Virginia, and American forces took control of the city on July 11, 1782.

THE ANTEBELLUM ERA

The Revolutionary War left Savannah a shambles, but the city recovered and prospered in the years between the end of that fight for freedom and an even grimmer struggle in the 1860s. Much of Savannah's prosperity in the years after the Revolution and before the American Civil War was due to a machine invented in 1793 on a plantation west of the city. While serving as a tutor at Mulberry Grove—a plantation owned by the widow of Revolutionary War general Nathanael Greene—a Connecticut schoolteacher named Eli Whitney perfected the cotton gin, a device for removing the seeds from cotton bolls. The machine helped revolutionize the cotton-producing industry and, in so doing, reinforced the value of slavery in the agrarian South—a circumstance that would bring disaster to the region and Savannah.

But in the early 1800s, cotton brought wealth to the city's port. On the subject of the city's transformation, Russell and Hines wrote, "In 1790 cotton exports were one thousand bales; by 1820 they were 90,000 bales a year. In 1794 Savannah's population was 2,000 with export revenues under $500,000. By 1819 she was America's 16th largest city with exports exceeding $14,000,000." As Savannah prospered, its residents built elegant homes and other imposing structures. Probably the most famed of the designers of these buildings was architect William Jay, who came to the city from England in 1818, stayed for seven years, and is responsible for existing masterpieces such as the Owens-Thomas House, the Scarbrough House, and the Telfair Museum of Art (see our Attractions chapter).

Savannahians experienced some giddy high points during the years between the wars. Among the highest was the transatlantic voyage of the SS *Savannah*, a vessel that was bankrolled by local merchants and propelled by steam and sail. The ship left Savannah on May 22, 1819, and arrived in Liverpool, England, a record-breaking 29 days and 11 hours later. On the return trip, the *Savannah* shattered that record by four days. A much more lasting achievement involving transportation occurred in 1847 when the Central of Georgia Railway was completed, with Savannah as its eastern terminus. At that time, "Savannah reached its antebellum zenith," stated author Edward Chan Sieg.

"Now profits really soared and Savannah enjoyed a period of unprecedented growth. In addition to cotton, other sources of income were tobacco, rice, corn, lumber, and naval stores. The population tripled, the city limits were extended, gas lighting made its appearance. Hospitals, churches, and orphanages grew in number for blacks and whites as excess wealth permitted the emergence of the charity traditions which were Savannah's birthright."

Other highly memorable moments occurred when two heroes of the Revolution visited the city. In May 1791, while he was serving as the first president of the US, George Washington came to town for four days and attended numerous get-togethers. One of these was a ball at which, according to William Harden's *A History of Savannah and South Georgia,* the Father of Our Country was "introduced to ninety-six elegantly dressed ladies." In appreciation of his stay, Washington presented the militiamen of the Chatham Artillery with two brass cannon used at Yorktown; they now occupy a spot on Bay Street just east of City Hall. The other visitor was Washington's French ally, the Marquis de Lafayette. He stopped over in March 1825 and was honored with a parade and many toasts.

Unfortunately, there were also some low points, including fires that destroyed large parts of the city in 1796 and 1820, deadly outbreaks of yellow fever in 1820 and 1854 (the epidemic of the former year killed 666), and a storm in 1804 that caused the drowning of more than 100 slaves, submerged Hutchinson Island, and greatly damaged many of the area's plantations. But as bad as those occurrences were, they were almost insignificant when compared to a disaster that was yet to come.

THE WORST KIND OF WAR

Disputes between Northern and Southern states over slavery and states' rights boiled over in the mid-1800s with cataclysmic results: the secession of Georgia and her Southern neighbors from the Union, the South's forming of a Confederacy, and the fighting of a war of the worst kind—a civil war. Although the war started in Charleston on April 16, 1861, when Confederate forces fired on and captured Fort Sumter, it was Savannah that, in the words of writers Russell and Hines, committed "the first belligerent act of the rebellious South."

Three months before Sumter, members of three militia outfits traveled by steamer from Savannah to Cockspur Island and seized Fort Pulaski, a large masonry edifice guarding the mouth of the Savannah River. Wrote Col. Charles H. Olmstead, who commanded the Confederates, "In due time Fort Pulaski was reached; its garrison, one elderly US sergeant, made no defense, and the three companies of the First Volunteer Regiment marched in with drums beating and colors flying, and so for them a soldier's life began." Olmstead and others thought Fort Pulaski was impregnable. But 15 months after its bloodless seizure, shells from rifled cannon emplaced on Tybee Island by Federal troops left the thick walls of the fort looking like Swiss cheese (see our Tybee Island chapter). After 30 hours of bombardment, Olmstead realized that holding the fort was impossible and surrendered it and its 385 defenders.

Following Pulaski's fall, the new occupants of the fort and their comrades in the Union navy began a blockade of Savannah. The city's exports of cotton and other goods were thus bottled up, and the residents spent most of the war enduring the hardships of the siege by sea and mourning the loss of relatives and loved ones who fell on faraway fields of fire. Among those who died were brothers Joseph C. and William N. Habersham, killed in fighting near Atlanta on the same day in July 1864.

i **The Green-Meldrim House on Madison Square is the site of the meeting in January 1865 that inspired the famed "40 acres and a mule" declaration, giving freedmen land in Georgia, South Carolina, and Florida.**

Later that year came Union general William T. Sherman's devastating March to the Sea across Georgia. The prize at the end of the trek was Savannah. Sherman took it on December 21, but not before a battle at Fort McAllister south of Savannah near Richmond Hill (see our Day Trips chapter) and a skirmish at what would become the town of Pooler. The Union commander also allowed a force of 10,000 badly outnumbered Confederate defenders to slip out of the city and into South Carolina. In an oft-quoted telegram to President Abraham Lincoln that the commander in chief received on Christmas Eve, Sherman wrote, "I beg to present you as a Christmas Gift, the City of Savannah with 150 heavy guns and plenty of ammunition; and also about 25,000 bales of Cotton."

Savannah was out of the war, and its citizens settled in to cope with the city's occupation by Union troops. For the most part, it was a benign affair. "The occupation was a model of order, even occasional pleasantry, with both sides generally behaving like ladies and gentlemen," wrote Russell

Close-up

Savannah: Style Central for Architecture Buffs

If anyone asks you about your vacation in Savannah and inquires about the architecture, whatever you tell them will be the truth. Stroll along the streets of Savannah's Historic District, and you'll be looking at a blend of buildings reflecting architectural styles prevalent in America during the late 18th and 19th centuries. Among these types were Federal, which was in vogue from 1790 to 1838; English Regency, 1811 to 1830; Greek Revival, 1820 to 1875; Gothic Revival, 1830 to 1885; Italianate, 1830 to 1900; Romanesque Revival, 1850 to 1890; and Victorian, 1860 to 1915. In summary, you will view all of these architectural styles in Savannah.

Probably the city's most outstanding example of the Federal style is the Isaiah Davenport House, with its central hallway and arched fanlight doorway. This brick and brownstone house at 324 E. State St. "reflects the balance and symmetry" of the Federal style, says Roulhac Toledano in *The National Trust Guide to Savannah,* and its double-entry stairway "must have set the standard for future graceful curving entry staircases leading to high stoops that dot the city in houses of all styles." The Davenport House, one of Savannah's many museum houses, was built in 1820; a successful effort to save it from demolition in the mid-1950s brought about the creation of the Historic Savannah Foundation preservation group. (Read more about the house in the walking-tour section of our Attractions chapter.)

The Regency style is best typified by the work of English architect William Jay and two of his designs, the Owens-Thomas House at 124 Abercorn St. and the Scarbrough House at 41 Martin Luther King Jr. Blvd. are open to the public. The porches and columns of these buildings are prime examples of the Regency style. A commission to build the house for cotton merchant Richard Richardson is what brought Jay to Georgia, and he "went on to create a series of buildings that qualify as the state's first architectural masterpieces," says Tom Spector in his book *The Guide to the Architecture of Georgia.* These two houses "rank among the best works produced in America" during the early 1800s. The Owens-Thomas House, which Toledano

and Hines. Regardless of this, however, some of the women of the town refused to walk beneath the American flag.

BOUNCING BACK AGAIN

Unlike some Southern cities, Savannah survived the Civil War without being decimated by shell fire or burned to the ground, although a fire that broke out a month after the city's surrender destroyed 100 buildings. But the war took its toll, leaving the city bankrupt and its people in need of food. However, within a year of the end of hostilities, said Sieg in *Eden on the Marsh,* "Savannah was rolling again," a beneficiary of

the rapid rebuilding of the South's railroads and a resurgence in cotton production. In Savannah, "exports for 1867 exceeded fifty million dollars," wrote Sieg. "The predictors of doom following the loss of slave labor were proved wrong as a rising market pushed cotton production to levels never realized" under slavery.

After the war, Savannah and the rest of the South entered into an 11-year period of Reconstruction during which radical Northern politicians hoped to build a power base with the support of former slaves. Ultimately they failed, and slavery was replaced by a caste system and the creation of a so-called deems "probably the finest example of English Regency architecture in America," was constructed in 1819, and the Scarbrough House was completed in the same year.

Greek Revival–style buildings are reminiscent of the temples of Greece with their long front porches supported by towering columns. To see two fine models of this style, take a look at the Aaron Champion House at 230 Barnard St. and the Sorrel-Weed House at 6 W. Harris St. Both houses were designed by Charles Cluskey, the Champion House in 1844 and the Sorrel-Weed House in 1841. Cluskey was Georgia's premier architect during the 1830s and 1840s.

Walk over to Madison Square for a look at what Toledano calls Savannah's "foremost Gothic-style house." The Green-Meldrim House at 14 W. Macon St., which can be toured by visitors, was designed by John S. Norris and built in 1853. Exterior features are the crenellated parapet, oriel windows, and the heavily detailed iron porch. (See our Attractions chapter for more on the Green-Meldrim House.)

The Mercer House at 429 Bull St. is another Norris design, but it is an example of the Italianate style, which has the look of an Italian villa—low-pitched roof, wide eaves, long porch, and cast-iron balconies. The house was designed before the outbreak of the Civil War but was completed in 1871 by two assistants of Norris. (For more on the Mercer House, see our Attractions chapter.) Another Italianate-style residence (and another of the city's house museums) is the Andrew Low House at 329 Abercorn St. (see our Attractions chapter).

The Romanesque Revival style is embodied by two Savannah landmarks, the Cotton Exchange at 100 E. Bay St. and the Chatham County Courthouse at 124 Bull St. Both were designed by William G. Preston. The Cotton Exchange, with its brick and terra-cotta facade and turned wooden posts, was constructed in 1886. Preston came to Savannah to build the courthouse three years later.

An interesting example of the gingerbread style of the Victorian period is the King-Tisdell Cottage at 514 E. Huntingdon St., which now serves as a African-American cultural museum. It dates from 1896.

separate but equal society that was more separate than it was equal. In Savannah, "blacks entered a long period of assimilation," said Sieg. "As a result, they developed their own culture, built their own institutions, formed their own business associations, created their own art, music, and literature—and in the process, developed a black elite that led the march into the twentieth century." Among the institutions founded was the Georgia State Industrial College for Colored Youth, which is now Savannah State University (see our Education section in the appendix).

Economically, the last quarter of the 19th century saw the rice plantations around Savannah go out of business, turpentine and rosin from Georgia's pine forests rival cotton as the city's chief export, and the port enhanced by the dredging of the Savannah River shipping channel to a depth of 26 feet from 14 feet at the end of the war. There was also a spate of disasters during the last 25 years of the 1800s: Yellow fever killed more than 1,000 people in 1876, and the city was damaged by five significant fires, a tornado, two hurricanes, and an earthquake.

RACING INTO THE 20TH CENTURY

Savannah focused international attention on itself early in the 20th century by hosting Grand Prix and Vanderbilt Cup automobile racing in 1908, 1910, and 1911. During the first decade of the new century, the city expanded in other ways: A new City Hall was built, and much of the present-day skyline took shape. In the years that followed, Savannah began stretching southward from downtown with the creation of the city's first residential subdivision, Ardsley Park, after World War I (see our Relocation & Real Estate chapter). In the African-American community, residents formed the Negro Civic Improvement League to clean up overcrowded neighborhoods and started their own businesses, including the Wage Earners Savings Bank, which by 1915 covered a downtown block. (The bank building is now the site of the Ralph Mark Gilbert Civil Rights Museum, which you can learn about in our Attractions chapter.)

Not all was rosy, however. By the early 1920s cotton production in the South had fizzled out as laborers moved to the industrialized North and the boll weevil decimated Georgia's cotton fields. Late in the decade came the Great Depression, and with it financial stagnation. During the 1930s, Savannah received an economic boost when the Union Bag and Paper Company set up shop just west of the city, bringing with it nearly 600 jobs and a payroll of $1 million. Union Bag, later known as Union Camp, was purchased by International Paper Company in the late 1990s and is still one of the city's largest employers. The company helped end Savannah's hard times, as did another, more far-reaching event—World War II.

ON THE HOME FRONT

Savannah contributed mightily to America's war effort. At the Southeastern Shipyard, some 15,000 workers built Liberty Ships. The city's little airport, Hunter Field, was appropriated by the military and turned into a huge air base. In 1943 it became a staging area for bomber aircraft and crews headed for duty in Europe; some 9,000 planes and 70,000 men were processed out of Hunter during the war.

With their airport gone, city officials began building another one in western Chatham County. It, too, was taken over by the government and became a training base for the crews of heavy bombers. Called Chatham Field, the base eventually became the site of Savannah/Hilton Head International Airport. Hunter continues to be used by the military and is now known as Hunter Army Airfield.

"The war turned Savannah from a sleepy, traditional, backward-looking town on a muddy river into a full-fledged, twentieth-century American city," wrote Sieg.

Old Fort Irish?

During your stay in our town, you might hear someone referred to as being "Old Fort Irish." This means the person is of Irish descent and grew up in the area of northeast Savannah where Fort Wayne once stood. According to local historian James Mack Adams, the fort, which was also called the Fort of Savannah and Fort Provost, was built about 1760 and was abandoned in the mid-1800s. A gas works was built on the site, and Irish immigrants flocked to the area because of low rents. The fort site at Bay and East Broad Streets is now called Trustees' Garden and is the location of shops, apartments, offices, and the Pirates' House restaurant.

"Savannahians gave what they had to the war effort, burying another generation of their youth and generously entertaining the youth of other cities." Savannah boomed, what with the influx of workers who came from the countryside to build ships and the city's popularity with military personnel from nearby bases, including the Marine Corps basic training complex at Parris Island, South Carolina.

The boom ended when the war did. The shipyard closed and most of the troops went home. "What remained was a partially deserted, once-fashionable Historic District," said Sieg. "Savannah had moved south to low-roofed suburbs, abandoning hundreds of high-ceilinged town houses to the dereliction of uncaring tenants, little or no maintenance, and, worst of all, unprofitable values. No wonder that the postwar business leaders reached the conclusion that if Savannah were to survive and flourish, the old city must make way for progress. But the preservationist attitude found its way into the lives of a handful of influential residents who became dedicated to the principle that demolition was not the only answer to decay."

PRESERVING THE PAST & MAKING PROGRESS

Savannahians reacted with shame in 1946 when Great Britain's Lady Astor called the city "a beautiful lady with a dirty face," a line that has continued to ring true occasionally to this day. They were moved to action when the town's City Market on Ellis Square was demolished in 1954 and replaced with a parking garage. The following year, a group of seven women led by Anna C. Hunter chartered the Historic Savannah Foundation for the purpose of saving noteworthy structures from destruction. By the time of the foundation's first general membership meeting in November 1955, the organization had 700 members.

Its first project was saving the Isaiah Davenport House (see our Attractions chapter), and it was successfully followed by many others. Of the group's efforts, Russell and Hines wrote, "The foundation determined to reawaken interest in Savannah's heritage, to convince the public of the economic benefits of restoration, and to promote tourism . . . During the next decade the foundation would deluge the city with a massive public relations campaign, arrange for a professional inventory of historic buildings, establish a revolving fund, and help establish a tourism and convention bureau within the Chamber of Commerce."

The group formulated a preservation plan that became a national model and the basis of the city's Historic Zoning Ordinance. By 1970 the foundation had saved more than 150 structures that were resold to individuals for restoration; the organization continues its efforts today from offices at 321 E. York St.

i **Savannah is the home of Girl Scouts of the USA, founded here by a woman named Juliette Gordon Low. Her childhood home is called "the Birthplace" and is visited by thousands of Girl Scouts each year. The home is also Savannah's first National Historic Landmark.**

In recent years, the Savannah College of Art and Design (SCAD) (see our Education & Child Care chapter) has stepped forward as a leader in historic preservation, and their work has been nationally and internationally acclaimed. Among the many buildings the college has restored to house classrooms and offices are former public school buildings, the old Chatham County Jail, and portions of what was once the Central of

Georgia Railway complex. In the 1970s the city government beautified River Street by creating Rousakis Plaza along the waterfront and started a revitalization of the Broughton Street shopping district that is a work in progress.

Since then, Savannahians have witnessed other progressive developments, including the construction of a new airport terminal, the replacement of the aging Talmadge Memorial Bridge across the Savannah River, improvements and growth at the city's port facilities, the revitalization of the Martin Luther King Jr. Boulevard corridor, and the construction of the Savannah International Trade and Convention Center on Hutchinson Island. In 1996 and 2004, Savannah found itself back on the international stage it had trod during the time of the great auto races: in 2004 as the news media and communications center for the G-8 summit meeting held on Sea Island, Georgia, and in 1996 as host of the yachting events of Atlanta's Summer Olympic Games. Fittingly, the opening and closing ceremonies of the games in Savannah were held at the eastern end of River Street, close to where James Edward Oglethorpe and his little band of colonists landed 263 years before.

ACCOMMODATIONS

There is perhaps no better way to experience Savannah's illustrious history than to stay in one of the Historic District's many bed-and-breakfasts, hotels, carriage houses, and inns. Disguised as elaborate mansions with architecturally stunning facades, these establishments are overflowing with charm and amenities that are unique to each property. Inside each, you'll find both atmosphere and modern amenities, along with historical features, original artwork, gourmet cuisine, and innkeepers who will see that you are well pampered during your stay.

Just as Mother Nature sprays the city in pastels each spring, Savannah hotels are in full bloom year-round, offering visitors everything from contemporary and chic accommodations to historic and convenient. No matter which you choose, the hotels are gift-wrapped in the splendor of history while modern amenities like wireless Internet, complimentary breakfasts, fitness facilities, and concierge services abound. If you're seeking a hotel that blends with the city's historical heritage, there are several within the Historic District furnished with antique replicas and housed behind centuries-old facades. Savannah hoteliers have done an excellent job marrying new accommodations with the flavor of this old city.

Most of the hotels and motels described here are situated in one of two locations: on or very near Bay Street in the Historic District or on or just off Abercorn Street near Oglethorpe Mall in the Midtown area. There are many other motels in several nearby locales: on or near the beach at Tybee Island, which is about 25 minutes from downtown Savannah; in the Southside on Abercorn between Oglethorpe Mall and Savannah Mall; and out on I-95, 10 or more miles from the heart of the city.

BED-AND-BREAKFAST INNS

The following listings are arranged in alphabetical order, and prices are indicated by the dollar-sign code explained earlier in the How to Use This Book section. You'll see a range of prices for some of these listings. Due to the wide variety of room options at some bed-and-breakfasts, it is not uncommon for one inn to offer both lower-priced accommodations and luxurious, upscale suites. Be specific when calling for details. The best deals are on weekday nights. If you are on a really tight travel budget, chances are many of the B&Bs listed here aren't the accommodations for you—amenities and atmosphere often

come with a price tag. These entries are not meant to be an all-inclusive list of city inns. Instead, it's a guide to help you get started. Chances are there are a few newcomers that have cropped up between the researching of this book and your reading of it.

AZALEA INN AND VILLAS, 217 E. Huntingdon St.; (912) 236-6080, (800) 582-3823; azaleainn.com; $$$–$$$$. Savannah's Azalea Inn and Villas is a pleasant and pretty blend of comfort and convenience. You'll receive a warm Southern welcome from innkeepers Teresa and Michael

Jacobson, the veteran hosts at this bed-and-breakfast located in a lush part of the Historic District near Forsyth Park. This Victorian home, circa 1889, offers eight rooms, two suites, three villas, and a two-bedroom second floor carriage house perfect for small families. The inn offers several friendly touches, including fresh fruit and finger foods that are available all day long as well as wine and hors d'oeuvres in the evening. The dining room is adorned with murals depicting Savannah's illustrious history, and the walls come to life in stories told each morning at breakfast, so be sure to ask. Breakfast is an experience in itself with some of the specialties well worth the trip. They include a beautiful orange cranberry croissant soufflé, creamy grits, and a delightful sectioned clementine with ginger syrup and mint! Rooms are tastefully elegant and not "overdecorated" with too many knickknacks. Several rooms offer working fireplaces and some offer spacious balconies and/or Jacuzzis. The innkeepers are particularly proud of their gardens that have been featured in several home tours. The shady courtyard garden is inviting, as is a refreshing swim in the pool after a day of sightseeing. Children over the age of 12 are welcome. The inn is nonsmoking throughout.

THE BALLASTONE INN, 14 E. Oglethorpe Ave.; (912) 236-1484, (800) 822-4553; **ballastone.com; $$$$$.** The Ballastone is a magnificently restored, four-story 1838 mansion just off Bull Street, one of the historic area's main thoroughfares. Arriving guests will notice the beautiful Queen Anne staircase in the entryway and the warm, lavishly decorated parlor off to the right. Ceiling fans, rice poster and canopy beds, marble-topped tables, and fireplaces are some of the things you might find in one of the 16 individually decorated rooms. The Victoria Room has a massive king-size bed and whirlpool tub.

Besides the wonderful surroundings, guests enjoy afternoon Victorian tea along with evening hors d'oeuvres. There is a terry-cloth robe waiting in the bathroom and nightly turndown service with chocolates and cordials. In the morning, you can choose to have continental breakfast in your room or a full gourmet breakfast served in either of the parlors or outside in the courtyard. Children 16 years of age and older are welcome at the Ballastone. The inn has been recommended by *Select Registry, Brides, Glamour, Gourmet,* and *Condé Nast Traveler.* This is one of Savannah's inns that more closely resembles a small European hotel. Jennifer Salandi is the innkeeper-owner.

i Reservations for the week of St. Patrick's Day should be made a year in advance. Bed-and-breakfast inns are perfect for your stay here during this colorful holiday!

BROUGHTON STREET GUEST HOUSE, 511 E. Broughton St.; (912) 232-6633; **savannahvillas.com; $$$–$$$$$.** Staying at the Broughton Street Guest House is an opportunity to have your own private home in the heart of Savannah's Historic District.

This property offers three bedrooms and a carriage house at the quiet end of Broughton Street, downtown Savannah's main thoroughfare. The master bedroom in the front of the home includes a four-poster bed, a spacious bay window overlooking the street, and a small whirlpool bath and shower combination. The middle bedroom has a comfortable sleigh bed surrounded by the old library. The rear bedroom has a queen-size bed with a view of the small rear courtyard. The carriage house rests on the rear of the property. It offers one bedroom and a sleeper sofa, and is decorated in a cozy, slightly more masculine style. Guests are allowed to utilize all of the house. There is a main parlor and dining room for relaxing. All the rooms are attractively decorated with antiques. The inn is not wheelchair accessible. Children are welcome. Housed in a circa-1883 town house, the inn was remodeled beginning in 1993. The home was operated as a bed-and-breakfast until 2004, and then was offered as a luxury vacation rental for families, wedding parties, and corporate retreats. It's the perfect place to stay for families or parade participants during St. Patrick's Day.

i Because of regulations passed by the local government, all new bed-and-breakfast inns opening in Savannah must provide off-street parking for their guests. That may be a headache for developers (not to mention a leg up to established inns that are "grandfathered"), but guests will ultimately benefit.

CATHERINE WARD HOUSE, 118 E. Walburg St.; (912) 234-8564; catherineward houseinn.com; $$$–$$$$. From the street, the Catherine Ward House is inviting. Like a freshly painted watercolor dotted with pinks and whites of Savannah's spring azaleas, the inn is a standout among houses on its block. There's a friendly porch with hanging baskets to welcome guests. Once you step inside, you'll discover that this inn meets and exceeds all the qualities one would expect from a fine Southern lodge. With nine rooms that range from modern and chic to traditional, each offers private baths, some with double showers. Less than a block from Savannah's resplendent Forsyth Park, the inn is equipped for business travelers and perfect those seeking a more restful stay. Nell's Room—a sunny space named for the former owner's housekeeper—offers a door leading to a private courtyard and a small fishpond. The Cosmopolitan Room is chic with a black

marble hearth, warm earth tones, a wet bar, and antique Asian nightstands. Just a note: The inn does not hold a liquor license, however, guests are encouraged to bring their own liquor or wine, and the innkeeper is happy to furnish glasses and ice.

EAST BAY INN, 225 E. Bay St.; (912) 238-1225, (800)-500-1225; eastbayinn.com; $$$–$$$$$. The striking design of downtown's East Bay Inn will catch your eye even if you're not looking for a place to stay. The exterior's tall windows and brickwork reflect the Greek Revival style, popular in Savannah around the time of the Civil War. The inn's entrance is friendly, and you're greeted with a warm welcome as soon as you step into the lobby. As typical with most commercial buildings of the period, the facade of the first floor is cast iron, as are the interior columns. Boasting the charm of a smaller inn with a cheery ambience in all of the common areas, this inn offers incredible style and service for a more moderate price. This inn, built in 1852, once served as offices for cotton merchants and housed cotton warehouses. In 1984, after several years of lying dormant, refurbishment began transforming the structure into the present-day East Bay Inn. Featuring 28 rooms—each with 18th-century-style furnishings, hardwood floors, mansion-style king and queen beds, high ceilings, and large, beautiful windows—this inn has become one of the city's most popular. Exposed brick walls, heart-pine floors, and plenty of comfortable places to rest, read, and dine, are factors in this establishment's success. Each guest room is tastefully decorated and meticulously kept. You will feel comfortable and safe whether your visit is for business or a nice romantic getaway. This is the perfect place to book a small wedding. You can have the ceremony in a private room in the restaurant below the inn, enjoy a reception

---

Rent a Part of History

One of the latest trends for families visiting Savannah for college graduations, weddings, and family reunions is luxurious historic homes that have been renovated for the purpose of renting out the entire home.

The **Mary O'Connor House,** at 507 E. Broughton St., is a fine example of one of those properties. Rates are $425 per night with discounts for a 5-night stay (or longer); holidays and weekends may have a minimum-stay requirement. Rates may also vary for special-event weekends. The house is updated to the very tee, with granite in the kitchen, shiny stainless steel appliances, and brick walls to round out the modern conveniences. Flat-screen TVs are in all rooms, and beds are decorated with high-thread-count linens and tastefully furnished with antiques.

The home is named for Mary Flannery O'Connor who was an American author born in 1925 who wrote two novels and 31 short stories. The house has a beautiful enclosed garden, three bedrooms, and a living and dining room. For more information on this beautiful rental home, call (912) 232-6633 or visit savannahvillas.com.

---

there, and book rooms for the entire wedding party.

ELIZA THOMPSON HOUSE, 5 W. Jones St.; (912) 236-3620, (800) 348-9378; eliza thompsonhouse.com; $$$–$$$$$. One of Savannah's most magnificent streets is home to the Eliza Thompson House, an inn that highlights spa-like amenities in each of its 25 recently restored rooms. Set amid a canopy of live oaks and stately residences, the original home was built in 1847 and restored to historical accuracy in 1977. Extending to two buildings, 12 rooms are in the main house, and 13 additional rooms carry over into the courtyard. Offering its guests premium soaps, bathrobes, and impeccable service, the inn is run with the efficiency and style of a small European hotel. Views from all rooms are a showcase of Savannah's natural flora: some tropical palms and flourishing live oaks adorned with hanging moss. Guests can enjoy Southern buffet breakfasts outside or, on those rare occasions when the weather does not permit, in a glass-walled alcove overlooking the beautiful fountain.

Wine and cheese are served in the parlor in the late afternoons, and dessert and coffee are provided in the evenings. Several guests and employees have reported seeing and hearing ghostly apparitions throughout the years. This is an all-adult property.

FOLEY HOUSE INN, 114 W. Hull St.; (912) 232-6622, (800) 647-3708; foleyinn.com; **$$$–$$$$$.** It is often the guest comments that define the success or demise of a property, and in this case, guests have praised the staff of this Savannah inn that stretches into two regal homes. The Foley House Inn's strengths—apart from a colorful, rich feel—come in the form of an outstanding staff (according to the comments) as well as luxurious amenities. The bedding is plush. The linens are fine. Several rooms offer private balconies and oversize Jacuzzis; most rooms have fireplaces. All offer plush bathrobes and lavish toiletries. When you first walk inside this 1896 brick home, you are struck by the rich burgundy and blue colors blanketing the walls and floors. The sumptuous design and detail extend throughout the parlor and all of the 19 individually styled rooms. Look out your window, and you will see beautiful Chippewa Square. Historic First Baptist Church is across the street, and a statue of Gen. James Edward Oglethorpe, the founder of Georgia, stands in the center of the square.

Tea and hors d'oeuvres are served each afternoon in the parlor, and guests can choose to have their continental breakfast there, in the small courtyard, or in their rooms. Particularly inviting are the garden rooms on the first level. They are bright, spacious, and convenient to a lush patio area. Evening cordials are also featured, as is concierge service for making all your dining and exploring reservations. The inn offers several packages that are inclusive of tour tickets, carriage rides, and restaurants. Visit the website for a full listing. Note that the inn is not wheelchair accessible.

FORSYTH PARK INN, 102 W. Hall St.; (912) 233-6804, (866) 670-6800; forsyth parkinn.com; $$$–$$$$$. The stately Forsyth Park Inn is made for savoring the views of a beautiful historic park and spending afternoons sitting and sipping ice tea on the porch. Built in 1893, the inn is surrounded by the exotic flora of Savannah, from gracious live oaks that frame the exterior to flourishing palms and lush azaleas (that bloom to their fullest in spring). Innkeepers will pamper you all day long, starting with their full gourmet-style breakfasts in the mornings. From fresh-fruit french toast and Florentine eggs Benedict served on the veranda or in the parlor, to afternoon tea and evening wine, this is an inn that has a long following of happy guests!

Ask for room number eight, which comes with a full balcony overlooking the gardens. If you're looking for ultimate privacy, ask for the Cottage, where children of any age (and pets) are welcome. The Cottage

overlooks the beautiful gardens and offers a living room with trundle bed, efficiency kitchen, and queen-size bed with private bathroom.

i Did you enjoy your romantic bed-and-breakfast stay? Hang on to those business cards! Weekends at these plush homes-away-from-home are a popular and different gift for newlyweds and others who are celebrating. Of course, the price may make such a gift more feasible as a group offering from the office or a gang of friends.

THE GASTONIAN, 220 E. Gaston St.; (912) 232-2869, (800) 322-6603; gastonian .com; $$$$–$$$$$. If there were space designated as paradise and set in Savannah, the Gastonian would be that place. This is an inn that fulfills the expectations of the most demanding traveler. Everything about the Gastonian invites relaxation and enjoyment, from the magnificent verandas that consume one side of the house to the impeccably landscaped courtyard and cheery, lavishly furnished rooms. From its lush gardens to its spacious porches, this inn has become one of the most highly acclaimed in the city. Fireplaces are lit (when the weather's right). Soft music plays at the day's end. Newspapers are delivered each morning. There is a friendly concierge who orchestrates your visit, from dinner to horse-drawn carriage tours. The inn is actually two historic, wonderfully preserved mansions next to each other along Gaston Street. This striking mansion is set in a residential neighborhood is just a short walk from one of Savannah's most beautiful parks—Forsyth.

Georgian and Regency period antiques fill the main parlors, while all of the 18 rooms are styled individually. Each has a working fireplace, wooden floors, and Persian rugs, and is named for a noted Savannahian.

French doors take you out to the veranda. Newlyweds often come to the Gastonian to have their pictures taken in the beautiful courtyard.

GREEN PALM INN, 548 E. President St.; (912) 447-8901, (888) 606-9510; green palminn.com; $$-$$$$. This small bed-and-breakfast plays up its name: The handful of rooms are named for different species of palm tree, and the inn overlooks Greene Square. That puts this inn on the eastern-most edge of the Historic District. It is one of the smallest and most affordable of the B&Bs. The house was built in 1887, and its renovation transformed it into a B&B in 1998. Look for atmospheric touches here like ultramodern bathrooms with air-jet tubs and showers (two of the smaller rooms have showers with multiple jets), a generous number of fireplaces (even in bathrooms), and British Colonial–style furniture. Guests can expect a hot breakfast as well as a delightful array of afternoon refreshments.

THE HAMILTON-TURNER INN, 330 Abercorn St.; (912) 233-1833, (888) 448-8849; hamilton-turnerinn.com; $$-$$$$. This glamorous Victorian inn boasts notable architecture, a prime location, and plenty of romance. The mansion—with an exterior as ornate as the Victorians could get it—was built in 1873, and among its claims to fame is the fact that it was Savannah's first house with electric lighting. Its location on Lafayette Square puts it square in the middle of the Historic District, with the Cathedral of St. John the Baptist as a neighbor and one of the city's most picturesque squares as its "front yard." The inn's grand-entrance steps empty onto a beautifully appointed parlor floor. The public rooms include a double parlor furnished with antiques and the front dining room, where breakfast is served. Breakfast is a full gourmet, health-oriented

Southern affair prepared by the inn's executive chef. Afternoon tea by request, evening wine with hors d'oeuvres, and late evening port are also served.

Most bedrooms boast the high ceilings and sweeping windows of the building's construction period. Exceptions, however, are on the ground floor, a level that Savannah terms the garden level. All garden-level rooms have individual private entrances from the gardens. The handful of rooms here feature brick walls and a cozier feel. This is an inn that offers excellent accommodations for disabled guests with a chairlift. An open-air elevator goes from the ground level to one of the parlor-level suites. Pet-friendly.

ℹ Reservations are a must, but while you are making them, be sure to check with the innkeepers regarding their cancellation policy. Some inns charge if you cancel, on the grounds that they turned away other reservations.

JOAN'S ON JONES, 17 W. Jones St.; (912) 234-3863, (888) 989-9806; joansonjones .com; $$$. Joan's on Jones is one of the most established of the smaller bed-and-breakfast inns in Savannah. Innkeepers Joan and Gary Levy have been welcoming guests to their Jones Street home since 1991. The inn features two suites, both with private entrances and ample room. You'll feel as if you have your own apartment in the heart of the city. These particular apartments are in a restored 1883 Victorian town house on one of the city's most scenic streets. The Jones Street Suite is painted a rich terra-cotta that Joan discovered in a local historic home and reproduced in her own. It is formally decorated and has pretty stained-glass windows and two fireplaces. Over one fireplace is a collection of old letters and other correspondence found behind the mantel during the restoration process. Reading lamps are over the bed for convenience, and there is a small kitchenette. The Garden Suite—just off a back courtyard that is perfect for relaxing with its lounge garden chairs—has a huge brick cooking hearth, queen-size iron bed, and exposed brick walls. There is also a full kitchen. This suite is less formal but more intimate and romantic.

Children are welcome, and well-behaved dogs are allowed in the back suites for a nonrefundable fee. A self-serve continental breakfast is available each morning.

THE KEHOE HOUSE, 123 Habersham St.; (912) 232-1020, (800) 820-1020; kehoe house.com; $$$–$$$$$. The Kehoe House stands catty-cornered to one of Savannah's preserved architectural treasures and house museums, the Davenport House, and has a commanding view of Columbia Square. The Kehoe House was constructed for an Irish immigrant who made a fortune in the iron foundry business. As his fortune and his family grew, he built this imposing brick Victorian. After its residential days, the building served other uses, including a stint as a funeral parlor. Former football star Joe Namath was one of a group of investors who held the property for a while.

The Kehoe has 13 rooms and is known for its European-style service. Guests are treated to a gourmet breakfast, afternoon tea, and evening wine with hors d'oeuvres. The fourth floor includes a party/banquet room, which is often the scene of brides-maids' luncheons and business meetings.

This inn is unusual in that it is outfitted with an elevator—an amenity you are sure to appreciate after you spend the day following our advice that the best way to see Savannah is on foot. Also, this inn touts its rumors of hauntings.

THE PRESIDENTS' QUARTERS INN, 225 E. President St.; (912) 233-1600, (800) 233-1776; presidentsquarters.com; $$$–$$$$$. Innkeeper Jane Sales has been in the business of pleasing Savannah guests for so many years, her delightful personality and vast innkeeping experience have carried over to one of the most satisfying accommodations in the city, the Presidents' Quarters Inn. This inn is one of the city's classiest, with not only a historical relevance, but also a high "chic" factor, exemplified by bathrooms with the latest and most modern fixtures (along with updated tile). Elevators make it easy for guests to get to their upstairs rooms. The twin townhomes of this Federal-style mansion are filled with surprises, and each room is named for a president. Overlooking Oglethorpe Square, the inn seems fresh and devoid of the mustiness some historic buildings in Savannah carry with age. There are 16 rooms, and most feature baths with granite countertops, high ceilings, fine linens, and a spaciousness often overlooked by other inns. My favorite is the George Washington Suite, a two-level loft with a wet bar, a large living space, and an upscale, tailored decor. Amenities include wine and hors d'oeuvres and complimentary turndown service. On St. Patrick's Day, the chef's delights spill out into the courtyard, making this one of the city's most desirable and festive places to stay during the holiday. Note: If that is your wish, book early.

ℹ️ Most bed-and-breakfasts provide DVD players in at least some of their suites. If aching feet or stormy weather is keeping you inside, why not check out a film made in Savannah? Check our Entertainment chapter for an inventory. Then settle back and see if you can spot your surroundings on the silver screen!

SAVANNAH BED AND BREAKFAST INN,
117 W. Gordon St.; (912) 238-0518, (888) 238-0518; savannahbnb.com; $$–$$$$. This charming and well-established bed-and-breakfast was an early comer to the scene. The circa-1853 Federal row house on Gordon Row adjoins innkeeper Bob McAlister's home in one of the most attractive areas of the Historic District. McAlister is a well-known host on the local scene, and his hospitality shows in this inn's operation.

Rooms are furnished with antiques to admire and reproductions for relaxation. (The innkeeper maintains antique chairs shouldn't be subjected to daily use, and guests shouldn't be subjected to antique chairs.) You'll love architectural details throughout. Renovation has enhanced the structure with a spacious deck that overlooks a beautiful courtyard. The garden suites are prime rooms, complete with full kitchens and living and dining areas. If you can get a room over St. Patrick's Day—regular returnees fill most of them—you're in for a real treat, as the breakfast party here is a favorite stopping-off point for locals (including many parade participants) heading to the festivities. Children are welcome in some of the guest rooms.

ZEIGLER HOUSE INN, 121 W. Jones St.;
(866) 233-5307; zeiglerhouseinn.com; $$$$–$$$$$. You can almost hear the "oh, how lovely" coming from guests who stay at the Zeigler House Inn! This small, cheery inn is situated in a glorious part of Savannah on Jones Street and proves to be the perfect place to stay for a quiet, relaxing visit to Savannah. Although there are only seven rooms, they are spacious and extraordinarily furnished. A special feature, among others, is the convenience of in-room kitchens, which offer the perfect place to store (and reheat) leftovers from some of Savannah's fine restaurants.

The inn is ideally located within a short walk to all of the major downtown attractions including shops, restaurants, Savannah College of Art and Design, museums, art galleries, Forsyth Park, City Market, and River Street.

Whirlpool tubs and private patios are unique features in several rooms. All accommodations have private baths, cable TV, CD/DVD player, refrigerator, microwave oven, toaster, and coffeemaker. Wireless Internet is available in all rooms and parking is free. Hors d'oeuvres and wine are served most afternoons, with coffee and tea available at any time. A continental breakfast with homemade baked goods and fresh fruit is provided in your room.

HOTELS & MOTELS

The motels at the beach are discussed in the Tybee Island chapter of this book. The accommodations between the malls and out on I-95 represent several major chains and should offer no surprises, but if your destination is Savannah and not the House of the Mouse or some other touristy spot in Florida, we recommend that you stay closer to our city and soak up some of the atmosphere of our historic old town.

You can be in the midst of that atmosphere by taking a room at a hotel or motel in the downtown area. In most cases, you'll pay accordingly for the location, but you can find some values if you're not too picky about the view from your room and the extras you receive. A rule of thumb: You'll pay more the closer you stay to the Historic District.

Another cost-saving option is to stay at lodgings in Midtown. You'll be out of the mainstream of tourism but not by much— the motels and inns in Midtown are only 5 miles from Bay Street, which is about 12 to 15 minutes of traveling time if you avoid rush-hour traffic. Although most of these establishments are geared toward people on business trips, the innkeepers are more than happy to have tourists stay with them. Another reason to take a room in Midtown is that parking is free. That's not necessarily the case if you stay in the Historic District.

All of the hotels and motels described in this chapter accept major credit cards and have wheelchair-accessible rooms.

The season generally runs from mid-March through October. Some establishments decrease their rates during the hot summer months, and others jack them up on weekends, so you should call in advance to ascertain how much you'll have to spend. If you're planning to stay here on St. Patrick's Day weekend, expect to pay considerably more than you would at any other time of year and make reservations months in advance. Some places set minimum stays of 2 or 3 days that weekend. (See the Annual Events & Festivals chapter for more information.)

Historic District

ANDAZ SAVANNAH, 14 Barnard Street; (912) 233-2116; savannah.andaz.hyatt .com; $$$$–$$$$$. This sleek new addition to downtown's hotel inventory is cutting edge, within steps (literally) of City Market and other attractions. Expect a modern, urban vibe, luxury accommodations, and a chance to rub elbows with locals at one of downtown's trendiest bars and restaurants. Pet-friendly. Parking is $23 daily; attached to city parking facility with $16 self-parking option.

THE BEST WESTERN PROMENADE, 412 W. Bay St.; (912) 233-1011; promenade savannah.com; $$–$$$. This is an older motel in perhaps one of the best sections of the Historic District. The Best Western Promenade fronts Bay Street, which is at times very noisy. However, with the noise

comes lower rates in comparison with many of the newer and pricier hotels nearby. It's the perfect place to bring small groups (i .e., Girl Scouts on tour, school field trips, etc.) as the rooms open to an outside walkway (hence, the name, Promenade) where there is no one to disturb. The rear building is on the western end of River Street, placing the three-story establishment about a block from the shops and restaurants along the river and in City Market (see our Shopping chapter). The establishment is a convenient stop for tour buses and trolleys that pick up at the front door.

The Promenade offers guests complimentary continental breakfasts, and there's a fenced-in heated pool for swimming and sunning on the River Street side of the property. Eighty-seven of the rooms have two full-size beds, and the rest have king-size beds. Parking is $15 per day.

THE BOHEMIAN HOTEL SAVANNAH RIVERFRONT, 102 W. Bay St.; (912) 721-3800, (888) 213-4024; bohemianhotel savannah.com; $$$$–$$$$$. The Bohemian is wowing guests who pull into a gated entryway with potted skyrocket junipers and attentive door attendants. This 75-room hotel overlooks the Savannah River and also features fine luxury bedding, lots of wood, brass, and leather design elements, as well as a rooftop bar (Rocks on the Roof) that has become Savannah's hottest spot for drinks and a tapas-style menu, and a full restaurant on the River Street level known as Rocks on the River.

THE BRICE, A KIMPTON HOTEL, 601 E. Bay St.; (912) 238-1200, (877) 482-7243; bricehotel.com; $$$. This massive brick building near the eastern edge of the Historic District started life as a soft drink bottling plant, but it was repurposed decades ago as a hotel. It has flown various hotel flags over the years, and veteran visitors probably remember it as the Mulberry Inn. The new Brice, a Kimpton Hotel, blew in in 2014 and added a cutting-edge modernity to the place. It's all fresh and luxe with a selection of king, queen, and suites available. The courtyard is lovely. Pacci, the in-house authentic Italian restaurant, has created a local buzz.

COURTYARD BY MARRIOTT, 415 W. Liberty St.; (912) 790-8287, (800) 932-2198; courtyard.com; $$$. The five-story Courtyard opened in late July 2001, adding 147 guest rooms and 9 suites to Savannah's inventory of overnight accommodations. The suites and 86 of the guest rooms offer king-size beds, with 9 of the rooms featuring spa-type bathrooms complete with whirlpool tubs. The other rooms have two queen-size beds.

The Courtyard, with a decor that's traditionally Southern in style, covers an entire block bounded by Martin Luther King Jr. Boulevard and Liberty, Montgomery, and Harris Streets. The main entrance is on Liberty, making the front door a short walk from the Savannah Visitor Information Center. The hotel's spacious courtyard—a lushly landscaped spot that creates an oasis in the heart of the downtown area—faces Harris Street and is also the site of a heated outdoor pool. Guests can relax here or at the hotel's spa, an exercise facility that includes a large whirlpool.

The Courtyard Cafe, which is in the northwest corner of the ground floor, is a roomy breakfast restaurant with plenty of windows to give diners a view of what's happening on Liberty Street and MLK. The Camellia Room is the setting for cocktails 5 to 10 p.m. Valet parking is available for $18 daily; no self-parking.

DOUBLETREE HOTEL, 411 W. Bay St.; (912) 790-7000, (800) 222-TREE; double tree.hilton.com; $$–$$$. The Doubletree Historic Savannah exudes the tradition of the finer homes of Savannah. With public areas that are bright and open, there are 151 rooms, all richly appointed with European-style furnishings. There are Irish and Celtic influences reflected throughout the common areas, and nautical hints in the rooms' decor. The hotel is an easy walk to City Market and River Street. There is an attractive restaurant and separate bar on-site, a business center, free wireless access, and more than 3,000 square feet of meeting space.

HAMPTON INN SAVANNAH, 201 E. Bay St.; (912) 231-9700, (800) HAMPTON; hamptoninn.com; $$–$$$. Fully renovated in 2009, this seven-story hotel blends well with the city's Historic District buildings. The stucco, brick, and ironwork of the exterior have the look of Old Savannah. The lobby has authentic gray bricks that were discovered on the site during construction. Other historical design elements include the hotel's heart-pine floors (retrieved from an old mill in central Georgia), antique and traditional furniture, Persian rugs, and a dark wood bar from England, purchased from a local antiques store. All of the hotels' 145 guest rooms have modern touches such as flat-screen TVs, high-speed wireless Internet service, and a refrigerator and microwave. The Hampton is at Bay and Abercorn Streets, a block south of River Street, a location that is perfectly situated between River Street and City Market. Check out the glorious view of the Savannah River, the Eugene Talmadge Memorial Bridge, and the Historic District from the rooftop pool, but wear shades on a sunny day—it's bright up there! The hotel offers a complimentary, deluxe hot breakfast each day from 6 until 10 a.m. There is a courteous valet staff to park your car for $20 per day.

HILTON GARDEN INN SAVANNAH, 321 W. Bay St.; (912) 721-5000, (877) 245-8854; http://hiltongardeninn1.hilton .com; $$–$$$. Just a few short steps from the trendiest restaurants, nightlife, shopping, and sights of the Historic District is the Hilton Garden Inn Savannah Historic District. This hotel offers a luxurious lobby on Bay Street. As found in most Hiltons, visitors have access to free wireless Internet, wireless phones with dataports, MP3-compatible clock radios, and ample desk space. You'll also find a microwave and refrigerator in every guest room. Upgraded rooms feature 32-inch LCD TVs and adjustable Garden Sleep System beds. The hotel offers a breakfast buffet at the Great American Grill. There's also an on-site concierge desk, and the Pavilion Pantry serves beverages 24 hours. Other amenities include room service (for lunch and dinner), a complimentary 24-hour business center, an outdoor heated pool and Jacuzzi, a fitness center, and three updated meeting rooms for groups of 5 to 80. Valet parking is $25 daily, with no self-park option.

HILTON SAVANNAH DESOTO, 15 E. Liberty St.; (912) 232-9000, (800) HILTONS; desotohilton.com; $$$. One of the city's most popular and elegant hotels, the Hilton Savannah DeSoto is situated directly in the center of the Historic District. Guests will literally be at the front steps of beautiful green squares, boutiques, local restaurants and pubs, grand mansions, theaters, historic sites, and more. The Hilton Savannah DeSoto has always maintained a tradition of luxury and Southern hospitality that starts in a grand lobby replete with trademark crystal chandeliers. There are 246 guest rooms decorated in a fusion of Southern and contemporary styles, with scenic views of Savannah's historic skyline. The hotel is the perfect place for groups, boasting 20,000 square feet of meeting space.

You'll enjoy a variety of Southern favorites at the DeSoto Grille inside the hotel, offering a lunch buffet, an outstanding Sunday brunch, and a diverse a la carte menu. If you're looking for something lighter, stop by for a quick Starbucks' coffee or freshly baked pastry at Beulah's, another eatery that offers wireless Internet and flat-screen TVs. In the evening, the Lion's Den Pub is both romantic and comfortable, featuring a variety of spirits served in a modern pub atmosphere. The hotel is within walking distance of River Street and City Market.

HYATT REGENCY SAVANNAH, 2 W. Bay St.; (912) 238-1234, (888) 591-1234; savannah.hyatt.com; $$$–$$$$. With an excellent management staff at the helm, you'll appreciate Hyatt Regency's hospitality whether you're dining, working out, or just hanging out in the beautiful atrium. Ironically, Gen. James Oglethorpe pitched his tent in a small park near the 347-room hotel, but that's not the main attraction of the Hyatt Regency—the hotel's drawing card is its location overlooking River Street and the Savannah River, constructed on the historic cobblestones that made the riverfront what it is today. This location places guests in the midst of Savannah's waterfront shops and festivals and affords terrific views of the river and the ships passing by. You'll pay extra for a room on the river, but it's well worth it for catching a bird's-eye view of the oceangoing vessels. On the fourth of the hotel's seven floors, you're at eye level with the decks of freighters and other ships as they make their way in or out of port.

There are also great views of River Street and the river from the Hyatt's Vu Lounge, a pleasant outdoor patio located off the lobby. The hotel's Harborside Ballroom, an 11,000-square-foot gathering place on River Street, offers floor-to-ceiling views. This is a popular setting for many wedding receptions and group meetings where guests can look out to the riverfront during their event. The Hyatt has a total of 33,000 square feet of meeting space, including two ballrooms, a junior ballroom, and breakout meeting space. The Hyatt also accommodates fitness buffs with a state-of-the-art exercise room and a heated indoor pool. Valet parking is $24 per day; there is no self-parking.

INN AT ELLIS SQUARE, 201 W. Bay St.; (912) 236-4440, (800) 542-7666; innatellissquare.com; $$$. This 252-room brick facility, situated conveniently between River Street and City Market, features 57 suites decorated in a traditional style and featuring reproduction Southern accents. The inn sits on the corner of Barnard and Bay Streets and occupies the circa-1851 Guckenheimer Building. The hotel's elegantly roomy, ground-floor public areas offer comfortable chairs, large fireplaces, Dominque's Lounge, and flexible meeting space accommodating 20 to 200 people. Other features are an on-site concierge and complimentary hot, deluxe continental breakfasts available daily. Garage parking is available on-site at $16 per day.

ℹ️ Savannah's first hotel was a place called the Mansion House on Bay Street. According to an article from a *Savannah News-Press* magazine of 1969 the city's "earliest inns were the Mansion House, City Hotel, and the Screven (House), all of them operating about the middle of the last century."

THE MANSION ON FORSYTH PARK, 700 Drayton St.; (912) 238-5158, (888) 213-3671; mansiononforsythpark.com; $$$$–$$$$$. Native son Richard Kessler added the Mansion on Forsyth Park to the Kessler Collection of luxury hotels in 2005. Kessler, who was born in Savannah and grew up in nearby Effingham County, created the Mansion on Forsyth Park by purchasing the 18,000-square-foot Kayton-Granger-Huger House on the park, then buying an adjacent property and building a four-story structure that houses the 125 rooms of his boutique hotel. The original brick and terra-cotta mansion, constructed in 1888, is now the site of the hotel's fashionable 700 Drayton Restaurant, which serves nouvelle American cuisine "with a Savannah flair." The restaurant is also home to Casimir's Lounge, the Carriage Wine Cellar, and the 700 Kitchen Cooking School. The hotel is associated with Marriott; however, it still retains its "boutique style" and the Kessler touch.

Among amenities available to guests are the Marble Garden Courtyard, waterfall, and outdoor relaxation pool; the Poseidon Spa, which offers massage therapy, rejuvenating body treatments, facials, specialty nail treatments, a cardio-fitness facility, and men's and women's locker rooms with steam showers; and the Grand Bohemian Gallery that specializes in sales of rare art and jewelry. The 700 Kitchen offers daily hands-on classes accommodating up to 16 participants. The school is open to both individuals and groups.

THE MARSHALL HOUSE, 123 E. Broughton St.; (912) 644-7896, (800) 589-6304; marshallhouse.com; $$–$$$. The Marshall House has the distinction of being one of Savannah's newest *and* oldest hotels. The 68-room luxury boutique hotel opened its doors August 1, 1999, after an extensive renovation. The hotel occupies the building that housed the original Marshall House, which was built in 1851 and closed in 1957; during its run it was also a hospital for Union soldiers.

The new Marshall House combines its historic past and sophisticated features. Rooms offer pine floors, minifridges, robes, and bathrooms with pedestal sinks. Also available are a 275-square-foot boardroom; a fully equipped business center; a 1,200-square-foot meeting room for corporate and social functions; and 45 Bistro, a fine dining restaurant. This is yet another of Savannah's most appealing places to host weddings and receptions. The quaintness of the hotel itself, combined with the historical elements, make it quite photogenic and convenient for traveling wedding parties. Valet parking is $20 a day, with limited self-parking in a garage behind the hotel.

PLANTERS INN, 29 Abercorn St; (912) 232-5678, (800) 554-1187; plantersinn savannah.com; $$$. Built in 1912 as the John Wesley Hotel, the Planters Inn has been thoroughly remodeled but retains the elegance and charm of the early days of the 20th century. The hotel's high ceilings, four-poster beds, lavish draperies, and antique furniture give you the feeling you've stepped back in time, but the friendly staff and the services they provide will make you aware you're very much in the present. Among the extras are nightly turndown service, complimentary continental breakfasts served in the hospitality room 6:30 to 10:30 a.m., and complimentary wine provided in the lobby 5:30 to 7:30 p.m. every day but Sun. Parking is available at a neighboring garage for $17.95 per night, and free valet service is offered.

RIVER STREET INN, 124 E. Bay St.; (912) 234-6400, (800) 253-4229; riverstreetinn .com; $$$–$$$$. Guests of this popular inn can experience a historic atmosphere in the midst of the activity of River Street. The rooms of this hotel occupy the top three floors of a renovated five-story cotton warehouse on the Savannah River. The main entrance to the inn and its "park side" rooms look out on to Bay Street. Thirty-two of the inn's 86 rooms face the river, and several of these have small French balconies you can step out onto for a grand view of the street and the waterway. (For an instant thrill, try popping out onto the balcony when you see a freighter approaching!)

The lower floors of the structure housing the River Street Inn were built in 1817 to store cotton for export, and the top three floors were added in 1853; the structure opened as an inn in 1985. Guests receive complimentary newspapers in the morning, use of an in-house exercise room, and homemade chocolates before retiring in the evening. There's a daily wine, champagne, and hors d'oeuvres reception in the afternoon. The inn can accommodate small meetings and conferences, with seating for 12 in its boardroom, 45 in its meeting room, and 64 for dinners. There is also room for a 125-guest reception. Parking is $15 per day.

SAVANNAH MARRIOTT RIVERFRONT, 100 General McIntosh Blvd.; (912) 233-7722, (800) 285-0398; marriott.com/ savrf; $$$–$$$$$. The atrium at the heart of the Riverfront hotel has 7,000 square feet of carpeted space that can easily accommodate themed events and trade shows attended by as many as 500 people. As many as 108 rooms on the seven upper floors of the hotel open onto balconies with views of the atrium, the north side of which looks out on the Savannah River through expansive floor-to-ceiling panes of glass. The hotel's 15,000-square-foot ballroom is the largest hotel ballroom and the second largest in the city overall, and there is an additional 21,000 square feet of meeting space in the form of conference rooms and boardrooms.

The real lure of the Marriott, though, is its location on the Savannah River and the river walk at the eastern end of River Street. A total of 60 of the hotel's 387 rooms have balconies facing north to the water, and for a little extra, you can be, as the Marriott folks say, "perched on the river" with a knockout view of passing ships. Special accommodations include rooms on the concierge floor and deluxe suites with walk-around wet bars, glass-topped dining tables, and large bathrooms featuring double vanities.

THE WESTIN SAVANNAH HARBOR GOLF RESORT & SPA, 1 Resort Dr.; Hutchinson Island; (912) 201-2000, (888) 625-4949; westinsavannah.com; $$$–$$$$. If you fly into Savannah, this hotel will probably be the first landmark that catches your eye. The city's largest luxury hotel, the Westin rises majestically above the Hutchinson Island waterfront across the Savannah River from the Historic District. The 16-story, 403-room hotel and its riverside neighbor, the Savannah International Trade and Convention Center, are the focal points of the island's Savannah Harbor development—the centerpieces of what is seen as the creation of a "second city" just north of (across the river from) Savannah's downtown area.

If you're staying for golf, the joys of playing the par 72 course—managed by Troon Golf—are almost as numerous as your spa treatment. The course plays more than 7,000 yards from its championship tees, and its clubhouse complex is the site of The Champions Grill, Legends Bar, a pro shop, an exercise facility, four tennis courts, and locker rooms with sauna and steam room. Additionally, the Westin's riverside oasis features a beautiful oversize and heated swimming pool, food and beverage service, and an extra large hot tub, as well as a zero-entry interactive dancing water children's feature. Cabanas are also available for rent, and include iced water and fresh whole fruit to help keep you cool under the hot Savannah sun.

The magnificent spa, the largest Westin has in North America, features 14 massage rooms, 2 steam rooms, 2 Swiss shower rooms, mud baths, body wraps, and more!

Southside/Midtown

COMFORT INN AND SUITES, 6800 Abercorn St.; (912) 356-1234; choiceprivileges .com; $$. At the Comfort Inn and Suites, the management serves a complimentary breakfast each morning that gives guests the opportunity to enjoy the glassed-in dining room looking out on the pool and patio. This hotel is convenient to both hospitals.

COUNTRY INN & SUITES BY CARLSON, 7576 White Bluff Rd.; (912) 692-0404, (800) 456-4000; countryinns.com/savannahga_ midtown; $$–$$$. Guest rooms offer two queen-size or one king-size bed, and there are three types of suites: the Jacuzzi Suite, with a two-person Jacuzzi tub and a king-size bed; the Guest Room with two queen beds or one king; and lastly, the One- or Two-Bedroom Suite, which has your choice of one room with a king or two queen-size beds, or two rooms, one with a king-size bed, and the other with two queens. All suites have a living room/ sitting area, full-size sleeper sofa, microwave, and minifridge. A particularly attractive feature of the Country Inn is its spacious indoor pool area, where you'll find a kidney-shaped pool, a whirlpool, and plenty of space for relaxing. The inn also offers a fitness room, a meeting room that accommodates 18 people, and a dining area where complimentary continental breakfasts are available 6 to 9:30 a.m.

HOMEWOOD SUITES BY HILTON, 5820 White Bluff Rd.; (912) 353-8500, (800) CALL-HOME; homewoodsuitessavannah .com; $$–$$$. The Homewood Suites by Hilton features 106 suites that are configured as either one-bedroom Homewood suites; Master suites, which have fireplaces; or as two-bedroom, two-bath suites. Each suite features a fully equipped kitchen with a two-burner stove, microwave, and full-size refrigerator; a sleeper sofa; and high-speed wireless Internet access.

In addition to the three-story building and two two-story buildings housing the suites, there is a spacious lodge that can accommodate 50 people for each morning's complimentary Suite Start Breakfast, as well as the Welcome Home Reception, held from 5 until 7 p.m. Mon through Thurs, which offers guests beer, wine, ice tea, lemonade, and a light meal with salad bar. A heated pool and whirlpool are situated just outside the lodge, and there is a court nearby where you can play basketball, tennis, or volleyball. The hotel has a fitness center and a business center.

OGLETHORPE INN AND SUITES, 7110 Hodgson Memorial Dr.; (912) 354-8560, (800) 344-4378; oglethorpeinn.com; $–$$. Although the Oglethorpe Inn and Suites (formerly the Masters Inn Suites) is near Oglethorpe Mall and nestled amid the shopping centers and office parks of the Southside, this three-story hotel looks and feels as if it belongs in downtown Savannah. This hotel is the perfect respite for families who need to stay in or near one of the city's two hospitals. It's built around an atrium decorated with palm trees, exotic plants, a gurgling fountain, and intricate black ironwork.

The Old South theme surfaces in the sitting rooms of the hotel's 51 suites. Each also contains a sofa, coffee table, easy chairs, and a small refrigerator, a microwave oven, and a coffeemaker. Six luxury suites have larger sitting rooms, king-size beds, and whirlpool bathtubs. All rooms are entered from the interior of the hotel. Guests can exercise in the outdoor pool at the rear of the hotel or in the fully equipped fitness room. Many of the guests are businesspeople, and there is a conference room capable of seating 45.

RESIDENCE INN BY MARRIOTT, 5710 White Bluff Rd.; (912) 356-3266, (800) 331-3131; marriott.com; $$–$$$. This Residence Inn has 66 one- and two-bedroom and studio suites under one roof. All suites have kitchens, and each of the two-bedroom accommodations has two full bathrooms, three televisions, and a wood-burning fireplace. Kitchens are equipped with refrigerators, microwaves, and coffeemakers, and the staff will do your grocery shopping for you. Just leave your shopping list at the front desk, and the groceries will be charged to your bill and deposited in your room by 6 p.m. Copies of *USA Today* and the *Savannah Morning News* are free, as is a hot breakfast buffet served in the Gatehouse sitting area. The Gatehouse is also the scene of social hours held 6 to 7:30 p.m. Mon through Wed—complimentary snacks, beer, wine, and other beverages are served. For those seeking recreation, you can enjoy an indoor pool and whirlpool, an exercise room, and an outdoor court for tennis, basketball, or volleyball. Pets are welcome, but there is a $100 nonrefundable cleaning fee.

SAVANNAH MIDTOWN COURTYARD BY MARRIOTT, 6703 Abercorn St.; (912) 354-7878, (800) 321-2211; marriott.com/savch; $–$$. Savannah's Courtyard by Marriott stands between two of the city's busiest thoroughfares, Abercorn Street and White Bluff Road, but the three-story hotel's beautifully landscaped grounds will give you a feeling of being away from the madding crowd. The centerpiece of the hotel is the courtyard with its quaint gazebo and swimming pool. Just off the pool is an enclosed whirlpool surrounded by lots of space for lounging, and there's a fitness room near the lobby that sports state-of-the-art exercise equipment. The Courtyard's large dining area is open for breakfast. There are 144 interior rooms including 12 suites. Rooms on the upper floors open onto balconies. There are two meeting rooms, each of which can accommodate 24 people seated at tables.

RESTAURANTS

Beyond the glitz of food television's Southern-cliché cooking shows, the realm of eating takes on a sophisticated flare in many of Savannah's restaurants. In other words, there's more to Savannah's cuisine than fried chicken, mashed potatoes, gravy, and lots of "y'alls." While this is a city that thrives on home cooking, there are even more culinary secrets to be found here! Word of the mild climate, romantic aura, and lower cost of living in Savannah has spread like butter on hot biscuits and has attracted gourmet chefs and creative entrepreneurs to the mix of tradition. The results: trendy cafes in historic facades, high-end restaurants, and enchanting eateries.

So how about the fare? What's new and what's Savannah's claim-to-fame with regards to dining? Apart from the Southern staples like creamy grits, corn bread, and pecan pie, many of Savannah's acclaimed provisions come from the sea. There's fresh shrimp steamed and spiced to perfection. There are crab cakes that take the cake. There's flounder served on an oversize plate, crispy and adorned with apricot glaze. And if your mouth isn't watering by now, there are hush puppies, made at least a hundred different ways.

So pull out your napkin, or better yet, bring an oversize bib. Buy your travel pants a size larger and with an elastic waist. You're about to be dazzled.

If your travels take you to nearby Tybee Island or Hilton Head, South Carolina, note that restaurants in those two locales are discussed in the individual chapters that cover those two island destinations.

AMERICAN

THE CAFE AT CITY MARKET, 224 W. St. Julian St.; (912) 236-7133; savannahcity market.com; $$. A classy local favorite for lunch or dinner is the Cafe at City Market. This European-styled bistro has maintained its popularity through the years with outstanding service and Old Savannah atmosphere. In the heat of summer, indoor dining is the choice. Within the original bricked walls, you'll feel cool and removed from the summertime humidity. Sinatra and Nat King Cole are often played in the evenings, making diners pause as they reminisce while they enjoy their favorite pasta, pizza, salads, or entrees. If the weather permits,

dine outdoors, and you'll be sitting under an awning on an open-air deck. At either location, you choose from a menu that's somewhat international in content and contains an item or two you've probably never encountered before, such as grilled cheese with artichoke hearts, mushrooms, and prosciutto or black bean pizza. Also featured on the lunch menu is the perennial-favorite Southern pecan chicken salad.

The dinner menu offers specialties such as stuffed chicken with asparagus, prosciutto, and provolone, and Cuban tuna with black beans. There's room for 65 diners inside and 45 on the deck; you can smoke outside.

Hours are Mon through Thurs 11 a.m. to 8 p.m.; Fri through Sun 11 a.m. to 9 p.m.

CAREY HILLIARD'S RESTAURANT, 3316 Skidaway Rd.; (912) 354-7240; careyhill iards.com; $. That there are six Carey Hilliard's in Savannah should tell you something about the popularity of these restaurants, which provide casual dining in an atmosphere geared toward families. Founder Carey Hilliard opened his first establishment in 1960 on Skidaway Road in what had been an A&W Root Beer stand. The drive-in, curb-service feature was retained, and all six restaurants offer it today. Order from your car, and you receive many of the amenities you would by dining inside, including china plates and silverware. Barbecue has always been, and still is, a big seller at Carey Hilliard's, which serves lunch and dinner, but seafood dishes account for about half the orders these days. Among customers' favorites are the fried shrimp, oysters, and deviled crabs. Seating at the restaurants averages 250. Beer and wine are available. Check the website for information on the other restaurant locations. Hours are Sun through Thurs 11 a.m. to midnight and Fri and Sat 11 a.m. to 1 a.m.

CHA-BELLA, 102 E. Broad St.; (912) 790-7888; cha-bella.com; $$. The trend toward natural and organic cuisine meshes with a balmy, natural setting at Cha-Bella, a local favorite and off the beaten path for tourists. Anchored by a lovely patio grill, the menu is amazing and filled with fresh and artfully presented appetizers and entrees such as Georgia white shrimp Carolina gold risotto, which is pan-tossed shrimp with asparagus and a light lemon Chardonnay and tarragon sauce. The hand-rolled pasta is fresh every evening and filled with natural, organic fillings. There's a grouper dish that features a hearty mound of gently seared fish with a farm pea, sweet corn, and lump crab

succotash. If weather permits, dine under the stars on the patio. There is an attractive bar inside. Hours are Sun through Thurs 5:30 to 9:30 p.m.; Fri and Sat 5:30 to 10 p.m. and Sun brunch 11 a.m. to 2:30 p.m.

CLARY'S CAFE, 404 Abercorn St.; (912) 233-0402; claryscafe.com; $. From the sidewalk, you'll see locals from this downtown neighborhood strolling to take their regular seats in this iconic Savannah eatery. Visitors know it as the original Clary's, the place where characters from *Midnight in the Garden of Good and Evil* congregated, but this cafe at Jones and Abercorn Streets was, as former owner Michael Faber once put it, "famous before the Book." Clary's opened in 1903 and, as a pharmacy and soda fountain, has been a hangout of Savannahians throughout its existence. Faber bought it in February 1994, during the week that *Midnight* hit the bookstores, and he renovated the building and converted the pharmacy into dining space.

The motivation for locals to flock here is Clary's famous breakfasts. Among well-loved specialties are the malted waffles and pancakes made with a special flour brought in from Michigan. For lunch, there are a variety of salads, burgers, sandwiches, and soups; and in the evening, featured items are the fillet of tilapia served on a seasoned oak plank, the old-fashioned pot roast, and the Triple Peaks salad, which has scoops of tuna, chicken, and shrimp salads on fresh greens with pasta salad. Hours are Mon through Fri 7 a.m. to 4 p.m.; Sat and Sun 8 a.m. to 4 p.m.

THE COTTON EXCHANGE, 201 E. River St.; (912) 232-7088; $$. The true Savannah experience should include a visit to the oldest restaurant on River Street, the Cotton Exchange. Quartered in a 1799 cotton warehouse, this is one of several eateries where you can dine and view the massive ships carrying cargo up and down the Savannah River. The Exchange opened in 1971 and for a time offered mainly sandwiches, but the restaurant later expanded into the dinner market, which has evolved into one of its greatest draws. Among the standouts on the dinner menu are the pasta dishes and many types of seafood entrees such as the baked, stuffed flounder, and the traditional Low Country Boil (steamed shrimp, sausage, corn, potatoes) and a small side of their home-made coleslaw. Lunch recommendations include outstanding sandwiches such as the Reuben and a char-grilled hamburger they call the Congress. With your sandwich, you get a choice of a side dish, and we recommend the zesty German potato salad. Hours are Mon through Thurs and Sunday 11 a.m. to 10:45 p.m.; Fri and Sat 11 a.m. to 11:30 p.m.

THE FIREFLY CAFE, 321 Habersham St.; (912) 234-1971; $$. This is a precious cafe that sits on the corner of beautiful Troup Square (named for Governor George Troup). The building, circa 1869, was constructed for John J. McDonough, who later became the mayor of Savannah from 1891 to 1895. Lunches are delightful, and outdoor seating is recommended for a true Savannah experience. The oriental chicken salad is a work of art with grilled chicken breast set atop shredded lettuce that has been mixed with sesame dressing, carrots, sweet peppers, mandarin oranges, scallions, and surrounded by fried wontons. The "Firefly" style corn chowder is one of the cafe's specialties: thick corn chowder with crab or chicken, topped with cheddar cheese, croutons, and scallions. For dinner, try the spicy sausage fettuccine with a thick tomato-cream sauce. There's a child's menu, which is a good thing since children will love the outdoor seating that often brings great views of passing horse-drawn carriages. A note: Late lunches are advised as delivery trucks unloading food

to this tiny restaurant are sometimes noisy and distracting. Hours are Mon through Sat 11 a.m. to 9 p.m. and Sun brunch 9 a.m. to 3 p.m.

THE PIRATES' HOUSE RESTAURANT, 20 E. Broad St.; (912) 233-5757; thepirates house.com; $$. Locals have been coming here, and steering tourists here, for decades. It once flirted with a stuffier atmosphere, but its market reminded it that it did just fine in the old incarnation. The restaurant is comprised of small dining rooms that wind throughout the building. (Legend has it some are haunted!) These quarters are Savannah's link to Robert Louis Stevenson's classic *Treasure Island*. When you have children in your party, it's hard to find a classier restaurant that accommodates younger patrons. The Pirates' House does this quite well, without damaging arrangements for adults out for a dress-up dinner. The menu is varied and includes lots of seafood. Locals head for the lunch buffet and always remember the fried chicken. The dessert menu is vast and intimidating: We suggest you consider dining here and skipping dessert, then making a return trip for dessert only before you leave Savannah. Nice casual will do for lunch, but brush up a little bit for dinner. There's full bar service. The restaurant also has a gift shop. If you're a new resident, this is a popular place to host children's birthday parties. The smaller rooms make ideal party places, and if you ask, your kids can meet a "real" pirate! Hours are Sun through Thurs 11 a.m. to 9:30 p.m.; Fri and Sat 11 a.m. to 10 p.m.

SOHO SOUTH CAFE, 12 W. Liberty St.; (912) 233-1633; sohosouthcafe.com; $$. Soho South Cafe is a Savannah staple of weekly lunch and Sunday brunch spots. The restaurant is named for the New York City neighborhood and is close to downtown shops and entertainment venues. Built as an automotive service station in 1945, the space was transformed into a restaurant in 1997 and recently remodeled to its existing state, which incorporates iconic archetypal New York City. The restaurant is described as having a "quirky, eclectic aesthetic with a sense of humor to the monumental, vast interior space." The building's original exposed elements, such as steel windows, iron trusses, and solid wooden garage doors, add to the casual dining experience. While the atmosphere hits the right mark, the food is an equal match, with salads, sandwiches, and entrees such as made-from-scratch chicken potpie. Hours are Mon through Fri 11 a.m. to 3 p.m.; Sat and Sun brunch 10 a.m. to 3 p.m.

ZUNZI'S, 108 E. York St; (912) 443-9555; zunzis.com; $$. Zunzi's bills itself as a mixture of international cuisines which comes from the owner's very different cultural backgrounds: Swiss, Italian, South African, and Dutch. Winner of many awards, Zunzi's brings together unique, fresh, and delicious flavors. It is best known for its Conquistador Sandwich, which was also featured on Travel Channel's *Best Sandwich in America*.

Zunzi's II, 9 Drayton St., is a larger version of the original. It features a full bar, outside deck, and live music. For hours call (912) 443-1554.

ASIAN

HIRANO'S RESTAURANT, 4426 Habersham St.; (912) 353-8337; $–$$. Japanese cuisine became a major hit in Savannah with the opening of this small storefront restaurant on Habersham Street. Folks stand in line for a chance to order simple, fresh food from a limited menu. Large servings and reasonable prices are hallmarks here. The food is prepared at open griddles behind the counter—this is not one of the showy knife-twirling restaurants. If you are eager

to get started, opt for a seat at the counter overlooking the cooking. Those seats come open more quickly than the small stock of tables. There is a separate sushi bar, but call ahead if you are interested—it tends to keep shorter hours. Hours are Mon through Sat 11 a.m. to 2 p.m. for lunch; 5 to 9 p.m. nightly, except Sun when the restaurant closes at 8 p.m.

BARBECUE

WALLS' BARBECUE, 515 E. York Ln.; (912) 232-9754; $. Ninety-five percent of the barbecue pork, fried chicken, deviled crabs, and other food sold at Walls' is taken out by customers. Walls' is essentially a building with a kitchen and counter on York Lane, which runs from Price to Houston Streets between York Street and Oglethorpe Avenue. If you want to eat in, there are three tables where you can sit. Walls' also offers fried fish, spareribs, and vegetable plates, and all the dinners come with three sides from among red rice, potato salad, fries, coleslaw, and vegetables.

Margaret T. Weston, who runs Walls' along with her daughter Teresa, says the business was started in the mid-1960s by her parents, Richard and Janie Walls, in a building in back of their cottage on York Street. "My daddy had a wood yard and he got tired of chopping wood, but he wanted security for my mother and me—he wanted us to be able to take care of ourselves." So the late Richard Walls started his barbecue business, choosing it, says Mrs. Weston with a smile, "because it was something he could get out of." Soon after the business opened, Walls began driving a taxicab, leaving Mrs. Walls and her daughter to do the cooking, and cook they have, much to the delight of Savannahians who love barbecue. Walls' is open Wed through Sat, 11 a.m. to 9 p.m. Call as days vary with the seasons.

BARNES RESTAURANT, 5320 Waters Ave.; (912) 354-8745; barnesrestaurant .com; $$. The folks at Barnes pride themselves on the fact that everything—from the barbecue sauce to the potato salad to the sweet ice tea—is homemade. The sauce on Barnes's chopped pork and sliced beef barbecue is made according to a recipe developed by restaurant founder Nesbert Barnes and perfected over the years by his son, Hugh; it's spread on meat that's slow-cooked at low temperatures over oak and hickory wood. There's a step-by-step guide for making the tea and an employee specifically designated to perform the task; if the tea maker is not present on a given day, the manager gets the job.

Today families, businesspeople, and retirees flock to Barnes for the barbecue and the tea for lunch and dinner. Chicken fingers, ribs, shrimp salad, and onion rings are other big sellers. Hours are Mon through Sun 10:30 a.m. to 10 p.m.

JOHNNY HARRIS RESTAURANT, 1651 E. Victory Dr.; (912) 354-7810; johnnyharris .com; $$. Stepping into the main dining room at Johnny Harris is like fox-trotting back into the late 1930s and the 1940s, when this establishment was an elegant supper club on the outskirts of Savannah. The bandstand that occupied the middle of the floor is gone, but the room retains the charm of that bygone era. Remaining from those good old days are the dark wood paneling of the Old English decor and a 30-foot-high ceiling adorned for a starry, night-sky effect. You can also still slip into one of the booths lining the perimeter of the oval-shaped room and place an order by pushing a service button that illuminates a green light overhead.

The restaurant has been a favorite of Savannahians for decades, and many patrons bring their grandchildren and great-grandchildren so they can experience the atmosphere, service, and food—in particular the barbecue, fried chicken, prime rib, and crabmeat au gratin (meat of the crab's claw folded in a cream and cheese sauce). Johnny Harris is the oldest restaurant in Savannah and one of the oldest in Georgia, but you'll notice it's not in the Historic District. It's in Midtown, on Victory Drive just east of Bee Road. That intersection is where the original restaurant was built in 1924 by a Southerner from out of town named Johnny Harris; the original wooden building was torn down, and the brick structure that houses the existing restaurant was built in 1936. Johnny Harris died in 1942, and the restaurant has been run by the Donaldson family of Savannah ever since. You might also consider purchasing some of the restaurant's barbecue sauce to take home with you. It's bottled hot and sold at Johnny Harris and other outlets in Georgia, South Carolina, and Florida, and it is shipped worldwide via mail order. Hours are Sun through Thurs 11:30 a.m. to 9:30 p.m.; Fri through Sat, 11:30 a.m. to 10:30 p.m.

WILEY'S CHAMPIONSHIP BBQ, 4700 US 80 East; (912) 201-3259; wileyschampion shipbbq.com; $$. No brag, just fact—this is the best barbecue in Savannah and maybe for a much larger radius. Wiley's is a little hole-in-the-wall joint in a strip shopping center on the way to the beach. The menu boasts chicken, beef, and sausage, but there's no need to go beyond the heavenly pulled pork. Sides are good too. Go with mac and cheese (considered a vegetable in the South) and collards and be aware the individual portions on the sides are too small for any but the daintiest of eaters, so bump your order up.

Perhaps the influx of thousands of college students has something to do with it, but area restaurants are now more likely to offer vegetarian, and even vegan, options on their menus. But if the menu doesn't actually use the word vegetarian, you might want to ask—Southern cooks traditionally use "side meat" such as salt pork or ham hocks as seasoning in vegetables.

BURGERS & DOGS

B&D BURGERS, downtown location 13 E. Broughton St; (912) 231-0986; bdburgers .net; $. There are times when the pocketbook and appetite dictate that mealtimes stray off the beaten path to the perfect burger. As an avid traveler myself, I speak with experience in recommending an out-of-the-box burger establishment that is both inexpensive and fun! In Savannah, your search brings you to a truly unique local burger joint downtown, B&D Burgers. There are burgers named for fountains and squares. There are burgers named for Savannah landmarks, and there are burgers named for famous Savannahians. Burgers at B&D are cooked to your liking, with an extensive build-your-own list along with an equally matched build-your-own hot dog selection. Breyers ice cream floats and shakes add to the yum. Now there are an additional downtown location at 209 W. Congress St. (912-238-8315) and two others at 11108 Abercorn St. (912-927-8700) and 238 Pooler Pkwy. (912-988-5560). Call for hours.

CAFES

GOOSE FEATHERS EXPRESS CAFE AND BAKERY, 39 Barnard St.; (912) 233-4683; goosefeatherscafe.com; $. This eatery offers so many delicious items that some local business folk have been known to dine there twice in one day. Our favorites

for breakfast? The bread pudding (although not for the calorie-conscious) is outstanding! The Belgian waffles are beautiful and tasty! There is fresh fruit with yogurt, as well as several variations of oatmeal combinations (like apples and cinnamon). For lunch, try the stuffed croissants, especially the spinach and feta or any of their trademark sandwiches such as the Hermitage, with cream cheese, cucumbers, sprouts, and tomatoes on multigrain bread. Winter begs for their tasty soups served in homemade bread bowls and accompanying sandwiches exploding with fresh vegetables. Be forewarned that you must stand in line (sometimes long, but always moving fast) to order. You'll take a tray with your drinks and a number and wait for your meal to be brought to the table. The Express opens at 7 a.m. weekdays and 8 a.m. weekends, closing 3 p.m. every day.

COFFEEHOUSES/BAKERIES

BACK IN THE DAY BAKERY, 2403 Bull St.; (912) 495-9292;.backinthedaybakery .com; $. Cheryl and Griffith Day, authors of the *New York Times* best-selling *Back in the Day Bakery Cookbook*, operate this funky, award winning bakery, coffee shop, breakfast and lunch destination. A foodie's haven, this spot serves up desserts and treats, artisan breads, award winning cupcakes, multicuisine lunch and free wireless access. Hours are Tues through Sat 8 a.m. to 5 p.m.

GALLERY ESPRESSO, 234 Bull St.; (912) 233-5348; galleryespresso.com; $. This is one of the city's first (and a personal favorite) on the coffeehouse scene. Coffee, both plain and in its multiple new forms, is augmented by a menu of baked goods and sandwiches, even wine. There's an occasional poetry reading or casual performance. The walls are home to displays by local artists, and the exhibits have grown in quality and importance over the years. At this cozy and good people-watching spot, the outdoor tables are particularly popular when the weather allows. Bring your laptop. It's usually open until 1 a.m. on the weekends. Hours are weekdays 7:30 a.m. to 10 p.m., weekends 8 a.m. to 10 p.m.

THE SENTIENT BEAN, 13 E. Park Ave.; (912) 232-4447; sentientbean.com; $. If political advocacy has a center in Savannah, this must be it. Of course it serves coffee (fair trade and organic, to boot) and light food, but that's the least of it. It hosts live music, film screenings, poetry slams, speeches, classes, and what have you. The schedule stays pretty full, and attendance can be pretty good, too. You might want to drop by just to read the flyers on the walls to keep up with events geared toward the young, the liberal, and/or the involved. There is both indoor and outdoor seating. The Sentient Bean is next door to Brighter Day, Savannah's oldest organic food store, and at the north end of Forsyth Park. Hours are 7 a.m. to 10 p.m. every day.

CUBAN

RANCHO ALEGRE, 402 Martin Luther King Jr. Blvd.; (912) 292-1656; rancho alegrecuban.com; $. This restaurant serves a variety of exotic-sounding dishes featuring chicken, beef, pork, and seafood, such as *pollo a la Juliana* (pepper chicken strips), *ropa vieja* (shredded beef slowly cooked in Creole sauce), *masas de cerdo fritas* (fried pork chunks), and *camarones al ajilio* (garlic shrimp). Most entrees are accompanied by rice, beans, and fried sweet plantains. We're betting this is also one of few places in town where you can get Cuban coffee, flan, and fried yucca. Live music is featured periodically. Rancho Alegre serves lunch and dinner Mon through Thurs 11 a.m. to 10 p.m., Fri and Sat 11 a.m. to 10:30 p.m., and Sun 11 a.m. to 9 p.m.

ECLECTIC

TOUCAN CAFE, 531 Stephenson Ave.; (912) 352-2233; toucancafe.com; $$. Nestled in the woods off Stephenson Avenue, the Toucan Cafe combines eclectic food, an interior that pulsates with the high-impact colors of the tropics, and an exterior with a classic Mediterranean look. The cuisine reflects the influences of several exotic cultures—Jamaican jerk chicken and Jamaican jerk tilapia, both of which are served with black beans and mango salsa; chicken farfalle and shrimp farfalle, both served in a basil cream with bow-tie pasta; and Hellenic stuffed chicken, made with spinach and feta cheese, served over rice and topped with marinated baby peas. Those are just a few of the dishes offered by owners Steve and Nancy Magulias who, in late 1998, moved the cafe to newly built quarters on Stephenson from a small storefront in nearby Eisenhower Plaza where the Toucan had been since 1994. The Toucan Cafe serves dinner and lunch Mon through Sat; reservations aren't required but will be accepted for parties of five or more. Hours are lunch Mon through Sat 11:30 a.m. to 2:30 p.m. and dinner Mon through Thurs 5 to 9 p.m., Fri and Sat 5 p.m. to 10 p.m.

FINE DINING

ELÊ FINE FUSION, 7815 US 80 East; (912) 898-2221; elerestaurant.com; $$$$. Elê opened in 2009 and since then, has established itself as one of the finer dining options in Savannah and surrounding islands. Well worth the drive from any part of town, this very contemporary and upscale eatery offers an enticing sushi bar. However striking the interior is, the draw for this restaurant is its food that is fresh and gourmet-like in its presentation as well as taste. Appetizers include a lightly battered and fried oyster plate, served with sweet chili sauce and cucumber salad, or the crispy lobster spring rolls. If you're indecisive, try Elê's tasting for two or four. You'll get a wonderful platter with chicken and steak kebabs, pot stickers, chicken spring rolls, and fried shrimp. Entrees are the real treat at Elê. The red curry chicken comes with red and green bell peppers, green beans, snow peas, bamboo, lime leaves, and basil, a sumptuous blending of spices! Elê's steaks are cut, prime, and premium grade and prepared and served with a red wine and portobello reduction sauce and steamed vegetables ($29.95 or $34.95, depending on the cut). Kobe steaks are pricey but well worth the outlay. These cuts are massaged with sake and so tender you can cut them with a fork. Desserts change weekly and you are urged to save room! Hours are Tues through Thurs 5 to 10 p.m.; Fri and Sat 5 to 10:30 p.m.; Sun, 5 to 9:30 p.m.

THE FLORENCE, 1B W. Victory Dr.; (912) 234-5522; theflorencesavannah.com; $$–$$$. Reality TV's *Top Chef* judge Hugh Acheson opened the Florence in 2014, filling a modern, industrial-themed space with a fine dining/casual mashup and an attached coffee shop. The cuisine is "Italian meets Georgia" but don't expect any recognizable pasta standards on the short and ever-changing menu. The pizza is well vouched for if the limited, complex list of entrees doesn't work for you. Rabbit, duck, and cuts of beef whose names you won't recognize are not uncommon. No disappointments, but it's pricy. Lots of attention has gone into the wine list and mixology.

GARIBALDI CAFE, 315 W. Congress St.; (912) 232-7118; garibaldisavannah.com; $$–$$$. The list of Savannahians' favorites extends to Garibaldi, a festive place that has played host to wedding celebrations, birthday galas, reunions, and friendly get-togethers for many years. In short, Garibaldi is usually the first place that comes to mind for locals seeking a special night out. Like a delightful European bistro, Garibaldi is located in what was once the Germania Fire House (circa 1871). It was reported that volunteers celebrated their firehouse with "toasts and jokes for several hours." This is precisely what Garibaldi is about today. Don't expect a quiet romantic dinner but rather a loud place where conversation and laughter defies traditional downtown restaurants. The dinner and wine list is filled with impressive selections. For an appetizer, try the corn crab cakes with mango relish and mango mint sauce. Don't leave Savannah without savoring the diamond-scored crispy scored flounder, an entire fish that is fried to a crisp and adorned with an apricot shallot sauce. (Other restaurants may claim to offer a similar dish, but no one prepares it better than Garibaldi.) Reservations are available, and dress is business attire on up. Dinner only. The restaurant opens at 5 p.m. daily.

THE GREY, 109 Martin Luther King Jr. Blvd.; (912) 662-5999; thegreyrestau rant.com; $$$. The Grey's setting almost overwhelms at first. So named because the building once housed the Greyhound bus depot, it has been meticulously restored. The result is a combination of movie set and time machine, minus the cheesiness and improbability. Executive chef Mashama Bailey, who earned her chops in New York's fiercely competitive restaurant scene, has Savannah roots. The menu changes monthly and evolves constantly. Dismiss the website claim of $30 and under per person—one entree goes for $28, another for $30, and others are north of that, without tips or drinks. It would be a shame not to give the Grey's high-performance bartenders some work.

LOCAL 11 TEN FOOD AND WINE, 1110 Bull St; (912) 790-9000; local11ten.com; **$$$.** Steps away from Savannah's Forsyth Park, this casual elegant restaurant serves popular Southern flavors using local and seasonal ingredients. Offerings include fresh seafood from the Georgia coast and fresh vegetables and herbs from local farmers. A contemporary design graces this 1950s-era former downtown bank. Open Mon through Sun 6 p.m. to 10 p.m.

NOBLE FARE, 321 Jefferson St.; (912) 443-3210; noblefare.com; **$$$$.** This foodie fantasy features locally inspired cuisine in an intimate setting. It is a favorite spot for fine dining locals and return out-of-town visitors with good taste. Hours are Tues through Thurs 5:30 to 10:30 p.m. and Fri and Sat 5:30 to 11:30 p.m.

FUSION

SKYLER'S, 225 E. Bay St.; (912) 232-3955; skylersrestaurant.com; **$$.** The co-owners of Skyler's—Nguyen Nguyet and Charles Coolidge—like to say their restaurant is "where East meets West." Nguyen, who's better known to patrons and friends as Ms. Moon, is a former resident of Saigon, and Charles is a native of Atlanta; they worked together as chefs at the Hyatt Hotel here and developed a cooking style Coolidge deems a "fusion of Asian-Continental cuisine with coastal dishes." They took that style with them when they left the hotel and opened the original Skyler's on State Street in 1990. The restaurant quickly outgrew that location, and Ms. Moon and Coolidge moved it in 1993 to the cellar of the East Bay Inn, where there was more room and the ambience of a onetime cotton warehouse—brick floors and walls and a ceiling dominated by thick wooden beams. Skyler's specializes in crab cakes, roast pork, teriyaki chicken, and Caesar salad, and seats its customers in Windsor chairs that make eating here an extremely comfortable experience. The main dining room accommodates 70 people, and there's a banquet room with seating for 60. Access to the restaurant is through the lobby of the East Bay Inn. Skyler's is open for lunch on weekdays 11 a.m. to 2:30 p.m. and serves dinner Wed and Thurs 5 to 8:30 p.m., Fri and Sat 5 to 9:30 p.m.

GREEK

OLYMPIA CAFE, 5 E. River St.; (912) 233-3131; olympiacafe.us; **$$.** This authentic Greek restaurant is a welcome respite from the glare and bustle of River Street. Although it resembles a fast-food eatery from the outside, on the inside brick walls and flooring, lots of plants, and soft lighting add to the atmosphere, but that's all incidental to the food. Favorites here include red snapper Aegean served with tomato sauce, spices, and feta cheese. Lamb chops marinated in olive oil and herbs before char-grilling are another favorite. *Spanakopita* is one of those dishes by which a Greek restaurant is measured, and you'll find this version of the flavored spinach pastry measures up well. On the lighter and less-expensive side of the menu, you can choose gyro sandwiches and chicken kebabs. Don't be confused when you arrive—Olympia Cafe also operates a quick-and-casual take-out place on one side and a 35-flavor ice cream parlor on the other. Hours are 11 a.m. to 10:30 p.m. daily.

ICE CREAM PARLORS

LEOPOLD'S ICE CREAM, 212 E. Broughton St.; (912) 234-4442; leopoldsicecream.com; **$.** Leopold's is an institution in Savannah, dating back to 1919, but the operation hasn't been continuous. Stratton Leopold reopened it with new digs within the old fixtures, and it's a real trip back in time.

Soups and sandwiches are on the menu. They make their own ice cream, along with fountain delights like banana splits and hot fudge sundaes. There are tables outside as well as in the nostalgic interior. Check out the decor: Leopold is a major Hollywood producer when he isn't making ice cream (really!), and he's decorated the place with memorabilia from movies he's been involved with. Hours are 11 a.m. to 10 p.m., (except it's open to 11 p.m. on Sat), and it's an easy walk from both the Lucas and Trustees theaters.

INDIAN

TASTE OF INDIA, 401 Mall Blvd.; (912) 356-1020; $$. Savannah has a substantial Indian community, including college professors, physicians, hoteliers, and operators of retail shops. As a result, the city has a small handful of Indian restaurants. Our favorite is Taste of India. The restaurant's quarters formerly housed a barbecue restaurant, so there's something just a little incongruous about lush Indian decor against a knotty pine background. But instead of appearing overdone, the overall effect is one of exotic luxuriance.

The menu is varied, with vegetarian dishes heavily represented. You can also choose from chicken, lamb, goat, and seafood entrees. On the appetizer side, try pau bhaji, a paste of mashed vegetables in garlic sauce that you eat on bread, or a chicken samosa, a spiced meat pastry. For entrees, dishes include lamb sagwala, which resembles a lamb stew in a creamy spinach base. Less-adventurous souls can safely opt for the chicken curry. Taste of India is open for lunch on weekdays, when it serves from a buffet, and for dinner 7 days a week. It has a full bar. Hours are Mon through Fri 11 a.m. to 3 p.m., dinner daily and weekends 5 to 10 p.m.

MOROCCAN

THE MIRAGE MEDITERRANEAN BAR AND GRILL RESTAURANT, 20 E. Broughton St.; (912) 236-5464; themiragesavannah.com; $$. If you're looking for a little local excitement that is out of the Savannah norm and convenient to the Historic District, check out this unique-to-Savannah restaurant, which includes a hookah lounge. The belly dancer comes on for short intervals throughout the evening, and the performances we've witnessed were interesting, entertaining, and quite decorous. The menu is heavily weighted with dishes like lamb cooked in honey and almonds, but even the less-adventurous palate will find an option here. Many dishes are variations on kebabs, in lamb, beef, or chicken (or opt for the dish featuring all three). For the appetizer course, try a salad sampler, which features six different salads or relishes. Open for dinner Sun through Wed 5 p.m. to midnight, Thurs through Sat 5 p.m. to 2:30 a.m.

PIZZA

BASIL'S PIZZA AND DELI, 216 Johnny Mercer Blvd.; (912) 897-6400; basilspizzaonline.com; $. This restaurant on Wilmington Island prides itself on being family operated (the name is derived from the Greek name of a son/grandson of the owners) and specializes in pizza and Mediterranean dishes. Among the combination pizzas are the Greek, eggplant Parmesan, and gyro varieties, and the menu also includes Hellenic-inspired fare such as *dolmades* and *spanakopita*. Basil's also offers delicious pasta, salads, and a broad array of sandwiches, and the pasta salad—made with bacon and broccoli—is as good as it gets. Basil's occupies a storefront in the Wilmington Island Shopping Center at the heart of the island. Basil's offers an excellent selection of domestic and imported beers.

An expansion includes Yo Basil's, a frozen yogurt shop and dessert cafe. There's outside seating on a screened-in porch. Hours are Sun through Thurs 11 a.m. to 9 p.m. and Fri and Sat 11 a.m. to 9:30 p.m.

SPANKY'S PIZZA GALLEY & SALOON, 317 E. River St.; (912) 236-3009; spankys .tv; $.

Ansley Williams, Alben Yarbrough, and Dusty Yarbrough opened the first Spanky's on River Street in 1976, intending to bring pizza to the area. They also served burgers and chicken sandwiches at the restaurant, which is housed in what had been a cotton warehouse. According to Williams, the chicken breasts used for the sandwiches were too large for the buns on which they were served, so the restaurateurs sliced off the excess chicken and, not wanting to be wasteful, battered and fried the strips of meat and sold them as "chicken fingers." Their concoction was a hit with locals. A warning: if you're not a fan of loud and boisterous restaurants with a sports bar atmosphere, you'll probably want to stay away from Spanky's. Hours are Sun through Thurs 11 a.m. to 10 p.m., Fri through Sat 11 a.m. to 11 p.m.

VINNIE VAN GOGO, 317 W. Bryan St.; (912) 233-6394; vinnievangogo.com; $$.

Vinnie's serves pizza with real character—thin crust with fresh ingredients, including such options as spinach, artichoke, and broccoli. Experiment with pesto instead of regular sauce. Dine in the cramped interior or at outside tables overlooking City Market (semi-enclosed when it's cold). Pizza is available by the slice, and one of those with the excellent spinach salad is an ample meal. A personal favorite among the pizzas is feta, sun-dried tomato, and black olive. Beer and wine are available. Your most casual duds are probably too dressy for Vinnie's, but the food's tops. Cash only; no credit cards. Hours are Mon through Thurs from 4 to 11:30 p.m., Fri and Sat noon to midnight, Sun, noon to 11:30 p.m.

PUB FARE

B. MATTHEW'S, 325 E. Bay St.; (912) 233-1319; bmatthewseatery.com; $$.

This once raucous bar called the Lamp Post is now thriving with old-city atmosphere and charm, a pub-like lunch and dinner menu, and a healthy array of imported beers on tap and in bottles. Starting with breakfast, their pancakes, omelets, and egg dishes are light and tasty! Sun brunch features an artichoke-and-goat-cheese omelet and apple, pecan, and bourbon chutney pancakes (served 9 a.m. to 3 p.m.). Lunch favorites include a Black-eyed Pea Cake Sandwich, a spicy combination served on fresh bread, and an apple–pecan chicken salad sandwich, and entrees like pecan-crusted chicken. Owner Brian Huskey bought the restaurant in 2006 and has constantly upgraded the facilities, making it one of downtown Savannah's brightest spots! Hours are Mon through Thurs 8 a.m. to 9 p.m., Fri and Sat 8 a.m. to 10 p.m. Sun brunch is 9 a.m. to 3 p.m.

CRYSTAL BEER PARLOR, 301 W. Jones St.; (912) 349-1000; crystalbeerparlor .com; $$.

Savannahian John Nichols revived the tradition of the Crystal Beer Parlor a few years ago, much to the delight of a close following of generations of fans. As best as he possibly could, Nichols tackled the challenge of returning it to the original look of an early-1900s burger joint with a vengeance, livening up the old place, while keeping the hometown feel alive. The original restaurant was one of the first American eating establishments to serve alcohol after the repeal of Prohibition. Today the walls are covered with photos of early Savannah. There's a Monroe Room, named for Monroe Whitlock, who was a server there for 45 years. Of course there's a bar here that serves a variety of draft and bottled beers. The rich and creamy crab stew is a specialty, but all the dishes on the large menu are delicious. The restaurant serves lunch and dinner Sun through Thurs 11 a.m. to 10 p.m., and Fri and Sat 11 a.m. to 11 p.m.

SIX PENCE PUB, 245 Bull St.; (912) 233-3151; sixpencepub.com; $$. With the charm of a true British pub, the Six Pence offers specials each day. Patrons have a particular liking for the shepherd's pie; the sausage (bangers, in England) and mashed potatoes; the French onion and potato soups; a meat pie made with mushrooms, peas, onions, and carrots; and beer-marinated beef. So if you're looking for Savannah-fare, you may want to dine somewhere else.

With a generous selection of beer on tap, the pub is filled with conversation-starting memorabilia, with most of it adorning the walls and bar. Among the Toby mugs, the coronation collectibles dating from 1898, and the pub signs, some of which are more than 200 years old, there's also a must-see ship's bell that's a replica of the one on the *Titanic*—a souvenir gift from that ill-fated vessel's maiden voyage. Hours are Mon through Thurs 11:30 a.m. to midnight; Fri and Sat, 11:30 a.m. to 2 a.m.; Sun 11:30 a.m. to 10 p.m.

SEAFOOD

DESPOSITO'S SEAFOOD, 187 Macceo Dr.; (912) 897-9963; $. If you're looking for a dive that has awesome steamed seafood, this is the place. On evenings when the weather's nice, the windows of the enclosed porch of this little cinder-block and wood eatery are opened wide. You can sit out there at tables covered with newspaper and eat boiled shrimp, crab legs, and steamed oysters as the breeze from the nearby Wilmington River wafts through the place.

Desposito's also serves deviled crab; homemade chili, pecan pie, and potato salad; and the Lowcountry basket, which is filled with shrimp, corn on the cob, sausage, and the aforementioned potato salad. In addition to the porch, there's a dining room and a bar that serves beer and wine. Desposito's is open for dinner daily except Mon and for lunch and dinner on Fri, Sat, and Sun but hours are variable. MasterCard and Visa only are accepted. It's on the eastern side of the Wilmington River and north of US 80.

DRIFTAWAY CAFE, 7400 Skidaway Rd.; (912) 303-0999; driftawaycafe.com; $$. The Driftaway Cafe is a casual place resembling someone's back porch that's been decorated with beachy knickknacks. The interior is cute without being cloying, with murals of local water scenes on the walls and a massive sculpture of a raging shark bursting through one wall. The best tables overlook the marsh at the rear, where you can see a real creek and a fake waterfall, a cat (or could it be a raccoon?) with some kitschy statuary scattered around. From the porch, you can also view (on a good night) some really large snapping turtles in the creek and the butterflies feasting on the landscaping.

Enough about the scenery. The menu covers salads, sandwiches, and full entrees, but you should start with the Herb River Crab Dip, a creamy blend of cheeses brimming with (real) crabmeat and spices. The dip is served with toasted bread, and it's a good thing they don't bring you much of it or you would forgo the entree and lick the dip bowl clean. There are chicken and steak dishes on the menu, but stick with seafood. There are shrimp quesadillas ($11), butterfly shrimp (fried and tossed in firecracker sauce, $11), and an Atlantic salmon grilled and served with jerk-grilled asparagus ($13). The fish tacos ($12) are phenomenal: grouper strips flash-fried in batter and served on flour tortillas with lettuce and some perfectly seasoned sauce. For a more formal meal, go for the crispy scored flounder, which is flash-fried and served with lots of spicy apricot sauce. Sides range from dressy (grilled asparagus) to down-home (homemade potato chips). There's a full bar and a large wine selection. Hours are Mon through Sat 11 a.m. to 10 p.m. and Sun 10 a.m. to 9 p.m.

THE FLYING FISH, 7906 US 80 East; (912) 897-2009; $$. Hush puppies, fried fish, and fried shrimp are served in a tropical-like atmosphere where flip-flops and T-shirts define the dress code. Don't expect anything fancy about this place as all food is served on throwaway dishes. Be sure to try the cheese grits with grouper fingers, fish tacos, and any of their fresh seafood, as well as the perfectly sweetened tea. There's a full bar and a decent beer selection and several outdoor tables if you're coming from the beach. Hours are 11:30 a.m. to 10 p.m. daily.

SOUTHERN

ALLIGATOR SOUL, 114 Barnard St.; (912) 232-7899; alligatorsoul.com; $$$. Attracted by an eclectic menu, locals and tourists enjoy the fabulous creations served at this Barnard Street eatery just north of Telfair Square. Try the fried green tomatoes—tasteful and beautiful with a crisp Parmesan and cornmeal–crusted covering, served sizzling over a delicious chipotle mayonnaise and garnished with a sweet relish. For dinner, try the shrimp and grits—shrimp sautéed in lemon butter and Creole spices and served over stone-ground grits with Tasso ham and cheese. Save room for dessert! The Alligator Soul Banana Beignets are served hot, and are perfect with coffee if you desire. Made with fresh bananas lightly coated with tempura batter, quickly fried, and served with banana ice cream, roasted cinnamon wonton crisps, and candied pecans, this dish is one of many

reasons to dine here. Open nightly, Mon through Sun 5:30 p.m. to "10-ish."

ELIZABETH ON 37TH STREET, 105 E. 37th St.; (912) 236-5547; elizabethon 37th.net; $$$. This 1900s Southern mansion that is both elegant and refined was made famous by the original owners, Elizabeth and Michael Terry. Now the operation is run under the same high standards by brothers Greg and Gary Butch, who were longtime employees of Elizabeth on 37th. With an incomparable menu starting with appetizers like a black-eyed pea patty with greens and tomato relish, mozzarella and tomatoes served warm with pecan pesto, and seasonal soups that are standouts, there's still prestige that comes with saying you're "dining at Elizabeth's." The atmosphere could be summarized as sophisticated and maybe a wee bit snobby. My favorite entree is the Spicy Savannah Red Rice with Georgia Shrimp and Half Moon River clams, sausage, grouper, and okra—a fancy way to say, Lowcountry boil . . . with okra. Another highlight is the Coastal Grouper Celeste, crisp sesame-almond crusted grouper with peanut sauce and roasted potato. This is a place that truly transforms the area's finest seafood into not-to-be-duplicated dishes. Before you leave, opt for the Chocolate Pecan Torte, a dark chocolate cream in a crushed pecan crust, topped with chocolate whipped cream. There is an elegant private dining room. Dress is business casual and reservations are always suggested. Hours are 6 to 10 p.m. nightly. Reservations are required.

HUEY'S, 115 E. River St.; (912) 234-7385; hueysontheriver.net; $$. This is a chain with a local flair! Huey's brings the Big Easy to Savannah with its New Orleans–style cuisine. With floor-to-ceiling windows right on the sidewalk, Huey's also offers a great view

Close-up

Regional Cuisine Offers a Taste of Savannah

When you're in Savannah, you might run across some cuisine you're not likely to find in other parts of the country. Two examples, the Lowcountry shrimp boil and the oyster roast, combine food with other elements you might have noticed being mentioned throughout this book: Savannahians' love of getting together and their fondness for being outdoors.

You can order Lowcountry boil in a restaurant, and the same goes for oysters, but perhaps the best way to experience them is by attending an outdoor party at which they are the featured components. Lowcountry boil—also known as Frogmore stew because it supposedly originated in Frogmore, South Carolina, which is about 90 minutes northeast of Savannah—consists of smoked sausage, corn on the cob, and shrimp all boiled together in a large pot. Some cooks add other ingredients, with new potatoes seeming to be the most popular.

Oysters served at an oyster roast are roasted on a big piece of tin or steel that's supported by cinder blocks. A red-hot fire is built under the sheet of metal, and the oysters are placed on it and covered with wet cloth—burlap sacks do nicely. The oysters will steam open in about 20 minutes, and they're ready to eat. Special oyster knives are used to help dig the oysters out of their shells, and it's a good idea to wear gloves to prevent being cut by the oyster's tough exterior.

The Southerner's way is to enjoy a Lowcountry boil or oyster roast by standing around a long table on a crisp day in autumn, chatting with friends, and diving into a pile of oysters or a big heap of sausage, shrimp, and corn that's been dumped on a table covered with newspaper. It doesn't hurt, by the way, if grilled hot dogs are nearby for those who aren't fans of the oyster.

Among other foods associated with this area are Savannah red rice, a dessert called trifle, and a cookie known as the benne wafer. The benne wafer has a taste all its own because it's made with benne seeds, which is what folks in the Lowcountry call sesame seeds. Trifle, a gift of the English colonists to Savannah, consists of pound cake that's been sprinkled with sherry, layered with custard, and topped with whipped cream.

Savannah red rice goes great with fried chicken and seafood. The following is a recipe for this distinctly local dish provided by Martha Giddens Nesbit, who edited and wrote much of the food section of Savannah's daily newspaper for more than a decade and is the author of the *Savannah Collection* and *Savannah Entertains* cookbooks.

In her recipe, which serves four people, Martha uses four slices of bacon that have been fried crisp, crumbled, and reserved, one chopped onion, one chopped celery stalk, a cup of raw rice, one 16-ounce can of tomatoes, three-quarters of a cup of water, a teaspoon of salt, and a quarter-teaspoon of cayenne pepper.

Fry the chopped onion and celery in bacon fat, then remove some of the fat, if desired, and add the rice, tomatoes, water, salt, and pepper. Combine the ingredients and transfer them to a 1.5-quart baking dish. Bake at 350 degrees for 20 minutes or until the rice is soft but not dry. Stir in the reserved bacon and serve hot or at room temperature.

Something else you're likely to encounter during mealtimes in Savannah is sweetened ice tea, which we call just plain ol' "sweet tea." Savannahians drink it year-round, and here's a good way to make a gallon-size pitcher full: Place three family-size tea bags in the basket of your automatic coffeemaker and brew up a full coffeepot of tea. Put about a cup of sugar in the pitcher and pour the hot tea on top. Stir it up and add a full coffeepot of water and stir again. When it cools, you've got sweet tea.

of the Savannah River, a circumstance that makes a breakfast of cafe au lait and beignets something special. For those unfamiliar with "N'awlins," beignets (pronounced "ben-yeas") are delectable French doughnuts.

Huey's also has some specialties for breakfast eaters with heartier appetites, including eggs Benedict and eggs Sardou, the latter consisting of a bed of creamed spinach with artichoke hearts on a toasted English muffin with two poached eggs topped with hollandaise sauce. For lunch and dinner, there are such dishes as red beans and rice served with andouille sausage, and Muffuletta, a sandwich made with freshly baked bread, Genoa salami, capocollo ham, provolone, and an olive dressing. The food is zesty but moderately spiced; if you want more zip, there's Tabasco sauce on your table. Hours are Mon through Thurs 7 a.m. to 10 p.m., Fri 7 a.m. to 11 p.m., Sat 8 a.m. to 11 p.m., Sun 8 a.m. to 10 p.m.

THE LADY AND SONS, 102 W. Congress St.; (912) 233-2600; theladyandsons.com; $$. Be sure to sample the food that made Paula Deen famous here at her restaurant, and remember, there are no guarantees that the diva will be there to meet you in person. There's an appealing menu at this Southern comfort-food eatery, but unless you're going to be in town long enough to return repeatedly, skip it and go directly to the buffet. This is the slow-cooked, perfectly seasoned stuff that Southerners consider real home cooking, which may define why there aren't many locals eating there. (They're eating it at home, too!) Fried chicken, squash casserole, seasoned greens, fried green tomatoes, hoecakes (ask if you don't know), cheese biscuits—you get the picture. Hours are Mon through Thurs 11 a.m. to 9 p.m., Fri and Sat 11 a.m. to 10 p.m., Sun (lunch buffet only) 11 a.m. to 5 p.m.

i You can take care of some of your souvenir shopping while you dine out. Many restaurants sell sauces featured in their prize dishes or cookbooks drawing from their menu.

MRS. WILKES' DINING ROOM, 107 W. Jones St.; (912) 232-5997; mrswilkes.com; $$. This restaurant is worth the wait because dining at Mrs. Wilkes' is about more than eating lunch; it's about experiencing the true, Southern Sunday lunch around the dinner table with family and friends. (At least they'll be your friends once lunch is over.) It's so special that President Barack Obama "popped in" with his entourage and dined with a table of surprised guests! Traditional Southern home-cooking restaurants in Savannah started at Mrs. Wilkes', and daughter Marcia Thompson does a fine job of seeing that her parents' famous traditions are ongoing. If you must visit one of the two restaurants during your stay in Savannah, try this one first. This place has been highly praised by national and international media through the years.

At our most recent visit to Mrs. Wilkes', the tables were loaded with fried chicken, barbecue chicken, beef stew, sausage, baked ham, collard greens, snap beans, black-eyed peas, squash, rice and gravy, okra and tomatoes, mashed potatoes, candied yams, pickled beets, apple salad, and macaroni salad. Mrs. Wilkes' doesn't take credit cards. Hours are weekdays 11 a.m. to 2 p.m. Be sure to arrive early to avoid waiting.

THE OLDE PINK HOUSE RESTAURANT & PLANTERS TAVERN, 23 Abercorn St.; (912) 232-4286; plantersinnsavannah .com; $$$. Savannahians who have traditionally enjoyed the Olde Pink House for its ambient downstairs bar and elegant, historical feel, are elated by the restaurant's expansion, an open outdoorsy bar with tables that spread out onto the sidewalk and under a canopy of trees. In fact, it's one of the trendiest and most in-demand places to dine in town. As the dining rooms inside have sometimes felt restrictive and crowded, the outdoor Pink House is exceptional. If it's winter, start downstairs in the Planters Tavern, a more casual and comfortable dining place and home to the restaurant's wine cellar. A fireplace is usually lit on each end of the room, and there is live piano music nightly.

The Olde Pink House serves regional cuisine in several elegant dining rooms occupying the upper two floors of the building. Examples of this type of cooking are the roast duck with wild berry sauce and hoppin' John, she-crab soup laced with sherry, Caesar salad with corn bread oysters, crispy scored flounder with apricot shallot sauce, and grilled pork tenderloin with collards and yams. Reservations are definitely recommended. If you're interested in dining in the restaurant's most romantic spot, ask for a table by a window in the second-floor Office Room—it has a view of picturesque Reynolds Square. Ask your waiter to share some of the varied ghost stories that are unique to this establishment. Hours are lunch Tues through Sat 11:30 a.m. to 2:30 p.m.; dinner Sun through Thurs 5 to 10:30 p.m. and Fri and Sat 11 a.m. to 11 p.m.

SWEET POTATOES, 6825 Waters Ave.; (912) 352-3434; sweetpotatoeskitchen .com; $. This casual restaurant, which offers lunch and dinner, is the downscale relative of the pricier and fancier Toucan Cafe (also described in this chapter)—but the food is still outstanding. The decor is simple and consists of bright paint and simple artwork. Basic meat and vegetables, cooked Southern style, are the mainstays here. There's a rotating list of daily specials, but you can count on some standard dishes as well. I recommend the vegetable plates, for which you select up

to four dishes, simply because it is so hard to find restaurants that offer good selections of vegetables and cook them properly. Consider the dilled lima beans or the collards. True to its name, the restaurant offers some variant of a sweet potato dish every day—baked sweet potatoes, sweet potato soufflé, mashed sweet potatoes, even sweet potato salad. If you're a fan of freshwater fish, try their fried catfish, cooked crispy (and not greasy). Beware, however, of the occasional offering of something called Wisconsin-style sweet potatoes—they are proof of the fact that while you can combine sweet potatoes and cheddar cheese, you really shouldn't. Hours are Mon through Sat 11 a.m. to 9 p.m.

VIC'S ON THE RIVER, 26 E. Bay St.; (912) 721-1000; vicsontheriver.com; $$–$$$. What a refreshing place to dine on the riverfront! Vic's on the River is not typical of other Savannah restaurants that are housed in historic buildings and oftentimes dark, musty, and cramped. Because this was once the top floor of a cotton warehouse, the rooms offer a spacious and airy feel with plenty of space to dine without bumping into the table beside you. The food is as refined as the atmosphere. Appetizers include a crab cake with corn, black-eyed pea salsa, traditional remoulade, and chervil; crispy calamari with pickled peppers and a citrus chile glaze with feta cheese; and fried green tomatoes. A favorite lunchtime entree is local shrimp and smoked cheddar stone-ground grits with smoked bacon and rosemary barbeque. The dinner menu standouts include many of the same entrees only doubled in price. There are also brown sugar–cured pork chops, a braised lamb shank, and a grilled rib eye for landlubbers. There's a bar within the restaurant, and the view of the Savannah River is outstanding. Hours are Sun through Thurs 11 a.m. to 10 p.m. and Fri and Sat 4 to 11 p.m. There is valet parking.

SURF 'N' TURF

BELFORD'S SAVANNAH SEAFOOD & STEAKS, 315 W. St. Julian St.; (912) 233-2626; belfordssavannah.com; $$$. Everything on the menu at Belford's is exceptional. Testifying to this statement are entrees such as shrimp, greens, and grits; a double-cut pork chop; and the stuffed filet—grilled filet mignon stuffed with shrimp and finished with béarnaise sauce. The crab cakes are among the city's best and, in fact, a consecutive award winner among professional writers. The light and airy atmosphere promotes casual dress. At first glance, Belford's architectural strengths are a standout, with the tall, arched, unadorned windows lining the City Market and Congress Street. The restaurant is housed in a former produce warehouse once frequented by local grocers. The name is derived from the Belford's Wholesale Food Company, which was an integral part of City Market in the early 1900s, and a portrait of the Belford family is among the framed artwork decorating the eatery. Brick walls, highly polished wooden floors, captain's chairs, and tables covered with linen add to the classical feel of the place. Belford's serves lunch and dinner daily, and breakfast Mon through Sat, with brunch on Sun. Hours are 11 a.m. to 10 p.m., 7 days a week.

THE RIVERHOUSE RESTAURANT, 125 W. River St.; (912) 234-1900, (800) 317-1912; riverhouseseafood.com; $$$. The Riverhouse and its bakery occupy four bays of an old cotton warehouse near the west end of River Street, and the bricks and thick wooden beams of the building lend charm to the upscale but casual atmosphere. Featured dishes include the grouper Florentine, which is served atop angel-hair pasta, and Atlantic salmon crowned with whipped potatoes and baked. Among the appetizers are the seafood strudel—a light pastry filled with spinach, feta, shrimp, and crabmeat—and shrimp served on grits with a tasso gravy. The restaurant serves lunch and dinner, and "dessert only" customers are welcome anytime in the bakery. Always save room for dessert here. The restaurant's forte is its Southern pecan pie, praline cheesecake, and fudge walnut pie (with ice cream if you like). Hours are daily 11 a.m. to 10 p.m.

THE SHRIMP FACTORY, 313 E. River St.; (912) 236-4229; theshrimpfactory.com; $$$. This restaurant near the eastern end of River Street offers "fine casual dining," meaning the atmosphere is relaxed but replete with special touches such as the salad being tossed tableside. The Shrimp Factory prides itself on its seafood, steaks, and chicken dishes, and as might be expected, you can find shrimp served "in so many ways" here—fried, with crab au gratin, with deviled crab, with sausage Creole, and with scallops. Pecan pie is a specialty of the house, as is the pine bark stew, which is best described as a "Southern bouillabaisse." The restaurant occupies the bottom floor of a warehouse built in the 1820s for storing cotton, rosin, and other products, and the building's heart-pine ceiling beams and rafters and brick walls give the Shrimp Factory a rustic feel. Hours are Mon through Sat 11 a.m. to 11 p.m. and Sun 11 a.m. to 10 p.m.

ENTERTAINMENT

In this chapter, we outline Savannah's major cultural organizations and venues for you, as well as how to kill a few hours in a pleasant way. We provide plenty of telephone numbers and instructions on how to tap into specific schedules. You might also want to check out our Annual Events and Festivals chapter for further suggestions for an artsy afternoon or evening. Keeping abreast of the local cultural scene is fairly easy. The *Savannah Morning News* offers its most comprehensive arts coverage in a Sunday Accent section. The *Morning News*'s Thursday Diversions section also contains event listings, but the coverage there tends to be more club and concert oriented.

Also, check out the Visit Savannah website (savannahvisit.com). It's an excellent resource for cross-checking event details.

Savannah's bar and entertainment scene falls into three general categories: River Street, a restored area along the Savannah River that was refurbished with just this sort of thing in mind; City Market, a restored quadrant of the Historic District that's heavy on clubs and bars as well as shops; and a variety of watering holes and entertainment sites scattered along routes to the Southside.

If you don't have something very specific in mind (say, jazz or a sports bar), our advice is to follow your ear, literally. Visitors will fare better on River Street and in City Market, where there are lots of nightspots clustered together. You can follow the music you hear spilling out the doors and wander conveniently from site to site. Which brings us to the question of alcohol and the law. Savannah's folklore stresses the city's hard-drinking reputation, with tales that the town was never dry, even during Prohibition (which lingered long in Georgia, where some counties are still dry).

Also note that city ordinances prohibit open bottles or cans on the street, but (as of this writing) if you want to wander out of a River Street watering hole or a City Market club, most places are glad to provide you with a plastic or foam cup. This "go-cup" leniency applies only to the downtown festival district—basically around River Street and City Market—and your bartender can fill you in on the finer points.

We've spent a lot of space covering alcohol, but we don't mean to give you the impression that all our entertainment has to do with booze. Savannah is home to an active Alcoholics Anonymous family: If you want to catch a meeting and talk first-hand about alcohol-free nightlife in Savannah, call (912) 356-3688 for the extensive schedule.

CLASSICAL MUSIC

SAVANNAH PHILHARMONIC, 30 W. Broughton St., Ste. 205; (912) 232-6002; savannahphilharmonic.org. The Savannah Philharmonic Orchestra is a professional group which presents a schedule of approximately eight major concerts each season (not counting chamber musical events), ranging from intense classical programs with notable visiting artists to the popular annual Holiday Pops, complete with sing-alongs. For a portion of its programs, it is joined by the Savannah Philharmonic Chorus, a community-based, auditioned group. Venues vary from the theater at the Savannah Civic Center to the Lucas Theatre to the sanctuary of the Cathedral of St. John the Baptist. Find out the schedule online; then order tickets online or via phone at (912) 525-5050 or pick them up in person at Savannah Box Office, 215 E. Broughton St. Mon through Fri 10 a.m. to 5 p.m. or an hour prior to the performance at the venue.

i Scan the local paper for listings of performances by the Savannah Arts Academy. This public high school puts on some surprisingly professional performances, often in the spring. Its Skylite Jazz Band is particularly good.

DANCING, NIGHTCLUBS & LIVE MUSIC

BERNIE'S, 115 E. River St.; (912) 236-1837; berniesriverstreet.com. This is a longtime riverfront hangout with a pub-like atmosphere that is truly Savannah. Situated within a pre–Civil War cotton warehouse, there's live music, a hefty beer selection, and easy access to the ballast stone sidewalks outside where you'll dash out to view passing ships. A full menu includes burgers, seafood, and hotdogs. Order a Bloody Mary and enjoy the astonishment when the bartender serves it to you in a mason jar with a sprig of pickled okra! Now, that's Southern! Hours are Mon through Thurs 11 a.m. to midnight, Fri to Sat 11 a.m. to 3 a.m. There's a second location on Tybee Island at 13 Tybrisa Street (912-786-5100).

CHURCHILL'S PUB & RESTAURANT, 13 W. Bay St.; (912) 232-8501; thebritishpub .com. An after-hours kitchen fire drove this little bit of England out of its original home several years ago, but it's back in new (well, not new, but different) and expanded quarters. The massive carved mahogany bar will make you feel to the manor born! Downstairs there are pool tables and dartboards. All in all, it's a nice, friendly place to have a drink, and the management is proud to point out that it's British owned.

Churchill's is also a restaurant that serves dinner, including such British fare as bangers and mash or roast beef with Yorkshire pudding. The menu also includes more conventional items such as fish dishes and sandwiches. They claim to have 20 beers on tap (we didn't count, but there's obviously no shortage). Churchill's opens daily 5 p.m. to 2 a.m.

CLUB ONE JEFFERSON, 1 Jefferson St.; (912) 232-0200; clubone-online.com. This was Savannah's first openly gay bar that also attracted a straight clientele. This address hosts a variety of features: a stage with a drag show and other performances, a high-tech dance floor, and quieter drinking spaces. Lady Chablis, the drag queen made famous in the book *Midnight in the Garden of Good and Evil* (and the movie, where she portrayed herself), periodically performs here. Hours Mon through Sat 5 p.m. to 3 a.m., Sun 5 p.m. to 2 a.m.

COACH'S CORNER, 3016 E. Victory Dr.; (912) 352-2933; coachs.net. The sports bar has become an American institution, and Coach's Corner is a fine example of a place where you'll find a pleasant mix of locals, students, sports fans, and a waitstaff that's been there for years (well, most of them). Don't expect the latest in audio/video capabilities as this is a small, locally owned sports bar; however, the pluses are many. Dark and cool, there are booths lined up on both sides, several pool tables, and an outdoor seating area and stage where bands and special events are held during the year. The true flair of Coach's is that no matter what obscure sporting event you're searching the airwaves for, the staff will more than likely find it for you. The chicken fingers (and chicken finger salad) are tender and lightly breaded, but the real draw here is the wings! They are possibly Savannah's most popular. Dress is always casual. Come by the Victory Drive site—it's in Thunderbolt, on the way to and from the beach—during Oct of a good season for the Atlanta Braves, and you can catch a giant motorized tomahawk chopping away, backed up by an occasional live chopper. Oh, and be sure to wear your colors! Hours are 11 a.m. to 11 p.m. daily.

THE JINX, 127 W. Congress St.; (912) 236-2281; thejinx912.com. This downtown bar has a hip vibe with eclectic live music and quirky decor. Hours are Mon through Sun 4 p.m. to 3 a.m.

KEVIN BARRY'S IRISH PUB, 117 W. River St.; (912) 233-9626; kevinbarrys.com. Savannah prides itself on its Irish heritage, not just during the elaborate St. Patrick's Day observance, but year-round. Just check out this pub. The stone-walled setting is dark and atmospheric, brightened considerably by a constantly changing program of authentic Irish performers every night (although we suggest calling ahead if this is essential to your evening; we've seen the schedule shift around a bit over the years). Count on acceptable food (including such Irish fare as potato soup and corned beef and cabbage), standard drinks, and an impressive collection of bottled and draft beers and ales. There's even a small gift shop for Irish goods. Brush up on your Irish history (and learn who the real Kevin Barry was) by reading the captions to the framed photos of figures who were either historic freedom

fighters or long-dead terrorists, depending on your outlook. Hours are Mon through Fri 11 a.m. to 3 a.m., Sat 11 a.m. to 2 a.m., and Sun 12:30 p.m. to 3 a.m.

ℹ️ Dressed up for an evening on River Street? You won't want to risk cobblestones in dressy shoes, so if you park above the street—as you probably will have to—take the municipal elevator down to the river level. It is tucked between City Hall and the Hyatt Regency Savannah Hotel.

LULU'S CHOCOLATE BAR, 42 Martin Luther King Jr. Blvd; (912) 480-4564; luluschocolatebar.com. Locals know when a sweet tooth and the need for an adult beverage collide. Desserts made daily with a full bar and martini specials are featured in a relaxed and fun setting. Hours are Sun through Thurs 2 p.m. to 1 a.m., Fri and Sat 2 p.m. to 2 a.m.

MOON RIVER BREW PUB, 21 W. Bay St.; (912) 447-0943; moonriverbrewing. This brewpub is Savannah's only on-premises microbrewery. You can get up to nine different (varying seasonally) fresh microbrews here in imperial pints and half pints. The building is pretty cool itself. The home of the former City Hotel, this is where the first post office was also housed. The building even served as a branch of the Bank of the United States. During the War of 1812, Winfield Scott, the Marquis de Lafayette, the first three commodores of the US Navy, and naturalist John James Audubon stayed at the hotel incarnation. Outdoor seating is available. Hours are Sun through Thurs 11 a.m. to 11 p.m. and Fri and Sat until midnight.

PINKIE MASTER'S LOUNGE, 318 Drayton St.; (912) 238-0447; pinkiemasters .net. Looking for a true dive in the city?

This modest neighborhood watering hole is legendary in Savannah as a political bar. Journalists once plied local sources with alcohol here; Jimmy Carter (yes, that Jimmy Carter) once gave a speech standing on the bar. What you'll find today is a small bar where regulars talk back to the television set. There's an eclectic jukebox, darts, and a few game machines, along with the beer and the booze. Check out the atmosphere: Christmas decorations that never come down, a stuffed crow (at least we hope it's stuffed—maybe it's just dead), a rogue's gallery of politicians' photos, and a soft-focus nude painting about which any of the regulars is willing to tell you lies. Drinks are cheap, the air is thick, and there's a sign above the bar that reads "TIPPING IS NOT A CITY IN CHINA." There's a lot to be said for a place that refuses to gloss up for tourists. Hours are Mon through Sat 4 p.m. to 3 a.m.

SAVANNAH SMILES, 314 Williamson St.; (912) 527-6453. Savannah Smiles brings something different to the Savannah night scene. It features "Rock 'n' Roll dueling pianos" in an audience participation format that is a mix of rock 'n' roll standards and light comedy (with food and drink in addition, of course). The show starts at 9 p.m., and the bar opens around 7 p.m. for ages 21 and up. Okay, so it's a bit hokey, but you're on vacation and you're never going to see these people again anyway, so have fun. If you don't leave here without singing along to at least one song, then you need to take a happy pill. This is a place that will make you smile, even if you're down. Hours are Wed through Sat 7 p.m. to 3 a.m.

i A walk on the beach can be a romantic conclusion to an evening out. Stroll out onto the Tybee Pier and Pavilion, lean against the rail, and watch the moon rise out of the Atlantic Ocean.

WET WILLIES, 101 E. River St.; (912) 233-5650. This high-volume River Street bar caters to the younger sector. The drinks are frozen concoctions with names like the infamous spring break potion, Sex on the Beach. Beware! Grain alcohol gives a single drink here the punch of at least two conventional alcoholic beverages. There's a light food menu, a small dance floor, and lots of loud recorded music. During the summer, students pour out onto the street in front of Wet Willies. It's definitely the "in" place, according to those patrons. A second location, complete with outdoor seating, can be found in City Market, 20 Jefferson St. (912-235-5651). Hours are the same at both locations: Mon through Thurs 11 a.m. to 1 a.m., Fri and Sat 11 a.m. to 2 a.m., Sun 12:30 p.m. to 1 a.m.

FILM

Georgia is in the midst of a boom in film and television production, and Savannah gets its fair share. The city has hosted at least 45 films since 1975, not counting some of the smaller projects. The entertainment industry has brought an array of performers ranging from Miley Cyrus (*The Last Song*) to Robert Redford (producer of *The Conspirator*) to town in recent years, not to mention Spongebob Squarepants.

Some of the earlier productions have been among the most critically acclaimed movies of their day and have starred the biggest names in the industry. Some have launched catchphrases into the lexicon of popular culture ("Life is like a box of chocolates . . ."). Examples of outstanding ones are *Glory*, the historically based account of African-American soldiers in the Civil War that won three Oscars; *Forrest Gump*, which claimed six Oscars and solidified Tom Hanks superstar status; and *Roots* (filmed here in part), which became the standard against which all mini-series are

Close-up

Savannah Filmography: 1975–2015

Note that accompanying dates are filming dates, not necessarily release dates.

2015: *Magic Mike XXL; The Spongebob Movie: Sponge Out of Water*

2013: *CBGB*

2012: *Savannah, A River Story*

2010: *The Last Song*

2009: *The Conspirator*

2000: *The Gift*

1999: *The Legend of Bagger Vance*

1998: *Forces of Nature; The General's Daughter*

1997: *The Gingerbread Man; Midnight in the Garden of Good and Evil; Claudine's Return*

1996: *Wild America*

1995: *Something to Talk About*

1994: *Now and Then*

1993: *Forrest Gump; Camilla*

1990: *Goldenboy; Love Crimes*

1989: *The Rose and the Jackal; Flight of the Intruder; Glory*

1988: *The Return of Swamp Thing; The Judas Project*

1987: *My Father, My Son; 1969; War Stories*

1986: *Pals*

1983: *Solomon Northup's Odyssey*

1981: *All My Children; Tales of Ordinary Madness*

1980: *The Slayer; White Death; Scared to Death; When the Circus Came to Town; Fear; East of Eden; Mother Seton*

1979: *Gold Bug; The Ordeal of Dr. Mudd; Orphan Train; Hopscotch; Carny*

1978: *The Double McGuffin*

1977: *The Lincoln Conspiracy*

1976: *Roots*

1975: *Gator*

measured. Going back to 1962, when location shoots were rarer, the original *Cape Fear* was partially filmed here. City Hall and the downtown business district and Isle of Hope were on display. The original movie, since remade, featured Robert Mitchum at his creepiest.

Savannah is well supplied with multiplexes for conventional movies, but if you want to see something really different, you have to have some detective skills (by which we mean web access and a little luck as far as scheduling). Alternative and revivals show up periodically. The Psychotronic Film Society of Savannah periodically screens nonmainstream fare at the Sentient Bean. The Lucas Theatre, now predominantly a live performance venue, brings some oldies back from time to time. Thursday's morning paper includes an entertainment section which will tell you if there are any offbeat film offerings.

PERFORMANCE VENUES

LUCAS THEATRE FOR THE ARTS, 32 **Abercorn St.; (912) 525-5040; lucasthe atre.com.** The restoration of the Lucas Theatre for the Arts seemed to take forever, but it has been well worth the wait. The theater

Park Smart

The Civic Center consumes an entire block between Oglethorpe and Liberty Streets, with entrances on Montgomery Street and facing the parking lot. A word of warning about parking is in order: Popular events at the Civic Center put parking at a premium. A city-operated multilevel parking garage opened in 2005 across from the Civic Center, and it is open at night when there are performances. Because it is easier to get out of a street-side parking space, many patrons prefer to park along the surrounding streets. You don't have to feed the meters at night, but be sure not to block the crosswalks leading to the squares or make up any imaginative parking spaces—lots of parking tickets get handed out on the evenings of big performances. Also, avoid the temptation to whip into the vacant parking lots of obviously closed businesses: Many businesses choose to defend those spaces at night and will have after-hours parkers towed.

was built in 1921 and rode the popularity of the silver screen for decades. Alas, it fell into disrepair as the 1970s came on, and after some ill-fated attempts to keep it running (such as a short stint as a dinner theater and a period when the lobby was a restaurant), the magnificent building went into mothballs.

But the Italian Renaissance–style building with its ornate interior was just too fantastic to let go, and a lengthy fund-raising campaign was started to get this grande dame back on her feet. Look for the 40-foot-wide ceiling dome, lots of gold leaf, and—a welcome sight to Savannahian eyes—the bars upstairs and down. It took 13 years to pull it off, but the end result is beautiful. The marquee, with its chasing lights, adds an exciting touch to Savannah's nightlife, and the theater has helped spur redevelopment of nearby buildings.

The Savannah College of Art and Design (SCAD) runs the theater, and while the college does use the facility for some activities, it remains open to the public for events. This venue serves as a major host for the Savannah Film Festival and the Savannah Music Festival, and it is also the site for events sponsored by the Savannah Film Society and the Savannah Concert Association, along with privately promoted touring productions and events brought in by SCAD but open to the general public.

SAVANNAH CIVIC CENTER, Montgomery and Liberty Streets; 301 W. Oglethorpe Ave.; (912) 651-6556; savannahcivic center.com. The Savannah Civic Center has two main components, plus various meeting rooms and a ballroom. The arena, named for the late Dr. Martin Luther King Jr., can seat up to 9,000, depending on the event configuration. The theater, which seats about 2,500, is named in honor of Johnny Mercer, the famed Savannah-born lyricist ("Moon River," etc.). By and large, the more formal events, such as dramatic presentations or one-person shows, play in the theater, with the arena going for large-scale, pack-'em-in audiences for such events as rock or country music concerts, wrestling matches, and monster truck shows. But that isn't a hard-and-fast rule: To keep up with what might be available during your visit, check the website or simply check the large billboard on the Liberty Street side of the building. The number listed here is for the box office, and tickets generally are on sale well in advance of performances.

SAVANNAH COLLEGE OF ART AND DESIGN, various addresses; scad.edu.

You may wonder what an art college is doing under the "Venues" heading. Actually, SCAD (as it is referred to locally) is a major player in the local arts and culture scene, not just for its own students, but for the general public. Two of the newest (including the most attractive and unique) theater entries are from SCAD. Trustees Theater, 206 E. Broughton St. (912-239-1447), is a circa-1946 movie theater that has been refurbished and reopened as a 1,100-seat performance venue capable of handling both stage productions and movie screenings. Its basic purpose is to house performances and classes for SCAD's performing arts majors, but it also offers performances to the public. Performers have included Tony Bennett, the Neville Brothers, and India.Arie. This is also a home venue of SCAD's annual film festival. The Lucas Theatre for the Arts, discussed elsewhere, is managed by SCAD.

SPECTATOR SPORTS

Auto Racing

OGLETHORPE SPEEDWAY PARK, Jesup Road off US 80; (912) 964-8200; ospracing .net. This speedway gives the green flag to stock car drivers competing in the NASCAR Weekly Racing Series every Fri night Mar through Sept. Special racing events are held Sat nights throughout the year.

You'll see more than 115 entries competing each week on the half-mile dirt track in Weekly Series ministock, street stock, pure stock, 440, and late-model division events. The speedway also hosts other motor sports events, concerts, and festivals on weekends throughout the year.

Oglethorpe Speedway is in West Chatham County. There's a park for recreational vehicles and primitive camping. The gates open at 5 p.m., and racing starts at 8 p.m.

Baseball

SAVANNAH SAND GNATS, Grayson Stadium, 1401 E. Victory Dr.; (912) 351-9150; sandgnats.com. The city's Class A minor-league baseball team, an affiliate of the New York Mets, plays 70 regular season games at Grayson, where the brick grandstand was built in 1941. At the eastern end of Daffin Park, the stadium stands amid tall pines and oaks dripping with Spanish moss, and it's a great place to sit back, relax, and enjoy the national pastime while sipping a cold beer and devouring some peanuts—the boiled variety being the most popular in this part of the world.

Despite its long history in Savannah, the future of professional minor-league baseball here is in limbo as of this writing. The team owners have threatened to leave if a modern stadium is not built for them—and that's a disputed call in a town with a track record of preserving and using the old. Will a new stadium be built? Will the current team leave and Savannah recruit another team for Grayson Stadium? The answers won't be clear until after 2015.

THEATER

You have to be pretty agile to keep up with drama groups in Savannah. They come and go, and always appear to be operating on a shoestring. The amazing thing, though, is not their occasionally temporary nature—it's their resiliency. One particular group may wither away, but there's always another in the wings. Right now, we know of three independent groups, not to mention the productions put on by the city of Savannah's Leisure Services. Several churches maintain

Close-up

Shoeless Joe Gets His Due in Savannah

Savannah did in 2003 what baseball has refused to do for decades—admit Shoeless Joe Jackson into a Hall of Fame.

Jackson, an all-time great outfielder who was banished from baseball following a gambling scandal involving the 1919 World Series, has been excluded from baseball's Hall of Fame in Cooperstown, New York, much to the dismay of fans who have sought his induction. His supporters point out that Jackson was never found guilty of charges of throwing the series.

But Shoeless Joe—a featured character in the films *Field of Dreams* and *Eight Men Out*—has found a place of honor in the Greater Savannah Athletic Hall of Fame (GSAHF). Although not prominently displayed, his plaque and likeness adorn a wall on the second floor of the Savannah Civic Center (301 W. Oglethorpe Ave.; 912-651-6556; savannahciviccenter.com), along with other members of the Hall's Class of 2003.

"There is only one athlete in any sport that interest is still being shown 80 years after he finished playing," states the inscription on his plaque. Also noted is that "his ties to Savannah began when he was sent here in 1909. . . . He loved Savannah and made it his home for years during and after his playing days."

Jackson, a native of South Carolina who died in 1951 at the age of 62, "owned and operated two businesses in downtown," his tribute states.

Shoeless Joe is among more than 200 athletes, coaches, mentors, administrators, executives, sportswriters, and organizations who have been inducted into the GSAHF since its founding by a group of 16 sports-minded residents in 1965.

The athletes participated in a wide array of sports—baseball, football, basketball, track, golf, swimming, diving, softball, automobile racing, weightlifting, and even lacrosse, kayaking, and racquetball. Those inducted range from media mogul Ted Turner, famed as a yachtsman and as the owner of professional sports teams, to a quintet of the University of Georgia's bulldog mascots—UGA I, UGA II, UGA III, UGA IV, and UGA VII.

You can find out more about Savannah's sports history and the folks who have contributed to it the most by visiting the GSAHF, which is free and open to the public during Civic Center operating hours.

---

highly successful theater programs featuring secular works such as Gilbert and Sullivan offerings, and there are also collegiate theatrical groups. Armstrong State University's Masquers produce reliably entertaining work. Check the event pages of the newspapers cited earlier for schedules and further information.

ASBURY MEMORIAL UNITED METHODIST CHURCH, 1008 E. Henry St.; (912) 233-4351. This venerable church was dying out as its congregation aged and the neighborhood changed, but it got a shot in the arm when a performance-minded pastor and the congregation opened their arms to the arts community. The church social hall serves as a performance arena. Don't mistake these productions for Sunday-school projects. They're at least on a par with the other local offerings (actually, all the local theater efforts involve different arrangements of essentially the same theater performers). Although the offerings often have a religious theme (*Godspell* and *Jesus Christ Superstar*), this group has also tackled Gilbert and

Sullivan and *The Fantastiks*. Ticket prices vary, usually around $15. Other local churches occasionally dip into secular drama, mainly to keep their youth groups involved, but this one definitely strives for and achieves a higher level.

THE MUSE, 703 Louisville Rd.; (912) 713-1137; musesavannah.org. Think of this repurposed warehouse space as a creative co-op that provides performance venues for visual, theater, cinema, music, dance, and poetry performances.

THE PUPPET PEOPLE, 3119 Furber Ave.; (912) 355-3366; puppetpeople.com. Puppets can be children's toys, but puppets can also be theater for grownups. Angela Beasley's Puppet People play to audiences of all ages. These are life-size creations that sing, dance, and vamp at everything from children's birthday parties to corporate bashes and retail openings. Beasley's been at it for 30 years, and her repertoire includes the characters around the Forsyth Park fountain, some very original Three Little Pigs, fish galore, and a Willie Nelson look-alike. These elaborate productions have been covered in the pages of *Southern Living* magazine and on cable network programming. The troupe does not perform on a regular schedule, but it is often featured at public events and festivals.

SAVANNAH CHILDREN'S THEATRE, 2160 E. Victory Dr.; (912) 238-9015; savannahchildrenstheatre.org. This is a thriving theater with two stages. Some performances at the Savannah Children's Theatre feature only children; others have adults in some roles. Some performances are culminating events in the classes the theater teaches; roles in others are open to aspiring young actors, child and adult, free of charge. The constant is the desire to expose children to the joys of live theater, whether onstage, backstage, or in the audience. It is housed in space carved out of a long-vacant department store in a small strip mall. Past productions have included *Beauty and the Beast, Seussical: The Musical,* and *Tarzan the Musical.* Actually, the list of past and planned performances is long: The theater is in almost constant production mode, and plays follow on one another's heels. Ticket prices vary, and they're $10 at the moment. You can buy them at the door, but it might be just your luck that's when the young star's entire extended family attends and the theater only seats about 150. You can also buy online. Limited concessions are available at most performances.

SAVANNAH COMMUNITY THEATRE, (912) 247-4644; savannahcommunitytheatre.com. Community theater standards and murder mysteries are among the staples of this community troupe. They perform in various venues.

SAVANNAH STAGE COMPANY, 36 Martin Luther King Jr. Blvd. (third floor of Ampersand restaurant); (912) 341-6496; savannahsstagecompany.com. This is the latest entry in Savannah's ever-fluid theater scene. Located atop a trendy restaurant, look here for edgier theater fare. The first performance of 2015 was John Hardy's *Poe*. Buy tickets online.

SAVANNAH THEATRE, 220 Bull St.; (912) 233-7764; savannahtheatre.com. This professional troupe came to town in 2002, with a show titled *Lost in the '50s,* originally developed in Branson, Missouri. Since then, the bill has changed periodically, but stayed within the same framework. The group puts on an oldies-based review, changing the name and some of the program each year or so. In late November and until Christmas, it presents a holiday-themed musical. Then, it goes dark for a break of a couple of weeks and reopens with a new show. The Savannah Theatre is billed as the country's oldest live-performance theater (stretching it a bit, since the only remnant of the original building would be its foundation, with the rest destroyed by fire long ago). Tickets are $35 for adults, $17 for ages 12 to 17, and $10 for ages 5 to 11, with younger children free. You can purchase a season's pass for $50. Major credit cards are accepted, and tickets may be purchased at the number above. Performances are at 8 p.m. Wed through Sat and matinees are at 3 p.m. Sat and Sun.

SHOPPING

If shopping is part of your vacation behavior, Savannah is your kind of vacation destination. Included in this chapter are the high points of lots of different kinds of shopping. Chain stores are largely excluded—you will know what to expect from those. Nor does this chapter claim to be complete: Savannah has way more stores than this. The purpose here is to get you started and whet your appetite for what this international port city's merchants have in store for you.

SHOPPING DISTRICTS

Before launching into our own category-by-category rundown of stores, here's a quick review of the major shopping locations with a few pointers along the way.

River Street

River Street is literally along the Savannah River. It is reached by street ramps that lead down from the bluff-level Bay Street. In between these two levels is Factors' Walk. River Street is a major part of Savannah's tourist scene, and you'll find it is a prominent player for restaurants, nightlife, and annual events. But don't forget shopping! This restored waterfront strip features a steady progression of shops all along its length, beginning at the west end across from a small out-of-commission power plant (whose smokestacks make handy landmarks) and extending eastward many blocks until you reach the Waving Girl statue that is a local riverfront landmark. Factors' Walk, which parallels River Street halfway up the bluff, also features shops, although more widely scattered.

Parking is scarce. There are a few small private lots, where you pay as you enter. There's limited street-side parking on the various roads leading to River Street. Lots of motorists park illegally along River Street itself, but it's a bad idea—the city has cracked down on the long-winked-at practice.

Opt to park in the parking garages that are within walking distance of Bay Street and City Market. The city of Savannah operates five parking garages. A favorite is the new Whitaker Street Garage across the street from the Hyatt Regency Savannah. This underground garage was built in 2008 on Whitaker Street between Bay and Bryant Streets. The garage has four levels underground and space for 1,065 vehicles. In my experience, it's never been filled. The daily rate is $2 per hour and well worth it for a clean and shady place to start the day. If you're heading down to River Street, cross Bay Street (at the light at Whitaker and Bay) and trot over to the Visitors' Elevator that runs alongside the Hyatt. Once you ride down to street level and leave the elevator, you'll find yourself dropped off on the tricky ballast stones of River Street. Wear appropriate footwear and opt for the elevator on your way back up. The stairs in each block are steep and irregular, and once you get to the rocks, you'll find them as hard to walk on as they are to drive over. The going is much smoother once you get to the River Street level where there are pedestrian-friendly sidewalks. There are public restrooms to your left as you reach River Street.

Don't expect much in the way of bargains on River Street but do expect some really cool shops. There are a variety of stores here to keep you busy for several hours. From tropical clothing to candy, charming eateries, and lots of merchants selling Savannah-themed memorabilia, you'll find it all.

City Market

This restored area in the commercial section of the Historic District runs from Barnard Street to Montgomery Street, north of Broughton Street. The complex is made up of nightclubs, restaurants, art galleries, and shops. The stores here tend to be more thematic—cat-motif merchandise, New Age, outdoor furniture and gifts, and so on—than their cousins a few blocks away on River Street.

Broughton Street Area & Historic District

Broughton Street was where Savannah shopped before malls seized control of the retail world. It suffered the same fate as Main Streets all across America but has begun a comeback as a home to restaurants, college activities, and trendy shopping, including a slew of antiques dealers. In fact, some of the very best recreational shopping in the city can be done on Broughton Street. New upscale offerings stand side by side with the small low-end shops that kept the street going in its hard-luck days, things like wig shops and cut-price clothing shops. You'll also find two of Savannah's retail grandes dames still in place. When other stores abandoned the main drag for suburban malls, **Globe Shoe Company** (17 E. Broughton St.) and **Levy Jewelers** (2 E. Broughton St.) dug in. These stores are where Old Savannah

bought her shoes for debutante parties and her bridal silver, and while both stores now have other locations as well, they never closed their doors on Broughton.

You'll find plenty of intriguing stores scattered throughout the Historic District. One quaint congregation of interesting shops is at the intersection of Bull and Liberty Streets near the Hilton Savannah DeSoto Hotel. The intersection of Jones and Whitaker Streets forms the nucleus for another appealing set that mostly specializes in arts and home decor. They call themselves, collectively, the Downtown Design District and capitalize on their proximity to both Mrs. Wilkes' eatery (see our Restaurants chapter) and Monterey Square. You'll also find individual shops, especially antiques shops, sprinkled throughout downtown.

Looking back over all these areas, let's put it in perspective: River Street is strong in local color and has lots of shops together, where you can walk out one door and into the next. There's a variety of merchandise aimed at all age levels, and the compact location makes it easy to keep groups— be they children or merely hard-to-herd adults—together. Broughton Street's offerings aren't as likely to appeal much to children and are more widely spaced, but the merchandise is actually several cuts better, and oddly enough, the prices are more reasonable. City Market falls between these two descriptions, but it's heavy on the souvenir shops, and you can stop by the other Historic District shops as you make your way around the city on tours, and so on.

Greater Savannah

Anything south of, say, DeRenne Avenue is dubbed the Southside by Savannahians. This is where you'll find the strip malls, discount houses, shopping centers, megastores, etc. **The Savannah Festival Factory Outlet Center** (11 Gateway Blvd.; 912-925-3089;

savannahfestival.com), a typical example of this new kind of strip mall, is at the far southern edge of the city, where Abercorn is better known as SR 204 and passes under I-95. This outlet center includes a Springmaid/Wamsutta factory store, Bugle Boy, and Bass Shoes, among many others.

East and west of Savannah, you'll find mainly grocery stores and other retail outlets in support of the suburban residential development there, with a few interesting shops thrown in and a large spate of beach-oriented shops at the end of the road on Tybee Island.

In West Chatham's Pooler, you will find Tanger Outlet Savannah. Set to open in 2015, stores include Michael Kors, Coach, J. Crew, the Nike Factory Store, and similar stores—85 in all. Pooler is also home to the recent development of just about every big-box store you can name.

MALLS & SHOPPING CENTERS

Savannah has two malls, both south of downtown in a heavily trafficked (by Savannah standards) area of suburban and chain-store development. There are various ways to get to them, but the most direct route from downtown and the one hardest to get lost on is straight out Abercorn Street from town. About 6 miles from the Historic District, you'll spot Oglethorpe Mall on your left (you really can't miss it). Another couple of miles south, and you'll spot Savannah Mall on the right.

As for that ubiquitous American retail staple, the strip shopping center, Savannah has its share scattered mainly in the Southside/Midtown area. Because you know what to expect in most of these—a grocery store, major discount retailer, chain or local drugstore, etc.—we have left most of them out as a rule. However, there are a few exceptions, with interesting stores or interesting stories, which we have included here.

ABERCORN COMMONS, 8108 Abercorn Extension; abercorncommons.com. At first glance, this V-shaped strip shopping center won't strike you as anything special. It looks new and houses several nationally known names like Michaels, Home Goods, Books-a-Million, and Panera Bread. What makes it interesting isn't immediately apparent: This is Savannah's first LEED-certified (Leadership in Energy and Environmental Design) retail development.

Developers took an aging and down-at-the-heels shopping center that wasn't living up to the potential of its location and, instead of just bulldozing it, tackled it as a "green" project. Demolition was held to a minimum, and conscious efforts were made to recycle or repurpose debris to keep it out of landfills. New buildings were designed to be energy efficient, pavement was made permeable, and xeriscaping, or the use of landscaping plants that can survive in the climate without artificial irrigation, was called into play. The stores that are moving into this work-still-in-progress include a mix of local and national names. But really, when was the last time you went to a shopping center where the parking lot design was actually interesting and significant?

ABERCORN WALK, Abercorn Street and Janet Drive. This narrow, deep strip shopping center is on Abercorn, just slightly south of the major intersection of Abercorn and DeRenne, which marks the southward sprawl of retail in Savannah. The stores here are going to sound familiar to veteran shoppers: the Fresh Market, Ann Taylor LOFT, Chico's, Jos. A. Bank, and Talbots. The significance is the upscale nature of the collected stores. It also rates mention because the Fresh Market is Savannah's first specialty grocery store (unless you count downtown's organic food shop, the venerable Brighter Day).

HABERSHAM SHOPPING CENTER, Habersham Street at 60th to 63rd Streets. This small strip shopping center runs along both sides of Habersham Street, from just after its intersection with 60th Street to 63rd Street. It appears modest at first glance—a small grocery store, a pharmacy, a dry cleaner, and other businesses clearly set up to serve the surrounding established neighborhoods—but look closer and you'll find some interesting specialty shops. They include Punch and Judy, a children's store; TailsSpin, an upscale pet supply store; and a candy store. It includes several appealing restaurants, with cuisine from Japanese to Italian.

OGLETHORPE MALL, 804 Abercorn St.; (912) 354-7038; oglethorpemall.com. Oglethorpe Mall is the city's original mall, and this one is thriving, with Sears, JCPenney, Belk, and Macy's as its anchors. There are more than specialty stores here, mostly on a single story, although some of the anchors have a second level. There's ample parking, but the multilevel parking deck comes in handy around the holidays and when it rains. You'll find a predictable array of stores inside (Gap, Victoria's Secret, etc.), along with a few restaurants and a food court. Barnes & Noble and its daily 9 a.m. to 11 p.m. hours—complete with coffee shop—have made this an unlikely but popular late-night adult hangout. On weekends, kids age 16 and under must be escorted by an adult, and yes, IDs are checked.

SAVANNAH MALL, 14045 Abercorn St.; (912) 927-7467; savannahmall.com. Savannah still calls Savannah Mall, which opened in 1990, "the new mall," although by most cities' standards it isn't new anymore. Bass Pro Shop, Dillard's, and Target are the anchors. Our count shows that Savannah Mall's specialty stores include Bath & Body Works, Victoria's Secret, Foot Locker, and Kay Jewelers, among others. Behind the mall are neighboring rival multiplexes totaling more than 20 movie screens, so the mall is a convenient place to kill some time while waiting for Hollywood's latest.

VICTORY STATION SAVANNAH, 1815 E. Victory Dr.; sjcollinsent.com. This is one of Savannah's newest shopping areas. Whole Foods anchors the development, where the Truman Parkway crosses Victory Drive. Stores and eateries include PetSmart, Chipotle, Zoe's Kitchen, Bruster's Ice Cream, and various other stores

SHOPPING SAVANNAH BY CATEGORY

Now that we've roughly covered the general shopping areas, let's get more specific. We've divided our featured stores into categories. Join us on a quick shopping trip.

Antiques

In this section, we cover a sampling of both high-end and low-end antiques dealers. Serious collectors with serious budgets should seek out the upscale places; collectors and browsers will have better luck in the more mainstream, less expensive stores.

THE ATTIC, 224 W. Bay St.; (912) 236-4879. Looking for antique fishing lures? Good examples can fetch $65 and up, and you'll find them among some of the other sports antiques here, along with fencing masks and old skis. It's an eclectic stock of mainly American antiques and collectibles—furniture, jewelry, glassware. It's not what you would call high-end, but it's fun. The location itself is of interest to fans of *Midnight in the Garden of Good and Evil*, since it was the site of the financially ill-fated Emma's, a piano bar featured in that bestseller. Hours are Mon through Sat 10 a.m. to 5 p.m.

COBB'S GALLERIES INC., 122 E. 37th St.; (912) 234-1582. This popular antiques shop keeps outgrowing its quarters. It is now housed in a Victorian mansion at the corner of 37th and Abercorn Streets, the allegedly haunted Krouskoff House. That's appropriate, because owner Al Cobb wrote a book, *Danny's Bed*, about a haunted bed that wreaked havoc in his household; you can buy a copy in the shop. Most of the stock is more conventional: an extensive collection of art pottery, about a thousand cookbooks, sports memorabilia, collectible liquor decanters, what have you. What's surprising about this shop is the sheer volume. Hours are Mon through Sat 10 a.m. to 3 p.m.

HABERSHAM ANTIQUES & COLLECT- IBLES MARKET, 2502 Habersham St.; (912) 238-5908. What was once a Savannah grocery store now holds a collection of some 70 antiques dealers who fill their booth space where Savannah's Ardsley Park matrons once bought canned goods and prime cuts of meat. The expansive building now holds old books, glassware, some antiques, and even vintage clothing. It's a great place to spend a rainy afternoon. Once a year, the enterprise expands, spreading to the neighboring parking lot with a spring festival that brings other vendors in booths. Hours are weekdays 10 a.m. to 6 p.m. and Sat 10 a.m. to 5 p.m.

LEE SMITH ANTIQUES AND DESIGN, 916 E. 72nd St.; (912) 352-4151; leesmith antiques.com. Lee Smith opened his 20-year-old warehouse and collection to the public, and if you're shopping or just browsing, it's worth a stop to view the English and continental pieces from the 18th and 19th centuries and fine art, porcelain, rugs, high-quality reproductions, and custom, made-to-order pieces he has amassed. The 4,500-square-foot warehouse is in Midtown. Hours are Mon through Fri 10 a.m. to 4 p.m.

SAVANNAH GALLERIES, 30 E. Bryan St.; (912) 232-1234; savannahgalleries.com. Native Savannahians own this gallery—in operation since the 1960s—where you'll discover more than 10,000 square feet of high-end antique English, French, and American furniture, silver, porcelain, and oriental rugs. Pieces range from elegant marquetry to rustic painted pine accents. The staff is friendly and will assist you in finding and building antique collections. They'll also clean, repair, and appraise your antique and modern oriental rugs. Hours are Mon through Sat 11 a.m. to 4 p.m.

37TH ABERCORN AND DESIGN, 201 E. 37th St.; (912) 233-0064; 37aad.com. This rambling yellow Victorian home houses collections from more than 50 dealers. Look for French country furniture, statuary, oil paintings, crystal, jewelry, and so on. This is a good browsing location with a wide price range— stuff for the serious collector and less-pricey offerings as well. Lately, this veteran store has taken on a more design-oriented feel. Hours are Mon through Sat 10 a.m. to 5 p.m. and Sun 11 a.m. to 4 p.m.

Art Galleries

Savannah has a large stock of art galleries. First listed are those with collegiate connections. Those will be followed by a few others of note. This is only a very small sample to get you started. The Sunday arts section of the *Savannah Morning News* usually offers a current listing of shows. And you'll stumble on others by accident: Lately half the coffee shops and little restaurants in town have turned their walls into impromptu galleries. For examples of this trend, check out Soho South and the Gallery Espresso on Bull Street at Chippewa Square.

SAVANNAH COLLEGE OF ART AND DESIGN, 345 Bull St.; (912) 525-5527; scad.edu. This growing art college's campus is scattered throughout Savannah's Historic and Victorian Districts. Among its holdings are multiple on-campus galleries featuring rotating displays in a variety of media. Some feature the work of students, both graduate and undergraduate, or the college's faculty. Frequently, however, these galleries host works by internationally known artists such as Jasper Johns, Robert Rauschenberg, and Dale Chihuly.

The flagship galleries, most likely to feature professional work, are shopSCAD and the Red Gallery. These exhibits are free and open to the public. Times vary, particularly in keeping with the academic year, so call one of the listed numbers for hours and information on what is currently on exhibit. Also, check out the media outlets discussed earlier in this chapter for exhibit details. Following is a rundown of SCAD's galleries. Consider this list fluid. As the college grows, the roles of its various galleries are subject to change—not to mention that it keeps acquiring new real estate.

i Looking for one of the Savannah College of Art and Design's galleries? Locals, for the most part, try to be helpful when visitors ask for directions on the street, but most of us simply don't know the names SCAD gives its buildings. We don't call it Poetter Hall, it's the old Armory to us; the Jen Library is known to old locals as the old Levy Department Store and to younger locals as the Maas Brothers Department Store; Habersham Hall is the old jail. Take the online SCAD tour at scad.edu to learn more.

SHOPSCAD, 340 Bull St.; (912) 525-5180. This gallery, housed in an old armory building in the center of the Historic District was among the first of the college's now-significant real-estate holdings. This gallery concentrates on visiting national and international exhibits and is among the easiest of the SCAD galleries for a visitor to find. If you are only doing one SCAD gallery, and the details on current exhibits don't give you a reason to pick one over another, visit this one. A look at the Rococo building is worth the trip by itself.

GUTSTEIN GALLERY, 201 E. Broughton St.; (912) 525-4743. This retail gallery, inside SCAD's library, features a variety of artists including SCAD alumni.

PINNACLE GALLERY, 320 E. Liberty St.; (912) 525-4950. This beautiful gallery space is used primarily for exhibits.

ORLEANS HALL GALLERY, 201 Barnard St.; (912) 525-5063. You'll find student work for sale at this gallery, which doubles as a reception facility.

Other SCAD exhibit galleries include:

ALEXANDER HALL GALLERY, 668 Indian St.

HAMILTON HALL GALLERY, 522 Indian St.

LA GALERIE BLEUE, 3515 Montgomery St.

MAY POETTER GALLERY, 342 Bull St.

PEI LING CHAN GALLERY AND GARDEN, 322–324 Martin Luther King Jr. Blvd.

A. T. HUN, 302 W. St. Julian St. (City Market); (912) 233-2060; athun.com. A staple of the City Market, this independent gallery is home to more than 25 artists in an electric, colorful, laid-back array. It's all contemporary, and the collection includes many larger pieces. The nudes that sparked the birth of the gallery aren't shocking, just a good reflection of how conservative Savannah can be. Potters, jewelers, and photographers are represented as well, and there is an affiliation with an English gallery so there is a regular exchange of international work. Don't look here for soft watercolors or memento landscapes of Savannah. It's young, funky, and even sells T-shirts sporting a Latin phrase that translates (roughly) as "We don't do snobby." Don't be misled, however; there's good stuff here. Hours Mon through Wed 10 a.m. to 9 p.m., Thurs through Sun 10 a.m. to 10 p.m.

GALLERY 209, 209 E. River St.; (912) 236-4583; gallery209savannah.com. This River Street gallery is the place to start your search for local artwork. Stuff here varies in quality, from some wannabe artists to the real thing. We especially like the enamel jewelry, such as a jewel-tone seahorse. In addition to paintings that run the gamut from very good to not very, you'll find fiber art and interesting and affordable ceramics. This stuff will appeal more to consumers than art museums, but what's wrong with that? Hours are 10:30 a.m. to 9 p.m. daily.

Bookstores

THE BOOK LADY, 6 E. Liberty St.; (912) 233-.3628; thebookladybookstore.com. Used and rare books are what you will find at the Book Lady, a quaint bookstore ideal for browsing. Besides art, architecture, religion, fiction, and the usual fare, you will also find sections called Pretty Books and Nice Old Books among the lot. The shop also carries new books and hosts author events. They stock several local titles on Savannah and the area. For that hard-to-find book, the store offers a search service. Free wireless access can be found in the cafe. Hours are Mon through Sat 10 a.m. to 5:30 p.m.

E. SHAVER BOOKSELLER, 326 Bull St.; (912) 234-7257. Book lovers will delight in this independent bookstore, which occupies the ground floor of a Historic District home. The shop has become a fixture for both downtown residents and tourists. An impressive array of hardcover and paperback books is available, and the knowledgeable staff offers solid advice. Local titles are well represented, and a whole room is devoted to children's books. Limited gift offerings include museum-style note cards, tote bags, and appointment calendars. This is what bookstores were before there were megachains. Hours are Mon through Sat 9:30 a.m. to 5:30 p.m.

EX LIBRIS, 228 Martin Luther King Jr. Blvd.; (912) 525-5770; exlibrisbkstr.com. Ex Libris is first of all a beautiful place to shop! Part of it is a coffeehouse, another part is a book and gift shop, owned and operated by the SCAD. The shop is on the western edge of the Historic District and may be a little out of your way, but it's worth the trip. After browsing through art books, posters, framed art, and many other eclectic and fun items you most likely won't find anywhere else in Savannah, you can sit and relax on the gigantic leather sofa and simply enjoy the beautifully restored building. A magnificent stairway takes up the center of the building and is the focal point of the room, along with "pillars" made out of hundreds of old books gracefully (and carefully) stacked. The store is especially beautiful during the Christmas season, when the college opens its holiday shop and offers decorations and other festive items. Hours are Mon through Thurs 7:30 a.m. to 8 p.m., Fri 7:30 a.m. to 6 p.m., Sat and Sun 11 a.m. to 6 p.m.

Candy

When we travel and need a gift for a hostess, or even a quick sugary snack, we often opt for pralines. No one can claim these super-rich candies (made of sugar, butter, cream, and pecans) are good for you, but given the prices, your purse will probably stop you before you do yourself too much harm. You can find them made and sold in two shops on River Street. Although the shops would scream to hear it, we can't taste any difference. Pralines are available at shops in Savannah's malls, but the ones on River Street taste better.

ℹ **Shopping for Georgia lottery tickets? Your best bets are small convenience stores and gas stations. Most lottery vendors have prominently displayed signs. Time your lottery shopping spree so that you avoid 6 to just before 7 p.m.—that's when the daily drawing for the Cash 3 game is held, and there's a line of hopeful last-minute gamblers at many lottery outlets.**

RIVER STREET SWEETS, 13 E. River St.; (912) 234-4608; riverstreetsweets.com. Savannah's oldest candy store, established in 1973, is located on the historic Savannah riverfront. There's a second, more recent location at 4515 Habersham St. (912-231-3654). Pralines are made right here, in full view, and there's usually someone near the door to offer you a sample. Display cases showcase other store specialties: confections of chocolate and nuts, spiced pecans, divinity, etc. There's a wide array of gift baskets and special packaging and an efficient shipping service. Hours on River Street are 9 a.m. to 11 p.m. every day.

SAVANNAH'S CANDY KITCHEN, 225 E. River St. and 318 W. St. Julian Street; (912) 233-8411; savannahcandy.com. Kids of all ages will run rampant in this large candy store, which fills several rooms. In addition to pralines and other store-made specialties, you'll also find gourmet jelly beans and a staggering selection of other mass-produced candy—the kinds you remember from childhood and assumed no one sold anymore. Choose from a wide selection of decorative tins to fill with goodies. Prepare to spend more than a few minutes here to take your time in selecting a bag of goodies to take back to the hotel. (This store also offers gift shipping if you'd prefer that your purchase awaits you at home.) Hours are 9 a.m. to 11 p.m. every day.

Clothing

GAUCHO, 251 Bull St; (912) 232-7414. When browsing through Gaucho, you might be reminded of those who believe you can never be too rich or too thin. Don't be discouraged, there's something there for every taste (and size), and you probably won't see these beautiful wares in a department store. Gaucho has a wide selection of hats and accessories, along with handpainted blouses and, in the back, shoes. Hours are Mon through Sat 10 a.m. to 6 p.m.; Sun noon to 5 p.m.

Gifts & Fun Shops

BYRD COOKIE COMPANY, 6700 Waters Ave.; (912) 355-1716; byrdcookiecompany .com. You can buy these well-known local cookies all over town, but the advantage of choosing them from this shop is that you can sample the wide range of flavors here: Key Lime Coolers, Benne Bits, raspberry, butter cookies, and so on. They're sold in decorative tins that are excellent choices for those obligation gifts. One is sufficient for a solid token gift, or you can assemble a collection if you need something more impressive. A locally popular favorite is the benne wafer, a subtly sweet concoction made of unhulled sesame seeds. There are oodles of gifts here, including a selection from the Gullah Gourmet line of easy-to-cook Southern treats (unique to this area). If you show up during a production run, you can even watch the manufacturing process through a glass window. In addition to Byrd Cookies, this shop features an array of pricey decor gifts. Hours are Mon through Fri 9 a.m. to 6 p.m., Sat 10 a.m. to 5 p.m., Sun 11 a.m. to 4 p.m. Adjacent to the store is the upscale B. Tillman Restaurant and Bar, offering what it describes as "sophisticated comfort food" for lunch and dinner 7 days a week. Satellite stores are located 102 E. Liberty St., 9 Mill Creek Circle in nearby Pooler, and 213 W. St. Julian St. in the Historic District.

FANNIES YOUR AUNT/BOB'S YOUR UNCLE, 305 E. River St.; (912) 232-9144 **bobsyouruncle.com.** As you can tell from the name, shop here for the branded clothing and items named Fannies Your Aunt, Bob's Your Uncle, and Life is Good. Look for brands such as Ty, Russ, Boyd's Bears, Enesco, and other, smaller lines. Upstairs you'll find 2,500 square feet devoted to baskets of every imaginable shape, size, and material. T-shirts include both Savannah-themed versions and witty (but not vulgar) novelty shirts. Other stock includes dolls (such as the Susan Wakeen line), books of local interest, and plenty of furniture perfect for toys. Other gift and novelty items, including voodoo dolls, are scattered in among it all. Hours are Sun through Thurs 9 a.m. to 10 p.m., Fri and Sat 9 a.m. to 11 p.m.

GO FISH, 106 W. Broughton St.; (912) 231-0609; **savannah.gofishretail.com.** This is a cheery shop filled with inspiring handicrafts that are reasonably priced. It grew out of a missionary family's interest in helping the artisans they encountered in developing countries and has expanded to a small chain (primarily in Georgia, Florida, and South Carolina) of stores selling Christian T-shirts and imported clothing, jewelry, and handicrafts. The friendly owners, Debbie and Lloyd Ryysylainen, welcome shoppers and carry the torch for the store's mission and focus. As illustrated in the literature scattered throughout the store, the Christian-themed T-shirts, handmade home accessories—Indonesian wood carvings, etc . . . are all priced very low. There's also a colorful like of line of elongated and brightly painted animal sculptures beginning at $25 and going up in height and price. There are, of course, a lot of fish items (paintings, carvings, etc.). The stock also includes beaded jewelry and clothing made from batik fabrics. Go Fish is a great place to bring traveling groups of adults and/or schoolchildren. Hours are seasonal: 11 a.m. to 4 p.m. from Labor Day through Christmas, and summers, Mon through Thurs 10 a.m. to 6 p.m., Fri and Sat 10 a.m. to 7 p.m.

HALF MOON OUTFITTERS, 15 E. Broughton St.; (912) 201-9393; halfmoonoutfitters.com. This unique outdoor clothing and equipment company has transformed a rather pedestrian storefront on the city's former main shopping drag to a modern and appealing space. It fills two levels, and the renovation job is worth a trip inside even if you aren't interested in camping, kayaking, or backpacking. All the gear is here, from clothing to kayaks themselves, along with food supplies and a large collection of books. The shop was acquired by Half Moon Outfitters, a small chain of outdoor stores based in South Carolina. The staff is made up of friendly, knowledgeable young people who practice the lifestyle they sell, which makes them good sources of information if you are in need of advice on where best to camp, canoe, or what have you in this vicinity. Winter hours are Mon through Sat 10 a.m. to 6 p.m. and Sun noon to 5 p.m.; summer hours are Mon through Sat 10 a.m. to 7 p.m., Sun noon to 6 p.m.

ONE FISH, TWO FISH, 401 Whitaker St.; (912) 447-4600; onefishstore.com. This little shop expanded to a bigger one and then got bigger still, offering an array of trendy and unique gifts and other unusual merchandise. We spotted gourmet goodies and gifts for pampered pets, and a few little jars of jellies and condiments for their human counterparts. The stock also includes trendy purses, ceramic flowers, and tons of other superfluous-but-so-desirable types of products. Look here for lavish linens and personal pampering items. One storefront down, but still within the same building, you'll find Circa Lighting, where you can buy lamps and lighting fixtures from a variety of periods and styles. It all adds up to a quaint and cozy little corner in which to browse. The restoration work, which stopped well short of the polished at a rustic and shabby-chic European look, merits a visit even if you are not in a buying frame of mind. Hours are Mon through Sat 10 a.m. to 5:30 p.m., Sun noon to 5 p.m.

PEANUT SHOP OF SAVANNAH, 407 E. River St.; (912) 232-8612. This is the perfect place to stock up on salty delights for your afternoon munchies attacks. Peanut brittle, roasted peanuts, and plain ol' peanuts, along with hard candy and key lime jelly, are just some of the many things you will find inside the Peanut Shop. If you aren't sure what kind of peanuts you want, don't worry, there are usually several samples out so you can try before you buy. Hours are Sun through Thurs 10 a.m. to 8 p.m., Fri and Sat 10 a.m. to 9 p.m.

THE PARIS MARKET & BROCANTE, 36 W. Broughton St.; (912) 232-1500; theparis market.com. If ever there was a beautiful store in downtown Savannah—carefully and lovingly restored to its full potential—this would be that store. The merchandise here is appealing, but the Paris Market is worth a visit just to see the primo restoration of the building that houses it. We remember when this store started as a small, crowded room-size shop in what is now called the Downtown Design District. Today, it occupies two spacious floors in a retail "palace" on a prominent corner of downtown's main street. The ground floor has nostalgic wood flooring and is crowded with a dazzling collection of chandeliers. Downstairs, the floors are brick, and mirrors and other elegant furnishings are showcased. It is a great setting for merchandise, and the selection includes some surprisingly affordable things. The stock is a mixture of new and vintage. There's also linen, dishes, soaps, decorating books, and more, much of it with a French or Parisian theme. In short, this is a nifty place to pick up a gift or for the house-proud to groom their nests. Hours are Mon through Sat 10 a.m. to 6 p.m., Sun noon to 5 p.m.

TRUE GRITS, 107 E. River St.; (912) 234-8006. Specializing in all sorts of nautical and Civil War items, there are lots of Savannah souvenirs packed into this rustic store. There are more than 250 different varieties hot sauce, each label claiming to be deadlier than the others. You'll also see plenty of shirts, toys, mugs, and plates with Savannah scenes. Also, you'll find items with nautical themes: lighthouse figurines and lighthouse needlework kits; large, realistic wooden ship models; tables made from hatch covers or using four-bladed brass props as bases; and antique telescopes. Civil War merchandise includes replica swords and hats, many history books, and three different versions of Civil War–themed chess sets. Hours are 8:30 a.m. to 11 p.m. every day.

24E, 24 E. Broughton St.; (912) 233-2274; 24estyle.com. Broughton Street and the directions it has taken with revitalization never cease to amaze us. In the street's shabbier days—post-mall and pre-refurbishment—inexpensive furniture stores and very expensive rent-to-own furniture places were one of the standard fixtures of the place, along with vacant storefronts. Now, those are mostly gone, and scattered along Broughton are a handful of upscale, high-fashion furniture stores where style (and price) rival anything you might find in a major metropolitan area.

The finest of the new lot is 24e, which has put its address to modified use as its name. In over two floors of what was once two separate storefronts, you'll find displayed everything from knickknacks (ceramic penguins that shop co-owner Ruel Joyner Jr. calls a season signature item) to truly unique furnishings. On the upstairs level, we found Italian leather sofas, overstuffed chintz armchairs, platform beds, and undulating chaise lounges. The accessory/gift-type stuff is on the lower level, including extremely expensive perfume lamps and reasonably priced glassware. Hours are seasonal so call prior to visiting; typically Mon through Thurs 10:30 a.m. to 7 p.m., Fri and Sat 10:30 a.m. to 8 p.m., Sun noon to 5 p.m. The website features much of the store's inventory.

i Roadside produce stands as well as regular grocery stores are good places to pick up Vidalia onions. These famous mild, sweet onions are grown only in and around nearby Vidalia and have acquired a dedicated national following of gourmets.

WILD BIRDS UNLIMITED, 8108 Abercorn St., Ste. 210; (912) 961-3455; http://savannah.wbu.com. Located in Savannah's Southside, this is a store for bird-watchers and enthusiasts. Stock up on birdseed, feeders, houses, binoculars, toys, gifts, and CDs here. This shop is geared to those who want to watch birds in the wild (including their own backyards), so it doesn't handle pet bird supplies. Some of the feeders and birdhouses double as lawn sculptures, including ornate, copper-roofed models. You'll also find a small stock of educational toys, and such unique items as hummingbird feeders and houses especially designed for butterflies and bats. Hours are Mon through Sat 10 a.m. to 6 p.m., Sun noon to 5 p.m.

i If you've got military privileges, you'll find a PX and commissary at Hunter Army Airfield in Savannah.

Thrift & Flea Markets

This kind of shopping isn't for everyone, just the most dedicated bargain hunters. If you don't mind rolling up your sleeves, these places can be real treasure troves. Of course, you'll occasionally come away empty-handed, but if you are into the thrill of the chase, you won't mind a bit.

KELLER'S FLEA MARKET, 5901 Ogeechee Rd.; (912) 927-4848; ilovefleas.com. Ever wonder where people buy velvet wall-hangings depicting the Last Supper, wild stallions, and dogs playing poker? We've found them here ($10 each). In fact, if you go often enough and search diligently, we're convinced you can find just about anything in one of the 400-plus booths. Some are just tables under shed roofs; others are enclosed mini-stores. Don't expect anything fancy—this is the base of the food chain in retail shopping. Still, we've made some real finds here and had fun people watching.

Among the booths you'll find the equivalent of yard sales, estate sales, and salvage sales. Some have new merchandise, including designer label stuff that doesn't appear very convincing and pure junk that isn't masquerading as anything else. Handcrafters, small-scale importers, and collectors set up here. Go early on Saturday, and you'll see the antiques dealers scouting for stuff they'll clean up (and mark up) for their own shops.

One section features exotic birds, reptiles, puppies, and chickens, but real animal lovers should give that section a wide berth. The market is open every Sat and Sun 8 a.m. to 6 p.m. Vendors set up at 8 a.m., and if you care to sell your own goods, spaces are only $5. Ogeechee Road is also US 17, and the market is in the county's far southwestern section. About 2 miles past Savannah Mall, you'll spot the exit for US 17. Take the exit, turn left at the end of the ramp, and you'll soon see the market on your left. Dress is casual.

ATTRACTIONS

We've decided to devote much of this chapter to one of the favorite Savannah pastimes, walking. This one could be addicting so be forewarned. Make sure your camera battery is fully charged and your feet are adorned in your most comfortable walking shoes. Then, set your sights high. Savannah's splendor is best viewed in the early morning or late afternoon.

First, a little direction. Since most of the city's best-known attractions are situated in the Historic District, this walking tour will take you to her most beautiful sights.

Here's the format: There are detailed listings of many of the popular historic sites downtown, and in between, explicit directions will appear in italics on how to get from one location to the next. The tour takes in a little more than 2.5 miles; how long it takes depends on how fast you walk and whether you decide to take a detour or two and further explore some sites. Along the way, you'll be treated to sitting spots on attractive benches that will allow you to take leisurely breaks. (If you stumble on a place that catches your fancy and is not listed in this chapter, chances are you can find out more about it in our Restaurants or Shopping chapters.) For another great dining option, pack a picnic before setting out. Each square you encounter—and we will cover nine—is perfect for relaxing near the magnolia trees while enjoying a good sandwich

There's a basic map at the front of this book. If you need a further visual aid, several good maps of the Historic District are available in shops around town and typically cost less than $5. The Savannah Visitor Information Center, 301 Martin Luther King Jr. Blvd. or the Savannah Area Chamber of Commerce offices, 101 E. Bay St. (912-644-6400) also provide a free visitors' guide that has a great map.

Following our Insiders' Historic District tour, there's information on other guided touring options in the city, plus a variety of other interesting attractions to explore both in Savannah's downtown and the outlying areas: the Islands, Southside, and West Chatham.

INSIDERS' HISTORIC DISTRICT WALKING TOUR

Whether you're approaching the Historic District via the Talmadge Bridge or you're already there and wandering around on foot, you can't miss the gold dome on top of City Hall. The tour begins at this landmark on Bay Street and the northern tip of Bull Street. So look up (or down, depending on your vantage point), and when you spot the gold dome, head in that direction. Once you arrive, don't be shy—wander inside for a quick look around. You'll be glad you did, and the office workers don't mind a bit. Also note that there are several ideal guided walking tours listed on the Convention and Visitors Bureau website: savannahvisit.com/getaways/tours/listing/0/419. Fees will vary

Victory Drive and Washington Avenue

If you're venturing south of the Historic District to do some sightseeing, be sure to take a drive down portions of two streets in Midtown—**Victory Drive** between Abercorn Street and Waters Avenue, and **Washington Avenue** between Bull Street and Waters.

You'll see stately homes set amid huge, graceful oak trees on both streets and, if you hit it just right during the springtime, medians and yards bursting with the color of azaleas in bloom. Palm trees were first planted along Victory Drive in 1906 when it was called Estill Avenue, and this thoroughfare—which starts at Ogeechee Road, runs to the Wilmington River, and continues to Tybee Island as US 80—was once reputed to be the longest avenue of palms in the nation. When Estill Avenue was widened and extended in 1922, it was renamed Victory Drive in honor of the Americans who fought and died in World War I.

with each walking tour. The one we share here is for an individual, self-guided tour.

CITY HALL, 2 E. Bay St.; (912) 651-6410. Local architect Hyman Wallace Witcover designed and built City Hall in 1905 for an estimated $205,167. This price was to include statues of chariots and horses on top of the structure, but budget constraints prevented them from being built. The exterior is composed of several materials, including rough-hewn granite blocks, colored limestone, and polished granite. The dome, rising 70 feet, was originally copper. However, in 1987 a local philanthropist donated $240,000 to the city, allowing the dome to be gilded with thin layers of 23-karat gold leaf. The gold was applied to the dome, cupola, and clock hands. The dome was renovated in 2007–8, so if it seems extra shiny, you'll know why. Usually, most of the faces of the clock have the right time—but if your group is splitting up to tour, don't depend on it for your rendezvous time!

Inside the foyer you will find a lovely and intricate mosaic on the floor. Look up in the foyer, and you will see more detailed tiles. Go farther into the rotunda and look up for a pretty, circular view all the way up

to the fourth floor and the stained glass in the dome. The original building directory is also in the rotunda on a giant tablet. Today, Savannah city offices are located throughout the community, but the second floor of City Hall is much like it was when the building was originally constructed. It still houses the mayor's office, clerk of council offices, and the council chambers. The stern and imposing council chambers have even stood in for courtrooms in a couple of Hollywood productions.

After leaving City Hall, head south on Bull Street. Look to your left while crossing Bay Street. The huge building on the corner opposite City Hall is the US Custom House.

US CUSTOM HOUSE, 1 E. Bay St. The magnificent columns in front of the Custom House each weigh 15 tons. Across the street are cannons presented to the Chatham Artillery in 1791 by George Washington. In 1972 the structure was designated a historic custom house by the US commissioner of customs. As you walk by, notice the wonderful ironwork fencing that not only decorates the building but also guards it. It is just one of many fine examples of wrought iron you will notice throughout your walking tour. Although it is a landmark, it's also the working home of the Customs office, busy tracking the business of Savannah's port.

Continue south on Bull Street in the direction of Johnson Square.

JOHNSON SQUARE, Bull Street, between Bryan and Congress Streets. This is Savannah's first square. It is named for Robert Johnson, the governor of South Carolina who helped the Georgia colony get established. During the early days of the colony, this was the hub of activity for the city. In the center is a monument to Revolutionary War hero Gen. Nathanael Greene, who died in 1786; his grave is here as well. Today the square is the center of banking in Savannah. Stand in the middle and you will be surrounded by several banks. If you need to pick up some cash, this is a good spot to find an ATM. This is also a popular square for downtown workers to lunch in, and in spring and early summer there is often lunchtime musical entertainment.

On the eastern side of the square, look for pairs of gigantic green doors and majestic columns. They belong to Christ Church.

CHRIST CHURCH, 28 Bull St.; (912) 236-2500; christchurchsavannah.org. Christ Church is known as Georgia's Mother Church. It was founded in 1733, on the exact spot where the first Christian religious service in Georgia was held. The current structure replaced two edifices that were destroyed. In 1735 John Wesley, the founder of Methodism, served as pastor here and founded what is believed to be the world's first Protestant Sunday school.

Also interesting: Christ Church has one of the rarest church bells in the entire country. It is known as a Revere Bell and was created by Paul Revere and Sons, the company owned by the noted "British are coming" patriot. It is one of about 130 Revere bells, the majority of which are found in New England; only a handful made it to the South. The bell in the tower is actually the third Revere Bell the church has owned. The first, purchased in 1816 for $716, cracked during shipment. The second cracked the second Sunday it rang. The third bell, as they say, was the charm. The church didn't have any significant problems with the third bell until 1995, when repairs needed to be made to the apparatus holding the bell. After a 2-year repair job, the bell was rung again in early November 1997.

Continue heading south on Bull Street, crossing Congress Street and proceeding to Broughton Street. This is Savannah's original business district, and after decades of decline, it is becoming a shining example of urban redevelopment. Look east and west to see many trendy shops and a restaurant selection that ranges from Thai to Moroccan to Italian (not to mention a good ol' hot dog place as well). Take a detour if you are hungry. If not, continue south on Bull Street to Wright Square, the second square on our trip.

WRIGHT SQUARE, Bull Street, between State and York Streets. Wright Square is named for Sir James Wright, the last royal governor of Georgia. The monument in the center is for William Washington Gordon, one of the founders of the Central of Georgia Railway. (The railroad's offices used to be about a block away; you will pass the site on this walking tour.) The large boulder, taken from Stone Mountain near Atlanta, marks the grave of Tomo-chi-chi, the Yamacraw chief who was instrumental in helping the founders get established in their new colony.

Taking up the entire western side of the square is the federal courthouse. Made of Georgia marble, its architecture is a conglomeration of many styles: Spanish, French, Itálian Renaissance, and Romanesque among them. On the eastern side of the square, you'll see the old Chatham County Courthouse, a light-colored brick building designed in 1889 by noted Boston architect William G. Preston. It now houses county offices. On the same side as the courthouse is Lutheran Church of the Ascension.

LUTHERAN CHURCH OF THE ASCENSION, 120 Bull St.; (912) 232-4151; ascensionsavannah.org.
Massive red doors lead into the Lutheran Church of the Ascension, formed in 1741 by German settlers. The current church was built between 1875 and 1879 and designed by George B. Clarke, using Norman and Gothic styles. One of the church's most striking features is the Ascension Window, depicting the Ascension of the Lord.

JULIETTE GORDON LOW BIRTHPLACE, 10 E. Oglethorpe Ave.; (912) 233-4501; juliettegordonlowbirthplace.org.
The Juliette Gordon Low Birthplace gives visitors an authentic glimpse of what life was like in the 1800s for one of Savannah's most prominent families—one that just happened to include Juliette Gordon Low, founder of the Girl Scouts.

But the Low Center isn't just about the Girl Scouts. This beautifully restored home, Savannah's first National Historic Landmark, is full of the Gordons' original belongings—from Georgian Revival chairs in the dining room to a painting of Niagara Falls by moonlight, a souvenir the Gordons bought some years after their honeymoon. When entering the main hallway, you will immediately notice the beautiful winding staircase with a rose-colored bull's-eye glass window in the background; it was installed in 1886 to give more light in the stairway. In the library is a brass chandelier original to the home. The south parlor, decorated in striking yellow, red, and green, has a pier mirror, installed in 1884.

Construction on the home began in 1818 in the newly fashionable English Regency style. William Washington Gordon and his wife, Sarah, were the first of four generations of the Gordon family to live in the home. William Gordon served as mayor of Savannah and is credited as a founder of the Central of Georgia Railway. The house was eventually inherited by William Washington Gordon II and his wife, Eleanor Kinzie Gordon, the parents of Juliette Gordon. Juliette spent her childhood here.

After passing through another generation of Gordons, the house was threatened with demolition in 1953. A concerned group of local Girl Scouts, including youngsters and adults, appealed to the national organization to save the birthplace of their founder, and the building was purchased by the Girl Scouts. It was restored and opened to the public 3 years later. Today, thousands of Girl Scouts from around the world make the pilgrimage to Savannah to visit the home of the group's cherished founder. The house is open Mon through Sat 10 a.m. to 4 p.m. (closed Wed from Nov to Feb) and Sun 11 a.m. to 4 p.m. Call for admission prices; Girl Scouts and their leaders get discounts. Recent renovations, which include a small elevator, have made the mansion relatively accessible to those with physical disabilities, unusual among historic attractions.

Continuing south on Bull Street, you will pass the offices for the local school district on the left, housed in a rambling brick building that was once home to a school and still sports nice frescoes above its entrances, and Independent Presbyterian Church on the right.

INDEPENDENT PRESBYTERIAN CHURCH, 207 Bull St.; (912) 236-3346; ip.csav.org. This church was founded in 1755 and is considered one of the most important Federal-style churches in the country. The original was designed by John Holden Greene of Rhode Island. It burned in 1889. The current building has an elevated mahogany pulpit, and the four Corinthian columns of the sanctuary were made from a single tree trunk that was carefully selected through exhaustive searches in the South. It's worth a peek inside just to view the pulpit. Woodrow Wilson married Ellen Axson, granddaughter of the church's pastor, here.

Continue south to Chippewa Square.

i For movie buffs, Chippewa Square is where Forrest Gump sat waiting for the bus. The movie-prop bench was placed on the far northern tip of the square. Next time you see the film, notice that traffic in the square is moving in the wrong direction! The bench can be seen in the Savannah History Museum.

CHIPPEWA SQUARE, Bull Street, between Perry and Hull Streets. General James Oglethorpe is immortalized in bronze in the center of this square. First Baptist Church, organized in 1800, is on the northwestern corner of the square. Across the park on the northeastern corner is the Savannah Theatre, home of a professional theatrical group that presents musical programs 5 days a week.

The beautiful building on the southwest corner is known as the Philbrick-Eastman House and is a fine example of Greek Revival architecture. It served as home for many prominent families; today, it houses a law firm. While walking south through the square, look to your left along West Perry Street, and you will notice a row

of magnificently restored private homes, among the many you will see on your trip today. You are getting into the more residential portion of the Historic District.

Continue south on Bull Street. After crossing Perry Street, notice a dolphin downspout on the home to your right. These interesting adornments to lovely houses are a common sight throughout Savannah. There are several boutiques, a coffee shop, and a few lunch spots in this area. Duck in to Gaucho to look for women's high fashion. Farther down Liberty Street is the Hilton Savannah DeSoto, built on the site of the DeSoto Hotel, which was razed in 1966. (Check the Shopping and Restaurants chapters for more information.) Next is Madison Square.

MADISON SQUARE, Bull Street, between Harris and Charlton Streets. Madison Square is named for James Madison, the fourth US president. When entering Madison Square you will notice the Sorrel-Weed House on the northwest corner of the square. It was completed in 1841 and is an example of Greek Revival architecture. In 1997 the home was purchased and underwent an extensive $2 million renovation that restored it to its original condition. This renovation included painting the home its original bright orange color, which did not please neighbors and members of a local historic review committee. However, the homeowner won out, as you will see when walking by.

On the northeastern corner is E. Shaver Bookseller, a popular locally owned bookstore. If you need a break, this could be a good place to take it. On the southeastern edge of the square is a gigantic redbrick building that once was the Savannah Volunteer Guards Armory. This structure and the large building across the street on the southwest corner of the square—the old

Close-up

Savannah's Mercer House Opens Its Doors to Public

During the height of the popularity of the book *Midnight in the Garden of Good and Evil*, **Mercer House** was under a sort of subdued siege. A thriving and opportunistic tourism subculture centered around the book was cashing in on the obsessive interest of fans. Nowhere could have been of more interest to those fans than Mercer House, the heart of John Berendt's loosely woven collection of Savannah stories centered on the colorful history of this magnificent mansion where among years of lavish Savannah parties, a fatal shooting occurred.

The sudden fame of Mercer House escalated when the book became a film. Tour buses blared their version of the story outside the sedate mansion that became the private residence of the late Jim Williams' sister, Dr. Dorothy Williams Kingery. Fans posed for pictures outside the house, or clambered up on the gate and low surrounding wall for better looks. Images of the house were reproduced on souvenirs of varying taste levels.

Kingery fought to restore the respect of her brother's home. She trademarked the facade of the house in an effort to deter its commercial exploitation. She even put the home on the market briefly, at a multimillion-dollar price.

The closest fans got for many years, at least legally, was through a gift shop in the home's carriage house. This two-story structure to the rear of the house was once the workshop where Williams worked on antiques. So things stood for the first decade after the publication of Berendt's book. An even larger percentage of the people featured in the book have died by now. The fan fervor had died down some. Then, in 2004, quietly, with no fanfare and an extremely low-key approach, Kingery opened the first floor of Mercer House (now increasingly known as the Mercer-Williams House) to paying guests.

Scottish Rite Temple—are now owned by the Savannah College of Art and Design. The armory was the first building the art school founders purchased when they came to town in the late 1970s. At the time, there was an old restaurant inside, so complete renovation was needed. It was the first in a long list of buildings purchased and restored by the school; you'll find them throughout the Historic District. Today the armory houses classrooms and Exhibit A, an art gallery that features artwork by students and professors and, at times, famous artists. It is open to the public free of charge.

Look to the northwest corner of the square. The Gothic brick mansion is the Green-Meldrim House.

GREEN-MELDRIM HOUSE, 14 W. Macon St.; (912) 233-3845; stjohnsav.org. Built in 1853 by architect-builder John S. Norris for a wealthy cotton merchant, the Green-Meldrim House is best known as being headquarters for Gen. William T. Sherman, who "gave" the city of Savannah to President Lincoln as a Christmas present. The famous telegram to Lincoln, dated December 22, 1864, reads, "I beg to present to you as a Christmas Gift, the City of Savannah with 150 heavy guns and plenty of ammunition; and also about 25,000 bales of Cotton."

Today the home serves as a parish house and is owned by its neighbor, St. John's Church. When you walk by, notice the beautiful and elaborate ironwork and the oriel windows that give light from three

The Mercer-Williams House is now the only private, occupied residence in Savannah that invites paying guests to tour it. Tours enter through the carriage house, where a guide leads small groups through the courtyard and into the home's first floor. At the moment, you'll sample the resplendence of the house, decorated with one-of-a-kind antiques and rare furnishings and accent pieces that were a part of Jim Williams's collection. British Colonial pieces are among the most distinctive. Kingery is enthusiastic about sharing the truth of the home's history and the tour guides are endorsed by her. They are knowledgeable about the home's interior features and the antiques displayed there.

At $12.50, the Mercer-Williams House is the priciest of the downtown house museums, although the price hasn't gone up in the years it has been open. But it's also among the more interesting and beautiful. This is a tour of Williams's house, and it focuses on his impressive role in the preservation and restoration of Savannah's architectural treasures. It is not—repeat, not—a facet of the *Midnight in the Garden of Good and Evil* notoriety. You won't hear the book mentioned, and questions about the subject should be withheld as a courtesy and out of respect to the family. The front of the house has no sign or other indication that it is open to tours. The carriage house is directly behind the house, and a small, discreet sign gives tour details. The shop is worth a browse, too. It offers home decor and gift items of good quality, not extravagantly marked up. Although it isn't really a bookstore, the things we've bought on our few visits have all been books. And, as a sign of how much things have changed, that small stock of books on sale now includes *Midnight in the Garden of Good and Evil*.

sides. Inside are American black walnut floors, elaborate moldings, marble mantels, and other original adornments. The home is open for tours Tues, Thurs, and Fri 10 a.m. to 4 p.m. and Sat 10 a.m. to 1 p.m. year-round. Admission is $10 for adults, $5 for students.

Continuing south on Bull Street, you will pass Jones Street, considered one of Savannah's most picturesque roadways. Notice the brick streets and wonderfully restored homes. It is well worth a short detour. It is also home to one of Savannah's most noted restaurants, Mrs. Wilkes', which is known for its Southern fare (see our Restaurants chapter).

Next is Monterey Square.

MONTEREY SQUARE, Bull Street, between Taylor and Gordon Streets. This is the final square on Bull Street. Its name commemorates the Battle of Monterey in the Mexican-American War. The square was laid out in 1847. In the center is a monument honoring Casmir Pulaski, a Polish nobleman who was killed during the American Revolution. He may or may not be buried under the monument that honors him; historians disagree. The monument was rededicated in 2001 after a restoration period of several years that saw its foundation standing empty.

During filming of the movie *Midnight in the Garden of Good and Evil,* set designers brought in their own monument. Now, when you see Monterey Square on the big screen, you'll know the monument is not the original. The square is surrounded by other significant sites used in the movie, including the home where the book's main plot unfolds, the Mercer-Williams House, commonly known as Mercer House, which is on the western edge of the square.

MERCER HOUSE, 429 Bull St; mercer house.com. Cited by the Historic Savannah Foundation as nationally significant for its architectural style, this home was designed by John S. Norris and completed in 1871. The striking ironwork—including cast-iron window pediments, eight cast-iron balconies, and the sidewalk fence—is one of the house's signature features. The house was named for Confederate Gen. Hugh Mercer, songwriter Johnny Mercer's great-grandfather, but General Mercer sold the house. He never lived there nor did any member of the Mercer family.

In 1970, after the house was neglected and empty for many years, Jim Williams, the antiques dealer, Savannah preservationist, and the central character in the book and film *Midnight in the Garden of Good and Evil* finished a complete restoration of the home. Today the private home is owned by Dorothy Kingery, sister of the late Williams. She opened the home to limited public tours in 2004. Tickets are $12.50, and entrance is through the carriage house. Tickets may be purchased on the website, where you will also find hours and contact information. For more details, see our Close-Up in this chapter.

Looking past Mercer House, on the southwest corner of the square, you will notice row houses along Gordon Street. One of these homes—7 W. Gordon Street—has also had a brush with celebrity. If you are a fan of the PBS show This Old House, *you may be familiar with the renovation that took place here in 1996 at*

the home of Mills and Marianne Fleming. For several months, Norm Abram, Steve Thomas, and the rest of the crew from the popular series were in town helping restore the 1884 home, which made headlines when it was built for being one of the first homes in the city to have indoor plumbing. Across the square from Mercer House, on the eastern side of the square, is Temple Mickve Israel.

TEMPLE MICKVE ISRAEL, 20 E. Gordon St.; (912) 233-1547; mickveisrael.org. Temple Mickve Israel began with a group of Spanish-Portuguese Jews who came to Savannah in 1733, just 5 months after the founding of the colony. It is the site of the first Jewish congregation in the South and the third in the entire US. It is also the only Gothic synagogue in the country. The temple was designed by Henry G. Harrison and houses the oldest Torah in the US. There are also hundreds of documents, historical books, and letters from Presidents Washington, Jefferson, and Madison in the museum adjoining the temple. Tours of the sanctuary and museum take place Mon through Fri 10 a.m. to 1 p.m. and 2 to 4 p.m. at a fee of $4 per person.

Continuing south on Bull Street, you will pass the George Armstrong House on the northwest corner of Bull and Gaston Streets. This massive building, constructed in 1920, was given to the city in 1935 and converted into Armstrong Junior College, predecessor of Armstrong State University, which subsequently moved to Savannah's Southside. Today it houses a law firm. Across the street, on the northeast corner of Bull and Gaston Streets is the Oglethorpe Club, a longtime private club. Straight ahead is Forsyth Park.

FORSYTH PARK, Bull Street, between Gaston Street and Park Avenue. This 30-acre park is an amazing postcard brought to life and filled with color! With azaleas, magnolia trees, walkways, and park benches, the park is one of Savannah's most beautiful spots. The park was laid out in 1851. One of its most recognizable and often photographed features is the white fountain near the center. Visit on the weekend, and you might see a bride and groom getting pictures taken beside the ornate swans and other creatures in the fountain.

The monument in the center of the park was erected by the United Daughters of the Confederacy and honors those killed during the Civil War. The park is also home to an amphitheater, a cafe, a Fragrant Garden for the Blind, and public restrooms. It is surrounded by beautiful and elaborately restored homes, many of which are Victorian in style. Across from the northwestern corner of the park is the Georgia Historical Society.

GEORGIA HISTORICAL SOCIETY AND RESEARCH CENTER, 501 Whitaker St.; (912) 651-2125; georgiahistory.com. Dr. William Bacon Stevens, a physician who later became the Episcopal bishop of Pennsylvania, and attorney I. K. Tefft are generally credited with organizing the Savannah-based Georgia Historical Society. The pair was soon joined by Dr. Richard D. Arnold, a founder of the American Medical Association. In 1839 the group incorporated one of the country's oldest (and the Southeast's first) historical societies.

Nearly 170 years later, the realization of their efforts can easily be seen in thousands of historic documents, artifacts, newspapers, and other source materials documenting Georgia's past. Visitors to the society will find everything in its massive archives, from copies of letters Gen. James Edward Oglethorpe wrote to the Trustees of the Colony, to the grapeshot that killed Casmir Pulaski and was extracted from the Polish war hero's leg. There are minutes from the first Georgia

Medical Society meeting, held in Savannah in 1804; photographs from the now-defunct YWCA; and family letters such as the one written by Garnett Andrews about the cotton gin Eli Whitney had invented.

The society also publishes, in cooperation with the University of Georgia, the highly acclaimed *Georgia Historical Quarterly,* a collection of scholarly articles. Entry to the Georgia Historical Society is free. The building is open to the public Wed through Fri noon to 5 p.m. and on the first and third Sat of each month 10 a.m. to 5 p.m. It is recommended that you call to confirm hours as they do change.

This is the midpoint of the walking tour. Time to travel north for the next portion of the tour, heading back in the direction of City Hall, where we started. Continue 1 block east onto Gaston Street, crossing Drayton Street. Check out the many beautifully restored homes. Head north by turning left onto Abercorn and stay on this street until you reach Calhoun Square.

CALHOUN SQUARE, Abercorn Street, between Taylor and Gordon Streets. The first of the Abercorn Street squares on our tour was named for John Calhoun, a South Carolina statesman. It was laid out in 1851. When entering the square, you can't help but notice Wesley Monumental Methodist Church on the southwestern corner of the square. This Gothic Revival church was named for John and Charles Wesley, early figures in the history of Methodism. The sanctuary was built between 1876 and 1890. It features a Wesley Window opposite the pulpit, which contains the busts of the men for whom the church was named.

On the southeastern edge of the square is the Massie Heritage Interpretation Center.

MASSIE HERITAGE INTERPRETATION CENTER, 207 E. Gordon St.; (912) 395-5070; massieschool.com.

Honored as Georgia's oldest school in continuous operation, the Massie Heritage Interpretation Center is also the only remaining original building from Georgia's oldest chartered school system. The Greek Revival structure is listed on the National Register of Historic Places. It was completed in 1856 and is known for its gable roof, wood cupola, and cornice, among other features. Today, an enrichment program is offered to increase student understanding of Savannah's historic and architectural heritage. The center is open to the public Mon through Sat 10 a.m. to 4 p.m. and Sun noon to 4 p.m. Self-guided tours are $7; seniors are $6; youth (5–17) $5; children (1–4) $2.

LAFAYETTE SQUARE, Abercorn Street, between Harris and Charlton Streets.

This square, which was laid out in 1837, was named for the Marquis de Lafayette, who visited Savannah in 1825. There are several significant buildings on this square, but when you enter it, you can't help but notice the Cathedral of St. John the Baptist, near the northeast corner.

CATHEDRAL OF ST. JOHN THE BAPTIST, 223 E. Harris St.; (912) 233-4709; savannah cathedral.org.

A few private moments in this magnificent cathedral should be on your priority list of Savannah's must-sees. This magnificent Gothic cathedral with its twin spires is one of Savannah's most noted landmarks. It is also the oldest Roman Catholic church in Georgia and the seat of the Diocese of Savannah. The parish organized in the late 1700s and erected its first church on Liberty Street. It wasn't until 1876 that the cathedral was built; tragically, it was destroyed by fire 20 years later. When the cathedral was rebuilt, the original designs were used. One of the cathedral's most striking features is its stained glass. Most of it was executed by Innsbruck glassmakers in the Austrian Tyrol and installed around 1900. Other features include an Italian marble altar, the stations of the cross (imported from Munich), and the coat of arms of Pope John XXIII. The building just underwent a massive restoration, indoors and out, and is now fully open in its restored glory. See the website for the mass schedule.

THE ANDREW LOW HOUSE, 329 Abercorn St.; (912) 233-6854; andrewlow house.com.

On the northwest corner of Lafayette Square is the Andrew Low House, built in 1848 this wealthy cotton merchant. Low's son, William McKay Low, married Juliette Gordon, founder of the Girl Scouts. In fact, the carriage house in back of the home is the first official headquarters of the Girl Scouts of the USA. Juliette Low left the building to the organization following her death.

The stunning home, with its elegant front gardens and beautiful ironwork, is built of stucco brick. It is now owned by the National Society of the Colonial Dames of America in the State of Georgia, whose members also donated its furnishings. Even the three-tiered fountain in the center of the square was donated by the organization. Some of the home's most noted guests have included Robert E. Lee and William Makepeace Thackeray. The home is open for tours from 10 a.m. to 4:30 p.m. Mon through Sat, and from 10 a.m. to 4 p.m. Sun. Cost to tour the house is $10 for adults and $7 for students, Girl Scouts, and Girl Scout leaders.

FLANNERY HOUSE, 207 E. Charlton St.; (912) 233-6014; flanneryoconnorhome .org.

Noted Southern author Flannery O'Connor was born in this high-stoop, 19th-century home on the outskirts of Lafayette Square. She lived here as a child until 1938.

The parlor floor has been restored to its original appearance and houses a small museum dedicated to the author. The home is open 1 to 4 p.m. every day except Wed and Thurs, and there is a $6 adult admission charge ($5 for students).

Continuing north on Abercorn Street, cross Liberty Street. On the east side of Abercorn Street is Colonial Park Cemetery.

COLONIAL PARK CEMETERY, 201 Abercorn St.; (912) 651-651-6843; savannahga .gov. Button Gwinnett, who signed the Declaration of Independence, and Edward Green Malbone, painter of miniatures, are two of the notable Georgians buried in this cemetery, the second public burial ground in Savannah. The cemetery, which takes up several blocks in the Historic District, opened in 1750; it closed to burials 100 years later. Visitors are welcome to tour the cemetery and glimpse the old tombstones and inscriptions.

After exploring the cemetery, continue north on Abercorn Street, crossing Oglethorpe Avenue. As you cross Oglethorpe, you will pass the city's fire department headquarters. Next is Oglethorpe Square.

OGLETHORPE SQUARE, Abercorn Street, between State and York Streets. Oglethorpe Square was named for Georgia's founder, James Edward Oglethorpe. It was laid out in 1742. On the northeast corner of the square is one of Savannah's most famous museum houses, the Owens-Thomas House.

OWENS-THOMAS HOUSE, 124 Abercorn St.; (912) 790-8800; telfair.org. Taking up an entire block on the eastern edge of the square is the Owens-Thomas House, considered to be one of the finest examples of English Regency architecture in the country.

The home, with its columned entrance portico, brass inlaid staircase, and more, was designed by architect William Jay from 1816 to 1819 for cotton merchant Richard Richardson.

The home is made largely of tabby—an indigenous, concretelike material made of lime, oyster shells, and sand. The exterior is English stucco. The interior, which includes three rare built-in marble-top tables that belonged to the Richardsons, has many stunning features, including an entryway with a brass inlaid staircase and a drawing room with an unusual ceiling that makes the room appear to be round. The carriage house, also open for tours, is one of the earliest intact urban slave quarters in the South and opens into an English-inspired parterre garden.

In 1830, after the home had been used as a boardinghouse, George Welchman Owens, a congressman and former mayor of Savannah, purchased it for $10,000. The property remained in the Owens family until it was bequeathed to what is now the Telfair Museum of Art. The home is open Mon noon to 5 p.m., Tues through Sat 10 a.m. to 5 p.m., and Sun 1 to 5 p.m. The cost to tour the house is $15 for adults; students (K–college) are $5, and children under 5 are free (as are members of the Telfair). Note that this house museum is part of the Telfair's three holdings—the other two are art museums, and the best bargain is the $20 adult ticket that gets you into all three.

One of Savannah's other noted museum houses is just around the corner from the Owens-Thomas House on East State Street. If you would like to detour to this house, head east on State Street and cross Lincoln. One block on your left will be the Davenport House.

ISAIAH DAVENPORT HOUSE, 324 **E. State St; (912) 236-8097; davenport housemuseum.org.** As you walk around today in the Historic District enjoying the beautifully restored homes and other sights, know that it was the Davenport House that was largely responsible for the preservation of this national treasure. In the 1950s, when developers came up with a plan to demolish the house, sell the brick, and put in a parking lot, seven local women banded together to stop it. That group, which later became the Historic Savannah Foundation, raised $22,500 to purchase the home; such were the beginnings of restoration efforts in Savannah.

At the time of the rescue purchase, the home was a tenement, divided into small apartments and full of people. The Federal-style home was originally built in 1820 by master builder Isaiah Davenport, who used it as a kind of showcase for his work. One of the incredible features of the house is the delicate and ornate molding and plasterwork found throughout. The Davenport House is open Mon through Sat 10 a.m. to 4 p.m. and Sun 1 to 4 p.m. Cost is $9 for adults, $5 for children.

After viewing the Davenport House, head west on State Street to Abercorn Street. Again, travel north on Abercorn. As you cross Broughton Street, you'll notice a large building on your right. Savannah College of Art and Design has transformed this former department store into a library. Continuing along Abercorn Street, you will come to the Lucas Theatre.

LUCAS THEATRE, 32 Abercorn St.; (912) 525-5040; lucastheatre.com. This Savannah landmark, built in 1921, served not only as a theater but also as a general center of entertainment for the city. It had floors of imported marble, a dome ceiling surrounded by 600 incandescent lights, and 36 ornate boxes. However, it deteriorated with the rest of downtown after World War II. A group of citizens—Lucas Theatre for the

Arts Inc.—banded together to reopen the theater and has been raising the millions of dollars needed to complete the project. As part of their fund-raising efforts, when the crew filming *Midnight in the Garden of Good and Evil* was in town in 1997, it participated in a fund-raiser for the theater. Among those in attendance were director Clint Eastwood and actor Kevin Spacey. The theater is now in full operation under the management of Savannah College of Art and Design. Check the schedule and plan to enjoy the beauty of this theater if there's an event going on during your stay.

After passing the Lucas Theatre, you will enter Reynolds Square, the last square on our walking tour.

REYNOLDS SQUARE, Abercorn Street, between Bryan and Congress Streets. Reynolds Square was named for Capt. John Reynolds, who served as governor of Georgia in 1754. In the center is a statue of John Wesley, the founder of Methodism. On the northwestern corner of the square is the Olde Pink House, a popular eatery.

Continuing north on Abercorn Street, you will reach Bay Street. Look to the west and you will once again see the dome on City Hall, where the tour began. Directly across Bay Street is Factors' Walk and River Street.

FACTORS' WALK AND RIVER STREET, Bay Street. Factors' Walk is named for the cotton brokers (or "factors") who bought, sold, and shipped their wares along the banks of the Savannah River. This unique row of buildings, erected on the bluff overlooking the water, rises two or three stories on the street side and three or more stories over the riverfront.

The focal point is the old Cotton Exchange, a redbrick building with the name

Cotton Exchange etched along the top of the facade. It was constructed in 1886 by William G. Preston and was one of the first buildings in the US to be erected entirely over a public street. At one time this building was where the world price for cotton was set. While the brokers set the price of cotton, the lower floors served as cotton and naval warehouses with entrances at several levels, including on River Street.

Today both River Street and Factors' Walk are full of shops, restaurants, and galleries, all housed in the restored warehouses. It is a favorite spot for visitors. Take a stroll on the river for a fitting end to our tour.

GUIDED TOURS

Savannah abounds with guided-tour companies. Their offerings are varied—general history, ghosts and hauntings, African-American history, you name it. Modes as well as subjects vary: travel by air-conditioned minibus, open-sided pseudo trolley, horse-drawn carriage, riverboat, or plain old shank's mare (walking, in other words). The latest addition to the local tour scene is the Segway, those motorized "people movers" that look like a scale in a doctor's office, except they carry you around.

This is a very fluid industry. New tours are added constantly, schedules and itineraries change, etc. Although the following is not a comprehensive listing, it will get you started.

Boats

SAVANNAH RIVERBOAT CRUISES, 9 E. River St.; (912) 232-6404, (800) 786-6404; savannahriverboat.com. This hour-long cruise takes you up and down the Savannah River on a replica riverboat, either the *Savannah River Queen* or the *Georgia Queen*. It's one of many ways for a tourist to get a firsthand look at the industrial and shipping side of the city—the bread and butter for many of us who live here. You can also get a waterfront perspective on historic structures. River Street from the water lends itself to good panoramic photos; however, realize that the tours may not be narrated. Depending on river traffic, you may get to see some of the massive ships that make the port of Savannah among the busiest in the nation.

The daytime sightseeing cruise is narrated. Wear sunscreen! This company also offers a variety of other cruises, keyed around dinner and dancing, Sunday brunch, or even gospel music with a buffet dinner. You'll need to check the website for current themed cruises since they vary. Prepaid reservations are required for most tours, except the daytime sightseeing. Note: All cruise schedules are subject to change, vary seasonally, and can be affected by the weather.

i Florence Martus is forever immortalized by the Waving Girl statue on River Street. For many years during the late 1800s and early 1900s, she greeted the ships that passed through the port of Savannah by waving a white cloth during the day and a lantern during the night, hoping to be the first to greet her returning husband (or, by some accounts, her returning fiancé). The Altrusa Club erected this statue in her honor.

Buses

Although most tours will take credit cards, some bus drivers do not have the means of processing them. If you plan on paying by plastic, mention that while making your reservations, because it may impact your selection of pickup locations. Also, prices don't include tips for the guide/driver, which most of the brochures and onboard signs shamelessly hustle for; they are strictly optional.

The Gospel Cruise

After several years of hearing about the Monday night **Gospel Dinner Cruises** advertised by the Savannah Riverboat Company, I ventured out to see if there was any truth to the positive reviews I had read. First, let me say this: These riverboats cruise waters along a working, industrial pathway, so if you're expecting to see postcard-like settings along the way, be forewarned. The Georgia Ports Authority's various working terminals and supporting shipping vendors will consume more space in your camera's memory than any wildlife or old buildings. You may pass working barges, and briefly, old Fort Jackson, but other than the historic cotton warehouses along River Street, there's not much beauty to behold.

The cruises board around sunset, which can be spectacular from the boat's third deck. This is where you'll want to enjoy your pre- and post-dinner time. Although the advertised boarding time is 6 p.m., board around 5:30 so you can spend a little time exploring the vessel's outside decks and maybe catch a dolphin or two in between the rustic commercial riverfront industrial sites. On Gospel Night, you'll be greeted by the sounds of about a dozen singers from varying Savannah churches who have been livening up the riverboat for the past several years. There are several lead singers, and let me tell you this, they can sing! From old hymns like "Tis So Sweet to Trust in Jesus," to favorites like, "Swing Low, Sweet Chariot" and "This Little Light of Mine," you'll be rocking right along with them as you dine on Southern favorites like fried chicken, mac and cheese, greens, and biscuits, buffet style. When it's all said and done and the group has sang its last amen, you'll wonder why you even thought about a view.

OLD TOWN TROLLEY TOURS OF SAVANNAH, 234 Martin Luther King Jr. Blvd.; (912) 233-0083, (888) 910-8687; trolley tours.com. It's exciting to tour the city in an open-air vehicle, and Old Town Trolley Tours of Savannah offers colorful and comfortable trolley-style vehicles. This 90-minute tour offers re-boarding options throughout the Historic District on orange and green trolley-style vehicles. A 1-day ticket costs $25 for adults and $10 for children. Most popular is the Paula Deen Tour, which includes dinner, $50 for adults and $26 for children. The tour company also operates a gift shop downtown and offers a ghost tour on a trolley, Ghosts and Gravestones, for $25 for adults and $10 for children.

OGLETHORPE TROLLEY TOURS, 215 W. Boundary Rd.; (912) 233-8380; oglethorpe tours.com. This group offers a 90-minute narrated, on-off trolley tour of Historic Savannah for $19 for adults and $11 for children. They also offer a Land and Sea Savannah Package, which includes a 1-hour narrated Sightseeing Riverboat Cruise along the Savannah River ($39 for adults and $20 for children). Historic Savannah Haunted Trolley Tour and Haunted Savannah packages are also available. Tickets for these are from $20 for adults and $12 for children.

Horse-Drawn Carriages

Although children generally don't jump up and down at the prospect of a guided tour of historic sites, we've found horse-drawn carriages up the appeal significantly. Who knows? You may be lucky enough to see a chartered and decorated carriage ferrying a bride and groom from a wedding at one of the Historic District churches. Tours are not given during the threat of thunderstorms, rain, or extreme heat.

CARRIAGE TOURS OF SAVANNAH, (912) 236-6756; carriagetoursofsavannah.com. Narrated tours are about an hour in length. Options include a daytime historic tour ($22 for adults, $12 for those ages 5–11), evening historic or ghost story tours ($22 for adults, $12 for children), and private carriage tours for couples (call for pricing). Hours vary.

HISTORIC SAVANNAH CARRIAGE TOURS, 2 W. Bay St.; (912) 443-9333; savannahcarriage.com. Pickup service can be arranged at hotels or at downtown locations. Fees are $23 for adults and $12 for children. Variations include private romance (Wine and Roses Tour) and Champagne Proposal tours. Standard departure is from the Hyatt Regency Savannah on Bay Street, or for private tours, by arrangement in the Historic District.

Walking

FREEDOM TRAIL TOUR, PO Box 1484, Savannah, GA 31402; (912) 398-2785. This tour lasts about 2 hours and visits historic churches, the Ralph Mark Gilbert Civil Rights Museum, slave burial grounds, and sites of particular importance in African-American history. Available 7 days a week, there are two tours daily in the winter and an extended schedule during other months. Prices are $18 for adults, $12 for children, $15 for seniors. Departures are from the Visitor Information Center, 301 Martin Luther King Jr. Blvd.

GHOST TALK, GHOST WALK, 4401 Montgomery St.; (912) 233-3896, (800) 563-3896. The ghost tour is the mainstay (there are actually two different versions). They depart from Reynolds Square, beside the statue of John Wesley (one wonders what the famous preacher would have thought of it). Tours depart at dusk, varying according to the time of year, so call for information. Fees are $10 for adults and $5 for those younger than age 12. No credit cards. Other available tours include a Civil War version, a botanical tour, a historic architecture walk, and a literary walking tour. Rates vary; check when you make reservations.

THE SAVANNAH WALKS, 37 Abercorn St.; (912) 238-9255, (888) 728-9255; savannahwalks.com. This walking-tour firm offers a varied menu with different meeting points. Be sure to check on these things when you make your reservations. Fees are $15 for adults and $7 for children ages 6–16. Options include general tours, a Midnight tour, a ghost tour, a Civil War walk, and one featuring gardens. The historic homes walk is slightly higher ($22 adults, $14 children) because it includes admission to one of the city's house museums.

SIXTH SENSE SAVANNAH, (866) 666-3323; sixthsensesavannah.com. Lots of companies offer Savannah tours on a ghostly theme. This walking-tour company does it with a mixture of deadpan seriousness and arch humor (like the phone number, which spells out 666-DEAD). This company does not adopt the "all in fun" approach of many other ghost tours: These folks profess to believe and even offer metaphysical readings on premises. The tour founder is Shannon Scott, who has hosted some cable network TV programs on hauntings. Scott helped convince the American Institute of the Paranormal to hold its annual convention in Savannah in 2002, and the group went on to bestow its "America's Most Haunted City" title on us. Tours start at 7:30 and 9:30 p.m. Prices start at $25 for adults and $15 for children 12 and under.

OTHER SAVANNAH ATTRACTIONS

It almost seems like Savannah attractions are endless! One of the most distinctive draws of this city is that many of her attractions are either free or cost very little. So keep your hiking shoes on and discover what lies beyond the walking tour.

Historic District

BEACH INSTITUTE, 502 E. Harris St.; (912) 234-8000; kingtisdell.org. The Beach Institute was established in 1865 by the American Missionary Association to educate newly freed slaves. Built in 1867, it was the first school in Savannah for African Americans and became a public school in 1919. The institute is an African-American cultural center and houses art, sculpture, and artifacts. The star of its exhibits is the 238-piece collection of wood carvings by the late Ulysses Davis, a Savannah folk artist. Stay tuned to an updated schedule for lectures and other fascinating programs via the website. The Beach Institute is open Tues through Sat noon to 5 p.m. Admission is $4 for adults, $2 for children.

FIRST AFRICAN BAPTIST CHURCH, 23 Montgomery St.; (912) 233-6597; first africanbc.com. Overlooking Franklin Square is First African Baptist Church. This church, which is still active, is descended from the oldest African-American congregation in the US. George Leile, a slave, began making missionary visits to plantations up and down the Savannah River as early as 1774. A permanent congregation was formed at Brampton

Plantation in 1788—the first black missionary Baptist church in Savannah. Eventually, the congregation constructed the current building. It is the first brick building erected in Georgia by African Americans for African Americans; it was built by slaves who worked on it at night after being in the fields all day. The sanctuary has beautiful stained-glass windows framing the back of the altar, which displays pictures of the founding pastors. In the balcony are original pews with markings left by the slaves who built the church. The staff of this church is friendly and will invite you to visit their Sun services at 10 a.m. Tours are Tues through Sat at 11 and 2, Sun at 1 p.m., $7 for adults and $6 for students and seniors.

THE GEORGIA STATE RAILROAD MUSEUM, 601 W. Harris St.; (912) 655-6823; chsgeorgia.org. Your children will love seeing the locomotive collection at the Georgia State Railroad Museum! It houses the oldest and most complete antebellum railroad manufacturing and repair facilities still in existence in the US. Take a moment and imagine you are standing there in the 1800s. Watch as the area's largest staff of professional historic preservationists works daily on more than a dozen historic structures. This site was the Savannah repair shop for the Central of Georgia Railway, and 13 of the original structures, which were built beginning in the 1830s, are still standing. Included are a massive roundhouse and operating turntable (where the engines were turned around) and the 125-foot brick smokestack. Various activities are offered daily at the site, including tours inside railcars, a train-ride tour of the museum, and rides on a handcar; call for schedules. The site is a National Historic Landmark operated by the Coastal Heritage Society. It is open daily 9 a.m. to 5 p.m. Admission is $10 for adults and $6 for children age 2–12.

KING-TISDELL COTTAGE, 514 E. Huntingdon St.; (912) 234-8000; kingtisdell.org. Built in 1869 by W. W. Aimar, this cottage, with its original gingerbread ornamentation, is in the Beach Institute neighborhood of the Historic District and serves as a museum dedicated to preserving the African-American history of Savannah and the sea islands. Inside the small home you will find art objects, documents, and furniture of the 1890s. It is open Tues through Sat noon to 5 p.m. Admission is $7.

LIVE OAK PUBLIC LIBRARY, 2002 Bull St.; (912) 652-3600; liveoakpl.com. The opening of an $8.3 million expansion and addition to the circa-1916 main branch on Bull Street revitalized the entire library system. The building's addition is clad in marble and features park views from massive clerestory windows. The collection had drifted off into inadequacy and obsolescence until the renovation project gave it a shot in the arm—and a $3 million injection of public and private monies to stock the new shelves. While you may not think of libraries as places to visit while vacationing, there are resources here of interest to the traveler. Foremost among them is the local history and genealogy collection. Those in search of the dirt on their ancestors have been known to make the trip just to get into those records. Visitors can use the resources of the library without charge and can even check items out if they pay the nonrefundable temporary card fee for out-of-towners. Branches are located throughout the county; check the website for locations.

RALPH MARK GILBERT CIVIL RIGHTS MUSEUM, 460 Martin Luther King Jr. Blvd.; (912) 777-6099; savcivilrights.com. More than 40,000 people toured Ralph Mark Gilbert Civil Rights Museum during its inaugural year of 1996. The museum chronicles the story of Savannah's civil rights struggles during the 1940s, 1950s, and 1960s. Along with traveling exhibits and special programming, it spotlights how Martin Luther King Jr. Boulevard, formerly known as West Broad Street, was once the center of the city's thriving African-American business community. Besides educating the community, the museum also serves as an educational resource for southeastern coastal Georgia.

Development of the museum took place over several years. More than $1.7 million went into it, which included the renovation of the Wage Earners Savings Bank building, where the museum is housed. The Wage Earners Bank is believed to be the second bank for African Americans in the nation. The museum is the brainchild of the late local historian and activist W. W. Law. It is named after the Reverend Ralph Mark Gilbert, a pastor at First African Baptist Church, who pioneered Savannah's modern civil rights movement. Admission is $8 for adults, $6 for seniors, and $4 for students. Hours are Tues through Sat 9 a.m. to 5 p.m. Guided tours are available upon request.

ℹ️ **The Pirates' House at 20 E. Broad St., which is now home to a restaurant featuring a mysterious maze of rooms, is a former sailors' tavern built in 1794. Peer down into the secret tunnels and you might find a dead pirate!**

SAVANNAH HISTORY MUSEUM, Savannah Visitor Information Center; 301 Martin Luther King Jr. Blvd.; (912) 651-6825; chsgeorgia.org. Cool off and delve into Savannah's past at the Savannah History Museum, located in the old passenger station of the Central of Georgia Railway that also houses the Savannah Visitor Center. The structure, a National Historic Landmark, features a variety of exhibits, including an 1890 steam locomotive that is still sitting on the original Central of Georgia tracks. A genuine antique cotton gin is on display, along with artifacts from the Civil War and other eras. Enjoy a colorful film that provides an overview of the city's history in the small theater. The museum is open weekdays 8:30 a.m. to 5 p.m. and weekends 9 a.m. to 5 p.m. It costs $7 for adults and teens, $4 for children ages 2–12. Kids younger than age 6 are free.

The Battlefield Memorial Park

After your visit to the Georgia State Railroad Museum, walk the grounds nearby where 800 troops fought and died in 1779, when soldiers from three different armies battled for control of Savannah. Within this area, approximately 2,500 British defenders faced down the allied force of 5,500 French and American troops who fought fiercely, and when the battle was over, more than 8,000 troops had fought and many died or were wounded, and Savannah remained in the hands of the British. It's quite a sight to view the granite markers that represent the soldiers who lost their lives. There's also a wooden sign greeting visitors at the Spring Hill Redoubt, a representation of the British fortification in the battle. There is no charge to walk the grounds; however, donations are always accepted.

SHIPS OF THE SEA MUSEUM, 41 Martin Luther King Jr. Blvd.; (912) 232-1511; shipsofthesea.org. Scarbrough House and its related garden (a true undiscovered treasure) have added a lot of tone to this museum, previously housed on River Street.

The exhibits are more formal now, showcasing paintings and intricate models. The collection also includes scrimshaw, ancient navigational tools, and a china cat figurine with its own risqué story to tell. Learn about Savannah's maritime history while exploring this museum. The home, built in 1819 for the principal owner of the *Savannah*, the first steamship to cross the Atlantic Ocean, was designated a National Historic Landmark in 1974. Cost is $8.50 for adults, $6.50 for children age 6 and older (if you have a college ID you can get the discounted rate). Children 5 and under get in free. The museum is open Tues through Sun 10 a.m. to 5 p.m.

THE TELFAIR MUSEUMS, 121 Barnard St.; (912) 790-8827; telfair.org. The Telfair Museums is the overarching title of three jointly operated but very different and distinct museums. The Owens-Thomas House is a house museum of historic and architectural importance. Savannah has several house museums, and in case you are unfamiliar with the term, consider them "lifestyle" museums that capture the home decor and flavor of life in the period of the usually significant homes they occupy; you could build a case that the Owens-Thomas House is the finest example in Savannah. The Telfair Museum of Art is a splendid hybrid: part house museum, complete with some of the original furnishings on its parlor floor, while the upper and lower floors display 19th- and 20th-century art. Round out this trio of museums with the Jepson Center, a modern setting for modern art, and you've met the whole set. Because the Owens-Thomas House is discussed in more detail elsewhere in this chapter, it is omitted from further review here so we can summarize the other two more fully.

TELFAIR MUSEUM OF ART, 121 Barnard St.; (912) 790-8800; telfair.org. The Telfair is the oldest art museum in the South. Its permanent collection of paintings, prints, sculpture, and decorative arts is housed in a mansion designed by English architect William Jay for Alexander Telfair, son of Georgia governor Edward Telfair. The family lived here until 1875.

Among the museum's holdings are paintings by Childe Hassam, Frederick Frieseke, and Gari Melchers, along with Robert Henri, George Bellows, and George Luks. The museum also has a decorative arts collection that includes American and European objects from 1790 to 1840, including a rare Philadelphia suite of maple furniture, a secretary-bookcase commissioned from Duncan Phyfe of New York, and a dining table ordered from Thomas Cook of Philadelphia. The museum also holds the largest existing collection of the works of Lebanese mystical poet and artist Kahlil Gibran, best known for *The Prophet*. His patroness, Mary Haskell, made her home in her later years on Gaston Street in Savannah. Because of the fragile nature of the artwork (it was done predominantly in pencil), it is only on display occasionally. On a more contemporary note, the Telfair is the new home for the *Bird Girl* sculpture featured on the cover of John Berendt's *Midnight in the Garden of Good and Evil*. Fans of the book hounded it out of its original setting in a family plot at Bonaventure.

The Telfair is open Mon noon to 5 p.m., Tues through Sat 10 a.m. to 5 p.m., and Sun 1 to 5 p.m. Cost is $12 for adults, $5 for students, and free for children under 5. Note that the best admission prices are those that cover all three Telfair Museums sites: the Triple Site Pass is $20 for adults; $18 for seniors, AAA members, and the military; $15 for students k–college; or a family of two adults and two children, $40.

JEPSON CENTER FOR THE ARTS, 207 W. York St.; (912) 790-8800; telfair.org. The Jepson Center for the Arts adds 64,000 square feet to Telfair's assets. In addition to large galleries for traveling exhibitions, it has space for regional and community work, outdoor sculpture terraces, classrooms, a 200-seat auditorium, a cafe, and a store.

In 2006 a city that made its reputation by preserving and restoring its historic architecture also offered something significant from the modern side of the architecture spectrum: the freestanding ultramodern Jepson Center for the Arts on the same historic square as the Telfair Museum of Art. The Jepson concentrates on 20th- and 21st-century collections, both owned works and traveling exhibitions. The permanent collection was bolstered on opening with the gift of more than 20 works on paper by major contemporary artists honoring the late Kirk Varnedoe, a former Museum of Modern Art curator and native Savannahian. Included in that impressive gift were works by Jasper Johns, Roy Lichtenstein, Robert Rauschenberg, and Richard Avedon, among many others.

Islands

BONAVENTURE CEMETERY, 330 Bonaventure Rd.; (912) 651-6843; savannahga.gov. "Bonaventure" means "good fortune," which may strike you as a strange name for a graveyard. But once you visit this serenely beautiful place, chances are the name will seem more appropriate. The massive cemetery (160 acres) stands under vast canopies of moss-draped shade where live oaks, thick with age, stand guard by row upon row of elegant statuary and headstones, culminating in a scenic waterfront view on the Wilmington River. Among famous residents in this cemetery are Pulitzer Prize–winning poet Conrad Aiken, whose grave is marked by a poetry-engraved bench, and the graves

ATTRACTIONS

of famed Savannah lyricist Johnny Mercer and his wife, Ginger.

Bonaventure was once an elegant plantation, but the grand home burned down more than once. Local folklore has it that the roof caught fire during a dinner party, and the guests finished the meal outdoors by the light of the burning building. If you are looking for ghost stories, there's a tale that you can still hear the revelry and breaking glass of that party at certain times. The property became a cemetery in the 1800s and was put into city hands in 1907. It is still an active cemetery with an occasional burial, but the few remaining spaces are generally taken—don't get attached to the place. You may encounter a real funeral on your visit to this beautiful cemetery, and your decorum is appreciated.

Many important figures from the history of Georgia and the nation are buried here. There's Noble Jones, who arrived with James Oglethorpe at the beginning of the colony; several members of Georgia's Liberty Boys; and a number of prominent physicians, including Brodie Herndon, chief surgeon of hospitals for the Confederacy and the first doctor to perform a caesarean operation in the US. John Walz, sculptor of many of the impressive funerary statues in Bonaventure and other local cemeteries, is buried here. Ironically, there is no headstone at his grave.

Park with care, as there is a lot of tour-bus traffic. There's a small lot behind the office building just inside the gates if you are the hiking kind; there's also a grassy parking area for a few cars that's near the water and not far from the Aiken plot. Although we haven't heard of any trouble, it's an isolated spot between tours, so it's probably a good idea to lock your car and bring a friend. Cemetery hours are 8 a.m. to 5 p.m. daily. The Bonaventure Historical Society's visitor center is open Sat and Sun 10 a.m. to 4 p.m. Free guided tours are provided by the society on the second Sun of each month and the preceding Sat. Sat tours are at 2 p.m. Sun tours are at 2, 2:30, and 3 p.m.

If you like what you see at Bonaventure, there's more. Another historic city of Savannah cemetery is Laurel Grove Cemetery, 802 W. Anderson St. (912-651-6772), resting place of those from all walks of life in Savannah's history. Many Confederate soldiers and veterans are buried there, along with such notables as Girl Scout founder Juliette Gordon Low and "Jingle Bells" composer James L. Pierpont. You'll find the same elaborate statuary standing under some of the most impressive oaks Savannah has to offer.

OATLAND ISLAND EDUCATION CENTER, 711 Sandtown Rd.; (912) 898-3980; oatlandisland.org. A visit to Oatland gives you a good idea of what Georgia's first European settlers might have seen when they landed in 1733. Walk the 1.75-mile trail through the center's 75-acre forest of oaks, pines, and magnolias, and you'll encounter enclosures providing natural settings for animals native to the state: shorebirds, alligators, panthers, birds of prey, white-tailed deer, black bears, timber wolves, and bison. The enclosures are large and wooded, and the inhabitants are often hard to spot, but getting a look at them in their environment is worth the effort. The trail leads you to the Heritage Homesite area, where two log cabins (built in 1835, moved to Oatland, and restored there) convey a feeling for life on the farm during pioneer days. Another Oatland feature is a small barnyard where youngsters can see and feed farm animals. Be sure to check out the Wolf Wilderness Exhibit where you can view, firsthand, a pack of five wolves!

Although Oatland's main focus is on teaching students from local and out-of-county public and private schools, it is open to the public 10 a.m. to 4 p.m. every day of the week. Guests can remain on the grounds until 4:30 p.m. Admission to Oatland is $5 for adults and $3 for children (ages 4–17), and seniors age 65 and older and active military also pay $3. Children under the age of 4 are admitted free. The tour of the center's animal habitats is self-guided and takes about 90 minutes.

OLD FORT JACKSON, 1 Fort Jackson Rd.; (912) 232-3945; chsgeorgia.org. Georgia's oldest standing brick fortification perches right on the banks of the Savannah River—built there so its guns could fire on any vessel coming into Savannah—and chances are good you'll get an up-close view of an oceangoing ship during your visit. This is a great place to pose for personal pictures and then walk on the parapet of the fort and investigate the structure's many nooks and crannies. Two powder magazines and most of the casemates are open to the public, and they contain displays of weaponry and tools used at the fort and artifacts from the CSS *Georgia*, a Confederate ironclad whose remains lay on the river bottom a few hundred feet away. Inspect 11 cannons. The 9-inch Dahlgren cannon is the largest functional piece of Civil War–era heavy artillery in the US. Cannon-firing programs are presented in the summer; call for more information.

For a thorough rundown on the history of the fort, watch the 15-minute film that's shown in one of the powder magazines. The fort is not on an island, but we've placed it in this section because it's 3 miles from the Historic District on the way to the eastside islands. To get there, take President Street Extension (also known as Islands Expressway) east to the red, white, and blue Fort Jackson sign; then turn left onto Woodcock Road and follow the brown signs to the fort. The fort is open 7 days a week 9 a.m. to 5 p.m., but it is closed on Thanksgiving,

Christmas, and New Year's Day. Entry is $7 for adults and $4 for kids age 2–12.

PIN POINT HERITAGE MUSEUM, 9924 Pin Point Ave.; (912) 667-9176, (912) 355-0064; pinpointheritagemuseum.com. This museum highlights the community of Pin Point, a Gullah/Geechee enclave founded by first generation freemen. This small fishing community centered around the now-closed A.S. Varn & Son Oyster and Crab Factory on Moon River nearing Skidaway Island. This museum celebrates the life, work and history of the people of Pin Point. One of the Pin Point native sons is Associate Supreme Court Justice Clarence Thomas. The museum is open Sat 9 a.m. to 5 p.m.

Southside/Midtown

BETHESDA HOME FOR BOYS, 9520 Ferguson Ave.; (912) 351-2005; bethesda academy.org. Bethesda, America's oldest children's home, reposes on 600 oak-filled acres overlooking the Moon River (yes, that Moon River, the one made famous in the song by Henry Mancini and Savannahian Johnny Mercer). You can stroll or ride around the well-kept grounds of the main campus and visit the Bethesda museum and chapel, but the home's administrators ask that you report to the office after you arrive so that they know you're there. The museum—located in what was once the dining room of Burroughs Cottage, which was built in 1883 and is the oldest standing building at Bethesda—contains documents and artifacts pertaining to the history of the home and of coastal Georgia. Whitefield Chapel was completed in 1925 and is named for George Whitefield, one of the home's founders. It's a reproduction of Whitefield's church in England, and with its straight-back wooden pews, brick floor, and airy interior, the chapel is a small but beautiful place in which to spend a few moments in

Close-up

Wormsloe Historic Site

You'll be amazed and astounded when you approach this magnificent attraction. After driving under a large masonry arch at the entrance to Wormsloe, you'll travel down an "avenue of oaks," a wide, crushed-stone road lined with majestic live oak trees. After 1.25 miles, the road narrows to a walking trail. At this point, you'll find a parking lot and the Wormsloe museum. Discover the last architectural remnant of the Oglethorpe era in Savannah at **Wormsloe Historic Site** (Isle of Hope, 7601 Skidaway Rd., 912-353-3023; gastateparks.org), which is at the end of Skidaway Road on the doorstep of the Isle of Hope, about 10 miles south of the Historic District.

Continue on foot down the trail about 0.25 mile, and you'll be looking at the remains of a fortified house where construction was started in 1739 during the 10-year span James Edward Oglethorpe spent founding and nurturing the colony of Georgia (see our History chapter). The builder and owner of the house—a physician, carpenter, and surveyor named Noble Jones—came to the new colony in 1733 with Oglethorpe and the first boatload of settlers. Three years later, Jones leased 500 acres from the Trustees of Georgia, land that would be part of a plantation he called Wormslow. The name was changed to Wormsloe in the mid-1800s by his great-grandson, and the plantation eventually grew to cover nearly 900 acres. Jones's descendants donated 822 of those acres to the Nature Conservancy in 1972, and the property was transferred to the state of Georgia, which manages the site via the Parks and Historic Sites Division of the Department of Natural Resources.

meditation. The chapel is open year-round; museum hours are Mon through Fri 9 a.m. to 5 p.m. There's no admission fee, but donations are accepted.

COASTAL GEORGIA BOTANICAL GARDENS, 2 Canebrake Rd.; (912) 921-5460; coastalgeorgiabg. Called the Bamboo Farm through the years by Savannahians because of the groves of the tropical plants grown there, the facility has a large collection of daylilies, a xeriscape garden, a cottage garden, and bamboo, of course—140 varieties of it. The bamboo collection is the largest in the US open for viewing by the public, and there's also a grove of giant timber bamboo—the reason the farm was purchased for the US Department of Agriculture in 1918. The bamboo grove, where stalks can reach a height of more than 70 feet and a diameter of 6 inches, originated with three seedlings planted on the site in 1890; 25

years later, it attracted the attention of plant explorer David Fairchild, who bought the 46-acre farm where the bamboo grew and donated it to the government. The farm offers a self-guided walking tour that will take you to (among other botanical treasures) the bamboo collection and grove, beds of ornamental and turf grasses, an experimental grove of different species of banana tree, a collection of crape myrtles that's probably the largest in coastal Georgia, and a variety of other interesting trees.

The gardens are open Mon through Fri 8 a.m. to 5 p.m., Sat 10 a.m. to 5 p.m., and Sun noon to 5 p.m. Admission is free, and donations are accepted. The facility is on US 17, about 13 miles south of the Historic District.

MIGHTY EIGHTH AIR FORCE HERITAGE MUSEUM, 175 Bourne Ave., Pooler; (912) 748-8888; mightyeighth.org. It's not unusual for veterans of World War II

The house Jones completed in the mid-1740s was a five-room, one-and-one-half-story dwelling built into a fort-like rectangular wall intended to protect its inhabitants from attack by the Spanish. The house and wall were made of tabby, a concoction of oyster shells, lime, and sand mixed with water. You can see parts of the foundation of the house and large portions of the wall. Other points of interest at Wormsloe are the museum and theater, where you can learn more about the site and the early days of the colony; a stone monument marking the first Jones family burial plot; nature trails; and the Colonial Life Area, which contains re-creations of outbuildings characteristic of Wormsloe's early period. This area is also the site of living-history demonstrations and programs presented during special events.

During your drive down the avenue of oaks, you may notice an elegant, two-story frame house on the eastern side of the road. This structure was built in 1828 and is home to the ninth generation of Jones's descendants; it is closed to the public. Wormsloe is open Tues through Sun 9 a.m. to 5 p.m. Admission is from $10 for adults, $9 for seniors, $4.50 for youth 6–17. This site is operated as part of Georgia's state parks system.

After you visit Wormsloe, take a few minutes to drive through nearby Isle of Hope, a community of narrow streets and beautifully preserved houses. Turn right after leaving Wormsloe, and you'll be on Parkersburg Road, which meanders through Isle of Hope until it reaches Bluff Drive, one of the prettiest streets in the Savannah area. A jaunt down Bluff Drive, which runs alongside the picturesque Skidaway River, is worth the time it will take to make this short detour.

aerial combat to leave this museum's Mission Experience exhibit with tears in their eyes. This re-creation of an Eighth Air Force bombing mission brings back vivid memories to those who flew over Europe—recollections of heavily defended targets, stricken aircraft, and fallen comrades. The panoramic, eight-screen theater and its B-17 flight are a featured part of the 90,000-square-foot museum in Pooler near the intersection of I-95 and US 80 (exit 102 from I-95).

Besides the Mission Experience, the museum's exhibit area contains presentations featuring more than 15 units that were part of the Eighth; a mural and a scale model depicting a World War II bomber base in England; areas dealing with escape and evasion, prisoners of war, and the contributions of African-American airmen; a diorama portraying the raids on the Ploesti oil fields; a PT-17 Stearman trainer and a Messerschmitt Komet rocket plane on static display; and several other theaters. There's also a research library stocked with books pertaining to aviation and air warfare, an art gallery, Memorial Gardens, a chapel, store, and restaurant. The museum is open daily 9 a.m. until 5 p.m. except for New Year's Day, Easter, Thanksgiving, and Christmas. Admission to the exhibit area is $10 for adults and teens and $6 for children ages 6–12, with those younger than age 6 admitted free. There are discounts for members of the military, senior citizens, and groups of 20 or more. The library is open 9 a.m. to noon and 1 to 4 p.m. Mon through Fri.

SAVANNAH BOTANICAL GARDENS, 1388 Eisenhower Dr.: (912) 355-3883; savannahbotanical.org. See more than 900 varieties of trees, shrubs, and flowering plants when you visit this Savannah Area Council of Garden Clubs project on the Southside. The clubs maintain 10 acres of gardens featuring roses, perennials, herbs, and vegetables, and separate gardens devoted to flowering plants that bloom during the different seasons of the year. There's also a garden for plants such as ferns that grow best in spots that don't get much sunshine. Some of the plants are labeled, so neophyte gardeners will be able to tell what they're looking at. A tabby walkway meanders through the gardens, and a small pond and a nature walk add to the ambience of this spot, which is nestled in a fairly well-developed part of town. The garden center is headquartered in an 1840s-era farmhouse that was moved to the Southside from a downtown location in 1991. The center and gardens are on Eisenhower Drive at its intersection with Sallie Mood Drive. Hours are from sunup to sundown 7 days a week. Admission is free, but donations are appreciated.

SAVANNAH-OGEECHEE CANAL MUSEUM AND NATURE CENTER, 681 Fort Argyle Rd.; (912) 748-8068. Listed on the National Register of Historic Places, the Savannah-Ogeechee Canal, which played a role in the commercial development of Savannah during the 1800s, lay virtually forgotten for a century until a group of Chatham Countians reclaimed a third of it from the tangle of foliage that had grown over it. These volunteers started their work in 1992, and now, organized as the Savannah-Ogeechee Canal Society, they oversee the continued development of the waterway as a historic and recreational area.

You can get a splendid idea of what the southern portion of the canal was like by visiting the society's museum and 184-acre nature center, which is on Fort Argyle Road (better known as SR 204), a little more than 2 miles west of exit 94 off I-95. The museum, a converted bungalow, has two exhibit rooms, one depicting the history of the canal and another displaying reptiles and amphibians that inhabit the area the waterway runs through.

Within view of the museum is Lock 5, which is on a trail you can follow for 0.4 mile along the canal south to Lock 6 and the Ogeechee River; this trail is the towpath that horses and mules trod while pulling barges more than 100 years ago. The Tow Path is one of several trails you can walk while at the nature center. The museum and nature center are open 9 a.m. to 5 p.m. each day of the year. Admission is $2 for adults and $1 for students and senior citizens; children age 5 and younger are admitted free.

ANNUAL EVENTS & FESTIVALS

Savannahians love to party. They love their history. They also love getting outdoors and taking advantage of coastal Georgia's congenial climate. Is it any wonder, then, there's almost always something going on in Savannah? That something might be a festival attracting thousands of people or the commemoration of a historic event drawing a few hundred, but a week seldom passes in which there's nothing to do in Savannah.

We admit things slow down a tad during the summer months because of the heat, but that doesn't mean you can't get out and enjoy yourself. Grab your suntan lotion, cooler, and lounge chair, and head for a day at the beach on nearby Tybee Island, just as Savannahians have been doing for more than a century.

Savannah's biggest party is its celebration of St. Patrick's Day, a green-hued blast bringing about a half-million visitors to the city in mid-March. Because we want to be sure you don't miss any of the fun, we've included in this chapter a full rundown on the main event—the parade—and the constellation of events that surround it.

We need to mention one thing before taking you through our month-by-month rundown of events and festivals: Dates, times, and admission fees can change, so it's best to call ahead for the most current information. The telephone numbers included with the following write-ups are the numbers of the individuals, organizations, or agencies sponsoring or coordinating the events.

JANUARY

Historic District

EMANCIPATION DAY SERVICE, Historic First Bryan Baptist Church; (912) 234-6293, (912) 236-3173; firstbryanbaptist church.com. By holding a special church service on New Year's Day, Savannah's Emancipation Association commemorates the signing of the proclamation that ordered the freeing of slaves in the Confederate states. During the 11 a.m. gathering, held at a different church each year, a participant reads the Emancipation Proclamation, a mass choir sings hymns, and speakers deliver addresses concerning the significance of that historic day in 1863. Call for additional information.

MARTIN LUTHER KING JR. OBSERVANCE DAY ACTIVITIES, various locations; (912) 234-5502. This monthlong tribute to civil rights leader Martin Luther King Jr. features a parade through downtown starting at 10 a.m. on the third Monday in January, the national holiday in his honor. The observances wind up with the Freedom Ball at the Savannah Civic Center on the last Friday of January. For more information or for the parade route and schedule, visit savannah now.com or call the number above.

ℹ If you're looking to uplift your spirits during what can sometimes be a depressing time of year—late January—consider attending "Hymns for Hope," a musical program usually held on the Sunday before Super Bowl Sunday. Featuring local church choirs and gospel singing groups, this presentation takes place in the afternoon or early in the evening. Admission is $10 and benefits the Interfaith Hospitality Network of Coastal Georgia, a volunteer organization that aids homeless families. You can contact the network and get the specific details on "Hymns for Hope" by calling (912) 790-9446.

FEBRUARY

Historic District

BLACK HERITAGE FESTIVAL, various locations; (912) 351-6320; savannahblackheritagefestival.com, savstate.edu. Various musical groups entertain with performances of gospel, reggae, blues, and jazz, and craftspeople gather at the Savannah Civic Center on the Grand Festival Day (a Sat) to sell items related to African culture during this event, which is held during a week in early February. Funded by Savannah's Department of Cultural Affairs this event is star-studded with local celebrities and usually starts at noon and ends at 4 p.m. The concert portion of the show highlights the multifaceted contributions of African Americans in the areas of music, the performing arts, and cuisine. Admission is free. Stay tuned to the website for news of the current year's event.

GHS'S GEORGIA DAYS, various locations; (912) 651-2125; georgiahistory.com. This observance celebrating Georgia's founding and heritage unfolds during the first 2 weeks of February and usually focuses on the 12th of the month—the day on which the first colonists landed in 1733. Georgia Week opens on the first day of February with a ceremony in a downtown square featuring a portrayal of a significant figure in the history of the state and wreath-layings at monuments throughout the city. Programs at historic sites and a lecture focusing on the aforementioned historic figure are part of the celebration, which is presented by the Georgia Historical Society (GHS) in partnership with Chatham-Savannah public schools.

On the morning of Georgia Day, February 12, schoolchildren dressed as colonists and the Native Americans who welcomed them walk in a procession from Forsyth Park up Bull Street to City Hall on Bay Street. Contact the GHS regarding events and further information.

SAVANNAH BOOK FESTIVAL, savannahbookfestival.org. The Savannah Book Festival brings authors of national status to Savannah, from the best-selling authors whose work keeps you amused on long flights to serious biographers and historians. It is held the Fri, Sat, and Sun of Presidents' Day weekend. Saturday is the busiest day, with authors scheduled for presentations throughout the day in a cluster of downtown venues within walking distance of one another—the Telfair Museum of Art, Jepson Center, Trinity United Methodist Church, and other churches and venues around Telfair, Chippewa, and Wright Squares. This event attracts such authors as Anne Rice, P.J. O'Rourke, Janet Evanovich, Mary Kay Andrews, and Tavis Smiley. For schedule details and venues check the website.

SAVANNAH IRISH FESTIVAL, Savannah Civic Center, Liberty and Montgomery Streets; (912) 651-6556, (800) 351-7469; savannahirish.org. This family-oriented event uses song, dance, and recitation to emphasize the heritage of the Irish and the contributions of Irish immigrants here and throughout the US. In addition to the main stage, where much of this activity takes place, there are stages for children's entertainment and readings and discussions involving Irish culture and history. Vendors market Irish clothing, jewelry, and artifacts, and members of local Irish organizations prepare and sell food, including shepherd's pie, Irish stew, and other ethnic dishes. The festival is on the second or third weekend in Feb 10:30 a.m. to 8 p.m. Sat, and noon until 7 p.m. Sun. Admission to the festival is $12 per day or $16 for a 2-day ticket. Children ages 4 and younger are admitted free.

Islands

COLONIAL FAIRE & MUSTER AT WORMSLOE, Wormsloe Historic Site; 7601 Skidaway Rd.; (912) 353-3023. Historical reenactors clad in the garb of Georgia's colonists make music and demonstrate craft skills, such as making candles and musket balls, at this program held in an open area near the marsh on Isle of Hope, overlooking the Skidaway River. At the visitor center, you can view artifacts excavated from Wormsloe's tabby ruins and watch an audiovisual show about the founding of the 13th colony. The program takes place 10 a.m. until 4 p.m. on the first Sat and Sun in Feb. Admission is free.

MARCH

Historic District

CELTIC CROSS CEREMONY, Emmet Park; Bay and Price Streets; (912) 233-4804; savannahsaintpatricksday.com. Members of the city's Irish organizations gather at the Cathedral of St. John the Baptist for mass at 11:30 a.m. on the second Sunday of the month, then march in procession to Emmet Park, where they lay a wreath at the Celtic

Cross and listen to a speech about their heritage. The cross, officially named the Irish Monument, was carved from a single piece of Irish limestone in County Roscommon, Ireland. The Savannah Irish Monument Committee erected the Celtic Cross in 1983, the 250th anniversary of the founding of Savannah and Georgia, to commemorate Georgians of Irish ancestry. The ceremony starts about 1 p.m., and it's open to the public.

FIRST SATURDAY, Rousakis Plaza, River Street; (912) 234-0295; riverstreetsavan nah.com. Browse through the wares of artisans and craftspeople from throughout the Southeast and listen to various forms of music during First Saturday on the plaza on River Street. While enjoying the breeze blowing off the Savannah River, you might find yourself staring at a large cargo ship as it glides along the waterway, so close you'd swear you could reach out and touch it. The 40 to 60 open-air arts and crafts booths on the plaza offer a variety of treasures, everything from original oil paintings and watercolors to rocking horses fashioned from wood scraps. If you can't turn up something that catches your fancy among the artists' booths, visit the shops in the renovated cotton warehouses lining River Street.

Hungry? You have your choice of restaurants dishing up a variety of cuisine. The Savannah Waterfront Association presents First Saturday festivals 9 a.m. to 6 p.m. on—what else?—the first Saturday of each month, with the exception of January and February. Some are part of expanded, more distinctive festivals: the Fine Arts festival in April, the Savannah Seafood Festival in May, Oktoberfest in October, and Christmas on the River in December. By the way, a fireworks display is staged at dusk every first Friday. Admission is free.

ST. PATRICK'S DAY PARADE, various downtown streets; (912) 233-4804; savannahsaintpatricksday.com. You'll know it's March if you choose this month to arrive in Savannah. The flowers will be in full bloom, painting the town with blazing colors. Strolling locals will shed their winter coats in exchange for green sweaters. Irish tunes will ring from the walls of St. Vincent's Academy as the girls practice their salute to the upcoming St. Patrick's Day Grand Marshall. Sidewalks will be adorned with green and white souvenirs that spill out of shops proclaiming that the day is upon us. Closer to March 17 (St. Patrick's Day), fountains will turn to green, and the demeanor of Savannahians will turn from ho-hum to jovial. It's a time when the Irish Catholic community comes together, and those who aren't join in the festivities.

On the morn of St. Patrick's Day, even the most introverted will come out. Adorned with everything from "boingy" shamrocks to green beads, green and white buttons, and fake beards and moustaches, some celebrants even dye their dogs green. On St. Patrick's Day in Savannah, people eat green grits and drink green beer.

Savannah's biggest annual event, the parade, lasts upwards of 4 hours and involves thousands of participants. Some 250 units take to the streets for the parade, including marching bands, floats, and the city's numerous Irish organizations. The parade starts about 10:15 a.m. at Forsyth Park and winds its way around several of Savannah's squares and down its main thoroughfares.

ST. PATRICK'S AT CITY MARKET, Jefferson and St. Julian Streets; (912) 232-4903; savannahcitymarket.com. City Market celebrates the big day with live music and dancing in the courtyard. This laid-back party occurs over a span of time that includes St. Patrick's Day and can last as long as 5 days, depending on when the holiday falls. On St. Patrick's Day, the bands crank up as soon as the parade passes nearby. It's free.

i The water of the Forsyth Park fountain is traditionally dyed green each year for St. Patrick's Day, but don't expect the Savannah River to be treated in similar fashion. The last and only attempt at turning the river green occurred in 1961 with less than desirable results. A thousand pounds of the chemical uranine was used, and the outcome was a striped effect.

ST. PATRICK'S DAY ON THE RIVER, Rousakis Plaza, River Street; (912) 234-0295; savwaterfront.com. The Savannah Waterfront Association sets up food booths on the plaza and brings in nationally known entertainers to perform, but the biggest attraction of St. Patrick's Day on the River isn't eating or listening to music—it's being part of the crowd that jams River Street. This 9-block party is free for nondrinkers, and it's the place to be during St. Patrick's Day festivities if you like to rub elbows with people—literally. Those wishing to drink beer outdoors will have to purchase $5 wristbands. The merrymaking is at its peak on St. Patrick's Day and the weekend closest to the holiday; the party cranks up about 10 a.m., and food sales and scheduled entertainment end at midnight.

SAVANNAH ASIAN FESTIVAL, Savannah Civic Center, Montgomery and Liberty Streets; (912) 651-6417; savannahga.gov/arts. A response to the contributions of Savannah's growing Asian community, this 1-day event features displays and entertainment reflecting the heritage of people of Chinese, Filipino, Indian, Japanese, Sri Lankan, Nepalese, Korean, Thai, Pakistani, Taiwanese, and Vietnamese

Close-up

Why St. Patrick's Day

You might be wondering why St. Patrick's Day has evolved as the most festive day of the year in Savannah. That is a valid question. It's not enough to say that a large segment of Savannah's population is, or has been, Irish or of Irish descent. That's true of lots of cities that don't make anywhere near the fuss over St. Patrick's Day as Savannah does.

Part of the reason for the popularity of the day might stem from the fact that it's been celebrated here for a long time, longer than in most American cities. According to the late William L. Fogarty, who wrote a history of the local observance entitled *The Days We've Celebrated*, the first celebration here was in 1813 when the Hibernian Society, formed by Irish Protestants seeking to help their impoverished countrymen, held a private procession. The city's first public procession, which is recognized as Savannah's first St. Patrick's Day parade, was also held by the society and took place in 1824.

"Why and how this celebration could possibly have carried on these many years is perhaps one of the most fantastic mysteries of all," wrote Fogarty in 1980 as he attempted to answer questions regarding the parade's origin. "I don't know of anyone who could really give the actual reason . . . Perhaps the answer would be the 'Pride of the Irish' has sustained it."

Although the celebration remains religious in nature (many Savannahians begin the day by attending morning mass at the Cathedral of St. John the Baptist on Lafayette Square), the observance has become more secular over the years and has been adopted by other segments of the population, leading to the saying that "everyone's Irish on St. Patrick's Day."

The celebrating that is part of St. Patrick's Day festivities in Savannah occurs over a span of 3 or 4 days. St. Patrick's Day is always observed on March 17, and the annual parade is held on that day except when it falls on Sunday—in that case, the parade is on Saturday, March 16.

Most of the merrymaking happens on the day of the parade and the weekend closest to it. When the parade is on a Monday, Tuesday, or Wednesday, the partying will be on that day, the weekend before, and the day or days before. When the parade is on a Thursday or Friday, the celebrating will be on that day, the day after, and the weekend following. On parade day and weekends, River Street and City Market are packed with celebrators.

Have a parking plan in place before the morning of the parade. Parking will be expensive and hard to come by. Consider parking at Oglethorpe Mall on Savannah's suburban Southside, where a special Chatham Area Transit (CAT) bus shuttles paradegoers and partiers back and forth all day.

The parade is an all-year planning project by the St. Patrick's Day Parade Committee, and you can get a progress report on the upcoming edition of the parade at savannahsaintpatricksday.com.

descent. A Vietnamese dragon dance ceremony, an Asian fashion show, martial arts demonstrations, and Vietnamese fan dancing are highlights. Representatives of the Asian cultures, some of them clad in native dress, display and sell arts and crafts at tables set up in the Civic Center arena and host workshops. You can purchase samples of Asian cuisine at food booths. The festival runs Fri and Sat in late March.

It's sponsored by Savannah's Department of Cultural Affairs and Armstrong State University. Admission is free.

SAVANNAH MUSIC FESTIVAL, various locations; (912) 234-3378; savannah musicfestival.org.

The Savannah Music Festival—formerly known as Savannah Onstage—enhances the beauty of the city with 2.5 weeks of jazz, classical, blues, gospel, zydeco, and other traditional American performances during late March and early April. The cornerstone of this steadily growing festival is the American Traditions Competition, which features solo vocalists presenting music that has played a significant role in forming the cultural heritage of the US. Each year additional major events are incorporated into the festival. Performers have included Jazz at Lincoln Center Orchestra with Wynton Marsalis, guitarist Buddy Guy, bluegrass singer and mandolinist Ricky Skaggs, the Dave Grisman Quintet, the Tallis Scholars, the Blind Boys of Alabama, and the Derek Trucks Band, and among past productions were a new and imaginative version of George Gershwin's *Porgy and Bess* and *An Evening With Beethoven,* featuring actress Mia Farrow and the Beaux Arts Trio. The festival also reaches students with free concerts and provides preconcert talks, films, and lectures about the heritage of American music to children and adults.

THE SAVANNAH TOUR OF HOMES AND GARDENS, Parish House of Christ Church; 18 Abercorn St.; (912) 234-8054; savannahtourofhomes.org.

This granddaddy of Savannah's seasonal tours brings you to a different neighborhood on each day of its 4-day run. Each 3-hour, self-guided walking tour takes you to approximately six private homes and/or gardens in the Historic District. Hours are 10 a.m. until 5 p.m. on Thurs, Fri, and Sat and 11 a.m. to 4 p.m. on Sun, and participants are encouraged to stroll from site to site at their own pace and in any order they choose. Special events such as luncheons, seminars, cemetery tours, and teas are also presented, and they vary from year to year. The event is held in late March. Begun in 1935, the event is sponsored by the Episcopal Church Women of Christ Church, along with the Historic Savannah Foundation, and proceeds benefit outreach ministries of the churchwomen and the foundation's preservation efforts. The fee for each walking tour is $40, and it's essential to order tickets for the tours and other activities ahead of time. The tours always—yes, always—sell out. You pick up your tickets at tour headquarters, the Parish House of Christ Church.

TARA FEIS IRISH CELEBRATION, Emmet Park, Bay and Price Streets; (912) 651-6417; savannahga.gov/arts.

The city of Savannah's Department of Cultural Affairs puts the emphasis on family-oriented activities at this Irish festival on the Saturday before St. Patrick's Day. Irish music and dancing, crafts demonstrations, storytelling, and poetry recitations fill the spotlight. Youngsters can participate in hands-on activities with a Celtic touch and enjoy carnival rides. Alcoholic beverages are prohibited in an effort to enhance the family-day atmosphere. The event, in sun-dappled Emmet Park, runs 11 a.m. to 5 p.m., and admission is free. In case you're wondering, feis is pronounced "fesh."

Islands

SHEEP TO SHAWL FESTIVAL, Oatland Island Education Center, 711 Sandtown Rd.; (912) 395-1212; oatlandisland.org.

While musicians fiddle and strum up a storm on the porch of a log cabin built in the 1830s, visitors watch an old-fashioned sheepshearing. This activity on a Saturday in March takes place at the center's Heritage Homesite and is an ideal activity for families.

The main events occur about 11:30 a.m. and 2 p.m. when workers clip the sheep with hand-operated shears. Members of the Fiber Guild of the Savannahs card wool from the previous year's shearing, spin it into yarn, and, using a 150-year-old loom, weave yarn spun beforehand into a shawl. The shawl is raffled off, and the winner is announced near the end of the festival, which runs 10 a.m. until 4 p.m. The center invites children to try their hand at carding and spinning wool. Anyone interested in viewing Oatland's wild and domesticated animals can walk the facility's 1.75-mile nature trail and visit the barnyard. Admission is $7 for adults and $5 for children, seniors, and the military.

Southside/Midtown

ST. PATRICK'S DAY RUGBY TOURNA-MENT, Daffin Park, Victory Drive and Bee Road; (912) 234-5999; savannahrugby .com. Billed as one of the largest tournaments of its kind in the US, this event is staged by the Savannah Shamrocks rugby club on the weekend closest to St. Patrick's Day. About 75 teams participate. There's no charge for roaming the sidelines and learning about this sport that's akin to American football and has been called "a ruffians' game played by gentlemen." The action starts about 9 a.m. on both days of the tourney, which was first held in 1979.

APRIL

Historic District

HISTORIC DOWNTOWN FINE ARTS ON THE RIVER, Rousakis Plaza, River Street; (912) 234-0295; riverstreetsavannah .com. Artists from throughout the nation display their paintings, photographs, and crafts during this festival on River Street's Rousakis Waterfront Plaza the end of April

or on the first weekend in May. Wine tasting, live music, and sales of food prepared by River Street restaurants add to the festivities. Admission is free to this event, a production of the Savannah Waterfront Association.

NOGS HIDDEN GARDENS OF SAVAN-NAH TOUR, Garden Club of Savannah; (912) 961-4805; gardenclubofsavannah .org. For more than 20 years, the members of the Garden Club of Savannah have, via this tour, enabled folks to glimpse a part of the city they would not otherwise see. As its name implies, this self-guided walking tour is your chance to get a look at some of the elegant gardens hidden behind the walls and gates of downtown homes. Chosen because of their beauty and unusual arrangement, eight gardens are opened to the public by their owners for only the 2 days of the tour.

You buy your tickets online or on the day of the tour at the Green-Meldrim House, 14 W. Macon St. A splendid way to end your walk is by finishing at the Harper-Fowlkes House on Orleans Square and attending the tea served there, a treat included in the $40 ticket price. A visit to the Massie Heritage Center and its garden is included on the tour, which is presented on a Fri and Sat in late April, about the time Savannah is in full bloom. The gardens are open 10 a.m. until 4 p.m., and light refreshments are served at the tea 2 to 4 p.m. By the way, NOGS stands for North of Gwinnett Street, the locale of all the gardens on the tour.

SIDEWALK ARTS FESTIVAL, Forsyth Park; (912) 525-5231; scad.edu/experi ence/events/sidewalkarts. The normally sedate slabs of the sidewalks leading through Forsyth Park pulsate with color for one precious day in late April, when the Savannah College of Art and Design stages its Sidewalk Arts Festival. SCAD students, alumni, prospective students, children, and preteens cover the concrete with chalk drawings, creating an immense art exhibit on the ground. You'll see everything from reproductions of famous masterpieces to the flights of fancy of 5-year-olds as you stroll through the park. Nearly 1,000 artists participate. Other attractions include the music of various bands and art projects for young children and preteens. The festival starts at 11 a.m. and ends at 5 p.m.

MAY

Historic District

RIVER STREET SEAFOOD FESTIVAL, Rousakis Plaza, River Street; (912) 234-0295; riverstreetsavannah.com. Fresh seafood prepared at booths on River Street's Rousakis Plaza is the main attraction of this event on the first weekend in May. Menus feature shrimp, crab, and crayfish—much of it caught in local waters. Festivalgoers munch away as they check out sales of arts and crafts, boogie to the beach and Cajun music provided by bands playing on the plaza's main stage, and enjoy the oystershucking contest. Hours are Fri and Sat 9 a.m. to midnight and Sun 9 a.m. to 6 p.m. Admission is free.

Southside/Midtown

SCOTTISH GAMES AND HIGHLAND GATHERING, Bethesda Home for Boys, 9520 Ferguson Ave.; (912) 233-6017; savannahscottishgames.com. Although tests of strength and dexterity are the focal point of the Scottish Games, there's more to the event than brawny lads tossing long poles ("cabers") and heaving sheaves of hay into the air. Aye, there are winsome lassies performing the dances of the Highlands, and stouthearted bagpipers playing their melancholy tunes. Also, members of more than 50 Scottish clans bring a touch of plaid to the green fields of the Bethesda Home

for Boys as they gather to parade, socialize, and celebrate their heritage during this festival on the first Saturday in May. The event runs 9 a.m. to 3 p.m. The tickets are $12 for adults and $5 for teens and children. Tickets, maps, and directions may be found on the website.

JUNE

Historic District

FIRST SATURDAY, Rousakis Plaza, River Street; (912) 234-0295; riverstreetsavannah.com. See our March listing for more information on this monthly event.

i If you happen to be near Johnson or Wright Squares around noontime on a Friday during the summer, amble on over and you'll likely be treated to some mighty fine sound provided by members of the local chapter of the American Federation of Musicians. From ragtime to jazz, their performances make lunchtime a special outdoor treat. They're on their outdoor "stages" 11:30 a.m. to 1:30 p.m. during most of June, July, and August.

JULY

Historic District

FANTASTIC FOURTH CELEBRATION, River Street; (912) 234-0295; savwaterfront.com. The sky above the Savannah River explodes in fireworks as folks gather on the plaza to celebrate the nation's birthday on July 4. Technicians shoot off shells 3 to 6 inches in diameter, including the largest projectile fired in Georgia, from nearby Hutchinson Island. Bring a radio and tune in to (FM) KIX 96.5, MIX 102.1, E 93, MAGIC 103.9, the Ticket, and WBMQ as the fireworks will be choreographed to music simulcast live on these local radio stations. Come early to stake out a good spot for viewing the show, and bring lawn chairs and a picnic supper to participate in what resembles a gigantic tailgate party. While you're waiting for the fireworks, you can listen to live music and people watch. The free event opens about 5 p.m., and the rockets start bursting in air about 9:30 p.m.

FIRST SATURDAY, Rousakis Plaza, River Street; (912) 234-0295; riverstreetsavan nah.com. See our March listing for more information on this monthly event.

AUGUST

Historic District

FIRST SATURDAY, Rousakis Plaza, River Street; (912) 234-0295; savwaterfront .com. See our March listing for more information on this monthly event.

OLD FORT JACKSON LABOR DAY LOW-COUNTRY BOIL AND AUCTION, Old Fort Jackson, 1 Fort Jackson Rd.; (912) 232-3945; chsgeorgia.org. An evening of fun, history, and food at the oldest standing brick fort in Georgia on the Saturday before Labor Day. The easygoing event takes place within the brick walls of the structure, which was manned in the War of 1812 and used during the Civil War as a headquarters for the Confederacy's defense of the Savannah River (see our Attractions chapter). A silent auction is offered, and visitors can chow down on Lowcountry boil, barbecue, and all the trimmings. The youngsters enjoy themselves scampering around in what amounts to a walled playground, and there's a cannon firing to further liven things up. Proceeds from the sale of food and drinks are used for the preservation of the fort.

Islands

TOOLS AND SKILLS THAT BUILT THE COLONY, Wormsloe Historic Site, 7601 Skidaway Rd.; (912) 353-3023; gastate parks.org. Wormsloe staff members in colonial attire demonstrate carpentry, blacksmithing, cooking, weaving, flint knapping, leatherworking, woodsmen's skills, pewter casting, and other abilities essential to the development of Georgia. This living-history program is offered 10 a.m. until 4 p.m. on the last Sat and Sun of August. Admission is $5 for adults, $3.50 for senior citizens, and $2.50 for children ages 6–18. Those under age 6 are admitted free.

SEPTEMBER

Historic District

SAVANNAH JAZZ FESTIVAL, Forsyth Park; (912) 651-6417; savannahjazzfes tival.org. Forsyth Park and other venues heat up with the sounds of jazz during the last full week in September when many of the finest musicians in the Savannah area and the South perform their special brand of American music. The park's the place to be for Blues Night on the Thursday of the festival, for lively presentations on Friday night and Saturday afternoon and evening, and for a special Sunday afternoon session for children. The festival is funded by the city's Department of Cultural Affairs and organized by the Coastal Jazz Association, a nonprofit, community organization that depends on volunteers to run the event. Sessions are free.

i Wear comfortable shoes to outdoor festivals, especially those on River Street, where you'll be walking on the ballast stones and uneven pavement. Be careful if you use the steps leading from Bay Street to River Street—they seem to have been designed for people with long legs and short feet.

SAVANNAH PRIDE FESTIVAL, Rousakis Plaza, River Street; (912) 234-1134; savpride.com. This celebration of alternative lifestyles centers in Forsyth Park, but events happen in various venues. The festival features dozens of entertainers and guest speakers addressing topics pertinent to the LGBT community. More than 60 vendors are on hand, including folks representing community service agencies and those involved in sales of food, arts and crafts, and other merchandise. The event, held on a Saturday in early-Sept, starts at noon and progresses into the evening.

OCTOBER

Historic District

OKTOBERFEST, Rousakis Plaza, River Street; (912) 234-0295; riverstreetsavannah.com. If you happen to have a dachshund handy, you might want to enter it in the Wiener Dog Race, a comical competition that's become a featured part of the Savannah Waterfront Association's Oktoberfest event. Some 200 low-slung pooches "sprint" down the 50-foot racecourse as they seek to win prizes for their masters. The race—run in heats of four to six dogs until an overall winner prevails—benefits the local Friends of the Animals organization. Watching is fun even if you don't have a dog running: Some pups never get out of the starting gate, and others wander around instead of heading for the finish line. The race is staged on the Saturday morning of the festival, which occurs during the first weekend of the month.

There will also be German food and music and plenty of beer. Booths manned by employees of River Street restaurants sell wiener schnitzel, sauerbraten, bratwurst, and German chocolate cake, but there is also food for those whose tastes aren't Teutonic. Oompah-band members decked out in lederhosen and Tyrolean hats provide much

of the music, and festivalgoers are invited to join them in doing the arm-flapping, head-bobbing "Chicken Dance." Also, a headline entertainer usually performs at Oktoberfest. Admission is free, but the food is not. Hours of operation are Fri and Sat 9 a.m. to midnight and Sun 9 a.m. to 6 p.m.

PICNIC IN THE PARK, Forsyth Park; (912) 651-6417; savannahga.gov/arts. Wine and dine under the stars and enjoy a pops classical concert by the Savannah Sinfonietta at this event on a weekend evening in early October. The more elaborate your picnic meal at tree-filled Forsyth Park, the better. Judges rate the best picnic, and festivalgoers seek to outdo one another with table settings and setups ranging from the elaborate to the unexpected. Candelabra, chandeliers, and chafing dishes make appearances, and some folks opt to embellish their picnics with formal rugs and dining room suites. Others get creative, building tropical huts for luaus or laying out an early Thanksgiving spread. If you prefer to simply sit on a blanket and nibble on a sandwich, that's okay, too. The concert and your seats on the grass are free of charge, courtesy of Savannah's Department of Cultural Affairs; you provide the food and drink.

SAVANNAH FILM FESTIVAL, Trustees Theater, 216 E. Broughton St.; (912) 525-5050; scad.edu/filmfest. Hosted by the Savannah College of Art and Design, this presentation of film and video productions takes place during a week's time in late October and/or early November. The latest in feature-length films, shorts, animations, documentaries, and student work are screened at the Lucas Theatre and Trustees Theater in downtown Savannah, with workshops and gatherings at various other venues. Look for the trendy, the indie, the oldie, you name it. This week is always good for celebrity watching. Every year, the stars who attend to pick up awards become more A-list.

SHALOM Y'ALL JEWISH FOOD FESTIVAL, Forsyth Park; (912) 233-1547; mickveisrael.org.

Congregation Mickve Israel presents this opportunity to sample Jewish foods such as blintzes, potato latkes, matzo ball soup, knishes, kosher hot dogs, pastrami sandwiches, challah bread, and, of course, bagels with cream cheese and lox. These delectable items are sold from booths set up in Forsyth Park.

While you're strolling the park, be on the lookout for a booth manned by Arnold Belzer, the rabbi of the temple, who'll be dishing up portions of his own specialty, a type of stir-fry he calls "Ahmein Lo Mein." Live entertainment and activities for children add to the event, which runs 11 a.m. until 3 p.m. on a Sunday in late October. Admission is free, and you purchase food and beverages by buying tickets at the park, or you may call in advance to pick up tickets before the festival. Note that the best food sells out early.

Islands

HALLOWEEN HIKE, Oatland Island Education Center, 711 Sandtown Rd.; (912) 898-3980; oatlandisland.org.

If you're seeking a tamer Halloween experience for your child, take advantage of this walk along the trails and through the "Friendly Forest" at Oatland Island Education Center. As they frolic through the woods, young trick-or-treaters meet adults costumed as animal characters, who greet the children with hugs and goodies. Admission is $5 for adults and $10 per child, and the center provides bags for collecting treats. You or another adult must accompany your child, and the little ones are encouraged to wear costumes and comfortable shoes. The center holds the hike on the Friday and Saturday before Halloween.

Southside/Midtown

COASTAL GEORGIA BOTANICAL GARDENS ANNUAL FALL FESTIVAL, 2 Canebrake Rd.; (912) 921-5460.

Paint your face, buy some plants (perennials and fall annuals), or purchase sugarcane syrup at this celebration of autumn in late October at the Bamboo Farm. For those seeking a bite to eat, there's a snack bar and a smoked pork luncheon featuring greens, roast pork, sweet potatoes, corn bread, and ice tea, and a hot dog lunch. The kids will enjoy hayrides, pony rides, a bounce house, and storytelling in the cottage garden. Adults might opt for the garden lecture and plant vendors. The last few years have featured workshops on the findings of an ongoing research program on growing bananas in Savannah—it can be done, with luck and skill.

SAVANNAH FOLK MUSIC FESTIVAL, various locations; (912) 786-6953; savannahfolk.org.

The focal point of this completely free 3-day musical jamboree is a concert at the Georgia State Railroad Museum in downtown Savannah. The concert consists of four to five acts featuring nationally recognized musicians. Folks such as singer-musicians Tom Rush, Mike Seeger, John Jackson, and Robin and Linda Williams have graced the stage. Don't let the threat of rain scare you away; the museum affords plenty of shelter, so inclement weather won't stop the singing, picking, and grinning.

For more information, check the website.

SAVANNAH GREEK FESTIVAL, Hellenic Center, 14 W. Anderson St.; (912) 236-8256; stpaulsgreekorthodox.org.

When we think of the Savannah Greek Festival, we can taste the baklava melting in our mouths. Those scrumptious pastries are just a sample of the tasty concoctions offered for sale at the Hellenic Center adjacent to St. Paul's Greek Orthodox Church in Midtown

Savannah during the third Thursday, Friday, and Saturday in October. Among other favorites of the festival's patrons are the Greek salad, gyro sandwiches, and a spinach pie called *spanakopita*. While you're enjoying the food, sit back and watch the Hellenic Center's dance groups perform. You can also tour the church. Festival hours are 11 a.m. until 9 p.m. Call or visit the website for updated admission pricing.

NOVEMBER

Historic District

FIRST SATURDAY, Rousakis Plaza, River Street; (912) 234-0295; riverstreetsavannah.com. See our March listing for more information on this monthly event.

ROCK 'N' ROLL SAVANNAH, runrockandroll.com/savannah. Thousands of runners hit Savannah streets in early November for the nationally popular Rock 'n' Roll marathon and half marathon. The event stretches over 2 days; Saturday for the marathon and Sunday with Rock 'n' Roll 5K and 1-mile run. Both days feature live music, post-race entertainment, medals and bragging rights for participants.

ⓘ You can drink alcoholic beverages in public in the parade festival area (bordered by River Street on the north, East Broad Street on the east, Jones Street on the south, and West Boundary Street on the west), but drinks must be in paper, Styrofoam, or plastic cups of no more than 16 ounces in volume.

SAVANNAH CHILDREN'S BOOK FESTIVAL, Forsyth Park; (912) 652-3600; liveoakpl.org. Award-winning children's book authors and illustrators from around the country converge on Forsyth Park for this free daylong event. Besides meet-the-author events, the festival includes arts and crafts, costumed characters, and a variety of food and entertainment. Past years have featured such authors and illustrators as Lois Lowry, Rosemary Wells, Bruce Degen, and Marc Brown. The event is sponsored by Live Oak Public Library and the city of Savannah.

TELFAIR ART FAIR, Telfair Square, 121 Barnard St.; (912) 790-8800; telfair.org. The Telfair Museums' annual fair attracts artists from throughout the US. They compete for cash awards and sell their creations to the public from displays under tents set up around Telfair Square. You can find paintings, sculpture, photographs, fabric, jewelry, and other fine arts at this exhibition, which takes place early in November. Hours are Sat 10 a.m. to 5 p.m. and Sun 12:30 to 4:30 p.m. The fair is free.

Islands

CANE GRINDING AND HARVEST FESTIVAL, Oatland Island Education Center, 711 Sandtown Rd.; (912) 898-3980; oatlandisland.org. Get a glimpse of the pioneer life of 1830s Georgia and do some early Christmas shopping by ambling through the Oatland forest and visiting the Heritage Homesite on a Saturday in November. At the end of your walk through a wood thick with oak, magnolia, pine, and vines of the Muscadine grape, you'll find yourself in a small clearing where sugarcane is being processed. Farmers grind the cane into juice at a mill powered by a horse, then boil it into syrup. You can watch the entire operation, then buy a bottle of the sweet-smelling nectar to pour on your Sunday morning pancakes.

You might also want to poke your head into the cozy interiors of the two log cabins at the site and watch weavers at work and costumed women preparing corn bread, or you might hunker down on a bench and listen to members of the Savannah Folk Music Society as they perform songs from Georgia's past. Complete your day at Oatland by walking the nature trail to the wild animal habitats and visiting the center's barnyard. If you need to get off your feet for a while, take a hayride through the forest. The festival opens at 10 a.m. and closes at 4 p.m. Admission is $7 for persons 4 and older; those younger are admitted free.

DECEMBER

Historic District

CHRISTMAS FOR KIDS, City Market, Jefferson and St. Julian Streets; (912) 515-2489; savannahcitymarket.com. It's been said that Christmas is for children, and City Market takes that to heart by offering a program for young people 11 a.m. to 2 p.m. on the first Saturday of the month. This event gives youngsters the opportunity to make ornaments to take home, have their faces painted, enjoy a petting zoo, decorate cookies, and visit with Father Christmas in the Carriage Tours of Savannah Cinderella Carriage, and hear a choir performance. The entertainment varies from year to year, with puppet shows and performances by cloggers in the mix. Carriage Tours collects toys for their annual Toys for Tots promotion. It's all free.

CHRISTMAS ON THE RIVER, Rousakis Plaza, River Street; (912) 234-0295; riverstreetsavannah.com. Usher in the Christmas season on the first Saturday in December by shopping for gifts created by artists and craftspeople and watching a lighted parade starring Santa Claus. The arts and crafts vendors start selling at 9 a.m. on the riverfront plaza, and the parade begins at 6 p.m. on the western end of River Street. The parade lasts from an hour to 90 minutes and also includes high school bands, color

guards, floats, dance troupes, antique cars, and last, but most important, St. Nick riding in a carriage. After the parade, Santa poses for photos, and strolling musicians and local choirs perform throughout the day. Enjoy the parade but keep an eye out for flying candy flung from the floats to youngsters lining the route. Arts and crafts booths remain open until 6 p.m. In keeping with the spirit of the season, there is no charge for admission to this holiday festival.

i Get a unique view of activities on River Street and stay out of the crowds by renting a hotel room facing the Savannah River, but be prepared for some late-night noise from musicians and merrymakers.

DOWNTOWN NEIGHBORHOOD ASSOCIATION HOLIDAY TOUR OF HOMES AND VICTORIAN TEA, Hilton Savannah DeSoto Hotel, 15 E. Liberty St.; (912) 236-8362; dnaholidaytour.net. Many of the homes on the tours offered during this mid-December event are decorated for Christmas in ways reflecting the lifestyles of their owners. The self-guided walking tours are on Saturday afternoon and evening and Sunday afternoon, with a different set of six to nine private homes featured on each day. The sponsoring Downtown Neighborhood Association selects homes in the Historic District that present a diversity of architectural design and decor. Call or check the website for more info.

HOLIDAY OPEN HOUSE, City Market, Jefferson and St. Julian Streets; (912) 525-2489; savannahcitymarket.com. On the first Friday evening of December, the courtyard at City Market glows with the soft light of more than 500 luminarias as shop owners open their doors and offer complimentary refreshments to visitors. Strolling

Prime Parade Watching

Some Savannahians have made careers out of saving spots in the squares for family tents. The whole process has become quite a chore, if the truth is told. That being said, the city of Savannah and the police department have been clamping down on "camping out in the squares" in recent years. Today no one is allowed to stake out their parade-watching plot until 6 a.m. the day of the parade. It's quite a sight to see the clock strike 6 and a mad rush for space, but it happens. Watch it on the news and save your energy. There are lots of spaces up and down the stretch if you'll just take your time (but get there at least by 8 a.m.).

Here are some good places for parade watching, as detailed by the *Savannah Morning News*.

The 600 block of Abercorn Street—where "the parade's performers aren't tired yet. The bands step higher; the people waving from their floats aren't yet suffering from arm fatigue."

East Broad Street between Broughton and Bay Streets—"a good place to see the picturesque variety of parade spectators . . . SCAD (Savannah College of Art and Design) students tend to be in full bloom around here. Green dogs abound. So do green people."

Bay Street between East Broad and Bull Streets—"The closest convenient spot for those who've been cavorting down by the river."

We would also like to make this suggestion: To obtain a unique view of the parade, try getting a spot on the southern side of Calhoun Square (Abercorn and Gordon Streets), Lafayette Square (Abercorn and Charlton Streets), or Oglethorpe Square (Abercorn and York Streets), or on the northern side of Wright Square (Bull and State Streets) or Chippewa Square (Bull and Hull Streets). You'll be watching the parade come straight at you rather than viewing it from the side, and it's a perspective that can be quite enjoyable.

---

carolers sing Yuletide classics while Father Christmas—resplendent in his green velvet robe and red velvet cape and hat—talks with children about the spirit of the season and their plans for the holidays. This festive atmosphere takes place at City Market's Holiday Open House, which starts at 6 p.m. with the lighting of the luminaries and ends about 9 p.m.

NEW YEAR'S EVE AT CITY MARKET, City Market, Jefferson and St. Julian Streets; (912) 525-2489; savannahcitymarket .com. A live band creates a party atmosphere at City Market during the hours leading up to midnight on New Year's Eve. It's an outdoor party and filled with all the color Savannah can muster. For Savannahians, this is as close as it gets to being in Times Square. The event is free, and the partying starts about 7 p.m. and lasts until 1 or 2 a.m.

SAVANNAH RIVER BRIDGE RUN, various downtown streets; (912) 355-3527; savannahbridgerun.com. Participating in the Savannah River Bridge Run will give you a unique view of Savannah—on foot from the Eugene Talmadge Memorial Bridge, a 1.4-mile span that rises 196 feet above the water. Races are the 5K, 10K, Double Pump, Kid Race, and Team Challenge. Check out the website for additional information and schedules, registration, and packet pickup dates. You can register ahead of time and save money or enter on the day before the race. More than 2,000 people compete. The race is particularly popular as it offers runners a safe way to see the sights from the towering bridge that is normally closed to foot traffic. Savannah's terrain is flat, so the steep slope of the bridge is another novelty for local runners.

Islands

COLONIAL CHRISTMAS AT WORMSLOE, Wormsloe Historic Site, 7601 Skidaway Rd.; (912) 353-3023; gaastatepaarks.org.
A Christmas celebration, 18th-century style, complete with caroling and dancing, and the burning of the Yule log, is one of the highlights of the Savannah holiday special events. This holiday program on the second Sunday in December runs 2 to 5 p.m., and admission is $10 for adults, $9 for senior citizens, and $4.50 for those ages 6–17. Children younger than age 6 are $2.

KIDS

Savannah is the place to bring your kids when you want them to put down their Wii controller, walk away from the television, breathe in the salt air, and discover all the fun they've missed staying stuffed up inside. Although the romance and historical elements of this city are plenty to satisfy the more mature visitor (and this is indeed nothing close to Disney World), there are lots of fun options for the kids.

That's great news for many travelers. Here are some suggestions to get them out in the air, and keep them safe, occupied, and entertained while they're here. The beach is within easy striking distance, a water-oriented outdoor lifestyle that puts crab traps and fishing poles in the youngest of hands, a local theater scene that makes room for kids, you name it. Savannah also offers that increasingly rare opportunity of growing up in a place that has a sense of identity and uniqueness.

In this chapter, we'll focus on history, wildlife, sports, flavor, and last, but not least, the paranormal (yikes!). If you are traveling with children, we recommend spending at least part of your stay at Tybee Island, the local beach. We've got a whole chapter on options there. Any child who tags along dutifully on historic site tours and antiques shopping rounds deserves a chance to dig in the sand and splash around in the ocean, even in winter. Shark tooth scavenging is an awesome way to spend a cold but sunny afternoon!

HISTORY FOR KIDS

You'll need your video camera to capture your child's face as he stares into the sunlit spray of a fountain, tossing pennies into the flow. The mesmerizing task can be an activity that accompanies a picnic under the live oaks in Johnson Square. This is just one of many activities that will make fond vacation memories.

When the picnic ends, sign up for a tour! Enlist the help of a carriage tour driver to color up the commentary and opt to see Savannah by horse-drawn carriage. Two really good options: carriage tours or ghost tours. If your children are old enough—say, at least second or third grade—you should check out the ghost tours, especially the walking or carriage versions. The stories are

tame enough that they are unlikely to inspire screaming nightmares. Actually, these popular tours have proliferated in recent years, and gotten hokier and sillier in the process, perfect for a group of mischievous children.

With younger children, you can add interest to historic sightseeing with the help of a bright, intriguing book for children, *Savannah Safari* (savannahsafari.com), the work of locals Polly Wylly Cooper and Emmeline King Cooper. It is a slim paperback volume, designed to serve as a coloring book if you so desire, that sends kids on a scavenger-style hunt for "animals" while touring the Historic District. The "animals" are the iron downspouts shaped like dolphins, the sculptured herons in the Forsyth Park fountains, and so on. Stretch the interest for older children by chipping in one of those disposable cameras so they can photograph their "animal" finds.

Savannah Safari is $6 and available in local bookstores, which you'll find listed in our Shopping chapter. It's time to don your backpack, hold that little hand, and gallop off to a wonderland that they'll love, even if it is in an old city.

i If you visit in the summer, the various branch libraries are in full swing with summer programs for kids. Call (912) 652-3600 to find the branch nearest you. Visitors are always welcome, and with a temporary card, you can even check out books, videos, and tapes.

JULIETTE GORDON LOW BIRTHPLACE, 10 E. Oglethorpe Ave; (912) 233-4501; juliettegordonlowbirthplace.org. If your children are, have been, or aspire to be Girl Scouts, don't miss this wonderful house museum. In fact, it's your best bet among the museums for entertaining children. The birthplace and childhood home of Juliette "Daisy" Gordon Low is a virtual mecca for Girl Scouts from throughout the country, and you'll spot field trips full of them trooping around Savannah all the time. As a result, the staff at the center is experienced in the art of entertaining children without boring their adult escorts.

The elegant and beautifully preserved home of the wealthy Gordon family, which includes a masterpiece of a garden, works well for both age groups. Call for hours and prices, which vary.

SHIPS OF THE SEA MUSEUM, 41 Martin Luther King Jr. Blvd.; (912) 232-1511; shipsofthesea.org. The kids can learn all about Savannah's maritime history at this museum, which has been relocated to one of Savannah's historic old residences. The more upscale setting probably lowered the kid appeal here, but it should still work. Cost is $8 for adults, $6 for students and seniors. Family rate is $20 (two parents and any siblings under 18). Children younger than age 7 are free. The museum is open Tues through Sun 10 a.m. to 5 p.m.

WILDLIFE

BULL RIVER CRUISES, 36 Wilmington Island Rd.; (912) 898-1800, (800) 311-4779; bullriver.com. This marina offers a variety of eco-cruises and charters, and bills itself as experienced in working with Girl Scout troops. Call for reservations. They're essential because these trips are keenly affected by the weather. No one can guarantee you a dolphin sighting, but it is highly likely. The real challenge is to make the trips long enough to justify the price and short enough to remain interesting if the local wildlife choose not to perform. Winter visitors are less likely to find these trips an option, although the marina will arrange custom trips, birthday parties, fishing charters, and other boating recreation excursions. Private charters run from $80-$125, depending on the size of the group.

LAZARETTO CREEK MARINA & CAPT. MIKE'S DOLPHIN TOURS, US 80 East (just across Lazaretto Creek Bridge), Tybee Island; (912) 786-5848, (800) 242-0166; tybeedolphins.com. While enjoying the scenery of Fort Pulaski and the North Beach of Tybee Island, see friendly bottlenose dolphins playing in their natural habitat. There are sunset cruises and special offerings for Girl Scouts. The 90-minute tours cost $15 for adults and teens and $8 for children age 12 and younger. Diving and deep-sea/inshore fishing charters are available.

River Street Kidstuff

River Street, especially by day, can appeal mightily to the young tourist. All along the river are lots of shops, and while they are stocked with expensive gift items with the usual tourist-area markup, there are also plenty of wares geared toward kid tastes and kid pocketbooks. Follow them from shop to shop here and watch them buy candy and trinkets.

If luck is with you, your young entourage will get to spot one or more of the giant container ships, escorted by a team of tugboats, on its way upriver to the Georgia Ports Authority. These ships are such an imposing presence that even jaded teenagers will stop in their tracks to stare.

OATLAND ISLAND EDUCATION CENTER, 711 Sandtown Rd.; (912) 395-1212; oatlandisland.org. You are virtually guaranteed to spot your alligator here at a natural-habitat facility operated by the local school system as an educational center. Other once-native animals—buffalo, wolves, birds of prey—and an authentic colonial farm setting, complete with livestock, can also be seen. A self-guided outdoor hike takes you through marshes and around to the different animal and plant exhibits. Admission is $5, and free for those age 3 and younger. The center, which hosts many popular programs, is open daily 10 a.m. to 4 p.m. As teachers, the staff members are good with kids, so don't miss this attraction. Bring your own bug repellent, though—you'll need it.

SAVANNAH NATIONAL WILDLIFE REFUGE, SC 170; (843) 784-2468; fws.gov/savannah. Take a coastal safari through the 29,174-acre Savannah National Wildlife Refuge. It's full of freshwater marsh, tidal rivers, creeks, and bottomland hardwood swamps. While driving through the refuge, see if you can spot alligators, owls, hawks, turtles, snakes, or maybe even a bald eagle. The refuge is managed by the US Fish and Wildlife Service. It is open Mon through Sat 9 a.m. to 4:30 p.m. (except federal holidays), and visiting is free. The refuge is about 9 miles from downtown.

TYBEE ISLAND MARINE SCIENCE CENTER, 14th Street parking lot, Tybee Island; (912) 786-5917, (866) 557-9172; tybeemarinescience.org. Stroll the beach, toss a net into the ocean, then learn about what you find during a beach discovery walk held daily at the center. A tour guide leads the way and explains about Tybee's marine life. Don't forget to check out the stuff inside the center, too—you'll find a touch tank, aquariums, and shark displays. This isn't Sea World—expect a small, personalized experience. Open daily 10 a.m. to 5 p.m. Admission is $4, with those under 3 admitted free. Check the website for the latest listing of "walks, talks, and treks" and other special programs.

i If you dare, take your children to see the huge live alligator collection at the Crab Shack at Tybee Island. At last count, this restaurant had at least a hundred gators in captivity. These air breathers are lively and not considered to be man-eaters, despite what you may have heard. The colorful website will get your kids excited about their visit. Check it out: thecrabshack.com.

THE UNIVERSITY OF GEORGIA MARINE EDUCATION CENTER AND AQUARIUM, 30 Ocean Science Circle; (912) 598-FISH (3474), (912) 598-2496; marex.uga.edu/aquarium. Scout out Georgia's marine life at the aquarium at Skidaway Island. This small facility, operated by the University of Georgia Marine Extension Service, also includes a picnic area (which you may appreciate, because it is quite a drive out to Skidaway) and a walking trail. See 200 live animals—including fish of all shapes and sizes, turtles, and maybe even a small shark in the many wall tanks lining the exhibit hall. You owe this one to your kids if they have never seen a live flounder, our candidate for weirdest-looking fish in the world. Then go outside for a stroll along the Jay Wolfe Nature Trail, which passes by scenic marshes. The aquarium is open 9 a.m. to 4 p.m. on weekdays and 10 a.m. to 5 p.m. on Sat. It is closed on Sun and holidays. The cost is $6 for ages 13 and older, $3 for children, military, and seniors; children ages 3 and younger enter free. No credit or debit cards.

OUTDOOR ADVENTURE

CHILDREN'S HISTORY MUSEUM, 655 Louisville Rd; (912) 651-4292; savannah childrensmuseum.org. Outdoor activities such as arts and crafts, story time, and water play are offered for children of all ages. Hours are Mon through Sat 9 a.m. to 2 p.m.

FORSYTH PARK, Bull Street between Gaston Street and Park Avenue. Thirty acres perfect for letting off some steam are set aside in the Historic District. There are swing sets, slides, and other contraptions for youngsters needing to get rid of some energy, along with plenty of open space for just plain running, and beautiful magnolia trees and scenery for Mom and Dad to enjoy, too. May we suggest a picnic?

LAKE MAYER, Montgomery Crossroad and Sallie Mood Drive; (912) 652-7308.

Bring your bike and take a spin around the 1.5-mile trail at Lake Mayer, located in the 75-acre community park of the same name. While there, you can also play tennis or basketball, frolic on the playground, or feed the ducks swimming in the lake.

i Let the kids try their luck at fishing. The dock at the Lazaretto Creek pier is a popular "hole" and sits along a picturesque section of Tybee where there are usually fish biting on any given afternoon. Fishing gear, bait, license, and snacks may be purchased at Wal-Mart on US 80 at Whitemarsh Island.

SKIDAWAY ISLAND STATE PARK, 52 Diamond Causeway, Skidaway Island; (912) 598-2300, (800) 864-7275; gastateparks .org. Camping sites, picnic areas, trails, an interpretive center, and three playgrounds can be found at 533-acre Skidaway Island State Park, the only state park in Chatham County. Maps of the park and trails are available at the park office. If you don't want to tackle the trails alone, free guided hikes are available with advance reservations. Park hours are 7 a.m. to 10 p.m. Office hours are 8 a.m. to 5 p.m. Cost to enter the park is $3 per car, except on Wed when it is free.

TYBEE ISLAND LIGHT AND STATION, 30 Meddin Dr.; (912) 786-5801; tybee lighthouse.org. Hike 154 feet to the top of Tybee Lighthouse for a great view of Tybee and Savannah. You'll also learn a few things about one of America's historic light stations. It opens at 9 a.m. and sells the last ticket at 4:30 p.m. (it closes at 5:30). The cost, which includes admission to the Tybee Museum, is $9 for adults, $7 for seniors, military, and children ages 5–17; children under 5 are free.

THE GREAT OUTDOORS

Savannah's natural tropical diversions are tempting, and the loveliness of the islands, with sago palms, hibiscus, and towering pines, can be found throughout the city, not just in a gated park, but within the downtown, Southside, and surrounding communities. Simply said: This is the ideal place to spend time with nature. For starters, salt marshes are begging for kayaks. Embark on a trip by water, abundant with sea life and splendid birds, comical fiddler crabs, and all kinds of fish. There are the endless waterways just waiting on your discovery. Tybee Island offers a serene shoreline for surf fishing, and there's even a National Wildlife Refuge where freshwater rivers and cypress swamps intercept saltwater. The city is blessed with parks and parklike areas of every description and in every jurisdiction—national, state, regional, county, and city—and these provide settings for picnics and play and trails for hiking, biking, and jogging. Golfers and tennis players will find numerous venues that are open to the public.

On the following pages, you'll also find information concerning the parks and activities we've mentioned. While you're reading, keep in mind that a big part of the beauty of the area's recreational offerings is that, because of Savannah's mild climate, they're available to you just about every day of the year, and most are free of charge.

PARKS & NATURE TRAILS

Historic District

FORSYTH PARK, Drayton and Gaston Streets; (912) 651-6610. This is probably the most famous and beautiful of Savannah's parks. This downtown park on the southern boundary of the Historic District has sort of a split personality, but it's a delightful one. The northern portion consists of 11 acres filled with trees and shrubs and has an ornate fountain as its focal point. Splashing waters and shady sidewalks make this part of the park, which was laid out in 1851, a wonderful spot for strolling, relaxing on benches, and just plain goofing off.

The southern portion has a more active persona. Here you'll find a large playground, basketball and tennis courts, and wide-open spaces often used by students and locals engaged in softball, team Frisbee, and other athletic pursuits. The southern portion, a drill field for local military units before it was made part of the park in 1867, is also the site of monuments commemorating the Confederacy and honoring Georgians who served in the Spanish-American War.

Two dummy forts, structures built in 1909 and used for military exercises before World War I, straddle the line dividing the two areas. The fort on the western side of the park was renovated in 1963 as the Fragrant Garden for the Blind; the eastern fort has been converted into a restaurant, Park Cafe, open 8 a.m. to 5 p.m. daily (912-233-7848). Here, too, are public restrooms and a playground designed for younger children.

The park was laid out on the site of a pine forest that was at the southern reaches of the city, a wood that made "sad and sea-like music," when stirred by the breeze," according to a historian of the late 1800s.

Over time the pines were removed, died out, or were uprooted by storms. Of the park's numerous existing trees—44 per acre in the northern portion—a few are pines, but you'll see many more oaks, sycamores, and magnolias when you visit. Particularly impressive are the live oaks (a particular species of oak) that line the central walkway stretching from the park's northern end at Gaston Street to its southern end at Park Avenue.

The monuments are on this wide promenade, as is the much-photographed fountain, which features a female figure surrounded by water-spouting swans and tritons (men with the lower bodies of fish). The fountain, said to be the largest in the US when it was unveiled in 1858, is modeled after one in the Place de la Concorde of Paris. A lighted sidewalk that's much favored by walkers and joggers who live or work downtown borders Forsyth. According to the city, the distance around the park is 1.5 miles. The park is also the site of major annual events, including the Sidewalk Arts Festival.

i Although most city parks such as Forsyth and Daffin don't have gates that can be shut to keep people out at night, there is an ordinance stating that parks are open from sunrise to sunset. Lighted areas in Forsyth Park are open until 11 p.m.

Islands

OLD SAVANNAH-TYBEE RAILROAD HISTORIC AND SCENIC TRAIL (MCQUEEN'S ISLAND RAILS TO TRAILS), US 80 East; (912) 652-6780; parks.chathamcounty .org. When you walk, jog, or bicycle on this 6.5-mile trail, you're traversing the roadbed of a railroad that took passengers from eastern Savannah to Tybee Island for nearly 50 years starting in the late 1800s. Chatham County maintains the palm-lined, limestone trail on McQueen's Island as part of the Rails

to Trails program created beginning in 1991, an effort to transform abandoned railroad rights-of-way into recreational areas. A trip along the entire length of the trail takes you past 18 fitness stations and 30 wooden picnic tables and across 10 wooden footbridges. Besides what it offers in the way of exercise, the trail presents visitors with vistas of marshland and the south channel of the Savannah River, opportunities for fishing and crabbing, and glimpses of wildlife indigenous to the marsh. Keep your eyes peeled for creatures such as the eastern box turtle, the diamondback terrapin, the American alligator, the red-tailed hawk, the brown pelican, and the great blue heron, and don't be surprised if you walk up on a rattlesnake or two (they enjoy sunning themselves on the trail).

The railroad was built over 17.7 miles of salt marsh, rivers, and tidal creeks by a group of investors led by Savannahian D. G. Purse, who in 1885 owned a good portion of Tybee Island and was trying to find a way to transport people there that was faster than the 2-hour ride by steamboat. His solution was to build a railroad, and the idea was considered a harebrained scheme by local folks; they were convinced it was an engineering feat that couldn't be accomplished. But Purse persisted, and his Savannah and Tybee Railway began making regularly scheduled runs in July 1887.

A few years later, the line became part of the Central of Georgia Railway system and was operated from then on as the Savannah and Atlantic Railroad. The last passenger excursion was in July 1933; by then, the advent of the automobile and the construction of a road to Tybee (now US 80) had made the railway obsolete. But in its heyday, the little railroad carried thousands of Savannahians and out-of-towners to Tybee for days of sunning and swimming at the beach and nights of dancing at the Tybrisa

Pavilion. The entrance to the trail places you at its midpoint and is on US 80 just east of the Bull River Bridge. The highway is well traveled, and there is not much space at the trail entrance, so be careful when you pull off the road to park. The trail is off-limits after darkness falls and not safe, so make sure you plan to visit when you have plenty of time to complete the walk or run before dark sets in. Plans are to extend the trail all the way to Tybee Island itself, but that's in the future.

SKIDAWAY ISLAND STATE PARK, 52 Diamond Causeway; (912) 598-2300, (800) 864-7275; gastateparks.org/Skidaway. Get back to nature on the Big Ferry or Sandpiper Trails at Skidaway State Park. Walking either will give you a good look at a maritime forest and the salt marsh, their plants, and possibly some of their animals, including fiddler crabs, egrets, deer, and alligators. The trails also take you to earthwork fortifications built as Confederate defenses during the Civil War and the remains of a moonshine still. Big Ferry can be hiked in either a 2- or 3-mile loop, with the latter taking about 90 minutes to walk. Sandpiper is a mile long, takes about 20 minutes, and can be traversed by people using wheelchairs (with a little help) and parents pushing baby strollers. A path connects the trails, enabling hikers to get in as much as a 5.5-mile walk. Contact the park for guided hikes.

The 533-acre park, created during the early 1970s and opened in 1975, is in the western portion of Skidaway Island and borders a stretch of the Intracoastal Waterway called the Skidaway Narrows. Other features of the park include a museum featuring the skeleton of a giant sloth, picnic sites, interpretive nature programs, and campsites. In addition to the picnic sites, there are five covered shelters available on a first-come, first-served basis. If you don't want to take a chance, you can reserve one at $35 a day;

a group shelter accommodates 150 people and rents for $150–$300 per day. The park has three new cabins priced at $135 per day and 87 tent/trailer/RV campsites priced at $26 to $45.

The park is open 7 a.m. to 10 p.m. 7 days a week. There's a $5 parking fee (more for buses). If you're planning to come here often or visit other state parks and historic sites in Georgia, you might consider purchasing an annual Georgia Park Pass for $30 ($15 for those age 62 and older). That will get you unlimited admission to all state parks.

Southside/Midtown

DAFFIN PARK, 301 E. Victory Dr.; (912) 351-3841. When Savannah's Park and Tree Commission members conceived plans for Daffin Park in 1908, the recreational area was on the outskirts of the city. Now, Daffin is in the middle of Midtown, and it's a magnificent place for residents to stroll and enjoy the outdoors; it's shady and covered with giant live oaks, and there's a well-kept lake and plenty of benches. The park, which is maintained by the city of Savannah's Leisure Services Bureau, covers 77 acres bounded by Victory Drive, Waters Avenue, Washington Avenue, and Bee Road.

Opportunities for enjoying the outdoors in a residential setting abound at Daffin, which has a large playground; grassy fields that accommodate softball, baseball, football, soccer, rugby, and, on occasion, cricket; basketball courts; nine tennis courts; a pool; a 4-acre lake where you can fish for bass, bream, and catfish; and a pavilion on the lake that can be reserved for $125 per day for a variety of gatherings. Call (912) 351-3837 for reservations.

The eastern portion of the park is the site of Grayson Stadium, and a picnic area shaded by towering pine trees. The playing fields on the southern side of the park— once the site of polo matches and a landing strip for airplanes before the city built its first airport in 1929—are also fine for flying kites and driving golf balls, when the fields are not otherwise occupied. You'll also find a popular dog park. If you're into walking or jogging, you'll find room to roam on the 8-foot-wide, 1.5-mile-long sidewalk surrounding the park. For a shorter jaunt, try the lighted sidewalk around Daffin Lake, which is a third of a mile long. A note: For safety reasons, don't walk the park at night, especially alone.

LAKE MAYER COMMUNITY PARK, 1850 Montgomery Crossroad; (912) 652-6780; chathamcounty.org. As the name implies, the centerpiece of this 75-acre park on the Southside is the lake, but there's more here than recreational offerings involving water. Lake Mayer is surrounded by a 1.5-mile walking and jogging track dotted with 18 fitness stations. The park grounds provide space for eight lighted tennis courts, two lighted basketball courts, an unlighted ball diamond, a conditioning course and a basketball court for people using wheelchairs, a playground, a remote-control auto racetrack, and an outdoor skating rink designed to accommodate in-line hockey games. Picnic tables are sprinkled throughout the park, and two covered areas accommodate large groups: a pavilion with space for as many as 500 people and a shelter with room for 80 to 100. These can be reserved at fees of $175 and $150 respectively for 5 hours of usage; otherwise, they are available on a first-come, first-served basis.

Getting back to the 35-acre lake: Swimming is prohibited, but you can fish for bass, bream, catfish, and crappie if you have a freshwater license. The possibilities for boating abound; the lake is the site of the Savannah Sailing Center (see this chapter's Sailing section), which offers instruction to young people and adults, and of Red Cross classes in kayaking and canoeing. Windsurfing is

permitted on the lake, which is also where remote-control boat-racing enthusiasts come to compete.

Staff members at Lake Mayer present special events throughout the year, including egg hunts and kite-making and flying contests on the weekend before Easter; fishing rodeos in April, May, and June; Senior Citizens Day in May; Family Nature Day in September; and Christmas Camp in December.

Lest we forget, numerous ducks and geese call the park home, and they are more than happy to take stale bread off (and out of) your hands. The park is operated by Chatham County's Public Works and Park Services Department. It's open 8 a.m. to 11 p.m. in the spring and summer and 8 a.m. to 10 p.m. in fall and winter. Again, a reminder: Don't walk this park at night.

An Ecofriendly Day Trip

From time to time, the Friends of Ossabaw lead groups to discover the natural and human history of Ossabaw Island, the state's third largest barrier island. The island was designated a Heritage Preserve for natural, scientific and cultural study, research and education. Call for costs. To register or find more information about their exciting day trips, go to ossabawisland.net or call (912) 233-5104.

SAVANNAH NATIONAL WILDLIFE REFUGE, SC 170; (843) 784-2468; fws.gov/savannah. By traveling the Laurel Hill Wildlife Drive, you can see some of the refuge's 29,174 acres of freshwater marshes and hardwood islands, which are known locally

Close-up

See Wilderness Up Close!

Wilderness Southeast (WiSE) programs offer scheduled and private programs for getting close to Savannah nature without taking the risk of getting bit—or lost! For example, if you're into birding, you may wish to schedule a private birding tour with one of their guides. (Diana Churchill is the bird expert of Savannah, so ask for her.) A portion of every tour fee goes toward Fish Got to Swim, a science enrichment water quality course that they provide for Savannah's underserved public middle-school students. The company also offers a wide array of group (minimum of two people) coastal tours such as beaches, estuary, salt marsh, cypress swamps, and wetlands. They also investigate wildlife such as alligators, birds of all sorts, dolphins, and much less glamorous species. Throughout the year they offer various water-based (paddling, motorboating, beach, and some early morning birding) programs. They offer 13 set tours or a create-your-own-tour option, according to your interest. Two popular tours are the following:

- **Alligators and Others:** On this three hour tour, participants venture to the Savannah National Wildlife Refuge Visitor's Center to discover alligators basking in the sun while great birds fish serenely nearby. A certified naturalist will share alligator stories, and you'll discover the secrets of historic rice plantations and learn the importance of maintaining the old rice paddies for wildlife.
- **Blackwater River Paddle:** After basic canoeing instruction, your WiSE naturalist will lead the way downstream past stately tupelo and cypress trees. Their bright spring-green foliage and dark trunks reflect perfectly in the mirror-dark water. The tour participants will be on the lookout for turtles, herons, and noisy kingfishers diving for their next meal. There's beauty around every bend!

For more information and prices, check out this organization's colorful website (naturesavannah.org) or call the offices at 3025 Bull St., Ste. 302, at (912) 236-8115.

as "hammocks." This 4-mile gravel road is open to hikers, bicyclists, and motorists, and it takes you along dikes built during the late 18th and early 19th centuries by rice planters. The US Fish and Wildlife Service, which manages the refuge, maintains 3,000 acres of freshwater pools created by the dikes, areas that serve as feeding grounds for wading birds and waterfowl. Unless posted as closed, all the dikes are open to foot travel, as is the Cistern Trail, a winding path that runs off the Wildlife Drive; however, if you're planning on leaving the drive to hike or bike, call ahead to ascertain the condition of the dike system.

The Wildlife Drive is open sunrise to sunset throughout the year, except for 2 days during the fall, usually in October, when it's closed to the general public to allow a deer hunt by people using wheelchairs; you should check to see if this event falls at a time when you intend to visit the refuge. The drive and the dikes are great places from which to observe wildlife, in particular birds and alligators. A marvelous time for bird watching is late December and early January, when the refuge is visited by 13 different types of ducks in concentrations of up to 30,000 birds. The best times for viewing gators are in March, April, and October, when

It's a Swamp Thing

Occasionally, the Savannah-Ogeechee Canal park management team will host a "Swamp Thing Lantern Tour." This tour is comprised of a series of reenactments from different periods of the canal's history, including the local lore about the presence of a fictional creature said to live in the area—the Swamp Thing. The program, designed to create and promote awareness of the center, is offered at different times for several hours and covers a half-mile section of trail traversed in about 20 minutes. The first part of the reenactment recreates the 1831 opening ceremony of the canal. A Civil War scene follows where Sherman's army is shown stealing a local man's horse, and another illustrates Confederate defenders burning the bridge at the canal's mouth. Both scenes are dramatic!

There are others equally as enthralling, including one story with live actors about the moonshine era where participants suddenly come face-to-face with the Swamp Thing! For more information and to find out when the next tour will be scheduled, call (912) 748-8068.

the big reptiles crawl onto the banks of the refuge's canals to bask in the sun.

Laurel Hill Wildlife Drive and about half of the refuge are in South Carolina but right across the Savannah River from Chatham County; the entrance to the drive is only a couple of miles from the West Chatham town of Port Wentworth on SC 170, which is SR 25 south of the river. The drive is not far from downtown Savannah. To get to it from downtown—about a 15-minute trip—take US 17 north across the river to its intersection with SC 170, then turn south on SC 170.

You can fish from the banks of the Wildlife Drive and in the Kingfisher Pond year-round and in the remainder of the refuge's freshwater pools March 1 to November 30, but the angling at these spots isn't anything to write home about, and you'll need a South Carolina license. You'll get better results fishing in the Savannah River along the refuge's boundaries, and a Georgia license will suffice if you stay in the main channels. The refuge manages hunts for deer, feral hogs, squirrels, waterfowl, and turkeys during the fall and winter. Permits are required to hunt there and can be obtained by mailing requests

or applications to Savannah Coastal Refuge Hunts, Parkway Business Center, 1000 Business Center Dr., Ste. 10, Savannah, GA 31405.

SAVANNAH-OGEECHEE CANAL MUSEUM AND NATURE CENTER, 681 Fort Argyle Rd.; (912) 748-8068; savannahogeecheecanalsociety.org. This 184-acre nature center and its several trails will give you a look at three environments: pine woods, hardwood tidal river swamp, and sand hills. Two of the trails start in the pines at the museum and follow the southern portion of the canal, which dates from 1830, faded from usage near the end of the 19th century, and has since been cleared of brush and other overgrowth. These trails—the Tow Path and the Heel Path—are each 0.4 mile long and lead you past Locks 5 and 6 of the canal to the Ogeechee River. The only bridge across the canal is at Lock 5 near the start of the paths, so don't expect to walk to the end of one and back on the other. However, a trail created as an Eagle Scout project allows you to walk from the end of the Tow Path (on the eastern side of the canal) to the 0.5-mile-long Jenkes Road Trail. Jenkes Road, once a thoroughfare for wagon traffic, will also take you from the museum to the river. The road and the paths carry you through the swamp; you can see the sand hills by walking the mile-long Holly Trail. The nature center is open 9 a.m. to 5 p.m. daily. Admission is $2 for adults and $1 for senior citizens and children older than age 5.

BICYCLING

We mention in several places in this book that the Historic District, with its quaint streets and squares and its laid-back attitude, is an ideal place for walking. It follows that this area is also a wonderful place to see from the seat of a bicycle. But if you opt to ride a bike rather than stroll around the downtown, be aware that you'll be competing with traffic that seems to become increasingly heavier as Savannah grows in popularity as a tourist destination. To avoid the worst of the traffic, consider taking your ride on a weekend morning before the sightseeing starts in earnest. Also, be sure to observe the same traffic laws as you would when driving your car, and give serious thought to wearing a helmet. Georgia law requires kids younger than age 16 to use protective headgear; if you're older than the age limit, you can set a good example by wearing a helmet, and you might even save yourself a bump on the noggin. Keep in mind that adults are prohibited from riding bikes through Historic District squares.

Dedicated cyclists who delight in long rides will find that the city and county haven't done a great deal to accommodate them; however, there is a governmental committee on bikeways and greenways that's working to come up with facilities that will make bike riding more enjoyable. Until the committee devises some plans and officials implement them, however, bike riders will have to make do with the existing designated bike paths and bike trails at their disposal.

The city has two bike paths, each of which uses streets that are often heavily traveled by motorists:

- The West to East Corridor runs along 52nd Street to Ward Street to LaRoche Avenue to the entrance to Savannah State University.
- The North to South Corridor follows Habersham Street to Stephenson Avenue to Hodgson Memorial Drive to Edgewater Drive to Hillyer Drive to Dyches Drive to Lorwood Drive to Tibet Avenue to Largo Drive to Windsor Road to Science Drive at Armstrong State University.

The county offers a couple of trails for bicyclists:

- The McCorkle Bike Trail ambles for 4 miles over 10 acres on Wilmington Island. The eastern end of this trail is at Walthour Road near Concord Road, and the western end is on Cromwell Road just past its intersection with Wilmington Island Road.
- The McQueen's Island Trail runs between Bull River and Fort Pulaski and is part of the Old Savannah-Tybee Railroad Historic and Scenic Trail (see entry in the Parks section of this chapter). This crushed-stone trail is best suited to mountain bikes.

COASTAL BICYCLE TOURING CLUB, cbtc .org. This group of biking enthusiasts holds organized rides just about every weekend and special rides throughout the year. The club has about 150 members who meet monthly and receive a monthly newsletter.

BIRD WATCHING

Its location on the air route of migratory birds known as the Atlantic Flyway makes Savannah a splendid place for watching birds. The premier spot for this activity is the Savannah National Wildlife Refuge, a haven for thousands of mallards, pintails, teal, and as many as 10 other species of ducks that migrate here during the winter months. Transient songbirds and shorebirds stop by briefly during the spring and fall. The peak time for viewing ducks at the refuge occurs in late December and January. You might also do some worthwhile bird watching on the beach on the north end of Tybee Island during the spring, fall, and winter and on Skidaway Island during the spring and fall. Tybee's North Beach is a good place for spotting gannets and purple sandpipers during the winter, and you might find migratory shorebirds and neotropical songbirds at Skidaway Island State Park and along the 4-mile trail on the northern end of the island running from the Georgia Marine Extension Service aquarium to Priest's Landing. Wild Birds Unlimited, the locally owned franchise of the national birding supply store, has an expert staff willing to answer questions.

BOATING

Chatham County has about 86,700 acres of tidal marshlands laced by approximately 420 miles of navigable tidal waters. In other words, the area is a paradise for boaters.

Three of the most accessible scenic waterways are the Wilmington, Bull, and Skidaway Rivers, and they'll lead you to Wassaw Sound and the beaches of Wassaw, Williamson, and Beach Hammock Islands, where you can picnic, swim, sunbathe, and look for shells. The 7 miles of beach at Wassaw, a barrier island that's part of a national wildlife refuge and accessible only by water, are most inviting, particularly the "boneyard" on the northeast end where the bleached remains of toppled trees present opportunities for taking intriguing photographs. The southernmost and northernmost ends and the ocean beachfront of Williamson Island are open to boaters, but the middle of the island is a Critical Wildlife Area closed to humans; this area is reserved for birds such as the American oystercatcher. The basically pristine beaches of these islands are about a 25-minute trip from the marinas in Thunderbolt.

When you make a landing, you shouldn't have to worry about rocks, but be aware of what the tide is doing—if it's running out, you could get stranded for several hours if you're not careful. Also, be sure you're wearing shoes when you jump out of your boat into the water so oyster shells, broken glass, or the occasional stingray won't injure you.

The county maintains boat ramps at several locations that will provide you with access to local waterways. In the Islands area, there are two double ramps at Skidaway Narrows on the Diamond Causeway, and double ramps at Lazaretto Creek on US 80 East at Tybee Island and at Frank W. Spencer Park on the Islands Expressway just east of the bridge over the Wilmington River. In West Chatham, there are two double ramps at the Houlihan Bridge on US 25 at the Savannah River and at Kings Ferry on US 17 South at the Ogeechee River; and there is a single ramp at Salt Creek on US 17 South. All of the ramp facilities have restrooms and wooden docks. You'll find picnic areas at all the ramps (with the exception of Lazaretto Creek).

Downtown Via Boat

You can reach River Street and its shops, restaurants, and other attractions by boat via the Savannah River, but make sure to stay well clear of the commercial vessels using the shipping channel. These are huge ships, and they throw huge wakes. You can tie up alongside River Street at a 300-foot floating dock alongside Rousakis Riverfront Plaza.

The rate for using this city-owned facility varies by circumstance. For more information, call the city's Revenue Department,

Close-up

Reworking the Concept of the Ideal Vacation: The Caretta Research Project

If your concept of the ideal vacation involves lazing on a sandy beach with accommodations that include air-conditioning and a hot tub, then you probably won't want to spend a week during the summer serving as a volunteer for the Savannah Science Museum's **Caretta Research Project.**

On the other hand, if you don't mind paying at least $750 for 7 days and nights of no A/C, no hot water, no privacy, and lots of bugs, then working with the environmentalists who run this sea turtle monitoring program might be right up your alley.

For your hard-earned dough, your time, and your sweat, you get the satisfaction of helping save a threatened species—the loggerhead sea turtle. Depending on when you devote a week of your life to the Caretta Project, you have the opportunity to either see loggerheads crawl up the beaches at Wassaw Island and lay their eggs or watch hatchlings scramble down the beaches to take up residence in the Atlantic Ocean.

"People say the project changes their lives," said biologist Kris Williams, who serves as director of the undertaking. After their weeks on Wassaw, "many students have changed their majors to biology to work with sea turtles," she said.

The Caretta Project—*Caretta caretta* is the scientific name of the loggerhead—has had more than 2,520 volunteers from nearly every state and about a half-dozen foreign countries participate since its onset in 1973. It's one of the oldest sea turtle monitoring programs anywhere and the only one in the US whose volunteer sessions last an entire week and are thoroughly hands-on. Hands-on means that you'd better be ready to work if you volunteer. "We don't want people wanting to spend a vacation," said Williams.

Volunteers who participate in the sessions running from mid-May through early August spend their nights—we're talking from dusk to dawn—patrolling 7 miles of Wassaw's practically pristine beaches looking for turtles intent on digging a nest and laying eggs. Once a turtle is found, she is checked for an identification tag; tagged, if necessary; and measured. The turtle-monitoring team—which consists of six volunteers, a member of the Caretta Project staff, and an assistant—then either marks the nest and covers it with a screen to protect it from marauding raccoons or digs up the eggs and relocates them to a spot farther from the water's edge. Relocating

---

which can be contacted at (912) 651-6451. You'll also find a dock at the Hyatt Regency hotel that's 414 feet long and available for boats 25 feet or longer. There is a fee for using the hotel dock overnight; for info call (912) 238-1234.

Marinas

If you're traveling to Savannah by boat or looking for a place to dock during your visit, or if you need somewhere to store your boat, you can choose from several marinas.

BAHIA BLEU MARINA, 2812 River Dr.; **(912) 354-2283, (912) 434-1005; morning starmarinas.com.** Tie up at Bahia Bleu Marina and you're within walking distance of the restaurants and stores on the bluff at Thunderbolt. This facility, on the Wilmington River near Intracoastal Waterway mile marker 583, offers more than 3,000 feet of concrete the eggs is often necessary because erosion has caused a shelf to form along much of the beach at Wassaw; unable to climb up the shelf, the turtles sometimes dig their nests where the tide can wash their eggs out to sea.

"The eggs probably wouldn't hatch if we didn't move them," said Williams, noting that a major aim of the project is to maximize the survival of hatchlings. Seeing the hatchlings dash for the ocean is the lure for the volunteers who take part in sessions running from late July through mid-September. "We watch the nests and try to make sure we're there to ensure the hatchlings make it to the water," said Williams, explaining how volunteers ward off predators such as coons and ghost crabs. "We usually stay up until midnight, then get up at dawn to make sure no hatchlings are stuck."

While on Wassaw, a sea island southeast of Savannah that's accessible only by boat, volunteers sleep in a rustic one-room cabin that's not air-conditioned; there's no hot water, and the shower is outside. Team members share housekeeping duties, including the preparation and cleanup of supper, the only organized meal of the day. "We eat well," said Williams, noting that suppers revolve around hearty dishes such as beef Stroganoff, pizza, spaghetti, and vegetable lasagna.

The registration fee covers a volunteer's food, lodging, and transportation by boat from Skidaway Island to Wassaw and back.

Volunteers should be 18 years old or older, but Williams said the program will accept those age 16 or even younger, provided they are highly motivated and independent types. "This is not a summer camp," said Williams. "This is a working vacation—it's not fun and games."

There's no maximum age limit, but participants in the program must be in good health and have reasonably good night vision and the ability to handle a moderate amount of walking. "Perhaps most important is your mental attitude," states the program's informational literature. "The project requires upbeat, adaptable folks who can cheerfully endure close quarters, insects, rainstorms, and the heat and humidity of a week in the subtropics without air-conditioning."

If you fit that bill and you're interested in participating, you can start the process of volunteering by calling (912) 447-8655 or visiting the website at carettaresearch project.org. Project staffers start accepting applications in January, and the sessions do fill up, so it's a good idea to get yours in early.

"It's a very rewarding experience," Williams said of the volunteer program. "We've had people coming back for their 10th and 11th years."

dock and 240 enclosed racks, plus an extensive ship's store, restrooms, and showers.

BULL RIVER MARINA, 8005 Old Tybee Rd.; (912) 897-7300; bullrivermarina.com. This marina sits on the Bull River some 4 miles from the mouth of Wassaw Sound, which borders the Atlantic Ocean. The location makes the marina about halfway between Savannah and Tybee Island. The marina provides boaters with 80 deepwater slips, a

ship's store, restrooms, showers, live and frozen bait, gas, and diesel fuel. It offers private charters, boat rentals, inshore and offshore fishing charters, beach and island shuttles, and dolphin, sightseeing, and nature tours. The marina is just off US 80 at the western end of the bridge over the Bull River.

HOGAN'S MARINA, 36 Wilmington Island Rd.; (912) 897-FISH; hogansmarina.com. Situated on Turner Creek about 0.75 mile

147

from the Wilmington River—the Intracoastal Waterway—Hogan's has dry rack, wet storage, and launching capabilities. You'll find a store with nautical gear and fishing tackle, gasoline, restrooms and showers, live and frozen bait, a fish-cleaning facility, and ice and beverages. Hogan's also repairs engines.

ISLE OF HOPE MARINA, 50 Bluff Dr.; (912) 354-8187; iohmarina.com. On a picturesque bend of the Skidaway River sits the Isle of Hope Marina, which was established here in 1926 and installed concrete docks in 2003. The marina was the first dealer of Cris Craft boats in the nation and was the site of the dock scenes in the original production of the movie *Cape Fear*, the first in a long line of films made in the Savannah area. There are 100 wet slips and a ship's store. Gas and diesel fuel are available, as are showers, and there's an over-the-water pavilion available for rental. It's at Intracoastal Waterway mile marker 590.

SAIL HARBOR MARINA & BOATYARD, 606 Wilmington Island Rd.; (912) 897-2896, (912) 897-1914; sailharbormarina .com. As the name implies, Sail Harbor caters mainly to owners of sailboats, but this marina on Turner Creek near the Wilmington River will also accommodate powerboats. There are transient slips, showers, and laundry. There is no fuel here.

SAVANNAH BEND MARINA, Old Tybee Rd.; (912) 897-DOCK. This marina on the Wilmington River at Intracoastal Waterway mile marker 582 has transient dockage at 35 wet slips and a dry-storage building containing 262 racks for boats up to 29 feet long. The ship's store carries nautical apparel. You can relax and get a fine view of the river from one of the rocking chairs lining the porch of the store. Savannah Bend offers fuel service and has showers, laundry facilities,

and restrooms. The marina is in Thunderbolt near the eastern end of the bridge over the Wilmington River.

THUNDERBOLT MARINA, 3124 River Dr.; (912) 352-4931; thunderboltmarina .com. Yacht owners who dock at this marina, next to the boat works in Thunderbolt, get doughnuts delivered to them in the morning. The marina has more than 1,100 feet of dock space available for transient boaters. The marina offers a ship's store selling marine supplies, has gas and diesel fuel, will perform maintenance service, and provides a laundry and showers. Thunderbolt Marina is on the Wilmington River at Intracoastal Waterway mile marker 583.

BOWLING

AMF SAVANNAH LANES, 115 Tibet Ave.; (912) 925-0320; amf.com. Bowlers will find 50 lanes, a pro shop, a snack bar, and a full-service sports lounge at Savannah Lanes. This establishment in the Southside is the home of about 50 bowling leagues. Call for hours and prices. Savannah Lanes is open year-round.

CAMPING

SKIDAWAY ISLAND STATE PARK, 52 Diamond Causeway; (912) 598-2300, (800) 864-7275; gastateparks.org. The park has 88 pull-through campsites set amid the serenity of a maritime forest on Skidaway Island. Each has water, 30 amp and a limited number of 50 amp electrical hookups, cable television, hookups, and elevated tent pads; grills and tables are provided. You can build campfires in the fire rings found at each campsite, but please don't build them on the tent pads. The park is a popular spot because of its natural beauty and also because it's only about 35 minutes from the Historic District. Many campers use the park as a "bedroom" while they visit the city, so the sites tend to fill up on major holidays and the weekend closest to St. Patrick's Day.

FISHING

If you like to fish, you've come to the right place. Year-round, there's somewhere in Chatham County or offshore in the Atlantic Ocean where you can wet a line and catch something. Basically, we're talking about three types of fishing: inshore and offshore, which involve fish that live in salt water, and freshwater.

The inshore area stretches from the beachfronts into the tidal rivers and creeks and includes Wassaw Sound. This is where you'll find spotted trout, red drum (also known as spot-tail bass), flounder, sheepshead, tarpon, croaker, and spots in the summer and whiting in the spring and summer. If you're visiting or new to the area and want to do some inshore fishing, hire a guide to show you some good fishing holes, which local folks call "drops." There are countless drops in Chatham's inshore waters, and it pays to know where they are; if you don't, you might find yourself sitting in a boat doing nothing while anglers in a vessel less than 50 feet away are hauling them in.

It's also a good idea to consult the local tide charts before you go fishing inshore; Chatham County has a high tidal range, and when the tides are "springing" (i.e., rising to 8 to 10 feet), the fishing isn't good because the bottom is churned up and the water is muddy. Go fishing when the tides are in the 6- to 7-foot range and the water is clear. You can find tide charts on the weather pages of the *Savannah Morning News*.

When you fish offshore, you'll either be bottom-fishing or trolling for sport fish. Bottom-fishing will net you black sea bass, grouper, and a variety of snapper. The sportfishing is seasonal, starting in spring with bluefish, followed by cobia, king mackerel, bonito, wahoo, marlin, sailfish, amberjack, tuna, and Spanish mackerel. The sportfishing is good into November, and some veteran anglers say the optimum time to venture out is after Labor Day. Offshore angling is best in the Gulf Stream and at a particularly fishy live bottom called the Snapper Banks. The Snapper Banks are about 40 miles out, and a trip there from Wilmington Island will take about 2 hours; the Gulf Stream, the warm ocean current that flows from the Gulf of Mexico along the US coast to New England, is about an hour farther.

If you're after freshwater fish in Chatham County, head for the Ogeechee River above Kings Ferry and the Savannah River above Port Wentworth. You'll encounter largemouth bass, shad, bluegill bream, redbreast bream, shellcracker bream, and crappie.

Georgia Fishing License

Make sure you have a Georgia fishing license, which will cover both salt- and freshwater angling; you'll be fined if you get caught without one. Licenses can be purchased just about anywhere you can buy fishing tackle, including discount department stores and online at georgiawildlife.org. For more information, call (800) 366-2661.

Okay, now that you have what you need, gather up your license, gear and bait and go fishing!

AMICK'S DEEP SEA FISHING, US 80, Tybee Island; (912) 897-6759; amicks deepseafishing.com. Amick's offers mostly offshore fishing trips and can accommodate 23 passengers on its 41-foot custom-built Morgan, the *Scat II*. Full- and half-day trips are available for private parties or individuals, and the company also has a 31-foot Morgan, the *Scamp*, for offshore fishing. Amick's is based on Tybee Island, just off US 80 at Lazaretto Creek. Open-boat trips to the Snapper Banks take about 10 hours. Call for pricing.

COFFEE BLUFF MARINA, 14915 White Bluff Rd.; (912) 925-7474; coffeebluff marina.net. Even if you didn't take advantage of the services offered by Coffee Bluff Marina, the ride out to the end of White Bluff Road would be worth making just to get the panoramic view of the Forest River and the wide expanse of adjacent marsh. Anglers who make the trip will also find the marina's large convenience store with a supply of fishing tackle and equipment, a boat hoist, gas, oil, bait, and ice. The marina also offers boat storage in the water and in sheds, but there are no rentals.

i Crabbing is a favorite pastime of many Savannahians. It's a recreational pursuit that's relatively inexpensive, and you don't need a boat to do it. All you do need is a basket net, some bait (chicken parts, such as the necks, will do fine), and a tidal creek in which to crab. If you don't want to buy the basket net, you can affix your bait to a line with a lead weight attached, but you'll probably need a dip net for getting the crabs you catch out of the water.

MISS JUDY CHARTERS, 124 Palmetto Dr.; (912) 897-4921, (912) 897-2478; miss judycharters.com. Go fishing and have fun doing it with Miss Judy Charters. Why is it fun? Owner Judy Helmey, who started skippering boats in the mid-1960s at the age of 14, says it's because her company caters to customers by making them aware of their surroundings during trips, answering their questions, showing them rod and reel operations, and swapping a fish story or two. "They get to do everything that's fun and we take care of the hard stuff," she says. The Wilmington Island–based company—started in 1947 by Judy's father, the late Sherman I. Helmey—provides inshore and offshore fishing via the *Miss Judy Too,* a customized 33-foot Sport fisher, and from a variety of other boats. Trips leave from the company's dock on Turner Creek; the entrance to the road leading to the dock is on Wilmington Island Road about a mile south of Johnny Mercer Boulevard. Call for rates.

i It is customary to cash tip the mate on your fishing charter, 15 to 20 percent. When the charter is complete, don't blame him or her if the fish didn't bite! (Don't forget to tip the fish cleaner, as well.)

GOLF

If golf is your game, you have several public and semiprivate courses in Chatham County from which to choose—one downtown, one on the islands, four in Southside/Midtown, and three in West Chatham. There are also write-ups on a couple of courses in nearby Bryan and Effingham Counties for those golfers who don't mind taking about a 30-minute ride to the links. The following listings will give you an idea of what's available; greens fees include cart rentals, and yardage is from men's tees.

Historic District

THE CLUB AT SAVANNAH HARBOR, 2 Resort Dr.; (912) 201-2240; theclubat savannahharbor.net. As you might expect of a course that hosts Savannah's premier golfing event—the Liberty Mutual Legends of Golf—this layout on Hutchinson Island has an impressive pedigree. As the course matures, it becomes more and more beautiful. This semiprivate course, which opened in 1999, was designed by golfing legends Robert Cupp and Sam Snead and is operated by the highly acclaimed Troon Golf. Set on 250 acres in the middle of the Savannah River, The Club takes golfers through a marshland environment and affords them spectacular views of Savannah's riverfront. The 6,627-yard, par-72 course features wide fairways and large, flat greens, and each hole bears an intriguing name. No. 8, for instance, is "the Briar Patch," a 132-yard par 3 with lots of marsh and a long green. Snead is celebrated at No. 10, nicknamed "Slammin' Sammy." The hole has a kidney-shaped green fronted by a large bunker; it's a par 4 that covers 363 yards.

The club has a pro shop, chipping and putting green, and a driving range, and there's an attractive grill overlooking the course that serves breakfast and lunch daily and dinner on Fri. Walking is permitted at all times.

Islands

WILMINGTON ISLAND CLUB, 612 Wilmington Island Rd.; (912) 897-1615. Set amid the oaks, pines, and palms of southwestern Wilmington Island, this par-71 course rambles over 6,715 yards. Raised, undulating greens are planted in Tifton and Bermuda grass, and there's water on 10 holes, including No. 15 and No. 6, two of the course's four well-bunkered par 3s. The signature hole is 6, a 155-yard par 3 with a pond in front of the green and bunkers on the right.

Donald Ross designed the course, which opened in 1927 as part of a resort, the centerpiece of which was the eight-story General Oglethorpe Hotel on the Wilmington River. In the mid-1960s, the hotel was refurbished and renamed the Savannah Inn and Country Club, and the golf course was rebuilt and improved by Willard Byrd. The resort was later purchased by the Sheraton corporation, which gave the property a new name. The hotel closed in 1994, but the semiprivate golf club remained open under the name of the Sheraton Savannah Resort & Country Club. In May 1998, a family-run development company based in Macon bought the hotel and golf course and changed the name of the golfing facility to the Wilmington Island Club.

The developers built a $1.5 million clubhouse—a two-story, 25,000-square-foot building featuring gym and locker rooms, a card room, a lounge-grill area, a full-service kitchen, and a banquet room capable of seating 300 people. The course was upgraded with new cart paths and a new irrigation system, and a pro shop, lighted driving range, and practice green are also part of the layout.

Only club members are allowed to walk the course.

Southside/Midtown

BACON PARK GOLF COURSE, Shorty Cooper Dr.; (912) 354-2625; baconpark golf.com. Recently upgraded, Bacon Park's 27-hole layout presents golfers with three 9-hole courses—Cypress, Live Oak, and Magnolia—featuring narrow, tree-lined Bermuda grass fairways and elevated greens. Cypress and Live Oak carry pars of 36, while Magnolia is a 37, and the combined length of any pair of the courses is more than 6,000 yards. Donald Ross designed the original layout, which is in the midst of suburban Savannah; it's owned by the city and managed by O.C. Welsh Golf Properties Inc. The clubhouse contains a pro shop and full-service snack bar, and a driving range and practice green are available. You can walk the course on weekdays and after 1 p.m. on Sat and Sun.

Cypress Course is the shortest of Bacon Park's three courses at 3,001 yards, Cypress has water on seven holes, including No. 3, the signature hole. This 185-yard par 3 has a large expanse of water on the approach to the green.

Live Oak Course has a long and narrow first hole, a 384-yard par 4 with a green that's well bunkered. The ninth hole is the longest at Bacon Park, a 522-yard par 5 with a fairway that is crossed by a canal past midpoint; there's plenty more water along the remainder of the fairway and in front of the green. The course runs 3,163 yards.

Magnolia Course starts with a long hole, a 466-yard par 5 whose green has lots of water on the right. Another interesting hole is No. 8, which is crossed near midpoint by a canal that runs down the left-hand side of the latter half of the fairway. The total length of Magnolia is 3,035 yards.

HENDERSON GOLF CLUB, 1 Al Henderson Dr.; (912) 920-4653; hendersongolf club.com. Henderson—opened in March 1995 and owned by Chatham County—offers a good mix of lengths among its 18 holes, ranging from just 127 yards on the 15th to 522 yards on the first hole. The course was built on farmland in southwest Chatham that contained 240 acres of wetlands, so there's plenty of water to look at. In most cases, however, the water is an intimidation factor rather than a sheer hazard.

In laying out the 6,273-yard, par-71 course, designer Mike Young took advantage of the wetlands and an abundant number of native trees by weaving them in with fairways and greens.

Henderson has a pro shop, driving range, practice green, and a grill serving hot food and sandwiches. It's the home of the Savannah Golf School, which offers a variety of lesson packages and hosts golf camps for youngsters.

Walking at Henderson is permitted anytime Mon through Thurs, and after 1 p.m. on Fri, weekends, and holidays. The course is off SR 204 just east of the I-95/SR 204 interchange.

West Chatham

CROSSWINDS GOLF CLUB, 232 James B. Blackburn Dr.; (912) 966-1909, cross windsgolfclub.com. This semiprivate club boasts the area's only par-3 course, a 1,126-yard layout that's illuminated for nighttime play. The par 3 is suitable for families, people new to golf, and the occasional player, but it's challenging enough to allow veteran golfers to sharpen up their iron play. Water comes into play on five holes, and the par 3 has undulating greens similar to the club's 18-hole course.

The larger course at Crosswinds, which derives its name from its location—less than 2 miles from Savannah/Hilton Head International Airport—covers 6,032 yards and is different from most layouts in that it has four par 5s and five par 3s and is devoid of residential development. The front nine features tree-lined fairways, while the last nine holes offer a wide-open, Scottish links feel. Water is in play on 8 of the 18 holes, and No. 3, a par-4 514-yarder, might give you fits because of a small green with lots of slope that provides the potential for putting balls in the drink.

Crosswinds, which opened for play in October 2000, has a spacious clubhouse featuring a full-service restaurant. Also on the premises are a pro shop, an illuminated driving range, and putting and chipping greens. Walking is permitted on both courses. Hours affect rates.

SOUTHBRIDGE GOLF CLUB, 415 South-bridge Blvd.; (912) 651-5455; southbridge golfclub.com. Rees Jones designed this 6,450-yard, par-72 course, blending in the tall pines, graceful oaks, and wetlands of the West Chatham woodlands. Water comes into play on 11 holes on the course, opened in 1988 as part of the Southbridge residential community. The signature hole is No. 13, a par-3, 179-yarder involving a shot over water to an elevated green cut into three sections. The fourth hole is also challenging; it's a long par 5 typical of holes on the back nine. This hole was carved out of a thick forest. Water on the left side is involved in every shot on this 490-yarder, and bunkers guard the right side.

An antebellum-style clubhouse adorns the semiprivate course, and the building houses a pro shop and Vickery's at South-bridge, a full-service dining room. The course rents clubs and has a driving range and putting green. Walking is allowed daily.

ICE SKATING

SAVANNAH CIVIC CENTER, Liberty and Montgomery Streets; (912) 651-6550. Believe it or not, you can enjoy this winter sport in Savannah, even at a time when it's liable to be downright warm. During December and starting on the first day of the month, the arena of the Civic Center is transformed into an ice rink where intrepid Southerners try their luck—and ankles—at skating. The rink fee is prone to change over the interval of a year that separates sessions entitles you to the use of a pair of skates. Skating times vary, so call ahead for information on when the rink is available and pricing.

RUNNING

You'll see lots of people running and jogging in Savannah, particularly during the more temperate months of autumn, winter, and spring. Good spots for running—places where you won't have to worry about colliding with motorists—are the sidewalks around Daffin Park and Forsyth Park and the jogging track at Lake Mayer Community Park (see listings in the beginning of this chapter). Each of these facilities covers 1.5 miles, so you can get a good workout by making a circuit or two. Some of the more experienced local runners drive out to the north end of Skidaway Island, park at the marine science center, and take to the roads there. These thoroughfares are fine for running because they are in good condition and sparsely traveled by drivers.

Savannah is the site of several major races, principally the Enmark Savannah River Bridge Run, a 5K and 10K race held in December, Savannah Rock 'n' Roll Marathon in November and the Critz Tybee Run in February. If you're a competitive runner, you can probably find a race most weekends (except during the hot and humid summer months) within a 2-hour radius of Savannah.

SAVANNAH STRIDERS, PO Box 15785, Savannah, GA 31416; (912) 631-1532; savystrider.com. The Striders meet monthly, and many members get together for runs during the week. The club, whose membership numbers about 180, sponsors the Tybee Marathon, Half-Marathon, and 5K in February and the Women's Wellness Walk/Run 5K in September. Annual dues are $15 for individuals and $20 for families, and membership forms can be picked up at the Habersham Branch YMCA on Habersham Street. The listed telephone number is the Striders' information line, and calling it will provide you with data on club meetings and upcoming races.

SAILING

Sailing is smooth in Savannah, as you might expect from the venue for the yachting events of the 1996 Summer Olympics. The best sailing is in Wassaw Sound, which is where the Olympic competition was staged. The sound has lots of deep water and few hazards, and you can bank on getting a trade wind breeze in the afternoon. Another good place for sailing is the Wilmington River, which is the site of several local regattas. The following are great places to get started.

GEECHEE SAILING CLUB, (912) 727-2395; **geecheesailingclub.org.** The club sponsors two major sailboat races, the St. Patrick's Day Regatta on the weekend after the holiday and the Oktoberfest Regatta in early October, and organizes about seven extensive cruises for members each year.

Members meet at Tubby's TankHouse restaurant in Thunderbolt on the second Monday of each month at 6:30 p.m. About 70 people actively participate in club functions that include a heavy social agenda.

ℹ️ **Besides being fun and good exercise, kayaking is an excellent way to get a close look at the marshland environment. Kayaking continues to grow in popularity in coastal Georgia, and you can rent boats and paddle around the marshes by paying a visit to North Island Surf & Kayak (912-786-4000) or Sea Kayak Georgia (912-786-8732), both of which are on US 80 on Tybee Island.**

SAIL HARBOR MARINA & BOATYARD, 606 Wilmington Island Rd.; (912) 897-2896, (912) 897-1914; **sailharbormarina .com.** Sail Harbor is on Turner Creek, right around the corner from the Wilmington River and about 7 miles from Wassaw Sound. This marina, whose office is closed Sun and Mon, has 100 wet slips, 5 of them for transients; a ship's store offering a variety of sailing merchandise; and a laundry, showers, and restrooms.

Sail Harbor was the 1996 Olympic yachting marina, meaning it served as a shore base for officials coordinating the sailing events. The actual sailing was done from a floating marina in Wassaw Sound that was dismantled after the Olympics.

SAVANNAH SAILING CENTER, Lake Mayer, 1850 E. Montgomery Cross Rd.; (912) 231-9996; **savannahsailingcenter .org.** Youngsters and adults can learn to sail and sharpen their skills by participating in the programs offered by this community-based nonprofit organization. The center began operations in 1993 and trained all of the volunteers who served on the water for Olympic yachting in Savannah in 1996. Courses are taught at the boathouse at Lake Mayer. The center will accept children as young as age 5 if they know how to swim. The center offers instruction on Saturday during the summer and every other Saturday during the spring and fall. Call for programming and pricing details. Scholarships are available, as are discounts for multiple sessions and multiple family members.

SWIMMING

CHATHAM COUNTY AQUATIC CENTER, 7240 Sallie Mood Dr.; (912) 652-6793; **aquatic.chathamcounty.org.** The aquatic center is a 40,000-square-foot area containing an eight-lane, 50-meter pool and a six-lane, 25-yard recreational and instructional pool, both of which are accessible to the disabled. In addition to accommodating lap swimming, the large pool is used for district, regional, state, and national swim meets; there's seating for 976 spectators. The building also has men's and women's changing rooms, a pro shop, a snack vending area, and several offices.

The 50-meter pool keeps things calm with a water-motion stabilizer that minimizes swimmers' wakes, and a ventilation duct running around the inside of the center keeps the air temperature at 88 to 90 degrees and the humidity at comfortable levels. The center offers a variety of programs for swimmers of all ages, those who want to develop their strokes and train for competition, and those interested in aquatic fitness. Call or check website for hours, fees, and classes.

TENNIS

About 1,500 tennis players participate in the US Tennis Association league program here, making it the second-largest program in the state next to Atlanta's. A total of 150 of the teams in the program, more than a third of those involved, play at public courts. There are courts at city and county parks throughout the area, but the biggest public tennis complexes are at Bacon and Daffin Parks.

BACON PARK TENNIS COMPLEX, 6262 Skidaway Rd.; (912) 351-3850. Tucked into a wooded area on Skidaway Road, this public complex has 16 lighted hard courts open 9 a.m. to 2 p.m. and 4 to 9 p.m. Mon through Thurs and 8 a.m. to noon. on Fri, Sat, and Sun; however, hours are limited depending on league play. A pro shop sells tennis merchandise and beverages. Fees start at $5.35 per hour.

DAFFIN PARK TENNIS COURTS, 1001 E. Victory Dr.; (912) 351-3851. Daffin's six clay courts and three hard courts sit near the park's lake, so you can occasionally catch a breeze off the water. You can play for free on the lighted hard courts (available 7:30 a.m. to 10 p.m.), but there's a fee of $5 an hour for using the soft courts, which don't have lights and are open 8:30 a.m. until 5 p.m. 7 days a week. (Longer hours are available during the summer. Call for times.)

DAY TRIPS

You obviously will find plenty to occupy your time in Savannah, but if you want to go roaming a bit, you'll discover lots to see and do in the rest of coastal Georgia. To get you started on your explorations of the territory to the south of Savannah, we've mapped out trips to Richmond Hill–Liberty County and to Jekyll Island.

The spotlighted sites in the Richmond Hill–Liberty County area are within an hour's drive of Savannah. It will take a little longer to reach Jekyll, which is about a 90-minute jaunt from Savannah. For those inclined to head north into the South Carolina Lowcountry, we've included a trip to Beaufort, a charming, history-filled town 50 miles from downtown Savannah. Happy wandering!

RICHMOND HILL–LIBERTY COUNTY

Lovers of history and nature will enjoy a tour of Richmond Hill and Liberty County, an area of extensive marshlands, lush forests, and meandering rivers, where the past is rich in significant people and events. To adequately visit all the spots we'll be sending you to, you'll probably need more than a day. That said, you might want to split this tour into a couple of day trips or pick a few places that sound the most appealing and spend a day visiting those.

Begin your tour of the area by driving to the Bryan County municipality of Richmond Hill, a fast-growing town that's become a bedroom community of Savannah during the past 20-plus years. This onetime stomping ground of industrialist Henry Ford is 19 miles southwest of downtown Savannah and can be reached by heading west on I-16 to I-516. Then head south on I-516 to the Southwest Bypass (Veterans Parkway), south on the Southwest Bypass to SR 204, west on SR 204 to US 17, and south on US 17 to the highway's intersection with SR 144. Turn left from US 17 onto SR 144 and head

east through the heart of Richmond Hill; it's a mile to your first stop, the Richmond Hill Historical Society and Museum. The museum building, which once housed a kindergarten that was a project of Ford and his wife, is on the right on the corner of SR 144 and Timber Trail Road.

RICHMOND HILL HISTORICAL SOCIETY AND MUSEUM, SR 144, Richmond Hill; (912) 756-3697; richmondhillhistory.org. You'll learn the fascinating story of Richmond Hill's Henry Ford era (1925–51) when you visit this museum. The billionaire Ford purchased 85,000 acres in Bryan County in the mid-1920s, in effect buying the town of Richmond Hill, which was then known as Ways Station. Ford spent his winters there, living on a plantation that accommodated a laboratory where chemists attempted to transform agricultural products into goods that could be used by the automobile industry.

Ford revitalized an area where moonshining was one of the major occupations;

he put people to work on his plantation and at a sawmill that he refurbished, and he built medical clinics, houses, chapels, and the town's Community House. Ford also improved existing schools and built a trade school for boys and a grammar and high school for African-American youths. A museum staffer will tell you about Ford's accomplishments and their impact on the community while you look at photographs and artifacts from the period. You'll also learn about sites from the Ford era that you can visit, such as the Community House, which is now a funeral home, and one of the chapels, now a Catholic church.

Other sections of the museum depict the area's plantation era and offer displays of photos and some of the furniture used in the county's one-room schoolhouses and in a typical parlor of a Bryan County home in the early 1900s. One room is devoted to the re-creation of a country store whose shelves are filled with authentic tins and boxes that held products popular during the early 1900s, and if you're interested in the really distant past, be sure to check out the time-line mural depicting the history of the area from prehistoric times to the present. No admission fee is charged, but donations are accepted. The museum is open Wed through Sat 10 a.m. to 3 p.m.

i Some of the attractions on our Richmond Hill–Liberty County day trip are in somewhat remote areas that aren't near restaurants, so you might consider packing a lunch for the day. You can dine in relative comfort at picnic areas at several stops on this tour, including Fort McAllister State Historic Park, Fort Morris State Historic Site, the Midway Museum, and the Fort Stewart Museum.

After you've looked at the displays at the Richmond Hill Museum, hop in your vehicle and head east on SR 144 to Fort McAllister State Historic Park. To reach the park, you'll drive 4 miles into the countryside on SR 144 to SR Spur 144, then turn left onto SR Spur 144; the entrance to the park is 4 miles ahead, and the drive to it will take you past upscale Lowcountry-style and ranch-style homes, some of them with backyard boat docks on the beautiful and fast-flowing Great Ogeechee River, which can be seen on your left.

i Fort McAllister State Historic Park and Fort Morris State Historic Site are among the 18 bird-watching venues on the Colonial Coast Birding Trail, which stretches along Georgia's coast from Tybee Island in the north to Cumberland Island National Seashore and the Okefenokee National Wildlife Refuge in the south. You can see songbirds, wading birds, and waterfowl at Fort McAllister and Fort Morris, depending on what time of year you visit.

FORT MCALLISTER STATE HISTORIC PARK, 3894 Fort McAllister Rd., Richmond Hill; (912) 727-2339; gastateparks .org. This 1,725-acre park between the Ogeechee River and Red Bird Creek has two alluring identities: It's a recreational area featuring amenities for campers and picnickers, and it's also the site of an earthen fort where much of the Savannah area's most significant Civil War action took place.

Prior to 1980 these two attractions existed as Richmond Hill State Park and Fort McAllister Historic Site. That year, they were combined to form Fort McAllister State Historic Park, which today is operated by the Georgia Department of Natural Resources. There's a $3.50–5 parking fee to enter the park, which is open daily 7 a.m. to 10 p.m. (campers arriving later can register at their campsites). There are also seven homey cottages to rent at this park for $95–225 per night. Some are dog-friendly. The cottages have two double beds in each bedroom and sleep eight. There are fully equipped kitchens with microwaves and dishwashers, heat, and air-conditioning. One, in particular, also has a lovely screened-in porch that overlooks the marsh.

The Recreational Area

For day-trippers, the main attraction here is the tree-filled picnic ground running along a high bluff overlooking the Ogeechee River. Tall pines and hardwoods make this a shady, serene spot for walking or sitting in a glider-type swing and watching the river flow by. You'll find 50 sites with picnic tables and grills, a fishing pier that extends out over the river, and plenty of rustic-looking playground equipment for the kids in this area, which borders the main road leading to the fort. Across the road from this area is the start of a 3.5-mile nature trail complete with a primitive campsite that can be rented for $10 a night per person.

If you plan on making your visit to Richmond Hill–Liberty County last longer than a day and you like roughing it, consider staying at the park's Savage Island Campground, which has 66 campsites—54 for recreational vehicles and 12 with tent pads, and all with water and electrical hookups, grills, and tables. Two comfort stations provide campers with toilets, heated showers, and washer/dryers, and the campground also has a playground, nature trail, and dock and boat ramp on Red Bird Creek. The RV sites rent for $27–32 a nights.

The Historic Site

Fort McAllister is one of the best-preserved earthwork fortifications built by the Confederacy during the Civil War. The southernmost of the defenses ringing Savannah, the fort withstood several attacks by Union warships before being overpowered by Federal forces on December 13, 1864, at the end of Gen. William T. Sherman's March to the Sea. The site was once owned by Henry Ford, who began an extensive restoration in the late 1930s, and the fort eventually fell into the hands of the state of Georgia, which restored it to its 1863–64 appearance.

You can wander around the walls and through the interior of the fort and look inside its central bombproof bunker, but be careful not to climb on these earthen structures, which are extremely susceptible to erosion from foot traffic. Take the self-guided tour of the fort and check out a 32-pounder smoothbore gun that fired red-hot cannonballs and the furnace where these projectiles were heated; the reconstructed service magazine, which held shells, powder, and fuses for the rebels' 32-pounder rifled gun; and the fort's northwest angle, where the attackers placed the first US flag planted on the parapets.

The museum contains Civil War shells and weapons; implements such as those used in the construction of the fort; artifacts from the Confederate blockade runner *Nashville,* which was sunk in the Ogeechee by the Union ironclad *Montauk;* a diorama of the assault on the fort; a display depicting life at the fort as experienced by its 230 defenders; and exhibits involving the Guale Indians, who once inhabited the area, and Henry Ford's efforts to preserve the site. The fort is open 8 a.m. to 5 p.m. Admission rates are $9 for adults, $8 for seniors, and $5 for youths; children younger than age 6 are admitted free.

After visiting Fort McAllister State Historic Park, head back to Richmond Hill on SR 144 and then south to Liberty County and the Historic Liberty Trail. The first attraction on this tour of the trail is Fort Morris State Historic Site, and you can get there from Richmond Hill by turning left onto US 17 from SR 144 and driving 2 miles to I-95, heading south on I-95 for 11 miles, and leaving the interstate at exit 76. Next, turn left onto US 84/SR 38 (Fort Morris Road) and stay on it for 7 miles until you come to the entrance to the site.

FORT MORRIS STATE HISTORIC SITE, 2559 Fort Morris Rd., Midway; (912) 884-5999; gastateparks.org. This peaceful little spot on a low bluff on the Medway River was the scene of one of the classic rejoinders in American history. During the Revolutionary War, the British besieged the American earthworks of Fort Morris and the nearby town of Sunbury, and the redcoat commander demanded a surrender. The fort's commander, Col. John McIntosh, answered the demand in this defiant manner: "We, sir, are fighting the battles of America, and therefore disdain to remain neutral till its fate is determined. As to surrendering the fort, receive this laconic reply, 'Come and take it!'" Lacking some expected support from another British force and the exact knowledge of the strength of the troops at Fort Morris, the redcoats did not follow McIntosh's suggestion; instead, they retreated. Fort Morris, however, eventually fell to the British and was dismantled.

A smaller earthen fort, called Defiance in honor of McIntosh's reply, was built during the War of 1812 from the remains of Fort Morris, and you can explore it by visiting this site. Strolling around the walls of the fort under the majestic oaks towering over it, you have a wonderful view of the Medway and its marshes, and you might even get a glimpse of a shrimp boat trawling in the river. The interpretive center/museum at the site tells the saga of the fort and of Sunbury, the town it was built to protect, and there's also a mile-long nature trail through marsh and scrub oak forest.

The Georgia Department of Natural Resources, which maintains the 70-acre site, offers several special events during the year, including the Independence Day Colonial Faire in July and the "Come and Take It!" reenactment in November. Admission to the site is $4.50 for adults, $4 for seniors, and $3 for youths ages 6–17; entry for children younger than age 6 is free. Fort Morris is open Thurs through Sat 9 a.m. to 5 p.m.

While you're at the interpretive center at Fort Morris State Historic Site, be sure to view the award-winning, 12-minute video, Sunbury Sleeps: The Forgotten Town of Sunbury, Georgia. *This hauntingly beautiful tribute to one of Georgia's "lost towns" serves as the perfect introduction to the next stop on our day trip, the Sunbury Cemetery. The cemetery is a little more than a mile from the entrance to Fort Morris. After leaving the fort, turn right onto Fort Morris Road and keep to your left until you reach Sunbury Road. Turn left onto this dirt road and drive to Dutchmans Cove Road, then take a right and follow this unpaved lane a short distance to the cemetery.*

SUNBURY CEMETERY, Old Sunbury Road, Midway; exploresouthernhistory .com. This small cemetery is all that remains of the once bustling town of Sunbury, which in 1764 had 80 dwellings, three stores, several wharves, and a trio of town squares. By 1773, Sunbury was a seaport beginning to rival Savannah as a place of commerce. That year the town saw 56 vessels clear port as compared with Savannah's 160. Sunbury also had another claim to fame: All three of Georgia's signers of the Declaration of Independence had a connection to the town—Lyman Hall lived there, Button Gwinnett resided on nearby St. Catherines Island, and George Walton was confined there when Sunbury was made a military prison after its capture by the British during the Revolutionary War.

By the end of the war, most of Sunbury had been destroyed, and the town never recovered. There were fewer than eight families living there by 1855, and all evidence of the town eventually disappeared—everything but the cemetery and the 34 grave markers that remain standing. When we visited Fort Morris, we knew when we left that there wouldn't be a great deal to see at the cemetery. But after viewing the Department of Natural Resources video about Sunbury, we felt compelled to take a look and pay our respects, so to speak. Maybe you will, too.

Now it's time to get back on the Historic Liberty Trail and head to the town of Midway. We recommend, though, that while you're on the way, you visit Seabrook Village, which you can find by turning right off Fort Morris Road onto Trade Hill Road.

SEABROOK VILLAGE, 660 Trade Hill Rd., Midway; (912) 884-7008; seabrookvillage .org. This 104-acre site portrays the history and culture of African Americans living in coastal Georgia during 1865 to 1930. Using authentic buildings and displays of artifacts, Seabrook brings that period to life. Among stops on guided and self-guided tours of the village are Bowen's Farm, with its rice fields and a barn containing tools used in farming, gathering oysters, and making turpentine; the Ripley Corn Crib, where corn is ground into grits and meal; the Seabrook School, with its original wooden blackboard and desks made by former student John Stevens; the Gibbons-Woodward House, in which you can see a rural kitchen, a feather bed, and a replica of the original clay chimney; a mill and boiler house where stalks of sugarcane are ground by horsepower and cooked into syrup; the Delegal-Williams House, with its family photographs and local furnishings; and a train depot that was moved to the site from nearby Riceboro.

While you're visiting Seabrook, be sure to see the unusual artwork of Cyrus Bowen, with which he adorned local gravesites. Seabrook is open Tues through Sat 10 a.m. to 4 p.m. Group tours lasting 3 hours and conducted by costumed guides are available, as are 1-hour guided tours in the afternoon. Admission is $10 for adults, $8 for seniors, and $7.50 for children.

Midway was established in 1754 by a group of Congregationalists from Dorchester, South Carolina. Their Midway Society produced governors, cabinet members, US senators and congressmen, numerous ministers, and foreign missionaries. The parish they settled, St. John's, was a hotbed of patriotic fervor during the years leading up to the American Revolution, and two of its residents, Lyman Hall and Button Gwinnett, were among Georgia's three signers of the Declaration of Independence. Clustered just up the road are the Midway Museum, Midway Congregational Church, and the Midway Cemetery.

THE MIDWAY MUSEUM, US 17, Midway; (912) 884-5837; themidwaymuseum.org. This museum gives visitors an idea of what life was like for landowners in coastal Georgia during the late 18th and early 19th centuries. The museum building is an elegant, raised cottage-style house erected in 1957 and based on a sketch made in 1828 of a home in nearby Riceboro. The rooms of the house are filled with original 18th-century furnishings; among the unique items are a walking-cane gun that fired a .45 caliber slug and a set of musical glasses that are played by rubbing vinegar around the rims. A museum staff member will tell you about many of the items in the three first-floor rooms of the house and will play a tune on the glasses; you're free to look at the upper-floor bedrooms and displays in the ground-floor rooms on your own.

This attraction, which is operated by the Midway Museum Board of Governors, is open Tues through Sat 10 a.m. to 4 p.m. Admission, which includes access to nearby Midway Congregational Church, is $6 for adults, $5 for seniors and military, and $3 for youngsters ages 6–17; children younger than age 6 are admitted free.

MIDWAY CONGREGATIONAL CHURCH, US 17, Midway.

Built in 1792, this stately church reflects a style reminiscent of colonial New England (some of the founders of Midway were descendants of Puritans from Massachusetts who had settled in South Carolina). The existing building replaced a church that was burned by the British in 1778. The church is a short walk from the Midway Museum, and you can obtain a key from a museum staff member and take a look inside. The church has no heating system or artificial lights, but services are conducted there each April by the Midway Society. For inquiries and service times, email info@themidwaymuseum.org.

MIDWAY CEMETERY, US 17, Midway.

Researchers believe Midway Cemetery was laid out in the late 1750s and that it contains about 1,200 graves. Among those buried there are James Screven, a brigadier general in the American army who was killed in November 1778 in a skirmish with the British about a mile south of his resting place, and Daniel Stewart, who attained the rank of brigadier after fighting in the Revolutionary and Indian Wars and was the great-grandfather of Theodore Roosevelt. Fort Stewart, the US Army's military reservation at nearby Hinesville, is named after Daniel Stewart. The cemetery is open to the public, and a brochure featuring a map and self-guided tour of the site is available at the Midway Museum for 25 cents.

Midway Cemetery is also the burial site of Louis LeConte, who owned a rice plantation south of Midway where he created a botanical garden of great renown. You can reach the plantation by driving south on US 17 for 3 miles to the Barrington Ferry Road. Turn right onto Barrington Ferry and follow it for 5.5 miles to the entrance to the plantation site.

LECONTE-WOODMANSTON RICE PLANTATION AND BOTANICAL GARDENS, Barrington Ferry Road, Riceboro; (912) 884-6500; leconte-woodmanston.org.

In its heyday during the early 1800s, Woodmanston Plantation covered more than 3,300 acres and was the largest inland rice plantation in Georgia. Louis LeConte came into possession of Woodmanston in 1810, and the garden he planted there gained fame throughout the US and Europe.

The plantation was abandoned in 1869, but a restoration of a 63.8-acre site was begun in the late 1970s as a project of the Garden Club of Georgia. The project, being carried on now by the LeConte-Woodmanston Foundation, is a work in progress that so far has resulted in the creation of a 1.5-acre botanical garden featuring plants that LeConte might have grown and a 1-mile nature trail along a network of rice dams. The garden contains more than 100 different plants, including beds of older varieties of camellias and roses. Several structures that were part of the plantation—a chicken coop, a garden shed, a smokehouse, and a slave cabin—have been re-created on the site. Visitors can also stroll along a path through a 3-acre bog containing flowering plants native to the area and observe rice being grown on 2 acres of wetlands.

The plantation is open to the public Tues through Sun 10 a.m. to 4 p.m. and at other times by prior arrangement, and admission is $5 per person. Because LeConte-Woodmanston is in a somewhat remote spot, you might want to call ahead to the listed number before you visit, and you definitely should call to make arrangements for group tours. Also, be aware that the last 1.6 miles of the drive to the plantation is on dirt roads.

The last attraction on this tour is the Fort Stewart Museum, a military museum just inside the main entrance to Fort Stewart, the huge US Army post at Hinesville. From LeConte-Woodmanston, drive back to the intersection of US 17 and US 84 and head west on US 84 about 7 miles to Hinesville. Turn right onto General Stewart Way, which will take you to the entrance to Fort Stewart. The museum is on the post at the corner of Wilson Boulevard and Frank Cochran Drive.

FORT STEWART MUSEUM, 158 Cavalry Way, Ft. Stewart; (912) 767-7885; stewart .army.mil. Displays at the museum focus on the history of Fort Stewart and its current occupant, the Third Infantry Division (Mechanized). Fort Stewart, now the largest army installation east of the Mississippi River, was established in the summer of 1940 as Camp Stewart and served as an antiaircraft artillery training center during World War II and the Korean War. During the early 1960s, the post was the site of a variety of tests and training by military units, and in the latter half of the decade it served as a training area for Army helicopter pilots.

In the mid-1970s, the 24th Infantry Division (Mechanized) was activated at Fort Stewart, and the unit was based there until April 1996, when the post became the home of the Third Infantry. The story of the Third's service in the two world wars and Korea is related at the museum, portions of which are also devoted to the 24th Infantry and the military history of coastal Georgia. Uniforms, weapons, and other items used by the Third Infantry and their opponents are

on display in the museum, as is a T-72M-1 tank abandoned by Iraqi Republican Guard crewmen in an engagement with the 24th Infantry during the earlier war in the Persian Gulf. There are also exhibits featuring Operation Iraqi Freedom and Audie Murphy, a Third Infantry hero in World War II whose exploits won him the title of "America's Most Decorated Soldier." Outside the museum, you'll find static displays of equipment used in warfare, including an M4A3 Sherman tank, a UH-1 Huey helicopter gunship, and numerous Iraqi artillery pieces and vehicles captured by US forces during the Gulf War. Entry to Fort Stewart is open to civilians, and admission to the museum is free. Hours of operation are Mon through Sat 10 a.m. to 4 p.m. Museumgoers should enter the post via the visitor center at Gate 1 on General Screven Way.

JEKYLL ISLAND

Georgia's coastline is a fascinating and varied one. Savannah, which snugs up to South Carolina, marks its northernmost point. At the southern extremity, up against the Florida line, you'll find St. Mary's, with its access to Cumberland Island National Seashore. And in between you'll find the Golden Isles.

Four islands make up this cluster, accessible from Brunswick, a port and industrial city that retains a small historic district. It is the jumping-off point for the Golden Isles, reachable by causeway with one exception. St. Simons Island is the biggest and most developed of the isles, with beaches, motels, restaurants, and historic sites. Little St. Simons is accessible only by boat and is open to a limited number of guests (by arrangement). Consisting of largely undeveloped beaches and marshlands, this island is a real treat for environmentally minded tourists. Sea Island, largely residential and from a geographical point of view virtually part of

St. Simons, is home to the extremely tony resort known as the Cloister.

Jekyll Island is the southernmost of the four Golden Isles and has the same appeal to the same type of traveler who is attracted to Savannah. You'll find places to eat and sleep there, but development has not destroyed the natural beauty of the island. In fact, the state of Georgia owns the place, and the business and residential ventures there are really long-term leases. However, that policy is changing—in 2007 the state opened part of the island to high-dollar development. Enjoy the beaches (which are all public, at least at the moment) and consider a trip along the extensive network of bike paths a must-do (bike rental places abound; check the lobby of larger motels). Spend the night to enhance your day trip even more. It's a beautiful island and you'll probably hate to leave! Jekyll, like the rest of the Golden Isles, is also covered with golf courses, most of which are accessible to the public at large.

The **Jekyll Island Welcome Center,** 901 Downing Musgrove Pkwy. (912-635-3636, 877-453-5955), and the **Brunswick & the Golden Isles Visitors Bureau,** 4 Glynn Ave., Brunswick (912-265-0366, 800-809-1790), are two general sources that can provide additional information, including lodging details and how to get onto the golf courses. Expect to pay a $6 "parking fee" as you drive onto Jekyll. There's also a website: jekyllisland.com.

To get there, head south on I-95. It takes about 90 minutes. While it's not that long a trip (we know people who commute there from Savannah for work daily, in fact), it can be harrowing. This is the corridor that runs between the Northeast population centers and Florida, and it is always heavily traveled by time-conscious vacationers. Exits are clearly marked.

Jekyll and St. Simons Islands are not accessible from one another—you have to make the trip back to the mainland on the causeway and then take the other causeway to the next island. It's a pleasant drive through the marshes, watching herons and marsh rabbits, but it does take a little time.

St. Simons is a more developed beach community than Jekyll Island, but it has still retained its charm and individual character. There's a large year-round population, and they clearly cherish the winter months when the tourists aren't as prevalent. That doesn't mean visitors aren't welcome; it does mean a quieter pace of life in the winter. There's even a "downtown," a short strip of shops leading to the water and including the usual tourist stuff, an interesting toy store, a bookshop, etc. St. Simons has large, legible signs posted at key intersections, and the names of specific destinations are clearly listed. It's simple to get around on St. Simons. The King and Prince Hotel is a good lodging choice (the selection is rather limited). It's by no means as tony as the Cloister, the region's upscale resort, but they've got the amenities you'd expect in a beachside resort. The island offers multiple restaurant options, predictably leaning toward seafood. The exclusive Cloister Sea Island (seaisland.com/thecloister) resort was built just before the bottom fell out of Wall Street and launched the Great Depression. It has long been a traditional destination of the if-you-have-to-ask-you-can't-afford-it crowd. Not that there aren't bargains to be had: Honeymooners are extended the right to rent rooms on their anniversary at the rate that prevailed at the time of the wedding—so if you meet someone celebrating their 50th, they're in high cotton. The owners tore the whole thing down a couple years ago and rebuilt it, using salvaged materials when possible. The result is a new-that-looks-old resort with stunningly landscaped grounds.

Close-up

Cumberland Island

If you're feeling adventuresome, prepare to unearth one of this country's best-kept secrets, **Cumberland Island.** Travel south on I-95 to FL A1A (exit 373). Turn left at the light at the end of the ramp. Then, follow FL A1A East for 14.8 miles to Centre Street. Turn left onto Centre Street and go to the waterfront. Drop off your passenger and/or luggage to meet the boat captain at Dock 3 next to the "Lucy R. Ferguson" sign on the dock rail. Follow the directions on your parking pass to the parking area, then walk southwest across the train rail to the boat. (The ferry leaves the Fernandina Beach docks at 9:30 a.m., 12:15 and 5:30 p.m. daily.)

Cruising over to Cumberland Island is a treat in itself. Pack a light snack as the ferry ride takes about 45 minutes. As you make your way closer and closer to Cumberland Island National Seashore, you'll enjoy unparalleled views of the south Georgia shoreline. Cumberland Island is approximately 18 miles long and 3 miles wide, and is the nation's largest wilderness island. There are endless smooth, white beaches that stretch the entire length of the eastern shore, oftentimes nearly a mile wide. There are times when you'll hardly meet a soul as you stroll along the beach. Cumberland's dense forest, golden salt marshes, and pristine beaches provide sanctuary to a host of wildlife, including armadillos, bobcats, loggerhead turtles, herons, egrets, alligators, wild horses, turkeys, and hogs. There are still traces remaining of the Native Americans, Spanish missionaries, English soldiers, plantation owners, slaves, freedmen and freedwomen, and Gilded Age industrialists who called the island home over the centuries. Sand dunes are prevalent, and among them arises one of the most luxurious (and private) hotels in existence, the Greyfield Inn, a four-story, 16-room property, which is detailed below.

On the opposite end of the island stand the stately ruins of Dungeness, an original estate built by Thomas and Lucy Carnegie in the late 1800s. Thomas died before Dungeness was completed, leaving behind his wife and nine children. Mrs. Carnegie was a dominant figure on the island. Expanding her husband's initial acquisitions, she eventually owned 90 percent of the island. She initiated renovation of Dungeness and construction of four additional mansions built as island homes for her children. The Greyfield Inn was the home of Lucy R. Ferguson, the daughter of Thomas and Lucy Carnegie. Converted to an inn during 1962, the family still oversees the operation.

Once you arrive on the island, if you haven't booked a room in the idyllic Greyfield Inn (greyfieldinn.com), then you'll at least want to tour this magnificent treasure where John Kennedy and Carolyn Bessette spent their honeymoon in 1996 after getting married in a small historic chapel on the island. Voted one of the top 500 highest-rated hotels by *Travel + Leisure,* you'll feel right at home among the beautiful antiques, candlelit dinners, and comfortable, plush sitting areas. There's no cell phone service here, and don't even try to pick up a Wi-Fi signal. My tip is to purchase Greyfield Inn's "Georgia Golden Isles American Plan Package " that includes round-trip ferry transportation; a single/or double occupancy room (additional guests are $275 per night); all meals (breakfast, lunch, and gourmet dinner); hors d'oeuvres during the nightly cocktail hour; snacks; a naturalist-led tour; unlimited use of sports, fishing, and beach equipment; and parking. Rates are $475 to $635 per night and depend on the room you select for your stay (for one person, all inclusive). A 2-night minimum is required. Call (866) 401-8581 or (904) 261-6408.

JEKYLL ISLAND HISTORIC DISTRICT MUSEUM VISITORS CENTER, Stable Road, Jekyll Island; (912) 635-4036. Georgia was originally founded as a refuge for debtors, but the richest and most powerful men in the US originally developed Jekyll Island. They bought the island in 1886 and made it into a private resort where you need not apply unless your annual income included at least seven figures, all to the left of the decimal point, at a time when that was really a fortune. Names that are synonymous with American fortunes were among the Jekyll Island Club's members: Rockefeller, Gould, Morgan. And they didn't stay in rented quarters, although the club was (and now is again) a fine hotel. Instead, they built "cottages"—mansions that took advantage of beautiful views, cooling breezes, and balmy weather. This was, indeed, the playground of the rich and famous.

Types of tours vary by season. Call for details.

BEAUFORT, SOUTH CAROLINA

Beaufort is situated between Savannah and Charleston, South Carolina, and it exudes much of the charm of those two cities, but on a smaller scale. This town of about 9,500 residents has a historic district filled with elegant homes built in the 1700s and 1800s and a quaint but bustling waterfront shopping district that's brimming with intriguing stores and unique eating places.

The Beaufort area is rich in history. The Spaniards unsuccessfully attempted to found the colony of Santa Elena here in 1559, and French Protestants, led by explorer Jean Ribault in 1562, tried to start a settlement called Charlesfort on what is now Parris Island. It failed, and the Spanish returned to the area in 1566, building a fort, San Phillipe, and the Mission of Santa Elena at Port Royal. According to the Historic Beaufort Foundation, this settlement was, by 1580, one of the largest Spanish towns north of Mexico. It was abandoned in 1586 following attacks on Spanish Florida by the English privateer Sir Francis Drake.

The English laid claim to the area in the 1600s and by the turn of the next century had established a foothold at Port Royal. Beaufort was founded in 1711, and in the years leading up to the American Revolution, local planters turned profits by growing rice and indigo. During the Revolutionary War, residents of the area were sharply divided over the issue of independence from Britain and allegiance to the crown. British forces occupied Beaufort in July 1779 but evacuated later in the year. Cotton planting was introduced to the area after the Revolution. Subsequent crops made rich men and women of many of Beaufort's citizens in the years leading up to the Civil War. Early in the conflict, in November 1861, South Carolina's Sea Islands were invaded by Union forces, and Beaufort and the Port Royal area fell into Federal hands. Beaufort became the main base of Union squadrons blockading the South Atlantic. During the Union occupation, the first school for freedmen, which eventually became Penn School, was established east of Beaufort on St. Helena Island.

Beaufort is about 55 minutes from downtown Savannah by car. To get there, take Oglethorpe Avenue west and drive across the Eugene Talmadge Memorial Bridge on US 17 into South Carolina. It's 5 miles from the bridge to the intersection of US 17 and Alternate SC 170; turn right onto Alternate SC 170 and stay on it for 6 miles, where it becomes SC 170 (also SC 46). Continue 3 miles to where SC 170 leaves SC 46. Turn left onto SC 170 and enjoy the scenery—a narrow, two-lane road shrouded by the moss-covered branches of gnarled oaks. Take a good look, because this area might not be heavily forested for much longer; civilization and the developers of subdivisions and shopping centers appear to be taking over.

You'll be on SC 170 for about 20 miles, which will take you into the outskirts of Beaufort. While on SC 170, you'll pass country roads with fascinating-sounding names such as Bulltomb, Bufflehead, Heffalump, Old Bailey's, Crippled Oak, Bellinger Bluff, and Mudbar, and you'll catch glimpses of marshland and open water. You'll cross the picturesque Chechessee River, drive through relatively pristine Lemon Island, and then find yourself marveling at the majestic expanse of the aptly named Broad River, which is spanned by a bridge that's 1.4 miles long.

SC 170 will lead you to US 21 South (also known in these parts as Boundary Street); turn right onto US 21 and stay on it for a mile until you reach the traffic light at Ribaut Road. Turn right onto Ribaut Road and drive to the third stoplight, then turn left onto Bay Street, which will take you about a mile past stately homes and a bay dotted with sailboats and into Beaufort's waterfront district.

The focal points of this area are Bay Street, which is lined on either side with shops and restaurants, and Henry C. Chambers Waterfront Park, a pleasant, tree-filled swath of greenery lying south of Bay Street. The park, with its wide walkways, swinging benches, and elaborate children's playground, is a wonderful place for strolling or sitting and catching a breeze off the nearby water. Several of the restaurants that dot the south side of Bay Street open onto patios and porches that offer outdoor dining on the fringes of the park. Among these eating places are **Saltus River Grill** at 802 Bay St., which specializes in seafood; **Plum's** at 904 Bay St., which is known for its gourmet soups, salads, sandwiches, and homemade ice cream; and **Panini's Cafe** at 926 Bay St., which features pasta, pizza, hoagies, and, of course, panini-style sandwiches.

The stores along Bay Street and on the narrow lanes running to the north off Bay provide a plethora of shopping opportunities. There are several galleries; a unique one is the **Rhett Gallery** at 901 Bay St. In addition to selling prints and paintings, this gallery offers antique maps and nautical charts and Civil War art and artifacts, including pages from *Harper's Weekly* and *Frank Leslie's Illustrated Newspaper*. Specialty shops you might want to visit include the Craftseller, at 818 Bay St., which deals in local and regional arts and crafts, and the Cat's Meow Shoppe, a gift shop on Bay Street that caters to collectors of all things feline. If you're looking for books, stop in at McIntosh Book Shoppe in the refurbished Old Bay Market Place at 917 Bay St. It has a good inventory that features books related to the region, and a large selection of rare, out-of-print editions.

Those in search of history will find it throughout town in general and in two locations in particular:

i While visiting Beaufort, consider taking a side trip to nearby Penn Center, a 50-acre National Historic Landmark District on St. Helena Island. Penn Center is the site of Penn School, one of the most significant African-American institutions in the US and an active community center. The mission of the center is to preserve the history, culture, and environment of the Sea Islands. You can get there by taking US 21 east from Beaufort to St. Helena Island and turning right onto Martin Luther King Jr. Drive.

BEAUFORT MUSEUM, 713 Craven St., Beaufort, SC; (843) 522-2665; beaufort historymuseum.com. Housed in an arsenal that was completed in 1798, the museum tells the story of Beaufort's history through its exhibits and displays of artifacts.

Among the exhibits are those involving the Native Americans who lived in the area, the European colonization of the region, the development of the town in the era prior to the Civil War, the Union occupation during that conflict, and early-20th-century industries.

The museum has been situated in the arsenal since 1939 as the result of a WPA project to add a wing for a museum and relic room. The building was the site of National Guard musters until 1966, and it was acquired by the city of Beaufort in 1990 for the continued purpose of preserving the town's heritage and that of the surrounding Sea Islands. Hours are Mon through Sat 9 a.m. to 5 p.m., Sun 1 to 5 p.m. Admission for adults is $5, $4 for seniors, and children age 10 and younger are admitted free.

JOHN MARK VERDIER HOUSE MUSEUM, 801 Bay St., Beaufort, SC; (843) 379-3331.
Built in the late 1790s by one of the town's leading merchants, the two-story frame house rests on a tabby foundation and is an example of the Federal style of architecture. Interior features are the paneled reception parlor, first-floor dining room, graceful staircase, and spacious second-floor drawing room. The decor and furnishings reflect those of the period from 1790 until 1825.

The house was condemned in 1942, but public-spirited citizens spearheaded a drive to save the structure, and a restoration effort was begun in the fall of 1975. It was completed a year later. The house is open to viewing Mon through Sat 10 a.m. to 4 p.m. Admission is $6 for adults and $4 for students.

THE POINT. You can see more of Beaufort's elegant old houses—their exteriors, at least—by visiting an area called the Point, which is east of Bay Street. This oak-filled section of town is not large and doesn't take long to drive through, but it's abundantly graced with what the local historic foundation calls "Beaufort-style" homes. According to the Historic Beaufort Foundation, these homes were "designed for airiness and coolness" and "incorporated elements of Georgian and colonial architecture as well as those of Greek Revival and semitropical Spanish." The foundation's guidebook states that the Beaufort-style home "differs from the more urban designs of Charleston and Savannah in that the Beaufort house is freestanding on a large lot, frequently with a formal garden, and is oriented to take full advantage of the prevailing southwesterly breezes. It more nearly resembles the plantation house, brought to town, as some indeed were, and adapted to the summer heat and the dampness of the Lowcountry."

A wonderful way to view these homes and the rest of Beaufort's Historic District is on foot on your own; you can pick up free maps of the area at many of the downtown shops and at the visitor center, which is at the intersection of Congress and Carteret Streets. If you're looking for something that's a little more structured, there are numerous tours available, including those provided by appointment by the **Point Tours** at 1002-B Bay St. (800-979-3370) and by **Carolina Buggy Tours** (843-525-1300); **Spirit of Old Beaufort,** which conducts walking and van tours (843-525-0459); and **Southurn Rose Buggy Tours** (843-524-2900). **John Sharp** (843-575-5775) provides a spookier look at Beaufort, with a lantern-lit narrative conducted in the graveyard of St. Helena's church.

HILTON HEAD,
SOUTH CAROLINA

Hilton Head Island, a lush playground for wealthy individuals—many who own second homes there—is also a popular destination for visitors from all over the US. This is the South's answer to the tropics and, by all appearances, it's an island that was bred for fun! The foot-shaped barrier island is located off the Atlantic coast of South Carolina, approximately 45 miles north of Savannah, 90 miles south of Charleston, South Carolina, and 30 miles south of historic Beaufort, South Carolina. The island—12 miles long and 5 miles wide—was the first "eco-planned" destination in the US. What does that mean? To the average onlooker who is trucking onto the island with a mini-van filled with kids, luggage, and beach gear, it means that this is a place that has been delicately preserved, where nature has collided with man in a pleasant sort of way. It's a place where you can bring your kids to escape the world of video games and opt to spend afternoons together trekking through the island on foot or bike. There are no high-rise buildings or commercial, touristy strips. Billboards are few, and even the common places that you know (like Publix, Outback, and TJ Maxx) blend discreetly into the serene natural flora. Indeed, the developers of this island are to be commended! Hilton Head can be the perfect day trip, or better yet, the perfect place for an extended vacation. If you choose to drive over for the day, you might find yourself booking a private home, villa, or condo for a longer return visit! There are simply too many things to do here, and to do them well and enjoy the ride, one must commit to a few days, at the very least. If you're coming for the week, you'll be sad when the checkout day arrives.

HISTORY

In contrast to Savannah, most of the structures on Hilton Head are about 60 years old, the result of two momentous events in the island's history that occurred in the mid-1950s. One was the opening of a set of two bridges connecting the 42-square-mile sea island with the South Carolina mainland. The other was the start of the Sea Pines residential/resort community by a southeast Georgian named Charles Fraser.

"The opening of the bridge had a major impact on development," states Porter M. Thompson in the book *Hilton Head Island Images.* "Suddenly building materials, equipment and people were able to come and go freely—Hilton Head had lost its isolation and a new era had begun."

Sea Pines, in its basic form a residential area built around a golf course, set the tone for the other planned communities that would be created on Hilton Head and spurred the development of the island as a mecca for retirees and vacationers. Back in the early 1950s, Hilton Head was home to about 100 families, "little more than a quiet community of farmers and shrimpers," as author Richard Rutt put it in *Hilton Head Island: A Perspective*. Now the island—with its natural assets of marshes, wide creeks, hardwood forests, and 12 miles of beach—is the site of planned communities harboring a multitude of stylish homes and upscale condominiums known locally as villas. Hilton Head boasts 30 beautifully manicured golf courses, 300 tennis courts, 8 marinas, several large hotels, a bevy of villa-style resorts and midsize hotels and motels, more than 250 restaurants, and 36 shopping areas with more than 200 shops. Permanent residents now number approximately 39,000, many of them engaged in satisfying the needs of visitors, of whom there are 2.5 million annually, according to the island's chamber of commerce.

All this growth has occurred in a manner that places an emphasis on preserving Hilton Head's natural surroundings: live oaks, magnolias, pines, palmettos, and other flora. Following ideas originally credited to Fraser, most islanders continue to adhere to the concept that buildings must blend in with the environment and that the development is as unobtrusive as possible.

Although Hilton Head's modern era begins in the 1950s, the island's recorded history goes back considerably further—to the 1500s, when Spaniards and Frenchmen visited while exploring the area bordering Port Royal Sound, the large bay on Hilton Head's north shore that's one of the world's finest natural harbors. The Spanish and French fought over the sound for almost 50 years, with the Spaniards triumphing but never settling the area. That was left to the British, who in 1717 were responsible for the island's first English-speaking settler, John Barnwell.

Englishmen had been in the area well before that, however. In 1663 sea captain William Hilton sailed into the sound and came upon the island. He spotted a headland on the northeastern end and named it after himself. As time went on, the entire island came to be called by the name of this promontory, Hilton Head.

The settlers who came to Hilton Head in the 1700s eventually planted the land in cotton, indigo, sugarcane, rice, and other crops. They purchased slaves brought to North America from Africa and used them to create large plantations. According to Richard Rutt, there were 24 plantations on the island by 1860, most of them producing cotton. Also by that time, South Carolina was on the verge of seceding from the Union and leading the South into the Civil War, a conflict in which Hilton Head would play an interesting part.

The island was invaded by Union troops on November 7, 1861, 7 months after the war began, in an effort to control Port Royal Sound and establish a portion of the blockade of the Confederacy's Atlantic coast. In the Battle of Port Royal, a Union fleet of 15 warships and 31 transports and supply ships exchanged shots with 4 Confederate gunboats and 2 forts, one of them on Hilton Head. The Confederate guns were silenced, the forts were evacuated, and Union forces took possession of the island and held it until the end of the war.

The area near the fort on Hilton Head—called Fort Walker by the Southerners and renamed Fort Welles by its Federal conquerors—became a town during the Union occupation, when the population of Hilton Head mushroomed to 40,000. "Enlisted personnel—both soldiers and sailors—constituted the bulk of that population, or, 23–30,000 men," Rutt stated in his book. "The balance of Hilton Head's wartime population consisted primarily of freedmen who sought refuge on the island, civilian dependents, and Yankee tradesmen. The latter opened and operated a variety of business establishments, ranging from hotels, blacksmith shops, and theaters to photography studios, tattoo parlors, and bordellos."

The main street of the town, which was located in what is now Port Royal Plantation, was named Sutler's Row after the merchants who lined it. The military men who paid exorbitant prices for the sutlers' goods called it Robber's Row, the name now borne by one of the plantation's golf courses. Another settlement sprang up in what is now Hilton Head Plantation. It was called Mitchelville and consisted mostly of tents and barracks housing freed slaves who had fled to the island. When the war ended, the military and the sutlers left and, said Rutt, "the shops and houses of Robber's Row and Mitchelville rapidly disappeared from the island, no doubt torn down by freedmen seeking to build homes of their own."

From the end of the Civil War until the middle of the 20th century, Hilton Head was a sleepy sea island largely bypassed and forgotten by the rest of the world. All that began to change in 1950, when Fred Hack, C. C. Stebbins, and Lt. Gen. Joseph B. Fraser bought 8,000 acres of pine forest and formed the Hilton Head Company for the purpose of selectively cutting the pines. In 1956 the company's holdings were divided, with Fraser acquiring 4,000 acres on the southern end of the island. A year later Fraser's son Charles, a University of Georgia and Yale Law School graduate in his 20s, bought his family's holdings and another 1,200 acres and started planning and developing Sea Pines.

Meanwhile, Hack and O. T. McIntosh, who had purchased 12,000 acres on the northern end of the island in the early 1950s, began work on their own developments: Spanish Wells Plantation and Port Royal Plantation. (Sea Pines also used the term *plantation* in its name in its early years, as have many of the planned communities on the island; it refers to the antebellum plantations once located on the sites of the communities.)

"These few men," wrote Porter Thompson in referring to Fraser, Hack, McIntosh, and other developers, "began with the idea that large holdings of land could be subdivided into lots and sold for residential purposes. There was a twist to this. Hilton Head is ideally suited by climate and location for resort activity, so the communities developed would have to accommodate both resort and residential activities. Charles Fraser is largely credited with first developing the concept that a resort/residential community could be successful, if a few considerations were made. He embodied two excellent and highly compatible interests: the understanding of development and a love of nature and of the natural beauty of the island."

Under Fraser's direction, Sea Pines became, in the words of the Associated Press, "a big-time leisure landmark, a model for resort playgrounds and planned communities from Virginia to the Philippines." Other developers followed his lead, creating their own planned communities and, in the process, transforming Hilton Head into the world-renowned resort that it is today.

Note that the island is virtually "built out" today. Just about the only vacant land is that set aside for green spaces, so new construction generally requires demolition of something that's already there. This has led to upscale development spilling off the island and onto the mainland, in the form of gated "plantation" housing, golf courses, and shopping centers. Although this Hilton Head "sprawl" is well outside the actual Bluffton, this area is called Bluffton.

TRAVEL INSTRUCTIONS & RESOURCES

Some people arrive at Hilton Head Island by boat or fly directly onto the island, but if you're like most visitors, you'll be coming by car, either from home in your own vehicle or from the Savannah/Hilton Head International Airport in a rental. Whatever the case, here's how to get to the island.

By Car

Getting to Hilton Head by car is fairly simple because there's only one road onto the island, US 278, a four-lane that runs west to east through the South Carolina Lowcountry. Finding US 278 is easy, particularly if you're arriving at the airport in Savannah and renting a car for the 40-minute drive to the island (you can find information on flights to Savannah and car rentals in our main Getting Here, Getting Around chapter). US 278 is also easy to get to if you're coming from the south or north on I-95, or if you're arriving from the west via I-16 and I-95.

US 278 intersects I-95 just north of Hardeeville, South Carolina, so once you're on the interstate, all you have to do is watch for the exit for US 278 (exit 8). Take that exit and head east; it's an 18-mile straight shot to Hilton Head. You'll be on the island in 20 minutes and at the middle of it in about a half hour. To get to I-95 from Savannah/Hilton Head International Airport, take Airways Avenue west for a little more than a mile to the interstate. Get on I-95 and head north into South Carolina. The US 278 exit is 16.5 miles up the interstate from where you left Airways Avenue.

If you're visiting Savannah and succumb to the temptation to venture over to Hilton Head for the day or to spend a night on the island, you can drive there by following the I-95/US 278 route just discussed, or you can go the "back way." If you take the I-95/US 278 route, you'll be on multilane highways, and it will take about an hour and five minutes for you to get from Savannah City Hall to the Hilton Head Island Chamber of Commerce building at the middle of the island. (To

get to I-95 from City Hall, drive west on Bay Street through three traffic lights to Martin Luther King Jr. Boulevard, turn left onto MLK, and head south three traffic lights to the entrance ramp to I-16, then take I-16 west for 8.5 miles to I-95.)

The back way is shorter (about 55 minutes from City Hall to the middle of Hilton Head), more scenic, and a little more complicated. It involves traveling on roads that are under construction. If you want to try it, take Oglethorpe Avenue west to the Eugene Talmadge Memorial Bridge and drive north across the Savannah River into South Carolina. You'll be on US 17 for 5 miles from the South Carolina side of the bridge to the intersection of US 17 and Alternate SC 170. Turn right onto Alternate SC 170 and stay on it for 6 miles, where it merges with SC 46. Continue east on SC 46 for 12 miles to US 278. Turn right onto US 278 and head east—you'll be on the island in about 5 minutes. Along your way on SC 46 to US 278, you'll pass through piney woods, hardwood swamps, and the laid-back, offbeat little town of Bluffton with its Squat & Gobble restaurant (worth a stop for lunch and whimsy) and 30 mph speed limit (be sure to observe it). While in Bluffton, you'll come to a four-way stop; turn left to stay on SC 46. This route is an area of active, almost exponential, development, so you will be sharing the road with cement mixers and lumber trucks. Be careful and on your first trip; it's a good idea to plan to travel in daylight.

By Boat

If you're going to Hilton Head by boat, you can get there via the Intracoastal Waterway, which runs along the west side of the island; however, please utilize the resources of a map or ask at the marina for specifics. There are several public marinas and harbors where you can tie up and enjoy your stay while aboard your vessel. These include **Harbour Town Yacht Basin at Sea Pines** (843-363-8335; seapines.com), **Hilton Head Harbor RV Resort and Marina** at Intracoastal Waterway mile marker 20 (843-681-3256), **Palmetto Bay Marina** at 86 Helmsman Way (843-785-3910), **Shelter Cove Marina** at Shelter Cove (843-842-7001), **Skull Creek Marina** at Hilton Head Plantation (843-681-8436), and **Windmill Harbour** (843-681-9235). The length of the slips available at Windmill Harbour marina ranges from 25 to 70 feet, and the cost per night for docking runs from $1.90 per foot for boats under 50 feet, to $2.25 for boats over 50 feet. Call ahead for specific details for this and other marinas as prices change.

By Plane

Hilton Head has its own airport on the north end of the island. The Hilton Head Airport is on Beach City Road, which runs north off US 278, the island's main drag. Beach City Road is at mile marker 4 on US 278, and the entrance to the airport is about a mile from US 278. There is a fixed-base operator across the runway from the airport terminal that can accommodate private planes. The FBO is on Gateway Circle off Dillon Road less than a mile north of US 278.

HILTON HEAD AIRPORT, 120 Beach City Rd.; (843) 255-2950; hiltonheadairport .com. Hilton Head's airport has an up-to-date, spacious terminal that is served by two commercial carriers, as of spring 2010 (remember, air travel is a volatile business and things change a lot). The longest established there is US Airways Express (800-428-4322). US Airways Express offers 8 to 14 flights each day to and from Charlotte, North Carolina, and direct flights to and from Washington, DC, on weekends. Delta Connection (843-342-5380) offers three departures daily.

Six rental-car agencies maintain desks at the airport: Avis Rent A Car (843-681-4216,

888-897-8448), Budget Rent A Car (843-689-3737, 800-527-7000), Enterprise (843-689-9910), Hertz Rent A Car (843-681-7604, 800-654-3131), National Car Rental (843-681-7367, 800-CAR-RENT), and Thrifty Car Rental (843-689-9990, 800-847-4389). There are nine taxicab and shuttle services operating from the airport.

GETTING AROUND

I recall driving onto Hilton Head Island for the very first time. With visions of a "beach town," dancing in my visor-shaded head, I remember asking my husband time and time again when I would first see the ocean? Expecting a Daytona-like setting where high-rise hotels and condos sit right on the sand, all of which is within eyesight of the main drag, I learned that the beach itself is not within plain view. The beach is, in fact, hardly seen until you check into your oceanside hotel or villa. The main road to Hilton Head (US 278) cuts the island in parts, but it is far from scenic. Once you get to your destination, more than likely, you're within a bike ride or short walk to the strand.

The best way to get on to Hilton Head is by car, and in some cases, the car is your best way to get around once you're there. Where you're staying and where you're going will dictate whether you should drive or ride a bike. Taxi and limousine services are available; however, the surest and less costly way to assure your stay in Hilton Head is pleasurable is to rent a car.

Driving on the Island

Finding your way around Hilton Head is fairly easy, but actually finding the places you're looking for can be a challenge. At first glance that statement might not make much sense, but consider this: Most of what a visitor would be looking for can be found on or very near three main roads (US 278, Pope

Avenue, and South Forest Beach Drive), but spotting a specific restaurant, shop, or motel can be difficult because of town regulations limiting signage and promoting natural beauty. Businesses are not allowed to have signs off the premises, and the signs they do have must conform to strict rules involving size and lighting. These regulations, combined with the emphasis on preserving trees and foliage and having buildings blend in, can make it easy for you to drive right past your intended destination. This is particularly true when it comes to the island's main thoroughfare, US 278, a busy four-lane divided highway also known as the William Hilton Parkway. Most everything is set back off the road on tree-lined side streets that often resemble driveways; pay close attention as you cruise along the island.

William Hilton Parkway. Once you cross the Karl S. Bowers and J. Wilton Graves Bridges to Hilton Head on US 278, you're on William Hilton Parkway, which runs east for 5 miles to the northern end of the island, then bends south and continues 6 miles to Sea Pines Circle. This 11-mile stretch passes restaurants, motels, shopping centers, other businesses, and the entrances to resort communities such as Hilton Head Plantation, Port Royal, Palmetto Dunes, and Shipyard.

To aid motorists, the town has placed mile markers along the parkway, with the lower-numbered markers closer to the bridges and the higher-numbered ones closer to the traffic circle. In some write-ups on businesses on the parkway, we've included a mention of the mile marker nearest the business being discussed.

Sea Pines Circle. When you enter this traffic circle from William Hilton Parkway, you'll encounter exits to the Cross Island Parkway one-quarter of the way around, Greenwood Drive halfway around, and Pope Avenue

three-quarters of the way around. Greenwood Drive is the main road leading into the Sea Pines Resort community. The stretch of the Cross Island Parkway directly west of the circle, also known as Palmetto Bay Road, was widened into a four-lane highway in 1997.

Pope Avenue. Pope Avenue runs east a tad more than a mile from Sea Pines Circle to Coligny Circle. On Pope, you'll find a variety of restaurants, stores, shopping plazas, another entrance to Shipyard, and the entrance to the public parking lot at Forest Beach.

Coligny Circle. The Coligny traffic circle is practically on Forest Beach, and it routes motorists from Pope Avenue to South Forest Beach Drive (one-quarter of the way around the circle) and North Forest Beach Drive (three-quarters of the way around). North Forest Beach Drive is residential and leads to many of the older vacation homes and permanent residences on the island; short side streets run east to the beach, but access is private and public parking is a no-no.

South Forest Beach Drive. There are several resorts and restaurants along South Forest Beach Drive, which leads to another entrance to Sea Pines. Access to the beach via the side streets is private unless marked otherwise.

Cross Island Parkway. The Cross Island Parkway, a four-lane toll road that bypasses the southern portion of William Hilton Parkway and alleviates traffic congestion on that heavily traveled thoroughfare, opened in January 1998. The 6-mile, limited-access highway stretches from near the intersection of William Hilton Parkway and Spanish Wells Road, at mile marker 2 in the northwestern portion of the island, to Sea Pines Circle. Part of the Cross Island Parkway is a 65-foot-high bridge that crosses Broad Creek at Palmetto Bay. The toll for riding the length of the parkway (one-way) is $1.25 at the plaza and $1 at the ramp for cash customers. Each additional axle is $1 (plaza and ramps) for trucks and $3.25 for five-axle trucks.

Biking on the Island

Hilton Head has some 50 miles of paved public bicycle paths, and there are many more miles of paths within the island's resort communities. Among the public paths are those that run along William Hilton Parkway from Gumtree Road (just past mile marker 2) to Sea Pines Circle for 9 miles, along both sides of Pope Avenue from Sea Pines Circle to Coligny Circle for a total of 2 miles, along North Forest Beach Drive from Coligny Circle to the end of North Forest for 1.3 miles, along South Forest Beach Drive from Coligny Circle to Sea Pines' Ocean Gate for 1.4 miles, along the Cordillo Parkway from South Forest Beach Drive to Pope Avenue for 1.1 miles, and to the Folly Field Beach Park (see the Public Beach Access and Parking section in this chapter) from William Hilton Parkway for 0.8 mile. A 3.5-mile path along Gumtree and Squire Pope Roads in the northwestern part of the island was completed in 1998, as were a 1-mile stretch on Point Comfort Road and 1.1 miles of pathway on Arrow Road in the southern portion of the island. Also open for riding are a 2.2-mile path along Beach City Road and the wider paths along North and South Beach Drives.

You can make arrangements to rent a bike through the resort where you're staying or by calling one of the more than 20 bike rental outlets that can be found in the Yellow Pages of the local telephone directory. In season, expect to pay $25 to rent a bike for a week and $9.50 to $12 for a day.

Taxis & Limousines

In addition to the taxicab and limousine companies that serve the Hilton Head Airport, there are several other limo operators on the island, including Camelot Limousine (843-842-7777).

Taxi rates are not regulated by the city of Hilton Head and vary from company to company and point to point. To find out how much a trip will cost, tell the dispatcher where you are and where you're going and ask what the fee will be

Bus Service

The island is served by the buses of **Beaufort County's Lowcountry Regional Transportation Authority** (LRTA), but this public transportation service is mainly a means of getting working people from towns on the mainland on and off Hilton Head. These buses serve Hilton Head in the early morning and in the late afternoon, meaning the LRTA is not a means of conveniently getting around the island throughout the day. However, there is a limited-demand response system through which riders can schedule transportation by calling (843) 757-5782.

Public Beach Access & Parking

All beach access points, with the exception of Burke's Beach, are ADA approved. In addition, public restroom facilities are available at each beach access point or nearby community park. As far as parking on the rest of the island goes, there is an abundance of parking in the lots of restaurants, shopping centers, motels, and other commercial establishments, much of it shaded by trees, which can be a blessing in the summer months.

Alder Lane Beach Access. This access point is on South Forest Beach Drive. Metered parking for the access is on Woodward

Avenue, which is across South Forest Beach Drive from Alder Lane.

ℹ️ The city of Hilton Head asks that visitors help safeguard the island's flora and fauna by, among other things, staying off sand dunes and refraining from picking dune plants, feeding dolphins, or tampering with turtles' nests.

Burke's Beach Access. This access is at the end of Burke's Beach Road, which runs off of William Hilton Parkway between mile markers 6 and 7.

Coligny Beach Park. The access at Coligny Circle offers about 30 metered spaces and a parking lot with about 350 spaces.

Driessen Beach Park. Located at the end of Bradley Beach Road, which intersects William Hilton Parkway just past mile marker 6, this access is about a half mile from the parkway.

Folly Field Beach Park. This access is on Starfish Drive, which runs off Folly Field Road. Folly Field Road also runs into William Hilton Parkway at mile marker 6; it's a little more than a half mile from the parkway to the access.

SOURCES OF INFORMATION

HILTON HEAD ISLAND WELCOME CENTER, exit 8 off I-95 at 524 Independence Blvd., Hardeeville, SC; (843) 784-6333; hiltonheadislandwelcomecenter.com. Located at Exit 8 off of I-95 in Hardeeville, South Carolina, the new Hilton Head Island Welcome Center is open 7 days a week 10 a.m. to 7 p.m. and offers visitor services and information about vacationing on Hilton Head Island, along with maps, brochures, and opportunities for area attractions, golf, fishing, and accommodations. There is a

reception area with wide-screen televisions featuring Hilton Head Island activities, comfortable seating areas, a large lighted island map showing directions to major attractions and accommodations, and clean, oversize restrooms.

Pinckney Island National Wildlife Refuge

Travelers intent on hiking, bicycling, and observing wildlife will find a pleasing venue in the form of the **Pinckney Island National Wildlife Refuge,** located off US 278 a mile west of Hilton Head Island. The refuge offers more than 14 miles of trails and accommodates large concentrations of wading birds and an active bald eagle nest. Pinckney Island, the largest land mass in the refuge and the only one open to the public, covers 1,200 acres. Admission is free. The refuge is open every day; however, it is recommended that you exit prior to nightfall.

ACCOMMODATIONS

When you vacation at Hilton Head, you have the option of staying at hotels, motels, villas, or private homes that are being rented out by their owners. I prefer the villa rental or selecting hotels with kitchen suites. The costs are comparable with hotels, but on the downside you'll have to purchase your own staples as opposed to hotels where you'll receive daily maid service and have access to on-site eateries and restaurants. Another upside of condo rental is that they are more spacious than standard hotel rooms. You'll get more for your money, and there are literally hundreds of condos for rent, even if you're on a budget. The hotels and motels range from modern, well-maintained establishments on the island's main thoroughfares to full-blown resorts situated in or adjacent to Hilton Head's luxurious golf communities. The villas are fully furnished condominiums set in apartment buildings and town houses, many of them with pools and locations close to beaches, golf clubs, and tennis courts.

There's plenty to choose from—Hilton Head has more than 3,000 hotel and motel rooms, 6,000 villa units, 1,000 time-share units, and an array of rental homes ranging from oceanfront mansions to laid-back cottages. Here's a rundown of hotels and motels—places that offer nightly accommodations; for information on villas, time-shares, and private homes, which usually rent for longer-term stays (anywhere from 3 nights to 2 weeks), we suggest calling one of the island's numerous central reservations services. Among these are the **Hilton Head Condo Hotline** (843-785-2939, 800-258-5852), **Hilton Head Accommodations and Golf Hotline** (843-686-6662, 800-444-4772; hiltonheadusa.com), and **Hilton Head Vacation Rentals** (843-689-3010, 800-476-4485).

In general, rates for accommodations are higher from the end of April through September, although some places raise their prices starting in February, and others lower them after Labor Day. Call ahead to see what's available (well ahead if you're planning on staying during the summer, especially on weekends) and ask about special deals—many of the larger establishments have a variety of vacation packages from which to choose. Be aware that some motels and hotels will give you a lower rate if you stay with them early in the week when they might be struggling to fill up their rooms.

Most of the hotels and motels surveyed don't allow pets and have nonsmoking and wheelchair-accessible rooms; exceptions are noted.

Price Code

We have included a dollar-sign code with each entry denoting a price range for the average one-night stay, in season, for two adults. These prices do not include tax, gratuities, and add-on amenities such as room service.

$. . . . . less than $100
$$ . . . . $100 to $120
$$$ . . . . $120 to $175
$$$$ . . . . $175 to $225
$$$$$ . . . . more than $225

Unless we've indicated otherwise, you'll have to pay to play golf or tennis at the resort where you're staying. Most places have packages or special deals involving these sports, and you should inquire about these if you intend to play. The following properties are listed alphabetically.

BEACH HOUSE ON HILTON HEAD BY HOLIDAY INN RESORT, 1 S. Forest Beach Dr.; (844) 993-9730, (855) 474-2882; wbeachhousehhi.com; $$$. A view of the Atlantic Ocean from poolside is a plus at this moderately priced oceanfront hotel. This family-friendly spot also accepts pets, and kids eat free at the on-site restaurants. The contemporary decor of the inn's 202 rooms (all of which have refrigerators and open onto interior hallways) carry out the beach motif, as do the five-story motel's eating and drinking places which include the Porch, a southern kitchen and bar open 7 a.m. to 10 p.m. and the Shack, serving poolside bites and beverages.

The inn offers numerous recreational activities, some of them free and many intended for the younger set. A children's program that runs from Memorial Day to Labor Day provides kids with activities such as relays on the beach, sand-dollar painting, and underwater treasure hunts. The inn also has a children's pool, kids' playground, and Dolly the Dolphin, a mascot who greets guests and interacts with youngsters. The hotel is near several restaurants, including Antonio's Italian Cuisine, an island favorite!

COMFORT INN SOUTH FOREST BEACH, 2 Tanglewood Dr., (843) 842-6662, (800) 522-3224; choicehotels.com; $$. The Comfort Inn South Forest Beach is a convenient and inexpensive place to stay that is also pet-friendly and five minutes (by foot) from the beach. The five-story hotel is a comfortable, clean, and pleasant place to stay. There is a nice pool on the premises and many activities (such as a water park) within walking distance.

The 153-room hotel is situated on 6 acres graced by three lagoons and sits well back from South Forest Beach Drive, a block from the Coligny traffic circle. Guests can partake of deluxe complimentary continental breakfasts 7 to 10 a.m. in the registration building, which also houses 900 square feet of meeting space. Some of the rooms have refrigerators and microwave ovens, and there's a store (Bi-Lo grocery store) nearby where you can purchase food items. Golf packages are available.

DAYS INN, 9 Marina Side Dr.; (843) 842-4800, (800) 329-2613; daysinn.com; $. An older and more serene place to stay for families on a budget, the Days Inn offers 14 suites with a nice touch—French doors separating the bedroom from the large sitting room. The other 105 rooms at the three-story motel off US 278 just past mile marker 9 have king-size and double beds, and there is a small pool and fitness center. Guests in quest of another form of recreation might opt to play the adjacent Pirates Island miniature golf course. The Days Inn is centrally located and near a slew of restaurants and shops.

Harbour Town Lighthouse

The Harbour Town Lighthouse, Hilton Head's most enduring symbol, stands 93 feet tall and is visited by a quarter-million people a year. The observation deck perches 66 feet above the base floor of the lighthouse on Calibogue Sound, and you reach it by climbing 114 steps. Completed in 1970, the lighthouse was the first one built on the Atlantic coast in more than 150 years. Flashing a white light every 2.5 seconds, it's a navigational aid for the sound and the Intracoastal Waterway, even though it's not operated by the US government. (It's run by the company that owns Harbour Town.) The structure is open daily 10 a.m. to 9 p.m., and there's a $1 fee to tour it, which is highly recommended. The views will be etched in your fondest vacation memories. Learn more at (866) 305-9814, harbourtownlighthouse.com.

HAMPTON INN, 1 Dillon Rd.; (843) 681-7900, (800) HAMPTON; $$. If you're not particularly interested in going to the beach, the Hampton Inn might be for you. This two-story, 121-room motel just off US 278 at mile marker 5 caters to business travelers and people visiting the island for the golf of it. And if you do desire to take a dip in the ocean, the Atlantic is only a little more than a mile away at the Folly Field Beach access. There's an outdoor pool for those who want to stay close by to do their swimming, an indoor putting green, and a small but well-equipped exercise room for the fitness minded. The Hampton Inn, like all other Hampton Inns, offers deluxe, complimentary continental breakfasts 6 to 10 a.m. and free copies of *USA Today*. Some of the rooms have kitchenettes with microwave ovens and small refrigerators, and some have whirlpool baths. Ask for the family suite where a special children's room is connected to a king suite. A special feature of the Hampton is the "afternoon snack" of fresh-baked cookies.

HILTON HEAD MARRIOTT RESORT & SPA, 1 Hotel Circle; (843) 686-8400, (800) 228-9290; marriotthiltonhead.com; $$$$$. If you're searching for a nice hotel that's right on the ocean and in the midst of lots of family activities, the Hilton Head Marriott is an excellent choice, and the views of the Atlantic Ocean are spectacular. Situated within Palmetto Dunes resort, this hotel stands 10 stories high and is the largest oceanfront resort between Atlantic City, New Jersey, and Palm Beach, Florida. The property is overflowing with lush foliage, offering guests a tropical feel wherever they stroll. Boasting spacious and updated rooms (there are 513), this is also a popular place for group meetings with 46,000 square feet of meeting space.

There's an abundance of dining options within the Marriott's premises. Poolside, guests will find the Ocean Blu Restaurant, a great place to order sandwiches, wraps, salads, and tropical drinks during the day. In the evening, Ocean Blu turns elegant-casual as the sun begins to set. From hazelnut-crusted sea bass to pan-seared fresh sword-fish, this is a convenient and fun place to dine without ever leaving the property. For indoor dining, there's the Cafe for break-fast (fresh fruit, traditional eggs and bacon, oatmeal, yogurt, and muffins), lunch (an excellent selection of low-carb options are offered), and dinner (burgers and sand-wiches), and Conroy's for dinner and Sun-day brunch. Conroy's Lounge overlooks the ocean and offers nightly entertainment, named for the author Pat Conroy, who

is a nearby resident. Try the jumbo lump crab cakes, a specialty. If you're in need of snacks, try the Grocery, an offbeat little convenience store on the hotel's lower level. Other shopping opportunities are found at the Coastal Coffee Boutique. If you crave exercise, you can work out in the Marriott's well-equipped fitness center, play a round of golf at one of five courses within walking or shuttle distance, or hit the courts at the Palmetto Dunes Tennis Center. Be sure to ask about bike rentals at the hotel and enjoy the miles of trails within Palmetto Dunes.

INN AT HARBOUR TOWN, 7 Lighthouse Ln.; (843) 363-8100, (800) 732-7463; seapines.com; $$$$. As you check into your room at the Inn at Harbour Town, you'll feel special—there to greet you is a personal handwritten letter along with chocolates in a gold box. At this instant, you'll become one of many who will probably return due to the service at this hotel. Although there are 60 rooms, butlers will serve you throughout the day, doing most anything you ask. From bringing you drinks and sandwiches to see-ing that business papers are mailed, shoes are shined, and pants are pressed, these "services" are only a part of the delights of this inn. There are Anichini Egyptian-cotton linens and duvet covers, complimentary shoe shine service, iPod docking stations, granite vanities, Molton Brown toiletries, plush robes, and complimentary newspa-pers, for starters. Some rooms offer fabulous views of the Harbour Town Golf Links, and others open on to the beautiful palms and tropical landscaping. The butlers, some of them wearing Scottish attire in keeping with Harbour Town's Highlands heritage, are a big part of the concept of patterning the Inn at Harbour Town after small, fine European hotels. Make sure you save time to enjoy the plush furnishings in the Player's Library where you can read, catch up on business, or enjoy a sporting event on the large wide-screen TV.

The inn also has much to offer in the way of recreation. The hotel overlooks the first tee of the famed Harbour Town Golf Links, and the Sea Pines Racquet Club is a short stroll from the front door. Guests have access to the pool next to the Racquet Club and can take advantage of a complimentary shuttle service that will take them anywhere in Sea Pines at any time of day.

The inn serves a continental breakfast 7 to 11 a.m., and offers 24-hour room service. There are lots of restaurants nearby, including the Harbour Town Grill and the eateries at the Harbour Town yacht basin. The inn is a AAA Four-Diamond resort.

MAIN STREET INN AND SPA, 2200 Main St.; (843) 681-3001, (800) 471-3001; mainstreet.com; $$$$. Emulating a fine European hotel, the Main Street Inn is indeed a delightful retreat in the midst of a modern-day island destination, just off US 278 between mile markers 3 and 4. Elegance abounds in this inn. There are rich (and comfortable) furnishings, antique accents, fresh floral arrangements, a grand piano, and beautiful heart-pine floors. In short, it's a captivating place to stay. The Royal Queen Suite is bright and cheery with an iron bed and gold-framed artwork perfect for a couple seeking a spot for a romantic getaway. The Deluxe Queen rooms have fireplaces and balconies large enough for a wrought-iron table that's a perfect spot for breakfast.

The additional 33 rooms are luxuriously appointed with classic furnishings: wooden armoires handmade on Hilton Head; beds adorned with Italian linens, goose-down pillows, and comforters; and baths featuring pedestal sinks and Italian marble floors and shower walls. The inn's crowning glories are the four Courtyard King rooms with their whirlpool tubs, glassed-in showers, and

pine floors fashioned from the 150-year-old beams of a Lowcountry mill. In some Kings, French doors in the bathroom open onto an intimate courtyard abounding with fig vines, fruit trees, and jasmine. Guests staying in rooms on the upper two floors can step outside onto wide verandas complete with rocking chairs. From there, you'll see the Charleston-style gardens of the courtyard and an inviting pool designed for swimming laps; the view beyond is of the lush 15th green and 16th fairway of Hilton Head Plantation's Bear Creek Golf Course and of the forested wetlands of a nature preserve.

Your stay includes buffet breakfasts with eggs, bacon, fresh fruit, and pastries served 7:30 to 10:30 a.m. in the dining room/library, the dining room/lounge, or the courtyard. If all this isn't relaxing enough, try a massage, which is available on-site. For a firsthand look, the website offers a virtual tour of all rooms and exterior gardens.

OMNI HILTON OCEANFRONT RESORT, 23 Ocean Ln.; (843) 842-8000, (800) 845-8001; hiltonheadhilton.com; $$$$$. Try the tropics with a Southern accent. The Omni Hilton Oceanfront Resort, which just had a $17 million rejuvenation, combines the best of both worlds for a spectacular holiday on the ocean. Oversize guest rooms decorated in traditional Southern themes (shades of green, wooden accents, striped fabrics) are designed to give you a "beach house" feel with all the amenities of a luxury hotel, including full mini-kitchens, private balconies, wireless Internet service, and in-room safes. Open hallways are tranquil with flowing ocean breezes, and a maze of lagoons winding their way through the flourishing greenery give this beachfront Hilton Hotel at Palmetto Dunes a semitropical aura. The extra-large rooms have equally spacious balconies, each with at least a partial view of the beach and sea. All 296 rooms have ceiling fans in dining areas and separate vanities in bathrooms. Oceanfront suites offer the same amenities, only with 1,000 square feet of space and a separate bedroom, living and dining rooms, and extra-spacious balconies that overlook the beach. The five-story hotel is built in a horseshoe shape that opens onto the beach, and the nooks and crannies of the spacious garden within the horseshoe feature small courtyards, rambling wooden decks, and plenty of seating for quiet afternoons spent reading or napping.

Dining options are abundant here. For a fun and casual oceanfront cafe, try the Buoy Bar. There are fun tropical-themed drinks galore, artfully presented chilled salads, outstanding burgers, and an unspoiled view of the ocean! The Palmetto Market is new and boasts a trendy, luxurious atmosphere. This is where you'll dine for breakfast, lunch, and dinner. There's an adults-only pool for those seeking a quieter atmosphere. For more relaxation, try one of the two oceanfront whirlpool baths or the variety of services at the spa. With kayaking so popular on the island, the Hilton offers 10 miles of lagoons. When the day is over, schedule a treatment at the spa (843-341-8056). The Coastal Cabana Massage is performed in a private cabana beside the ocean. The 50- to 80-minute treatment is available for singles or couples. Call for rates.

The hotel offers special rates for golf and tennis at the courses and courts at Palmetto Dunes, and special activities for children via Seaside Adventures Club.

PARK LANE HOTEL, 12 Park Ln.; (843) 686-5700; hiltonheadparklanehotel .com; $$$. This hotel lies in the Central Park office complex just off US 278 between mile markers 9 and 10, convenient to area businesses and in the midst of Hilton Head's shopping and business district. Each of the 156 "Carolina-decorated" suites has a fully equipped kitchen with granite countertops (including a full-size refrigerator), fireplaces (in some), and trendy loft suites that are perfect for lengthier stays or for hosting guests. The lofts boast an enlarged dining area, a sleeper sofa, and a bedroom with its own bathroom. Take note: There are no dining options here so you'll need to come prepared with your own staples.

THE RAMADA HILTON HEAD, 200 Museum St.; (800) 345-2995; m.ramada .com; $. Located on the rapidly developing north end of the island, the Ramada boasts many of the features you might expect to find at a full-service hotel, along with a modern, clean look that complements Hilton Head's building ordinances. The hotel blends in discreetly with the environment and offers travelers a less expensive way to sample Hilton Head. Among the amenities here are an outdoor pool, a putting green, 2,000 square feet of meeting space, and same-day valet, laundry, and dry-cleaning service.

SONESTA RESORT HILTON HEAD ISLAND, 130 Shipyard Dr.; (843) 842-2400; sonesta.com/hiltonheadisland; $$$$$. Set on 11 acres, this beautifully landscaped family-friendly resort is a beachfront AAA-approved Four Diamond hotel. The Sonesta recently completed a $30 million renovation that highlights an elaborate swimming pool complex, spa, casual and fine dining, on-site bike rentals, and convenient access to world-class golf and tennis.

SOUTH BEACH MARINA INN, 232 S. Sea Pines Dr.; (843) 671-6498, (800) 367-3909; sbinn.com; $$$. Called South Beach due to its location at the southern tip of Hilton Head Island, the inn is small and rustic and decorated in the spirit of New England. In fact, were it not for the distinctly Southern foliage and marshlands within view, you might imagine that you are, in fact, in New England. The charming, 17-room hotel is part of a small complex of shops and restaurants patterned after a fishing village on Nantucket Island, Massachusetts. The rooms of the inn, a nightly rental property at Sea Pines, reflect the Yankee atmosphere via the highly polished heart-pine floors, brass beds, and colorful rag rugs.

All of the one- and two-bedroom accommodations have kitchenettes, and most have separate, cozy living rooms that will make you feel as if you've found a second home. Although the inn is deep within Sea Pines, the village and marina offer just about everything a vacationer would need. You could park your car and not leave, except to play a round of golf on the nearest course, which is a 5-minute drive. At your front door is the marina on Braddock's Cove, which offers various recreational opportunities for hire—boat rentals, charter fishing, parasailing, kayaking, and windsurfing. Also, just outside your doorstep, you will find a pool, a dozen tennis courts, and 15 miles of paved trails for hiking, bicycling, jogging, and in-line skating. You can walk to the beach in 3 to 4 minutes, and there are six restaurants within the village. All rooms are on the second floor; there are no wheelchair-accessible accommodations.

WESTIN RESORT HILTON HEAD, 2 Grasslawn Ave.; (843) 681-4000, (800) WESTIN1; westinhiltonhead.com; $$$$$. A recent $30 million renovation has freshened this property. The architecture of the sprawling Westin radiates the charm of a classic, turn-of-the-20th-century seaside hotel and is designed to complement the historic cities of Savannah and Charleston. A feeling of Southern hospitality carries throughout the five-story oceanfront hotel at Port Royal Plantation. The lobby features polished woods, palms,

elaborate chandeliers, and Asian porcelains, coastal-inspired color palettes, and a mix of comfortable seating offers an ambience characteristic of the homes of the Old South. The Gazebo Lounge looks out on the hotel's spacious courtyard, where swans swim in a pond set amid lush foliage. In the cooler months, the lounge and its comfy drawing-room furniture and wood-burning fireplace beckon to guests. When the weather's warm, the courtyard is the place to be. You'll find three pools and extensive wooden decks where you can sunbathe and have a bite to eat at calypso-themed Turtles Beach Bar & Grill or Turtles Poolside, where you'll get in the island spirit with tropical drinks and Caribbean fare (and even a massage by the pool if you like). There are pools galore, including an outdoor heated pool, a main outdoor pool, an outdoor whirlpool, and an indoor pool with a hydraulic lift for the physically impaired. Take advantage of the Westin Workout, powered by Reebok Gym.

Those seeking outdoor recreation can find it at the nearby Port Royal Golf Club, which has three championship courses, or at the Port Royal Racquet Club, which offers grass, clay, and hard-surface courts. A shuttle service is provided from the hotel to both sites. The hotel features six restaurants, from fine dining to poolside.

RESTAURANTS

Just as Hilton Head's resplendent image of gleaming white beaches, live oaks dripping with moss, and colorful flora convince you to spend a vacation here, come with the knowledge that this is an island that also shines for connoisseurs of fine cuisine. There are outdoor cafes set amid a backdrop of the dunes. There are restaurants rich in ambience. There are open-air seafood eateries on the rims of marinas, and yes, bakeries that will lure you with promises of sumptuous pastries. So save room for tempting dining options. Note that smoking is banned in all bars and restaurants in Hilton Head.

All restaurants listed (in alphabetical order) take most major credit cards.

Price Code

You can expect restaurants to be more expensive on Hilton Head Island than in Savannah. The price code is based on the cost of an average meal for two, excluding drinks, dessert, or tip.

$. . . . . less than $30
$$ . . . . $30 to $50
$$$ . . . . more than $50

ALEXANDER'S, 76 Queens Folly Rd.; (843) 785-4999; alexandersrestaurant .com; $$–$$$. Located on a lagoon at Palmetto Dunes, Alexander's invites a business-casual dress code in three splendid settings: a delightful, enclosed porch with magnificent lagoon views, an alluring wine bar with a fireplace, and a friendly dining room replete with a variety of tropical plants that accentuate a fine collection of vintage Harleys. This restaurant will fast become one of your vacation highlights. Enticing entrees include roasted Mediterranean chicken, crab cakes, and shrimp and grits. This is just a small sample of some of the over-the-top specialties. There are more than 100 selected wines from which to choose, and dinner starts at 5 p.m. nightly. Hours are 5 to 10 p.m. Reservations are suggested.

BIG BAMBOO CAFE, Coligny Plaza, 1 N. Forest Beach Dr., Ste. 210; (843) 686-3443; bigbamboocafe.com; $. Owners of this establishment might be accused of packaging all the fun you can think of having into one cool place. For starters, there's live music several times a week (check the

website for details). Then, there's the decor that may take you by surprise. According to the legend of the Big Bamboo, which appears on the front of the cafe's menu, this restaurant on the ocean side of Coligny Plaza shopping center has been constructed as closely as possible to the configurations of the original Big Bamboo, a bar and grill opened on the Pacific island of Tarawa in 1944 by ex–fighter pilot Jimmy Phipps. From the bamboo of the bar to the thatched palm fronds and camouflage netting of the ceiling to the World War II regalia tacked on the walls, Hilton Head's version of the Big Bamboo reflects the feel of the real thing—if there had been a real thing, that is. You see, the Big Bamboo of the Pacific is a figment of the imagination of a former owner, albeit one that has been brought vividly to life on Hilton Head.

What is real about this 85-seat dining room and bar is the food, featuring salads, seafood, burgers and ribs. Hours are Mon through Sat 11:30 a.m. to 2 a.m.

The Sweet Stuff

Make this bakery a sure stop when your sweet-tooth attacks. **Signe's Heaven Bound Bakery & Cafe** at 93 Arrow Rd. is indeed one of Hilton Head Island's main attractions. The mouthwatering creations are the truly angelic pastries and other goodies, such as the banana nut bread and the key lime pound cake, but Signe's also serves breakfasts, salads, and hot and cold sandwiches. There's seating inside or on the outdoor deck and a long list of loyal fans cheering, "Just like heaven." Give them a call at (866) 807-4463.

CHARLIE'S L'ETOILE VERTE, 8 New Orleans Rd.; (843) 785-9277; charlies greenstar.com; $$–$$$. If you're looking for a restaurant that has colorful character, fine cuisine created with the freshest ingredients, the charm of Europe, and a staff that locals know and love, Charlie's L'Etoile Verte fits the bill. And if you ask any islander where to eat on Hilton Head, the first word out of his or her mouth is more than likely to be "Charlie's." This busy bistro near Sea Pines Circle serves lunch Mon through Fri 11:30 a.m. to 2 p.m. and dinner 5:30 to 9 p.m.; Sat is dinner only, 5:30 to 9 p.m. Charlie's is billed as a "French kitchen" (*l'etoile verte* means "green star" in French), but this eclectic-looking cafe serves, as its affable owner Charlie Golson puts it, "whatever we feel like cooking"—"we" being Golson and his son, Palmer, the entre chef. They put their heads together and brainstorm during the day, a process that creates a menu that's different each night, written in longhand, and copied for distribution to diners.

Served cafe-style on linen covered tables with fresh flower sprays, among the most popular selections are the chicken salad, cobb salad, rack of lamb, pompano with mango sauce, and triggerfish in Parmesan crust. The Carolina red trout (with horseradish beurre blanc) is also tasty. Charlie's specializes in more than a dozen types of fish cooked in many ways.

CQ'S RESTAURANT, 140 Lighthouse Rd.; (843) 671-2779; cqsrestaurant.com; $$$. CQ's is a story and then an experience before it is a restaurant. As the first structure built with careful environmental forethought within Harbour Town, the restaurant was originally designed by Ralph Ballantine in 1970 for his studio. A transplant of Chicago and a recognized advertising illustrator, Ballantine's work includes illustrations of the Jolly Green Giant and the "good hands" of

Allstate, as well as the bull of Schlitz Malt Liquor fame. The restaurant was built from several materials from different Lowcountry buildings, i.e., roof beams from an old Savannah house and flooring from a Jasper County church. Modeled after a local rice barn, the two-story building also includes spindles from the staircase that reportedly once graced the interior of a house of ill repute in Savannah. Originally called Bal's Place, (a name for the studio), the building evolved into a restaurant at the urging of Bal's friend, "Sig" Winehandle, and the establishment is named after Sig's son, Courtney Quentin. Today each dining room reflects a name that is representative of its heritage. There's the Plantation Room, the Heritage Room, the Cotton Room, the Rice Room, and the Indigo Room.

Many of the dishes are American Southern, and among the featured entrees are the venison, lobster pasta, and crab cakes. There's also an extensive wine menu. CQ's has outdoor seating on a deck. Reservations are highly recommended at this well-known establishment, which serves dinner 7 days a week. Hours are daily 5 to 9:30 p.m.

THE CRAZY CRAB, 104 William Hilton Pkwy.; (843) 681-5021; thecrazycrab.com; $$–$$$. Colorful and festive, Hilton Head Island's two Crazy Crab restaurants serve fresh seafood and steaks in a rustic wharfside surrounding offering splendid views of the water. At the Crazy Crab on the William Hilton Parkway near mile marker 1, the view is of picturesque Jarvis Creek and its marsh. The other Crazy Crab is among the shops alongside the **Harbour Town Yacht Basin in Sea Pines** (Lighthouse Road, 843-363-2722), overlooking the scenic marina. The menus at both restaurants are the same, with the mainstays being the fried shrimp and the steamed seafood pot, which consists of half a Maine lobster, crab legs, shrimp, and oysters. They are open for lunch and dinner 7 days a week 11:30 a.m. to 10 p.m.

HILTON HEAD BREWING COMPANY, 7-C Greenwood Dr.; (843) 785-3900; hhbrew ingco.com; $.

Billed as South Carolina's first brewpub since Prohibition and the only one on the island, this establishment in Hilton Head Plaza just off the Sea Pines traffic circle always has five handcrafted beers ready for drinking: South Atlantic Pale Ale, Calibogue Amber, Old Duck Dark, Raspberry Wheat, and a seasonal brew. Although the pub takes on the atmosphere of a bar late at night, the restaurant offers casual dining for families at lunch and during the evening. Watching the turtles, ducks, and geese in the pond outside the pub's enclosed porch will keep the kids entertained. The menu yields a large variety of choices, including hand-tossed pizzas, burgers, steaks, huge sandwiches, and their award-winning chicken wings. Hours are Mon through Fri 4 p.m. to 2 a.m., Sat and Sun 11:30 a.m. to 2 a.m.

i It was once said that one shouldn't consume an oyster unless the month of consumption had the letter r in it. South Georgians and South Carolinians bank on this. You won't find many of us eating oysters in May, for instance. This is, however, folklore, and the rumor mill was probably born in the days when there wasn't adequate refrigeration and much spoilage resulted. So no matter what month it is, although there are always risks in eating raw shellfish, enjoy your "or-sters," as we jokingly call them.

HUDSON'S ON THE DOCKS, 1 Hudson Rd.; (843) 681-2772; hudsonsonthedocks .com; $–$$.

The emphasis at Hudson's—a fixture on the Hilton Head restaurant scene since 1967—is on fresh seafood, much of it caught locally, including shrimp hauled in on the boats you might see tied at the docks just outside. The vessels and Skull Creek can be viewed from the main dining room, one of three at the 335-seat restaurant, which also has an oyster bar. Forty percent of Hudson's business involves shrimp—fried, steamed, or boiled—but the steamed oysters, scallops, and crab cakes (made with 100 percent lump backfin meat) are also big sellers. As you might expect, the dining rooms at Hudson's have a nautical look, and the tables and the oyster bar are made from shrimp-boat doors, the wooden pieces of equipment used in trawling.

The Oyster Factory Dining Room occupies the site of an oyster processing plant built in 1912 and bought by J. B. Hudson in the 1920s. The Hudson family added shrimp to the processing operation in the mid-1950s and opened the restaurant with 95 seats in the latter half of the 1960s. Brian and Gloria Carmines purchased Hudson's in 1975 and have expanded it since then.

Hudson's serves lunch and dinner daily 11 a.m. to 9 p.m.

KENNY B'S FRENCH QUARTER CAFE, 70-A Circle BiLo Center; (843) 785-3315; eatatkennybs.com; $.

Kenny B's brings a touch of the Quarter to Hilton Head at its eatery in the BiLo shopping plaza at the intersection of Pope Avenue and Cordillo Parkway. The cuisine is Creole with some Lowcountry tweaking, and murals, ceiling fans, and lampposts create a Big Easy atmosphere. Entrees lend to the aura—there's crawfish parade; voodoo pasta, which features seafood over penne; and Taste of the Bayou, a medley of N'awlins favorites (gumbo, jambalaya, red beans and rice, and shrimp étouffée). Drop by Kenny B's daily for breakfast, lunch, or dinner. Hours are Sun 8 a.m. to 8 p.m. and Tues through Sat 8:30 a.m. to 9 p.m.

MARLEY'S ISLAND GRILLE, 35 Office Park Rd.; (843) 686-5800; marleyshhi .com; $. The food is as colorful and tasty as the atmosphere is fun at Marley's Island Grille. With indoor or outdoor dining, the festive atmosphere is enhanced with theatrics from the tropics as chefs prepare your dinner in the restaurant's open kitchen. If you watch, you'll marvel as they toss, chop, and create masterful culinary creations from the wood-fired grill and steaming kettles. As the reggae plays, your fresh shellfish— shrimp, mussels, clams, or a combination of all three—will merge with ingredients like traditional tomato sauce, an island curry, the house ale, and Old Bay, or in a broth of garlic butter and sherry. Try one of these other intriguing-sounding seafood dishes: tortilla-crusted tilapia, sesame-seared yellowfin tuna, or voodoo-spiced swordfish. From the wood grill, there are the red chili–rubbed flank steak, Havana cabana chicken, and Australian rock lobster. Marley's is famous for its drink selections. Check the website or call for live entertainment schedule. Hours are Sun through Thurs 4 to 10 p.m., Fri and Sat 4 to 11 p.m.

OLD FORT PUB, 65 Skull Creek Dr.; (843) 681-2386; oldfortpub.com; $$$. If you're looking for a romantic setting for a meal, your search ends at the Old Fort Pub. Set on a bluff along Skull Creek amid a tangle of live oaks, this restaurant offers evening-time diners candlelight, classical music, a rustic Lowcountry atmosphere, and spectacular sunsets over a creek and its marsh. There are great views of the water from the first-floor dining room, bar, and outdoor deck that get even better as you ascend to the second-floor Sunset Room and the rooftop widow's walk, a wooden deck reached via a cast-iron spiral staircase. Up there in the treetops, you'll find an ideal place for small cocktail parties, marriage proposals, and wedding ceremonies.

Old Fort Pub serves Lowcountry cuisine for dinner 7 days a week and offers brunch on Sun; reservations are a must in the evenings and should be made 3 to 4 days in advance. The dinner menu includes dishes such as Atlantic salmon, wild shrimp and pasta, and Sea Island bouillabaisse.

While you're at Old Fort Pub, which was built in 1974 in a style inspired by the architecture of the Lowcountry, take time to stroll around the remains of Fort Mitchel, a Civil War gun battery on the site adjacent to the restaurant. Pathways wind through what were once the bunkers and moats of a fortification constructed by the Union army after it captured the island in November 1861.

THE OLD OYSTER FACTORY, 101 Marshland Rd.; (843) 681-6040; oldoyster factory.com; $$. With its floor-to-ceiling windows, this multilevel restaurant offers splendid views of beautiful Broad Creek and the adjacent marsh from its 270 seats. Built of pegged timbers on the site of one of Hilton Head's oyster canneries and opened in 1989, the restaurant serves steaks and seafood, including oysters from surrounding waters prepared several different ways. At times you can view small family boats cruising by, continuing the tradition of shrimping that started generations ago. Shrimp is part of one of the restaurant's big sellers—the seafood medley, which also consists of scallops, oysters, and choice fish fillets. Another popular dish is the salmon *en croute* (in pastry), but you'll have to ask your server about it—it's not on the menu. The Old Oyster Factory is open for dinner daily and provides live entertainment on the dock from May through Sept. Hours are 4:45 to 10 p.m.

REILLEY'S GRILL AND BAR, 7-D Greenwood Dr.; (843) 842-4414; reilleyshilton head.com; $. The laid-back atmosphere of the Reilley's in Hilton Head Plaza on

Greenwood Drive is what you'd expect from a restaurant that has a deck once called the "Barmuda Triangle." First-class rustic, this is a restaurant that could double as a Boston bar. With dining that is indoors or outdoors, locals have labeled it "an institution." Reilley's menu, adorned with shamrocks and leprechauns, lists a wide variety of offerings including several variations of Blarney Burgers and Super Sandwiches. If you're in the mood for a dinner, flip to the Longtime Favorites section, where you'll find steaks and a couple of dishes suited to Gaelic tastes—the corned beef and cabbage and the cottage pie, which is ground chuck seasoned with mushrooms and onions and topped with peas, homemade mashed potatoes, and cheddar cheese.

Reilley's takes credit for organizing the island's first St. Patrick's Day parade, a celebration started in 1983, the year after the restaurant opened in the Gallery of Shops. In 1995 the restaurant moved to its existing location in Hilton Head Plaza just south of the Sea Pines traffic circle. Reilley's serves lunch and dinner daily and offers a champagne-and-eggs brunch on Sat and Sun. The menu and atmosphere are much the same at the Reilley's at Port Royal Plaza on Mathews Drive (843-681-4153), but there's no deck.

SAGE ROOM, 81 Pope Ave.; (843) 785-5352; thesageroom.com; $$$. Although the Sage Room nestles in one of the least-conspicuous locations of any restaurant on the island, that hasn't kept locals from flocking there. And if you make the effort to find it, you'll see why. Contemporary with shiny stainless accents, white linen tablecloths with black accents, this restaurant is an experience in behind-the-scenes food prep. The chefs work in an open kitchen, turning out a variety of dishes featuring seafood, fowl, and steak, plus Colorado rack of lamb and roasted pork tenderloin. Appetizers include some you won't encounter often—butternut squash soup, and the snow-pea martini (sautéed snow peas with a pineapple soy reduction). Hours are Mon through Sat 6 to 10 p.m.

SANTA FE CAFE, 700 Plantation Center; (843) 785-3838; sssantafehhi.com, $$–$$$. A delightful rooftop cantina is one of the highlights of the Santa Fe Cafe. With whitewashed adobe walls (inside and out), fireplaces, and tiled floors, this is a place for quiet conversation and fresh, authentic southwestern cuisine. Owner and chef Jim Buckingham spent his younger days in the Southwest, and he brings his appreciation for that region to his cooking. The upscale southwestern cuisine of his Santa Fe Cafe is spicy food based on many types of chiles, resulting in dishes such as grilled pork tenderloin with smoked habanero barbecue sauce, black beans, and sweet potato fries; herb-roasted free-range chicken with jalapeño corn-bread stuffing and roasted-garlic mashed potatoes; and grouper with chipotle (smoked chile) Parmesan au gratin. After several years of operating a limited chain of Mexican restaurants, Buckingham decided to concentrate his efforts on one establishment and in 1993 opened this cafe off William Hilton Parkway near mile marker 8. The stylishly southwestern Santa Fe serves dinner 7 nights a week (5 to 10 p.m.) and lunch Mon through Fri (noon to 2 p.m.); reservations are accepted.

STEAMERS SEAFOOD COMPANY, Coligny Plaza, 1 N. Forest Beach Dr., Ste. 28; (843) 785-2070; steamersseafood.com. $$. With a pleasant outdoor deck and live entertainment 7 nights a week, Steamers has become a Hilton Head tradition since 1991. Boasting an island decor, this reasonably priced eatery has grown its beer selection to 250 beers from around the world. That coupled with fresh fish, shrimp, lobster tails, and certified Angus beef makes it one of the locals' favorite places to dine. For shellfish lovers, there's a platter consisting of steamed oysters, clams, shrimp, crawfish, mussels, and snow crab. Barn and dock wood and corrugated tin on the walls and bars complete the pier-side look, and there's also a 70-seat raw bar for fans of steamed and raw seafood.

Hours are Mon through Sun 11:30 a.m. to 10:30 p.m.

STELLINI ITALIAN RESTAURANT, Executive Park, 15 Pope Ave.; (843) 785-7006; stellinihh.com; $$. This "little star" of an Italian restaurant shines forth from a wooded nook off Pope Avenue. Owner Joe Pesce and his partners have created the comfortable look of the Little Italy section of New York City at Stellini. Especially inviting is the 40-seat Carolina Room, a porch with views of the surrounding forest. The restaurant also has a main dining room for 50. The menu provides an extensive selection of northern Italian fare, including chicken pancetta, a chicken breast sautéed in a light cream sauce with pancetta bacon and broccoli over angel-hair pasta; veal Sorrento, medallions of veal sautéed in white wine topped with eggplant and melted mozzarella cheese in marinara sauce over angel hair; and zuppa di pesce, clams, shrimp, scallops, mussels, calamari, and grouper in marinara over linguine. One item you won't find on the menu is a special that's offered often: the veal chop stuffed with prosciutto and mozzarella. Pesce suggests making reservations to dine at Stellini, which opened in 1988.

THE TAPAS RESTAURANT, 11 Northridge Plaza; (843) 681-8590; $$. Ever wanted to try something a companion is eating but felt self-conscious taking it from him or her? When you dine at the Tapas, such behavior is not only acceptable, it's expected. Tapas are appetizers in Spanish cuisine, and the small dishes served at this cozy, elegant bistro in Northridge Plaza off William Hilton Parkway between mile markers 4 and 5 are perfect for sharing. Don't be overwhelmed when you see the menu of more than 50 items. Each colorful presentation is prepared on small plates, almost like an appetizer, so treat each dish as it is an appetizer. For instance, if you're dining with three other people and each of you orders three different selections, you may be tasting up to 12 different dishes. A word of warning if you've never dined at a tapas restaurant: Keep a mental tally of the meal as you go along so the final bill won't be shocking.

Among the dishes you might try are the veal Antonia (tenderloin of veal sautéed with garlic and mushrooms deglazed with sherry), and lobster seafood cake, served with sweet potato french fries and tangerine-balsamic drizzle. The Tapas, although housed in a shopping center, has surprising ambience. The ceiling is filled with a multitude of hanging wicker baskets, which makes it feel a little like being outside. The 56-seat restaurant is open for lunch Mon through Fri, and for dinner nightly; reservations are strongly suggested. Hours are Mon through Fri 11:30 a.m. to 2 p.m. and 5 to 9 p.m.; Sat and Sun 5 to 9 p.m.

TRUFFLES CAFE, 71 Lighthouse Rd.; (843) 671-6136; trufflescafe.com; $. Islander Price Beall has owned and operated this casually elegant restaurant (and two other similar ones) since 1983. With seating for 150, Truffles is larger than the typical cafe but retains the atmosphere of a bistro. It is jovial, and there are linen-covered tables and island artwork on the walls. The food is American in style, with specialties like chicken potpie made with fresh vegetables (broccoli, carrot, mushroom, sweet bell pepper) in white wine sauce and pasta New Orleans—a chicken breast served over pasta tossed with a spicy cream sauce. Other favorites of regular customers are the ribs, grilled fish, pasta dishes, and Caesar and Monterey salads, both of which feature grilled chicken. Lunch and dinner are served daily. Hours are 11:30 a.m. to 10 p.m.

Feel Free to Pig Out

If you need a bite to eat while traveling the "back way" to or from Hilton Head Island, consider stopping at the **Pink Pig** restaurant (843-784-3635) on Alternate SC 170 at a crossroads identified as Levy. This shockingly pink cinder-block eatery specializes in barbecue. You'll chuckle when you enter the front door to pink pigs hanging from all directions! You can't miss the place. Just look for the pigs on the simple one-story building on your right and come hungry.

ENTERTAINMENT

Arts & Culture

Hilton Head has for years radiated a vibrant cultural presence. Some 20 community groups—ranging from the Hilton Head Art League to the Hilton Head Orchestra—foster and promote an appreciation of the visual and performing arts. The community created a new artistic resource, the Arts Center of Coastal Carolina, which has become the cultural hub of the island.

ARTS CENTER OF COASTAL CARO-LINA, 14 Shelter Cove Ln.; (843) 686-3945; artshhi.com. A big-city facility on a resort island, this $10 million visual and performing arts center offers theatrical productions, performances by musicians and dancers, art shows, education programs, and community-service programs.

Each year the center's 350-seat Elizabeth Wallace Theater hosts up to six productions. Among previous presentations were *Say Goodnight, Gracie*, a one-man Broadway show; and *Bjorn Again: The Abba Experience*. Check the website for current events. The theater complex has dressing and costume rooms and a green room. A rehearsal hall has seating for 150.

The center brings islanders a series featuring local talent and regional and national touring companies. Six to eight art shows are exhibited annually in the center's 2,300-square-foot Walter Greer Gallery, which has 12-foot-high ceilings and flexible lighting for showcasing art. Through its education program, the center cosponsors residencies by professional artists in area schools and brings children on field trips to the center for performances. The center also offers services and assistance to artists and art groups from throughout the island, providing technical support and space for a variety of organizations.

The center further serves the island by presenting free events such as the Community Christmas Tree Lighting, Family Fiesta Latina, Youth ArtsFest, and Gullah-Fest. For tickets to individual events, call or visit the website.

HILTON HEAD ART LEAGUE, 106 Cordillo Pkwy.; (843) 681-5060; artleaguehhi.com. As part of its mission to provide artists with opportunities to hone their skills and exhibit their works, the Hilton Head Art League presents "minishows" every 4 weeks at its gallery in the Pineland Station shopping complex. Each of these exhibits features the work of a league member, and each opens with an evening reception. The league sponsors two major art shows annually at the Walter Greer Gallery of the Arts Center of Coastal Carolina. One of the shows is juried, and the event attracts more than 700 entries from throughout the Southeast. The league also presents workshops that attract nationally known artists from throughout the US (call 800-995-4068 for information). The Hilton Head Art League was started in 1972 by a handful of local artists. Today there are more than 950 members, 250 of whom are artists.

HILTON HEAD ORCHESTRA, 2 Park Ln.; (843) 842-2055; hhorchestra.org. The 70-piece Hilton Head Orchestra presents a 10-concert Monday Master Series, a 5-concert Sunday Series, and several special events, and sponsors a youth orchestra and international piano competition. About 40 percent of the musicians are from the local area, with the others traveling from Southern cities such as Savannah; Charleston, South Carolina; and Jacksonville, Florida, to participate in performances. Concerts are held at the First Presbyterian Church at 540 William Hilton Pkwy. The orchestra was founded in the winter of 1982 by a handful of local musicians who incorporated the organization as the Hilton Head Chamber Orchestra later in the year. The name was changed to Hilton Head Community Orchestra in 1983; 6 years later, it became the Hilton Head Orchestra. The Hilton Head Youth Orchestra was organized in 1996. The Hilton Head Island International Piano Competition was also started in 1996. The competition is held early in Mar at the First Presbyterian Church. About 150 pianists apply, with 24 selected as quarter-finalists.

Nightlife

Hilton Head is a resort that caters to families who are on the go throughout the day and to golfers with early-morning tee times, so it's not exactly a hotbed of nightlife activity.

Evenings are mostly spent with a good book, a family round of Monopoly, or ample porch sitting. If you're visiting, you might find yourself actually searching for late-night venues and maybe even commenting about how sleepy the island appears. There are, however, nightspots at several hotels and motels. Some of Hilton Head's restaurants also have lounges where you can hang out and catch live entertainment.

There are three movie theaters on the island: Coligny Theatre in Coligny Plaza, Northridge Cinemas at 435 William Hilton Pkwy. at mile marker 5, and Park Plaza Cinemas in the Park Plaza Shopping Center off Greenwood Drive. Coligny Theatre has 1 screen, Northridge has 10, and Park Plaza has 5.

If you've spent your day knocking a tennis ball around, pedaling a few miles on bicycle paths, and frolicking in the surf, and you still haven't pooped out, you might consider the following nighttime entertainment options.

THE JAZZ CORNER, The Village at Wexford; (843) 842-8620; thejazzcorner.com. This nightspot is literally tucked away in a corner of the Village at Wexford shopping complex. When you walk through the door (if you can get inside despite the lines of other people trying to do so), you'll immediately put on your happy face! Although tiny in size, this establishment defines fun and offers live jazz and Dixieland music and fine dining each evening of the week. Dinner is available, with entrees averaging $20 and including dishes such as crispy flounder, seafood-stuffed salmon, oysters Gillespie (named for trumpeter Dizzy, no doubt), and veal piccata. If you're out for dinner, it's recommended to dine early rather than later when the joint gets jumping! In fact, although the food is delicious, this is a great after-dinner place to go. Although the focus

Close-up

Hilton Head's Gone Gator

If you get near a body of fresh or brackish water on Hilton Head, which is hard not to do given the preponderance of the island's lakes and lagoons, there's a good chance you will see a creature that looks as though it has crawled right out of Jurassic Park. This is the American alligator, the largest reptile on the North American continent and one of the oldest surviving vertebrates on the planet.

Alligators abound on Hilton Head, where developers have provided readymade homes for them by creating the waterways that decorate the island's communities and golf courses. "If there's a mud puddle in the Lowcountry, there's an alligator in it," says Dean Harrigal, who coordinates the alligator nuisance program in the area. There have been no formal surveys of the alligator population on Hilton Head, but there are probably 2,000 to 4,000 gators living on the island, says Walt Rhodes, the alligator project supervisor for the South Carolina Department of Natural Resources.

Alligators, which are protected by state and federal law, can grow to a length of 12 feet, but most of the gators removed from Hilton Head under the nuisance program are from 6 to 8 feet long, according to Harrigal. Even so, if left alone, alligators pose little threat to humans, say Rhodes and Harrigal. "Gators are naturally shy of people," says Rhodes. According to the two alligator experts, humans are more of a threat to gators than vice versa.

If the state receives a complaint about a gator on Hilton Head, and the animal is deemed a nuisance because of its behavior or location, the reptile will be removed. Removed, in this case, means destroyed, not relocated. Relocating a gator doesn't work because of the animal's strong homing instinct: Gators have been known to travel as much as 30 miles to return to their nesting areas, Rhodes and Harrigal say. About 50 gators are removed from Hilton Head each year because of complaints against them, but the two say that wouldn't be the case if people were more tolerant of the animals, who were here first (present-day gators are direct descendants

is on the smooth jazz of the 1950s and 1960s, there's plenty of swing-era music. The Jazz Corner makes the most of an abundance of local talent while also presenting well-known performers.

THE LODGE BEER AND GROWLER BAR, Hilton Head Plaza, 7 Greenwood Dr.; (843) 842-8966; hiltonheadlodge.com. The island's only craft beer bar has an interior resembling a hunting lodge, and it's high on the popularity list of beer fans. With 36 rotating taps (and growlers to go), it's a popular place for locals and a quite festive place for visitors to the island. You can satisfy your competitive instincts at the billiards tables or try some shuffleboard, or you can relax in front of one of the two fireplaces with a drink from the full bar. In addition to wine by the glass, single malts, ales, cognacs, and bourbons, the bar serves a specialty drink—the chocolate martini. This establishment in Hilton Head Plaza, off Greenwood Drive near the Sea Pines traffic circle, opens at 5 p.m. daily.

SHOPPING

The shopping is plentiful on Hilton Head, which has stores of every description in large shopping centers, strip malls, and along the island's out-of-the-way streets and byways. To get you started, we've provided rundowns on a few of the bigger shopping of a creature that lived in what is now Florida during the Miocene epoch, which occurred 25 million years ago). People don't like gators for a number of reasons. For one thing, the alligator's appearance is not in its favor. The gator looks like a big lizard, only uglier, and it seems to have a malevolent smile permanently plastered on its bumpy face. "It's not Bambi," says Rhodes. "It's not warm and fuzzy, it's cold and scaly." For another, most people don't know much about alligators and their relatively placid temperament. Folks confuse gators with the crocodiles found on other continents, in particular the 14-foot crocs seen devouring water buffaloes in sensationalized nature flicks. Gators, says Rhodes, "will let you alone if you let them alone, and they'll see you first."

Humans have a tendency to bring out the aggressiveness in gators by feeding them. If a person feeds a gator enough times, the beast's golf ball–size brain begins to associate the human with food. This is, if you'll pardon the phrase, a recipe for disaster that can be harmful to the human involved and fatal to the gator. It's also against the law: If you're caught feeding an alligator, you can be fined $200 or sentenced to 30 days in jail. There are cases of humans provoking gators into attacking them. Rhodes tells of a golfer who hit his ball near a gator that was sunning itself on a Hilton Head fairway, then smacked the animal with his golf club in the process of recovering the ball. The gator bit the golfer. "The gator did what you would do if someone hit you with a golf club," says Rhodes. There have been reports of people being pursued by gators, but Rhodes says he's handled in excess of 3,000 of the animals and has never been chased.

Rhodes's rules for coexisting with gators: Don't feed them; they find plenty to eat in the form of insects, crustaceans, fish, and snakes. Don't tease them. For goodness' sake, don't try to pet them. Look at them all you want but do so from afar. "Give the animal the respect it deserves," says Rhodes. "It has as much right to be here as the deer, squirrels, and people."

areas and pointed out some of the stores you can find there. Also, Hilton Head offers two clusters of outlets. Both are located as follows: From Savannah, take I-95 to Hwy 278, South Carolina exit 8. Proceed for 13 miles. Tanger Outlet Center 1 (under renovation) is on the right, 2 miles before the Hilton Head Bridge. Tanger Outlet Center 2 is on the right, 1 mile before the Hilton Head Bridge. Tanger 2 offers more than 50 different stores with highly discounted items (tangeroutlet .com); open Mon through Sat 10 a.m. to 9 p.m. and Sun 11 a.m. to 6 p.m. Knock yourself out.

Shopping Centers

COLIGNY PLAZA, 1 N. Forest Beach Dr.; (843) 842-6050; colignyplaza.com. Sometimes it takes a rainy day to encourage you to change directions during a vacation on Hilton Head Island. It's those days that call for a trip to Coligny Plaza, one of the island's most popular places to shop, dine, and peruse the more than 60 retail stores and eateries. As the island's oldest and largest shopping center, it covers nearly 9 acres at the Coligny traffic circle on the south end of the island.

Coligny Plaza mixes specialty shops with conventional businesses and plenty of restaurants.

HARBOUR TOWN, Harbour Town Yacht Basin; (843) 363-8335; harbourtown.com. The iconic lighthouse at Harbour Town is your marker to spend an afternoon browsing the shops there. With more than 20 shops and eating places gracing the north side of beautiful Harbour Town Yacht Basin, there's plenty to entertain you all within a pleasant walk. When you're not busy wandering in and out of shops or restaurants, you can relax outside by plopping down in one of the many rocking chairs and watching the activity in the boat-filled marina. The Harbour Town shopping complex is in the Sea Pines Resort and hosts a variety of on-site entertainment during the summer months.

VILLAGE AT WEXFORD, 1000 William Hilton Pkwy.; (843) 842-2240; villageatwexford.com. If you're looking for upscale variety, you'll find it at the Village at Wexford, where the majority of the 30 stores and eateries are locally owned. This quaint-looking stucco retail-and-office complex sits on 9 wooded acres off the parkway near mile marker 10, and houses Le Cookery kitchen accessories, an Audubon Nature Store, Mum's the Word florist and gift shop, Pretty Papers stationery store, and Smith Galleries, which deals in artwork and jewelry. Several stores offer women's apparel, including Patricia's, and there's a men's clothing store, Teague's. Island Child specializes in clothing and shoes for children. The restaurants at the Village at Wexford range from those offering fast food to those devoted to casual and fine dining.

Bookstores

BARNES & NOBLE, 20 Hatton Place; (843) 342-6690; barnesandnoble.com. This branch of the nation's largest bookseller opened in July 1998 and offers islanders and visitors more than 175,000 titles, a mind-boggling selection of magazines, and a cafe where you can sit, read, and drink juice, tea, or coffee and munch on gourmet cookies. Special features of the 20,250-square-foot store are the storytime sessions for children. The store's Special Order Express service will order any book from more than 1.2 million in print, and deliveries usually take place within 7 days. This spacious store is just off William Hilton Parkway between mile markers 3 and 4.

RECREATION

Golf

Hilton Head is heaven on earth for golfers. There are 25 courses on the island, many of them world-class and all of them overflowing with natural beauty. Seventeen are open to the public, and information on these follows.

The courses we've described have amenities such as pro shops, practice greens, and driving ranges. Many do not allow walking, but we've pointed out which ones do and to what extent. The greens fees listed include carts, and they reflect rates during the most popular playing times (generally spring and fall).

The rates included are for players not staying at the resorts associated with the courses. You can make arrangements to play these courses by calling directly, through the resort where you're staying, or via central golf reservation services such as **Last Minute Tee Times** (843-689-2262; lmteetimes .com) and the **Golf Island Call Center** (888-465-3475; golfisland.com). Public and private courses are noted.

i These reservation services are extremely busy so make sure you check details for both services online, first, and if possible. There are times when the phone lines are tied up due to demand, so reservations for two or more players can be made online. In some cases, phone reservations must be made 7 to 10 p.m. the night before the planned outing.

COUNTRY CLUB OF HILTON HEAD (PUBLIC), 70 Skull Creek Dr.; (843) 681-2582; clubcorp.com.

Many of the greens on this par-72, 6,543-yard course at Hilton Head Plantation run near the Intracoastal Waterway, and the 12th is right on it. Designed by Rees Jones and built in 1985, the course has two holes that are almost 600 yards, including the uphill, par 4, 556-yard 18th. Greens and fairways are Bermuda grass.

GOLDEN BEAR GOLF CLUB (PUBLIC), 72 Golden Bear Way; (843) 689-2200; clubcorp.com.

What a great name for a golf course! Interestingly enough, the chief architect of this Jack Nicklaus design was not the Golden Bear himself but the late Bruce Borland. Players of this 6,643-yard layout at Indigo Run will find a real challenge in the 11th hole—it runs 430 yards and features a long dogleg to the left and water on the left side of the green. This par-72 course has fairways and greens of Bermuda grass set among lagoons and stands of pine and hardwoods. Be wowed as you tackle the course amid towering pines and mature cypress. Among the amenities are a bar and grill.

OYSTER REEF GOLF CLUB (PUBLIC), 155 High Bluff Rd.; (843) 681-1745; oysterreef golfclub.com.

This course was rated one of the top 25 new courses in America in 1983 and was designed by Rees Jones. The sixth hole at Oyster Reef—a par 3, 160-yarder—overlooks Port Royal Sound, giving golfers a fine view of that majestic body of water on the northern side of Hilton Head. The par-72 layout covers 6,440 yards at Hilton Head Plantation. The greens were converted to Tif Eagle Bermuda grass in 2000. There are 9 ponds and 66 bunkers for players to contend with. At the end of a round, players can relax at the club's bar and restaurant.

PALMETTO DUNES GOLF COURSES (PUBLIC), 1 Trent Jones Ln.; (843) 785-1136, (800) 827-3006; palmettodunes .com.

Palmetto Dunes offers golfers three 18-hole courses from which to choose, each of them named for their heavy-hitting designers: Arthur Hills, George Fazio, and Robert Trent Jones. You can cover them on foot if you want to. Unrestricted walking is allowed at all times of the day.

ARTHUR HILLS COURSE AT PALMETTO DUNES.

This heavily wooded par 72 was reconditioned during the mid-1990s, with all the greens being rebuilt. One of the most interesting holes is the 12th, a par 4 that's bordered by water along one side. The course measures 6,122 yards.

GEORGE FAZIO COURSE AT PALMETTO DUNES.

This course is ranked among the Top 100 in the country. Located inside Palmetto Dunes, it offers a 432-yard 1st hole and 462-yard 18th and is the only par-70 course on Hilton Head Island. The Fazio Course covers total 6,239 yards and is characterized by rolling fairways and lots of long par 4s—there are only two par 5s and three par 3s. The 18th is a challenge, ending with a hole where two bunkers provide a significant challenge.

ROBERT TRENT JONES COURSE AT PALMETTO DUNES.

Don't be surprised to view kayakers paddling quietly in the lagoons that run throughout this scenic course. If you like playing by the water, you'll enjoy this 6,570-yard course, which provides a winding lagoon system tied into 11 holes and a great view of the ocean from No. 10. Other hallmarks of this par 72 are open fairways and large greens. Doug Weaver is the pro and will be happy to offer pointers to steer your game to perfection!

Triple Play

Rather than paying individual greens fees for each course within Palmetto Dunes, book an Unlimited Golf Package that includes private villa accommodations and golf! You can play on three legendary courses: the Robert Trent Jones Course, the George Fazio Course, and the Arthur Hills Course. Stay 4 days and 3 nights in select resort villas, and receive three rounds of golf per person on three championship golf courses (includes green fees, cart fees, and warm-up range) with complimentary repeat rounds available on the same course, same day based on availability. For more information, call (866) 380-1778.

PALMETTO HALL PLANTATION CLUB (PUBLIC), 108 Fort Howell Dr.; (843) 342-2582; palmettodunes.com. The Palmetto Hall Plantation Club offers golfers the opportunity to enjoy a Lowcountry-style clubhouse and 36-hole courses designed by Arthur Hills and Robert Cupp. The 16,000-square-foot clubhouse is a repository of historic artifacts (both Lowcountry- and golfing-related), antiques, and paintings, and features a grillroom with the aura of a club.

ARTHUR HILLS COURSE AT PALMETTO HALL. The signature hole here is No. 18, a 434-yarder with water running up the left side of the fairway. It's a challenging par 4. Another hole featuring plenty of water is the 5th, but the water on this beauty is on the right side. The hole runs 490 yards and is a par 5. This 6,257-yard course was opened in 1991. Walking is prohibited.

ROBERT CUPP COURSE AT PALMETTO HALL. Unrestricted walking is allowed on this 6,042-yard course, which was unveiled 2 years after the Arthur Hills layout. Vistas of marshlands and forests of oak and pine are features of this par-72 course, along with its straight lines and sharp angles. The course, which opened in 1993, was renovated and reopened in the fall of 2005.

PORT ROYAL GOLF CLUB (PUBLIC), 10 Clubhouse Dr.; (843) 689-1760; portroyalgolfclub.com. This golf club at the Port Royal resort community has three 18-hole courses—Barony, Planter's Row, and Robber's Row—plus a bar and restaurant.

PORT ROYAL/BARONY COURSE. The long drivers will take a backseat to the shot makers on this 6,223-yard course, which has many small greens. The Barony, which was designed by George Cobb, presents players with a test of skill at No. 12, a par-4, 411-yard hole with water on both sides of the fairway.

PORT ROYAL/PLANTER'S ROW COURSE. Willard Byrd was the designer responsible for Planter's Row, where golfers finish on a par-5, 511-yard hole featuring woods and water. If that's not enough of a challenge, consider No. 12, a narrow, 419-yard hole where you've got to cross water to get to the green. The course measures 6,284 yards, and par is 72.

PORT ROYAL/ROBBER'S ROW COURSE. Robber's Row represents a team effort by designers George Cobb and Pete Dye. The course was built in 1967 and reconfigured in 1994 by Dye, who added several water hazards. This par-72 course runs 6,311 yards.

SEA PINES RESORT (PUBLIC), seapines .com. Sea Pines is the home of three of the island's most popular golf courses, including the Harbour Town Golf Links, which is the site of Hilton Head's number-one sporting event, the Verizon Heritage. Walking is allowed on all three courses.

HARBOUR TOWN GOLF LINKS, 32 Greenwood Dr.; (866) 561-8802. The signature hole at Harbour Town is the one you've seen countless times on television—the windswept 18th, a par 4 on Calibogue Sound where shots to the green often end up among the fiddler crabs in the adjacent marsh. Consistently ranked among the world's top courses, this one was designed by Pete Dye and Jack Nicklaus and has some outstanding par 3s. The yardage at this par-71 course totals 6,040.

OCEAN COURSE, 100 N. Sea Pines Dr.; (843) 842-8484, (800) 955-8337. The 15th hole on this oldest of island courses offers a terrific view of the ocean. It's the oldest course because it was designed by George Cobb in 1962 but was remodeled by Mark McCumber in 1995.

HERON POINT COURSE, 100 N. Sea Pines Dr.; (843) 842-8484, (800) 955-8337. You'll encounter wide fairways and lots of lagoons, trees, and marshes when you play this par-72 course, which was redesigned by Pete Dye and reopened after a year of work in September 2007.

i If you should somehow run out of golf courses to play on Hilton Head, be advised that there are several fine off-island layouts nearby. Among them are four on US 278, the road to the island—Eagle's Point (843-757-5900), Hilton Head National Golf Club (843-842-5900), Island West (843-689-6660), and Old South Golf Links (843-785-5353).

SHIPYARD GOLF CLUB (PUBLIC), 45 Shipyard Dr.; (843) 689-GOLF, (800) 2-FIND-18; hiltonheadgolf.net. Shipyard offers three interconnecting 9-hole courses appropriately named for three types of sailing vessels: Brigantine, Clipper, and Galleon. There is water involved on 25 of the 27 holes, which have Bermuda grass fairways and greens. There's a bar and restaurant on the premises.

BRIGANTINE COURSE. The work of designer Willard Byrd, the Brigantine is a 3,054-yard par 36 surrounded by private homes and rental condominiums that blend in with the natural environment. You'll be challenged by No. 6, a long par 4; and No. 9, which is a par 5 that runs 494 yards and has water on one side of the fairway.

CLIPPER COURSE. The 3,302-yard Clipper has a tough 9th hole with lots of bunkers. Water comes into play on all the holes except No. 6, which is a par 4, 415-yarder. George Cobb also designed this course, which carries a par 36.

GALLEON COURSE. Of the various interconnecting nines at the Shipyard Golf Club, the Clipper/Galleon Course is the largest. The greens of the Galleon Course are large and well bunkered. This George Cobb–designed, par-36 course is best known for No. 2, a par 5 with an elevated green fronted by water and with bunkers all around. Total yardage for the course is 3,146.

Tennis

If you fly in on through the Savannah/Hilton Head International Airport, you'll probably be surrounded by avid tennis players heading to "the island" for tennis vacations. This is a sport that brings thousands to Hilton Head to improve their game. The options for playing, as well as for formal instruction, are plentiful! Among those open to the public for play are the following:

PALMETTO DUNES TENNIS CENTER, 6 Trent Jones Ln.; (843) 785-1152, (800) 972-0257; palmettodunes.com. An array of instructional programs and daily round-robin tournaments are featured at the tennis center at Palmetto Dunes. The tournaments are billed as "lively afternoon social competition with the emphasis on fun." There are 23 clay and 2 Pro Bounce (a cushioned hard surface) courts, 8 of which are lighted.

PORT ROYAL RACQUET CLUB, 15 Wimbledon Ct.; (843) 686-8803; portroyal .com. The Port Royal Racquet Club offers three Grand Slam–type playing surfaces. There are 10 clay courts, 4 cushioned hard courts, and a new croquet court. The club offers a variety of instructional programs and will custom design clinics for individuals and teams.

Located at Port Royal Plantation, the club has a well-stocked pro shop that provides a varied selection of men's and women's tennis wear and the latest in equipment.

SEA PINES RACQUET CLUB, 5 Lighthouse Ln.; (843) 363-4495, (800) 732-7463; sea pines.com. Programs and instruction take center court at the Sea Pines Racquet Club. The flagship program is the Smith Stearns Tennis Academy, named in part after Stan Smith, the former US Open and Wimbledon champion who serves as the club's touring pro and tennis consultant.

There are various programs for every age group, and 23 clay courts are available for play. The club has five instructors. The club dates from the early 1970s. The pro shop offers players the latest in tennis fashions, equipment, and footwear. The website has a full listing of instructional packages, including several children's tennis programs.

VAN DER MEER SHIPYARD TENNIS RESORT, 116 Shipyard Dr.; (843) 686-8804, (800) 845-6138; vandermeertennis .com. Twenty courts set amid the lush surroundings of Shipyard Plantation await the tennis buff at this racquet club, which the US Tennis Association presented with its Outstanding Tennis Facility of the Year Award for 1997 and continues to live up to the honor today. There are 13 clay courts and 7 hard-surface courts outdoors and 3 DecoTurf courts indoors (a total of 8 courts have lights). The club also offers a variety of tennis getaway weeks and weekends, stroke of the day sessions, daily drills, and intensive drills available year-round. The intensive drills are geared for players with 4.0-plus ratings and are designed to take skills to the next level.

The Shipyard Racquet Club has a large pro shop displaying an extensive variety of items, and it's also the site of the US Professional Tennis Registry's International Tennis Symposium and $25,000 Championships, which are held annually during the middle of February.

VAN DER MEER TENNIS CENTER, 19 DeAllyon Rd.; (843) 785-8388, (800) 845-6138. This tennis center operated by well-known instructor Dennis Van der Meer provides a multitude of programs for adults and junior players in all stages of development, from beginners to aspiring professionals. There are 17 hard-surface courts, of which 4 are covered and lighted, with fees for an hour of play set at $15. The center has a pro shop and is the headquarters of the Van Der Meer Tennis University, which offers training programs for tennis teachers. The center is on DeAllyon Road, which runs off Cordillo Parkway on the south end of the island.

ANNUAL EVENTS & FESTIVALS

The island's most significant annual events occur during the spring.

HILTON HEAD ISLAND ST. PATRICK'S DAY PARADE, Pope Avenue; (843) 384-4035; hiltonheadireland.org. What started as a march by a few residents of Irish descent in 1983 has matured into the largest free spectator event held on the island. Some 26,000 onlookers gather to watch the 2-hour parade, which is held on the Sunday before St. Patrick's Day or on the day itself when the holiday falls on Sunday. If you go, expect to see marching bands, in the neighborhood of 30 floats, dance groups, a bagpipe band or two, local dignitaries, and maybe even Budweiser's Clydesdale horses. The parade starts at 2 p.m. at Coligny Circle and proceeds west on Pope Avenue to Office Park Road and into Park Plaza. Tom Reilley started the celebration when he and a few friends decided to march in honor of St. Patrick. Because they didn't have a parade permit, Reilley and his pals ran into some legal troubles with local officials, but they managed to straighten things out and resumed marching in 1985. Since then the parade has grown into the family-oriented event that it is today. Visit the website for more information.

HILTON HEAD ISLAND WINE & FOOD FESTIVAL, hiltonheadwineandfood.com. This weeklong event, held for more than 30 years, showcases the latest and greatest in wine and cuisine. There are wine-pairing dinners, cooking demonstrations, and island chefs showcasing their talents at the Grand Wine Tasting. Venues and prices can be found on the website.

THE RBC HERITAGE, Harbour Town Golf Links, 71 Lighthouse Rd.; (843) 671-2448, (800) 234-1107; rbcheritage.com. This event brings the PGA's 132 invited players and 125,000 spectators to famed Harbour Town Golf Links in the Sea Pines Resort during 4 days in April. In one of golf's most picturesque sites, this course has attracted international media since it started in 1969.

The list of Heritage champions of the past includes Jack Nicklaus, Greg Norman, Nick Price, Hale Irwin, Tom Watson, and Arnold Palmer, who won the tournament in its inaugural year of 1969 when it was known as the Heritage Classic.

Attending the Heritage involves more than watching a golf tournament. The event is usually held during the second week in April, when the weather is generally lovely and nature is putting on a springtime show. It's a terrific time to get outdoors, amble around the verdant Harbour Town course, visit the shops and restaurants at the Harbour Town Yacht Basin near the first tee and 18th green, gawk at the high-priced boats docked in the marina, and observe the hordes of spectators doing all of these things. Sometime during their day at the course, those attending are invariably drawn to the 18th hole, which overlooks Calibogue Sound and has the Harbour Town Lighthouse as part of its backdrop, to see how the players finish up and deal with the wind blowing off the water.

During the 3 days leading up to the tournament, which starts on Thursday and ends on Sunday, there are two pro-am events and a pro-am fishing tournament. On the Monday afternoon before Thursday's first round of play, the Heritage presents opening ceremonies focusing on golf's Scottish origins and the game's long history in South Carolina (the South Carolina Golf Club of Charleston was founded in 1786 and is reputed to be the oldest membership golf club in the US). The defending champion, tournament board members clad in plaid, and bagpipers from The Citadel military college parade along the yacht basin to the 18th green, where the defending champ gets the tourney under way by smacking a ball into Calibogue Sound as a Civil War–era cannon is fired. Pricing and more details can be found on the website.

TYBEE ISLAND

The drive out to Tybee Island from Savannah is a bit like being on a small adventure. With marshland on both sides, the natural setting is captivating, often luring drivers to pull over to the side of the road to take a quick photo of an egret standing in the mud with its neck outstretched or a turtle hatchling trying to cross the road. (This is not recommended.) The scene is often mixed with a little bit of disbelief as you make the 8- to 10-minute-long trek to this oasis called Tybee Island. Once you've arrived, you'll know it, as you'll quickly slow your speed down to 35 mph and begin taking in the colorful wooden signs, salty docks, and cheap souvenir shops that tell you that you've left civilization.

There are some things about Tybee that haven't changed in the past couple decades. City Hall is still City Hall. The North Beach is still vast, and beachcombers are few. The ships still blow their horns as they make their way into the mouth of the Savannah River right off Tybee's coast. You can still get a smooth ice cream cone (and chocolate dip) from a vendor on Butler Avenue, the main drag. And there's still plenty of beach to lie on, even when it's the Fourth of July.

While other beach communities succumb to high-rises, slick resorts, and gated communities with lawns pristine enough to putt on, Tybee has stubbornly resisted. Look around the town's beachside shops during summer and you'll see kites and flags hanging out the doors of souvenir shops that hawk seashells and bargain T-shirts for less than $10. You'll see sunburned kids slurping snow cones to music wafting from the Tybee pier. And you'll see locals strolling the strand every day because that's what they do.

An important reminder: No grilling, glass bottles, or dogs are allowed on the beach. Police officers routinely patrol the beach looking for violators who are issued hefty tickets for any infractions. The island does, however, have a dog park located at the intersection of Van Horne and Fort Streets.

HISTORY

Tybee is a place where folksy eccentricity is celebrated, and many things have been practiced. Gambling was one of those things, carried on in back rooms throughout Tybee until being exposed and cleared out in the early 1960s. A decade or so later, nearly every bar in town was shut down for staying open too late on Saturday night. Seems people were having too good a time to remember that selling beer on Sunday was illegal. That's the thing about Tybee Islanders—they just sort of do their own thing.

Through the years, there have been nicknames for Tybee that may, or may not, have been quite fair. Somehow, "Redneck Riviera" just doesn't seem appropriate for this beautiful place, where you can wear flip-flops year-round and everybody knows your name. Bluntly put, there are places at Tybee that are a little scruffy, but if you'll get your nose out of the air, you'll learn to appreciate the quirky appeal as the art of the island. You'll find million-dollar beachfront construction next door to cinder-block shacks (and don't necessarily assume the owners of the fancy home are the richer: Tybee knew shabby before it was chic). This is a beach run by locals who are glad to see tourists, and even happier to see them leave. Tybee is a beach of rituals. One such example is the Beach Bums Parade, wherein locals on makeshift floats armed with large-scale water guns do battle with spectators spraying garden hoses, marking the beginning of the tourist season—a fun, messy launch to the crowds of summer. Later, mid-September ushers back in "Tybee time," when the residents have the place to themselves and the particular pleasures of a warm winter beach.

If you think Tybee—with its whimsical cottages and wacky storefronts—is colorful, just wait until you read about her past. This island served a role in several wars and has been home to Lt. Col. George C. Marshall (creator of the Marshall Plan) and to a quarantine station for people with infectious ailments. In the early 1800s, scientists believed the marshes in and around the island held harmful vapors or miasma, which rose from the marsh vegetation and were carried by the wind into Savannah. However, it was also widely theorized that the vapors were counteracted by the healing properties of sea air. That was a notion that eventually played a role in Tybee's foray into tourism in the late 1880s.

Native Americans were the first Tybee Islanders. They settled this small island (2.5 miles long and about 0.6 mile wide) and also are generally credited with giving the island its name, which means salt, though there are other competing theories. Next came the Spanish in the 1500s, followed 200 years later by Georgia's founder, Gen. James Edward Oglethorpe.

Because of its location at the mouth of the Savannah River, Tybee was important strategically. Soon after his arrival, Oglethorpe ordered the construction of a lighthouse, which was completed in 1736. During the War of 1812, the lighthouse was used to warn Savannah of possible attack by the British, but this attack never materialized. A fortress known as a Martello tower, designed with round walls that supposedly would deflect cannonballs, was built on Tybee Island in 1815 to help guard the Savannah River from attack. It was one of only a few such structures in North America.

On the western end of the island, a quarantine station was set up to house sick passengers coming in off ships. This is how Lazaretto Creek got its name. *Lazaretto* is an Italian word for an institution or hospital for those with contagious diseases. "They kept them in quarantine there for four months," said James Mack Adams, local Tybee historian. "If they got sick and died, they buried them right there."

In 1829 construction began on Fort Pulaski. The fort, now a national park, stands off US 80 as you approach Tybee. It was constructed of 25 million bricks and has walls 7.5 feet thick. A young Robert E. Lee was one of the engineers who planned and supervised construction. During the Civil War, Union forces attacked the fort using a new weapon called "rifled cannon." It took only 30 hours of bombardment for the fort to fall into Union hands. The attack had such devastating effects on the brick fort that after the surrender, all forts like Pulaski were considered obsolete.

Following the war, Tybee turned its attention toward tourism. In its early years, Tybee was reached by boat, a voyage that could take 2 hours from Savannah. That changed in 1887 with the construction of a rail line through the marsh and over various creeks and rivers between the island and the mainland. That same year Tybee was officially incorporated as Ocean City. A year later it was changed to Tybee, only to be changed in 1929 to Savannah Beach. It wasn't until many decades later, in the early 1970s, that it became Tybee again. A reference today to Savannah Beach is likely to raise the locals' dander.

Day-trippers, as they were known, would come on the train, rent bathing suits from a local hotel, and spend the day at the beach. Some would arrive later in the day to dance to Big Band music supplied by outfits playing at one of the island's biggest attractions: the Tybrisa Pier. When the Tybee Road opened in 1923, the stream of people coming to the island continued to grow. In a column that ran in the local newspaper in 1931, E. B. Izlar reflected about the "good old days" on Tybee. "The decline of mosquitoes, of picnickers, of bars and of yardage in women's bathing suits constitute the most radical changes in reviewing the past thirty years on Tybee Island," the column stated. "Today, Mr. Izlar declares that mosquitoes, except in the dense wooded places, are rare, and he bears out his statement by remarking that he has only seen three this season."

Reminiscing on the bathing suits of the early years, Mr. Izlar lamented the time when suits were sold for $2.50 to $4 a dozen (except, of course, when special suits for women were as high as $12 a dozen) in the days when women "wrapped up" to cover everything. As for bars, Mr. Izlar said that though they abounded in bygone days, there was little disorder—only friendly fights. "There was not even need for a jail in those days."

While the islanders focused on tourism, the US War Department began construction of Fort Screven on the north end of the island. The fort was made up of seven gun batteries that ended up being fired only for practice, not for war. During World War I, part of the Eighth Infantry Regiment was assigned to Fort Screven. One of its commanders was Lt. Col. George C. Marshall, who after leaving Tybee became a five-star general and served as secretary of state, secretary of defense, and author of the Marshall Plan for rebuilding western Europe after World War II.

ℹ️ Tybee hasn't had a major hit from a hurricane in more than 100 years. The most damaging hurricane occurred August 27, 1881. It landed with a massive storm surge that covered the island and destroyed nearly every structure in its path.

In the meantime, Savannahians were beginning to build houses at the beach for the summer months. The ocean breezes would give them relief from the city's sweltering summer heat. Many of these magnificent old beach homes can still be found on the island today, and many are still owned by descendants of family members who were the original owners. Former resident Walter Parker recalls how empty the island was in those days. "I can remember in the winter you could go for several blocks before you saw a light on," said Parker. "No one lived here year-round."

Eventually, that began to change, and Tybee's year-round population slowly grew. However, several factors—beach erosion, pollution, the closing of Fort Screven— resulted in several years of decline on the island beginning in the 1940s. Residents cultivated an outlaw attitude during this era by engaging in back-room gambling and illegal drinking, which got the attention of the news media. It also helped fuel the island's reputation in some circles as Georgia's unruly stepchild. Eventually, local and state law enforcement agencies cracked down to curb Tybee's wanton ways. The pollution, gambling, and other sins were eventually cleaned up, and Tybee once again became a popular tourist spot.

> ℹ **Geologically speaking, Tybee is very young—only about 1,000 years old. Savannah's other islands, including Wilmington and Skidaway, are more than 40,000 years old.**

Since 1980 or so, the island's year-round population has been on the rise to its current level of around 3,000. Today, locals who have called Tybee home for generations live among a thriving community of artists and writers, most of whom migrated during the 1980s. There are also many retirees whose hometowns are places far away from Tybee. Every socioeconomic group is represented, from the poor to the very wealthy.

"I think Tybee is an easy place to live," said Parker. "I think it has more than its share of characters . . . But it has a small community feeling and most want it to stay that way."

TRAVEL INSTRUCTIONS & RESOURCES

Tybee is about 18 miles east of Savannah. There is only one road to get you there: US 80. You can reach it from the Historic District by heading east on Bay Street. In less than a mile, it will run into President Street, then President Street Extension. After about 3 miles, it merges with US 80 East. From Midtown, hop on Victory Drive and head east—you are also on US 80 East.

After entering Tybee, US 80 turns into Butler Avenue, the community's main street, which will take you past hotels, beach houses, and the small downtown area. You will know US 80 has become Butler Avenue after going around a fairly sharp curve that keeps you from driving into the ocean. You

can't miss it. Follow Butler a mile or so farther into downtown, and you will be deposited in a city parking lot next to the pier.

Most places you need to visit on Tybee should be accessible from this main strip. Near the beginning of Butler Avenue, streets running east and west are numbered, starting with 1st Street at the northern end of the city and ending with 19th Street at the southern end. These are crossed by north- and south-running streets that are named and numbered, starting with Butler Avenue closest to the beach and ending with 6th Avenue.

The city operates three parking lots, all accessible from Butler Avenue: at the end of Tybrisa (which used to be 16th Street), 14th Street, and at North Beach. The parking lots, and the streetside spaces near them, are equipped with pay-and-display meters. Parking is patrolled every day year-round 8 a.m. to 8 p.m. Like the Savannah authorities, the parking enforcers are very generous when doling out tickets. So if you don't want an expensive ticket, don't let your meter expire. It usually isn't too much trouble finding parking on Tybee, except for a few very busy weekends.

ACCOMMODATIONS

Affordable hotel rooms, sprawling beach houses, and ocean-view condos are some of the choices you'll find when searching for accommodations on Tybee Island. Tybee is known as a family beach, so a lot of what is available is geared toward those lugging not only beach chairs but high chairs as well. Regardless of where you land, more likely than not you'll be within comfortable walking distance of the beach.

Tybee's season runs typically from the middle of April through the middle of September. After that, the streets become less crowded and rates go down. Stay during the peak season, especially on weekends, and the rates are going to be higher. A few weekends, including July 4, are especially busy. Weekend hotel rates are considerably higher than weekday rates.

Tybee's accommodations scene is very atypical. There's a healthy scattering of hotels, but few in the way of major national chains and none that you would consider truly upscale. (In fact, lots of them are rather shabby, although you'd never guess it from their rates.) Nor is development moving in that direction. When a developer breaks ground on Tybee these days, chances are that developer is building condos. These run the gamut from strictly investment properties to purely private residences, but it's safe to say the tourist housing market on the island is skewing increasingly to condo rentals. At least one motel has converted to condos, in fact.

Price Code

Our price code is designed to make it easier for you to gauge the cost of staying at one of Tybee's hotels, motels, or bed-and-breakfasts. The dollar sign indicates the average cost for a one-night stay for two adults during peak season, typically mid-April through mid-September. Weekends cost more.

$. . . . . less than $50
$$ . . . . $50 to $100
$$$ . . . . $100 to $150
$$$$ . . . . more than $150

Hotels and Motels

There are only a handful of middle-class hotels and motels to choose from on the island. Most are smaller chains with names you will recognize and offer standard, sometimes modest accommodations. In all honesty, the majority of the few hotels on Tybee are plain, and far from luxurious. In other words, the term *renovation* might be defined

as new bedspreads and curtains at Tybee, so don't expect the Ritz here. The ones we list have nonsmoking and wheelchair-accessible rooms and come with free parking. Although Tybee is outside Savannah, it shares area code 912.

ADMIRAL'S INN, 1501 Butler Ave.; (912) 786-0700; admiralsinntybee.com; $$$–$$$$. A nice, two-story hotel, Admiral's Inn has 41 spacious rooms, a swimming pool, and is across the street from the ocean. The standard room comes with two queen-size beds, but if you need a little more space, deluxe king rooms with sitting areas are available. The hotel's meeting room holds up to 75 people. Computer, phone/fax, free wireless access and copy service are available for those unfortunate souls who have to work while at the beach. The hotel is within comfortable walking distance to "downtown Tybee."

DUNES INN & SUITES, 409 Butler Ave.; (912) 786-4591; $$–$$$$. Dunes Inn & Suites is across the street from the beach and a block or so away from Tybee's small-town shopping district, where you can find everything from a new swimsuit to suntan lotion. This motel offers 54 rooms: 33 in the main building and additional rooms in the Dunes annex. Some have balconies overlooking the pool, and a few kitchenettes are also available. There is a complimentary continental breakfast, wireless available in rooms, and Dunes is pet-friendly.

DESOTO BEACH HOTEL, 212 Butler Ave.; (912) 786-4542, (877) 786-4542; desoto beachhotel.com; $$$–$$$$. The only thing old about this place is the name, which once served one of Tybee's oldest hotels. Completely renovated in 2010, this is a delightful place to stay with freshly painted rooms, upgraded linens and furniture, and rooms that range from two bedrooms with king or queen-size beds, oversize balconies, and kitchenettes (Hernando DeSoto Suite) to deluxe rooms with two queen-size beds. The old is gone, but on this narrow sliver of land between condo developments, careful design has led to 37 rooms, most of which are technically ocean view and a few of which have a magnificent view. The hotel is on the ocean side of Butler, and it is one of the first motels or hotels you will encounter when driving onto the island. There's an oceanfront pool and a game room that's partially open to the elements.

OCEAN PLAZA BEACH RESORT, 1401 Strand; (912) 786-7777, (800) 215-6370; oceanplaza.com; $$–$$$$. This is Tybee's largest hotel, with 215 rooms, suites, and nearby luxury condos at the Brass Rail (offered under the umbrella of the Ocean Plaza). There are two swimming pools on property at the Ocean Plaza. It is also one of the few properties that offer direct room views of the ocean. Head out your door, walk through a parking lot, and within a few steps you are on the sand. Located on the southern end of the island, there are actually three buildings at Ocean Plaza, including two four-story structures facing the ocean. The rooms are spacious and decorated in bright pastel colors. All oceanfront rooms have balconies overlooking the Atlantic.

Many room options are available, including a single room with a king-size bed, one-room suites with queen-size beds, and two-room suites with one king-size and one double bed. Kitchenettes are also available. Regardless of the room type, all come with a choice of poolside or ocean-view location. There are minifridges in every room, complimentary parking, and free wireless Internet. The Ocean Plaza offers free HBO and a conference center. The Dolphin Reef Restaurant, bridging two of the motel buildings, serves breakfast, lunch, and dinner 7 days a week.

RIVER'S END CAMPGROUND AND R.V. PARK, 5 Fort Ave.; wwriversendcamp ground.com; (912) 786-5518, (800) 786-1016; cityoftybee.org/campground.aspx; $. This little campground is full of charm and has great access to the beach. The city of Tybee Island bought the park in 2006 to preserve its use as a campground, fearful of impending condo development. Aside from the unusual ownership arrangement, this is a standard campground. There are close to 100 RV sites with water and electric and 18 primitive campgrounds. Among the amenities are a swimming pool, air-conditioned bath houses, cable, wireless access, a laundry, and similar touches. Rates start at $29 a night for the primitive campsites, and go up to $74 for the most utility-rich RV sites. Rates are cheaper by the week, and even cheaper by the month. The campground stays pretty busy, so book early.

SAND CASTLE INN, 1402 Butler Ave.; (912) 786-4576, (866) GA-BEACH; sandcastle-inn.com; $$–$$$. The Sand Castle Inn is within walking distance to Tybee's "downtown." It is on the beach side of Butler Avenue—Tybee's main thoroughfare. The motel offers a pool and free continental breakfast each morning. The rooms are fresh, with bright colored bedspreads and white walls. Although just a short stroll to the beach, none of the rooms have ocean views.

Bed-and-Breakfast

THE LIGHTHOUSE INN, 16 Meddin Dr.; (912) 786-0901, (866) 786-0901; tybeebb .com; $$$$. Susie Morris and her husband, Stuart Liles, opened this charming B&B in the fall of 2000 in a circa-1910 home they have restored. It features three fully decorated guest rooms and baths, as well as a front porch for relaxing. The couple lives on the ground floor. The inn is close to the North Beach (a less-developed segment of Tybee's beaches) and the lighthouse (as the name no doubt cued you into). The North Beach Grill is also close by, and beach access is just a few short steps away.

Rentals

MERMAID COTTAGES VACATION RENTALS, (912) 704-4618; mermaidcottages .com. Owner Dianne Kaufman handles vacation rental homes that include historic houses and cozy cottages decorated with coastal charm in mind. Mermaid rentals include food celebrity Paula Deen's "Y'all Come Inn" and *New York Times* best-selling author Mary Kay Andrews's "Ebbtide" and "Breeze Inn." Many Mermaid listings are pet-friendly. Mermaid Cottages also sells a line of products such as Mermaid Morning Bliss Coffee, Beach Bum Biscuits, and Salty Sea Air Candles.

TYBEE BEACH VACATION RENTALS, 106 US 80; (912) 786-0100, (800) 967-4433; renttybee.com. This local company offers a large selection of beach cottages, homes, and condos. Like all the rental agencies listed here, inside the offices are lists of properties, pictures, rates, and other valuable information.

TYBEE COTTAGES, 1310 Jones Ave.; (912) 786-6746, (877) 524-9819; tybeecottages .com. Tybee residents Jim and Becky Heflin represent several appealing rental properties at Tybee Island. From quaint two-bedroom cottages decorated with typical brightly colored, Caribbean-type furnishings to two-story classic Tybee beach houses with their white-slat woodwork and expansive porches, most properties are located right on the beach or come with a pool, and each is supplied with all the conveniences you'll

need for a pleasant stay: i.e., linens, dishes, cookware, and washer/dryer. All properties can be viewed on their website.

TYBEE ISLAND RENTALS, INC., 203 1st Street; (912) 786-4034, (800) 476-0807; tybeeislandrentals.com. Beach homes, condos, and cottages of all shapes and sizes can be rented from Tybee Island Rentals. Check out the varied selection at their offices, located about 2 miles past the bridge onto Tybee. If you are looking for a romantic getaway for two or a place to bring the whole family for a week at the beach, you should be able to find something that suits your needs.

TYBEE ISLAND VACATION RENTALS, 1010 US 80 East; reservations: (877) 214-7353, office: (912) 786-5853; tybeevaca tionrentals.com. The team at Tybee Island Vacation Rentals handles a long list of vacation homes that offer the perfect getaway for families, individuals, and groups.

RESTAURANTS

Tybee's restaurant scene is evolving. Locals don't have to be that old to remember when most eateries were burger and ice cream joints where you could come in your bathing suit, and where you were likely to find the door locked shortly after Labor Day. Those places are still there, but they have been joined by a few reasonably priced family restaurants. One thing you won't find (and another personification of Tybee's individuality) is much in the way of fast-food franchises—with the exception of an Arby's.

Price Code

The price code listed below is based on the cost of an average meal for two, excluding drinks, dessert, or tip. Of course, prices vary to either extreme on most menus and you can tip the bill over into the next category.

$................. less than $30
$$ .... $30 to $50
$$$ .... more than $50

A-J'S DOCKSIDE, 1315 Chatham Ave.; (912) 786-9533; ajsdocksidetybee.com; $$. Dine on the deck overlooking Tybee's beautiful Back River or step inside to sit at tables or at the bar. Seafood is the main menu attraction. Call for info on live entertainment. A-J.'s is a local favorite where many gather each night to watch the sunset in style.

BREAKFAST CLUB, 1500 Butler Ave.; (912) 786-5984; breakfastclub.com; $. If you want to get a table at the Breakfast Club without waiting in line, you may have to get up a little early, especially during the summer months. Lines start forming outside this very popular eatery about 7 a.m. on weekends. During the week, sleep in much past 8:30 a.m., and you will most likely find yourself waiting outside with a handful of other people. Regardless, it is worth the wait. As the line (which moves fast) attests, this diner on the southern end of the island near downtown is one of Tybee's best. For more than 20 years, members of the Farrow family have been serving up breakfast specialties like chorizo con huevos (flour tortillas, sausage, sharp cheese, salsa, and sour cream) and pecan waffles, which are light and crunchy and the talk of the beach. Enjoy the surf and turf omelet, complete with fresh rib eye and local shrimp with garlic butter. While omelets are a menu favorite, you will also find many other choices, from grits to burgers. Chef Jodee Sadowsky, who purchased the diner from his mother, Helen Farrow, was named one of North America's 101 best cooks in *Cooking Across America*.

After the season, when the locals reclaim the island, you'll find them sitting here, sharing the gossip. Warning: This place doesn't look like much but don't let that mislead you. Hours are 7 a.m. to 1 p.m. daily, year-round.

THE CRAB SHACK, 40 Estill Hammock Rd.; (912) 786-9857; thecrabshack.com; $$. Going to the Crab Shack is as much about atmosphere as it is about seafood. Located in Chimney Creek, a hamlet off US 80 just past the Lazaretto Creek Bridge (you can't miss the signs), the Crab Shack's motto is, "Where the Elite Eat in Their Bare Feet." What started as a small, rustic restaurant on the marsh has grown into a giant tourist favorite. Now they've even added a licensed live alligator habitat. While munching on giant servings of seafood delicacies such as Georgia blue crab, snow crab, golden crab, Alaskan king crab, shrimp, and oysters, you can sit out on the huge porch overlooking the marsh. Oak trees decorated with white lights give the Crab Shack a casual, relaxed, fun flair. If you want to try a local specialty, try the Lowcountry boil, which includes boiled shrimp, corn, potatoes, and sausage. As for drinks, the frozen margarita is a good choice along with the piña coladas and daiquiris. Dress is beach casual. The restaurant can handle parties of up to 150 people and boasts a separate gift shop, dubbed (what else?) the Gift Shack. Hours are 11:30 a.m. to 10 p.m. daily, year-round.

FANNIE'S ON THE BEACH, 1613 Strand; (912) 786-6109; fanniesonthebeach.com; $$. This restaurant and outdoor bar, which commands an ocean view across a parking lot, added an upstairs outdoor deck for dining and a band on the weekend. It's open for lunch, dinner, and late night. Specialties include a shrimp burger—a concoction made of ground shrimp, sautéed onions, and celery. Quesadillas are meals, not appetizers, and include shrimp and scallop varieties. They also offer sandwiches, salads, and burgers, but the staff considers the pizzas to be the signature dish. You can get everything from the standard version to one sporting smoked salmon, capers, cream cheese, scallion, black olives, and sun-dried tomatoes. After dark, the club atmosphere comes to the fore, and the band cranks up in summer. Hours are Sun through Fri 11 a.m. to 11 p.m. and Sat 11 a.m. to midnight.

HUC A POO'S BITES AND BOOZE, 1213 US 80 East in the Shops Under the Tybee Oaks; (912) 786-5900; hucapoos.com; $–$$. This funky watering hole and pizza place bills itself as "a bar where everybody knows your name but can't remember it," but don't be fooled, the cooks here remember the recipe for great pizza by the slice or whole pies. Huc a poo's is a great place for people watching or just gazing at the interesting stuff displayed on the walls and ceiling. Pizza listings include the Odyssey, the Santa Cruz, and most everything in-between. The menu also offers salads, calzones, and other tasty selections. Hours are Mon through Thurs 11a.m. to 11 p.m. and Fri through Sun 11 a.m. to 3 a.m.

SEASIDE SWEETS, 18-B Tybrisa St; (912) 786-9861; seasidesisterstybee.com; $. This sweet spot offers Italian gelato made to order from scratch—nothing artificial. Don't forget the candy, from gummies and taffy to fudge and pralines. Shakes and smoothies round out the menu. Hours are seasonal. Look for Seaside Sweets' sister business, Sweetie Pie, next to Seaside Sisters on US 80 East.

SEAWEEDS ICE CREAM, 1405 Butler Ave.; (912) 786-8091; $. For an after-beach treat, check out this longtime favorite for ice cream, frozen yogurt, and snow cone venue. No credit cards. Seasonal hours.

STING RAY'S SEAFOOD, 1403 Butler Ave. (at the corner of Butler and 14th St.); (912) 786-0209; stingraysontybee.com; $$. This laid-back restaurant/bar offers seafood, live music, and drinks, inside and out. Menu selections include appetizers such as crab-stuffed mushrooms and bacon-wrapped scallops, a wide variety of sandwiches and dinner specials like salmon, mahimahi, and tuna steak as well as traditional seafood dishes like fried shrimp and oysters. To top it off, Sting Ray's is the perfect place to watch one of Tybee's many parades. Hours are weekdays 11 a.m. to 10 p.m. and weekends 11 a.m. "until."

SUNDAE CAFE, 101 US 80; (912) 786-7694; sundaecafe.com; $$–$$$. Several years ago, this former ice cream shop and deli in an unassuming strip center was transformed into one of the island's best lunch and dinner spots. Southern-inspired dishes focus on seafood, steaks, gourmet salads, pasta, and sandwiches. Don't miss the weekday lunch specials such as pot roast and chicken-fried chicken with vegetables on the side. Hours are Mon through Sat 11 a.m. to 3 p.m. and 5 to 9 p.m. Check out Sundae's sister restaurant/upscale sports bar, 80 east gastropub, 725-B 1st St. (912-786-4782).

THE TYBEE ISLAND SOCIAL CLUB, 1331 Butler Ave.; (912) 472-4044; $$. This restaurant/bar describes itself as "surf bungalow-meets-safari-plantation-setting." The menu is Latin inspired with a Southern coastal twist touting organic and locally sourced ingredients. Check out their sister restaurant, Tybee Island Fish Camp, in a renovated 1950s cottage at 106 S. Campbell Ave. (912-662-3477), specializing in a large domestic wine selection, regional seafood, and an "unabashedly delicious bone marrow companion to our house baguette." Hours of the Social Club are

Sun through Thurs 11 a.m. to 10 p.m. and Fri and Sat 11 a.m. to 3 a.m.

SHOPPING

Tybee isn't exactly a shopper's paradise, but you can buy what you need. Beach essentials and tacky souvenirs are easy to come by in a variety of stores clustered around the action. Some places merit more attention, however, and we mention a few of them here.

CHRISTY'S DEPARTMENT STORE, 1-3 Tybrisa St.; (912) 786-4204. Christy's is one of the island's oldest stores and located near the pier. The store sells beach gear, decorative items, clothing, and most everything in between. Call for hours.

DEBBIE BRADY ROBINSON SIGNATURE GALLERY & HALL OF FRAMES, Sundance Square, 1207 US 80; (912) 786-8944; debbiebradyrobinson.com. This shop showcases noted Tybee artist Debbie Brady Robinson who often can be spotted in front of the shop painting canvases or putting her special design on custom furniture. Inside are paintings, furniture, souvenirs, and other unique items. Debbie also offers full-service framing.

HIGH TIDE SURF SHOP, 406 US 80; (912) 783-6556; hightidesurfshop.com. High Tide specializes in surfboards, kiteboards, skimboards, skateboards, surf/skate apparel, wet suits, swimwear, sunglasses, and footwear. Call for hours.

LATITUDE 32, 1213 US 80; (912) 786-9334. This shop carries quality apparel, hats, children's clothing, and loads of other fun stuff.

SEASIDE SISTERS, Sundance Square, 1207 US 80 East; (912) 786-9216; seasidesisterstybee.com. This beach-inspired

gift shop has a collection of art, furnishings, clothing, and decorative items, in addition to a handful of vendors who offer antiques and gently used treasures. Call for hours that vary with the season.

SHOPS AT TYBEE OAKS, 1213 US 80 East. Situated under a canopy of moss-laden live oaks just as you drive onto the island, this cluster of shops includes something for everyone. You'll find clothing, souvenirs, shells, and other items. There is also a pizza place and a coffee shop.

T. S. CHU CO., 6 Tybrisa St.; (912) 786-4561. T. S. Chu emigrated from China in the 1930s and slept in the dunes until he got things going financially. And get them going he did. His early enterprise has grown to a prosperous local retail empire. For the most part, it's convenience stores and gas stations. But the original store remains on Tybee, a sprawling, dimly lit, and unconventional place that sells tourist junk and beach supplies near the door and lightbulbs, hammers, dishpans, and other housewares and hardware farther inside. Call for hours, which vary with the season.

TYBEE MARKET IGA, 1111 Butler Ave.; (912) 786-4601; tybeemarketiga.com. The mark of a dedicated Tybee Islander is a refusal to leave the island unless he or she absolutely has to. That makes Tybee's only grocery store (aside from numerous convenience stores) a godsend. Folks from Savannah have been known to drive to Tybee Market for their quality meats. Hours are 8:30 a.m. to 9 p.m. 7 days a week. Ordering online and grocery delivery are available.

THINGS TO DO

A vacation to Tybee Island should first be filled with lots of time for reading, shuffling about on the beach, kite-flying, fishing, and

Close-up

Hitting the Beach with "Crawfish" Crawford

There is good news for swimmers diving into the ocean off Tybee, according to John "Crawfish" Crawford, a University of Georgia educator and expert on Tybee and its marine life. The 30 to 40 species of sharks lurking in the waters offshore probably aren't that hungry. "We have well-fed sharks here," said Crawford. "The water is full of plenty of food which they would rather eat instead of fooling with something the size of a human being."

Words to live by. Although shark attacks are so rare they are nearly unheard of on Tybee, Crawford says to reduce your risk even further by avoiding swimming during twilight hours when sharks typically feed. Also, don't use a flutter kick—to a shark it could sound like a wounded fish.

Besides sharks, beachgoers might encounter an abundance of other marine life on Tybee, according to Crawford. Some of the more common things you might come across during your day at the beach include:

- **Sandpipers**—These tiny, fleet-footed birds seen running up and down the beach are born and nest in the Arctic tundra. They fly all the way to Tybee just to engage in a little 50-yard beach dash for food.
- **Ghost crabs**—Look near the dune line, and you might see whitish-colored crabs scurrying—then disappearing—into a hole. Besides spending their time digging their hole homes, these crabs serve as beach garbage collectors, picking up parts of dead fish and others things cluttering their front yards.
- **Jellyfish**—Several different species of jellyfish live in our waters. The cannonball variety has a brown rim around the edge, and you can't be stung by them. The sea nettle, which comes out typically in the late summer and has long wispy tentacles, is responsible for the most stings off Tybee. If you get stung, putting meat tenderizer on the sting helps ease the pain, according to Crawford.
- **Ghost shrimp**—If you run across tiny holes just above the low-tide line, you most likely have encountered a ghost shrimp. These tiny shrimp live in a network of burrows that twist and turn in the sand and are only three-fourths of an inch in diameter. Those little brown things you see near the entrance of the hole are their droppings.
- **Sand dollars**—These small disks are actually live animals. Many people mistakenly take them home while they are still alive, Crawford said. If you find a sand dollar on the beach and it is a greenish color on top and reddish on the bottom, it is still alive, so leave it on the beach. A white color indicates that the sand dollar has died.
- **Stingrays**—If you happen to see a stingray while swimming in the surf, don't panic—they aren't aggressive and won't bother you a bit. If you happen to be unfortunate enough to step on a stingray, however, they do consider this an attack and will sting. To avoid such a confrontation, shuffle your feet back and forth while walking in the surf. This gives them enough time to realize you are coming and head in a different direction.
- **Sea turtle nests**—Sea turtles regularly nest on Tybee Island. The city's public works department patrols the beaches for the nests to mark them with wire so people don't run over them. If you do come across a nest, don't disturb it.

of course, dining on the excellent seafood at local restaurants. The South Beach, where the most development (restaurants, shops, entertainment, etc.) and largest crowds are, and North Beach, which is more residential in nature, are your two options for hanging out on the beach. Go south for people watching, north for shelling. You're at South Beach when you park in Tybee's downtown, main-drag Strand area. North Beach parking is across from the lighthouse and behind the museum. At low tide, you can walk from one to the other, but if you miscalculate the incoming tide, it can be a long walk around.

During the season, Tybee's beaches have lifeguards. Hours and days depend on the weather and crowds. The lifeguard stands are clustered near the public parking. Early on, they're only staffed on weekends. Don't take it for granted that there's a lifeguard on duty, and even if there is, they call it a day when the crowd starts to thin. Be careful! Ocean swimming at Tybee Island can be tricky, even for the strong swimmer. Tybee is prone to riptides.

Beach regulations prohibit glass containers or cans. Dogs aren't allowed on the beach, either, and you'll get a ticket if you bring one. The beach is patrolled by officers in shorts and T-shirts, either walking or on all-terrain vehicles.

Vendors on the beach rent canvas rafts, umbrellas, boogie boards, and the like.

FORT PULASKI NATIONAL MONUMENT, US 80 East; (912) 786-5787; nps .org. Explore a 19th-century fort from top to bottom at Fort Pulaski. About 15 miles outside Savannah on the way to Tybee, the fort is remarkably preserved and gives a fascinating glimpse into coastal warfare. The fort was completed in 1847 and considered the ultimate defense system of its day. Audio stations provide information on the fort's pivotal role in the Civil War and how it changed defense strategy worldwide after an attack by Union forces. The 5,600-acre monument also provides picnic areas and nature trails, along with panoramic views of the Atlantic Ocean and scenic salt marshes. Bring your camera—this is one of the area's most photogenic spots. Expect to see abundant wildlife such as white-tailed deer that roam freely on the island, and alligators, turtles, and small marine life that inhabit the moat. There are numerous trails so bring a picnic if you're prone. The fort is open 9 a.m. to 5 p.m. The cost is $5, and the admission fee is good for up to 6 days of visitation. Children age 15 and younger enter free. There are group rates for commercial vehicles: 1–6 passengers, $25.

LAZARETTO CREEK MARINA, US 80 East, just across Lazaretto Creek Bridge; (912) 786-5848, (800) 242-0166; tybeedolphins .com. You'll be thrilled to see wildlife up close on Captain Mike's dolphin tours at Lazaretto Creek Marina. There are also fishing, diving, and sunset cruises. Dolphin tours are $15 per adult and $8 per child (12 and under); offshore fishing ranges from $250 to $850, depending on the length of the trip. Boats are not wheelchair accessible. Tours are conditional based on weather and wind conditions, so it's best to call ahead and confirm.

THE TYBEE ARTS ASSOCIATION, PO Box 2344, 7 Cedarwood Ave.; Tybee Island, GA 31328; (912) 786-5920; tybeearts.org. This nonprofit group is dedicated to developing and promoting arts throughout the area. Besides operating the Lighthouse Gallery near Tybee Lighthouse, the organization holds exhibits and gives art classes for adults and children. Adult classes can include pottery, stained-glass making, and painting, while children's classes include wearable art, make-your-own puppet, sand and beach art, and painting and drawing, among other options. Contact the association for information on classes, art shows, and sales. Stay tuned for current events posted on the organization's website.

Hole-In-One

There's no golf at Tybee. There are no water parks. There is no minigolf course here. The fun lies within your imagination. However, if you're looking for a fun place to take your family that is clean and safe, try the **Island Mini Golf** on US 80 and Walthour Road (912-898-3833; islandminigolf.com). There are bumper go-karts, softball and baseball batting cages, a Moonwalk bounce, a clean and refreshing arcade with snacks and hot dogs, a private party room, and an 18-hole miniature golf course! Hours are Sun through Thurs 11 a.m. to 9 p.m., Sat 11 a.m. to 10 p.m.

TYBEE ISLAND LIVE OAK BRANCH LIBRARY, 405 Butler Ave.; (912) 786-7733. Chances are there aren't too many public libraries around with an ocean view. Granted, you have to have pretty good eyes to see it, but the view is there, along with an impressive entryway sculpture by ironwork artist Ivan Bailey. (Look up!)

Local library regulations are very kind to guests. Here, as elsewhere in Chatham County, nonresidents can buy a temporary library card with full privileges. Some paperbacks and children's books can be borrowed without a card.

TYBEE ISLAND LIGHT AND STATION, 30 Meddin Dr.; (912) 786-5801; tybeelighthouse.org. Throughout history there have actually been four Tybee Island lighthouses. The original was completed in 1736, but it sat too close to the shore and was washed away during a storm. Hurricanes, fires, and even an attack by Union forces during the Civil War led to partial or complete destruction of two other stations. In 1866 the fourth Tybee lighthouse—a combination of old and new—was authorized. It used the lower 65 feet of the 1773 Tybee light as the base, then 94 more feet were stacked on top. The light, a first-order Fresnel lens, was displayed for the first time on October 1, 1867, and it has been there ever since. It is one of only two of the 15 original light stations built in Georgia that is still functioning.

Learn about the history of the lighthouse in the refurbished facilities and take a 154-foot climb to the top for a wonderful view of the area. Hours are 9 a.m. to 5:30 p.m. daily (last ticket sold at 4:30 p.m.) except Tues, when it is closed. Closed for major holidays (St. Patrick's Day, Thanksgiving, Christmas, and New Year's Day). Cost is $9 for adults, $7 for seniors, military, and children ages 6–17; children younger than age 6 get in free. The price includes admission to the Tybee Museum.

i The Tybee Lighthouse was one of five southeastern lighthouses featured on a set of US postage stamps in June 2003.

TYBEE ISLAND MARINE SCIENCE CENTER, 14th Street Parking Lot; (912) 786-5917; tybeemarinescience.org. Learn about Tybee's marine life at the Tybee Island Marine Science Center. Just steps from the sand, the center has aquariums with species indigenous to the area, such as starfish and jellyfish. There is a small library, a touch tank, and displays featuring such things as sharks and shells—always favorites with the kids. Don't expect anything polished or Sea Worldish, but it is informative. Beach walks are one of the most popular programs offered. Folks are invited to stroll the beach to learn about the things that inhabit it. The center staff also throws a seine net into the ocean to see what they might catch. The center is open daily 10 a.m. to 5 p.m. Admission is $4 for all, but kids 4 and under are free.

ℹ Like to collect seashells? According to expert seashell hunters, Tybee's North Beach provides the best bounty.

TYBEE MUSEUM, 30 Meddin Dr.; (912) 786-5801; tybeeisland.com. Besides learning about Tybee's history, visitors to the Tybee Museum get to walk around one of the few remaining structures at the former Fort Screven. Inside Battery Garland, one of the original seven-gun batteries built at the fort, you can learn about hundreds of years of Tybee lore—from the arrival of Native Americans to Tybee's role in the Civil War to the beginning of tourism on the island. Open Wed through Mon 9 a.m. to 5:30 p.m. (although the last ticket is sold at 4:30 p.m.);

closed major holidays (note that St. Patrick's Day is a major holiday in these parts). Admission is $9 for adults; $7 for seniors, active military, and children ages 6–17; children ages 5 and younger get in free. Members of the US Coast Guard are free. The fee includes admission to the Tybee Island Lighthouse just across the street.

TYBEE PIER AND PAVILION, Tybrisa Street. This $2.5-million wooden pier was unveiled in time for the 1996 Summer Olympics, when the yachting events were held in the area. It was built in almost the exact location of the Tybrisa, Tybee's former pier and pavilion that was known for its Big Band concerts before it burned down. Wander out to the end of the pier, and you will witness anglers casting into the ocean to see what they might catch. You can rent fishing poles and bait on the pier, and you can pick up a snack, too. The pier's pavilion, a large wooden platform you cross before heading out over the ocean, is also a popular spot for concerts. Concerts are often free (and even when they aren't, you can sit on the beach and listen in). It's also a good place for a romantic evening stroll without getting your feet wet.

Appendix

LIVING HERE

In this section we feature specific information for residents or those planning to relocate here. Topics include real estate, education, health care, and much more.

RELOCATION & REAL ESTATE

Savannah is a popular relocation destination. Retirees come here, drawn by the weather, the availability of military benefits resources, the golf. Military discharges often opt to stay. Vacationers get hooked on what they see and come back year after year, putting down roots here. And, in a phenomenon we probably couldn't document but which we would vouch for after 30-plus years of anecdotal observation, people who are reared here return to live here, despite the appeals of better-paved career paths, larger cities, and lower humidity. See a Savannah girl marry a beau from college in the Northeast and then strike out for California? Sure. Give her a few years—she and that husband will be back here to raise their kids.

If you are looking to relocate yourself, you want an area that has shown up on relocation radar. It's not that you are looking to follow the rest of the migrating herd—it's just that when you look at an area with a tradition of welcoming in new populations, you find a relocation industry already in place. The banks are all going to have packets welcoming you to the community; everyone from the voter registration folks to the library is going to be versed in helping newcomers; and chances are your kid won't be the only new face to turn up in class this year.

OVERVIEW

When you are starting out on a relocation quest, the first thing you want is information—lots of it. That's what this section is all about.

SAVANNAH AREA CHAMBER OF COMMERCE, 101 E. Bay St.; (912) 644-6400; savannahchamber.com. The chamber can provide you with its standard relocation packet via mail and free of charge. No one ever accused a chamber of being excessively unbiased, but this is still a good starting point. Materials and references will largely be restricted to chamber members, but with a few exceptions that doesn't lead to major omissions. Be sure to stress, when making your request by telephone, that you are looking for relocation info, not just tourist material, since the chamber, through its

Visit Savannah operation, handles tourism materials, too.

SAVANNAH MORNING NEWS, 1375 Chatham Pkwy.; (912) 236-9511; savannah now.com. Don't even think of relocating anywhere without reading the daily newspaper there for a period of time. An online subscription is currently $29 a year. With registration you'll get full access to the website and can also get the "e-edition" which recreates the actual pages—meaning you can see virtual stuff like grocery circulars and other ads of interest to newcomers.

Speaking of news, you might also want to check out Savannah's television stations via their websites. Four of them run local news (we're skipping the small one that doesn't have a news operation). In ratings pecking order, they are WTOC (CBS, wtoc .com), WSAV (NBC, wsav.com), WJCL (ABC, wjcl.com), and WTGS (Fox), which currently has a joint operating agreement with WJCL, although recent corporate shifts mean that's likely to change. The stations are improving their websites constantly, and you can stream the most recent of the newscasts on WJCL and WTOC.

THE BASICS

Consider this section a quick community review. You can read more in our chapters covering the area overview, history, education, and health care.

When you are talking Savannah, you are essentially talking three counties and multiple municipalities. Chatham County (population 251,120 in 2008, spread out over 451 square miles) is the biggest one in the area, and the sixth most populous in the state of Georgia. Savannah is the county seat, but you'll also find incorporated communities to the east and west—Thunderbolt, Tybee Island, Vernonburg, Pooler, Bloomingdale, Garden City.

Effingham and Bryan Counties make up the rest of what statisticians call the Savannah SMSA, or Standard Metropolitan Statistical Area. Both were established rural counties in their own right before becoming bedroom communities for Savannah as well. Effingham's county seat is Springfield, but the SUVs that commute into and out of Savannah are likely coming from Guyton and Rincon, for the most part. Bryan County's seat is Pembroke, but the smaller municipality of Richmond Hill—south of Savannah's Southside—is the town you'll hear of most often.

Other counties—hey, Georgia boasts 159 counties—play a role in the local scene, too. Most prominent is Liberty County (county seat: Hinesville), which is home of Fort Stewart, to which Savannah's Hunter Army Airfield is attached in all but geography.

On the South Carolina side, essentially two counties play in the regional mix—Beaufort County, with its county seat of Beaufort and townships of Hilton Head Island and Bluffton, and Jasper County, home of Ridgeland and Hardeeville.

Hilton Head Island pioneered the concept of planned communities designed for relocating early retirees. As the island has increasingly built up, you'll find similar upscale buildings spilling onto the mainland side, where the address is Bluffton. Next in line for the advent of gated communities will be Jasper County, which currently isn't heavily developed.

A geography review seems in order for those who are relocating from other parts of the country. Not for nothing is this section of South Carolina called the Lowcountry, and the land doesn't get any higher when you cross the Savannah River and hit Georgia. Invest in flood insurance wherever in this region you buy, and carefully evaluate the flood risks of any property you are considering buying. Remember that Savannah and environs all fall within hurricane impact zones. True, the last hurricane to really strike Savannah was David in 1979, and that was sort of a glancing blow. But Hurricane Hugo (1989) and Hurricane Floyd (1999) prompted evacuations before striking elsewhere, and the potential is there every fall.

In fact, put drainage at the top of your list of questions when looking at property. It doesn't take a particularly heavy rainfall to cause localized flooding, if it comes during a high tide when all the drainage ditches (we call them canals) are filled up with tidal water. Paving and development have increased the flood risk and drainage problems in some areas. Investigate thoroughly.

INFRASTRUCTURE BASICS

Next up for review are infrastructure issues.

Electricity in this section of Georgia is provided by Georgia Power, a division of Southern Company. Natural gas is a deregulated industry in Georgia, as of several years ago. The result was a glut of marketers, confusing pricing, and billing fiascoes. Things have shaken out a bit now, but as a new resident you'll find yourself choosing among providers.

By the way, when investigating a new home, review your energy system seriously. The hot, humid summers make good air-conditioning a serious quality-of-life issue. And despite the fact that there may be a palm tree growing outside a house, winters can include some serious cold snaps—and many older homes lack good insulation.

The city of Savannah sells water, sewer, and garbage service to its citizens, and also sells water and sewer services under contract to various developments outside its city limits. In fact, you'll find these services provided by most municipalities. If you wind up in the unincorporated areas of the county—such as the popular Islands area—you may find yourself in a spot served by a private water system, septic tanks, and private garbage contractors. Outside the city of Savannah, you may also encounter areas served by volunteer or combined pro and volunteer fire departments.

Chatham County and Savannah have consolidated their police forces, although there are periodic disputes. The smaller municipalities still maintain their own. All you really need to know is that 911 works countywide.

Comcast Savannah is Savannah's television cable service and offers phone and Internet service as well (comcast.com).

Does your new home involve construction or remodeling? Unless you are from some very isolated portion of the country, you're familiar with the idea and basic process of getting building permits. If your tastes have led you to the Historic District, be aware that the renovation permitting process can be extremely exacting—yes, you may find yourself (or your architect) having to defend the style of door handles you choose.

i As a new homeowner in the region, one of the first services you are going to need is pest control. Mild winters, wet weather, and lots of green spaces all add up to bugs. Most locals make their peace with them outdoors, and wage chemical warfare inside their homes.

SAVANNAH NEIGHBORHOODS

The real estate bubble burst all over the Coastal Empire in 2009. Values have recovered in some areas but not others. What matters is the various neighborhoods seem to have kept their places relative to one another—meaning the priciest real estate is in the Historic District or on the waterfronts, mid-range and upwardly mobile stuff in the still-developing suburbs and municipalities of West Chatham, and bargains are to be had in aging and built-out suburbs on Savannah's Southside and scattered around.

Historic District

The Historic District is a miniature city within a city. Inside the 2.5-square-mile area you will find restaurants, churches, antiques shops, museums, banks, government buildings, art galleries, and even some wildlife—that is, if you count the hundreds of squirrels who call the many squares and parks home. (They'll practically eat out of your hands!)

Of course, there are also the houses. Hundreds of homes painstakingly restored to their original 19th-century splendor fill the area. Within a few steps in the Historic District, you are apt to encounter wrought-iron balconies, brick courtyards, and other architectural delights such as historic downspouts shaped like dolphins that empty water into the street.

In addition to being a neighborhood, this is also a tourist attraction. Be aware that this is, or could become, a drawback of sorts: slow-moving and loud tour buses that the city does not regulate heavily; onstreet parking problems; walking tours that currently are at daggers-drawn with some irate residents; and so on. The charms outweigh the drawbacks, though.

The Historic District is also an area of great diversity. Some of Savannah's wealthiest and oldest families live a door or two away from art students who came to town from California or Ohio or Asia. In the Beach Institute area on the eastern edge of the district, many long-standing African-American families raise their children in homes that have been in the family for generations.

The stock of run-down homes in need of renovation has fallen in the main district, although there are still fixer-uppers in the Victorian District and other historic areas outside the traditional "landmark" Historic District. Don't expect to find anything renovated for less than $250,000, although you may find some bargains in new condos, townhomes, or downtown lofts. The same housing market slowdown that has hit elsewhere in the country began affecting this area, too.

A good dose of "buyer beware" is called for when buying a historic home. Antique mantels are adorable; antique plumbing and wiring are not. If you are not familiar with the mixed blessing that comes with being the keeper of historic architecture, make sure you seek out expert advice about things like lead paint, fire escapes, and the like. And if you plan renovations of your own, any changes visible from the street will be under the watchful eye of the Historic Review Board.

i Residents of the Historic District can apply for inexpensive parking stickers, which allow them to park their vehicles at meters near their homes without getting tickets. Everyone, residents and guests alike, however, needs to watch out for the posted weekly sweeping zone times, when parking is prohibited so the city street sweepers can do their job.

The Victorian District

Just south of the Historic District lies the Victorian District, roughly bounded by Victory Drive, Gwinnett Street, Martin Luther King Jr. Boulevard, and East Broad Street. Here you will find the Victorian ladies of architecture— two- and three-story wooden houses with porches and gothic touches.

There's still renovation work to be done here, and gentrification is an active struggle as well. Homeowners also confront the climate—Savannah's heat and humidity are a challenge to any paint job ever painted. The result is spotty: gorgeous homes next to boarded-up hulks, blocks that look homeless next to blocks that look pristine.

Some of these homes have as neighbors parts of the campus of Savannah College of Art and Design, which has spread beyond its Historic District roots to the Victorian District and even to surrounding industrial neighborhoods.

Starland. Once called "a cozy artists' neighborhood," this southernmost section of the Victorian District had not seen much in the way of restoration until a handful of visionaries began rebuilding the blighted area into a diverse and friendly mix of residence and business. The name comes from an old dairy plant in the area. Now, there are artists galore and it's become one of the city's hippest places to live and work.

Today you'll find the area still fairly early in the regeneration stages, with much of the work done by energetic sweat-investors rather than banks. There's a coffee shop, a dog park, art galleries (including a vet's office that sells art), and an eclectic feel of community.

If you are looking to buy here, come ready to do your own work—the stock of redone housing isn't large yet. But we suspect that to most Starland residents, that's sort of the point.

i **Savannah boasts two glossy magazines, both with high production values.** *Savannah Magazine* **appears six times a year (Jan/Feb, March/April, etc.), plus fall and spring special issues focusing on home decor and design. It also produces** *Savannah Weddings* **twice a year. Find out more at savannahmagazine.com.** *The South* **magazine also appears six times annually, on the opposite every-other-month schedule (Feb/March, April/May, etc.). It offers a slightly more regional focus. Its website is thesouthmag.com.**

Southside/Midtown

Ardsley Park. Ardsley Park is Savannah's original suburb. Laid out in 1911, the development is south of the Historic District and the Victorian District in what Savannahians call Midtown (an elastic term that means different things to different people). Although it was designed as a single residential subdivision, throughout the years it has grown to include a large area loosely bounded by Victory Drive on the north, Columbus Drive on the south, Bull Street on the west, and Waters Avenue on the east. Ardsley Park offers wide, tree-filled streets with many sizes and styles of older homes. Drive around and you will see large four- or five-bedroom mansions with elegant entrances, sunporches, and

several fireplaces selling for several hundred thousand. In other blocks, couples with young children live in very nice Craftsman-style bungalows with big yards. Because the area appeals to such a wide section of the community—from professionals to young families—it is a popular place to buy. In fact, as mentioned before, it is in the midst of the temporary curse of being trendy.

Looking in this neighborhood? Watch for flood-prone areas. Also, don't invest without checking the after-work parking situation. Many of the bungalows either lack garages or carports, or else had them converted to living space—which means competition for street parking in some blocks is downright cutthroat. Columbus, Washington, and 52nd Streets have become fairly heavily traveled east-west routes.

An additional note: Across Waters Avenue and for several blocks behind the city's major Daffin Park is a neighborhood called Parkside, where you'll find much the same types of homes at, at least for the moment, slightly lower prices.

Gordonston. Gordonston is a small, charming neighborhood nestled into Savannah's eastside. It is a popular spot for many local professionals including professors and others working in education.

Bordered by Skidaway Road, Gwinnett Street, and Pennsylvania Avenue, it was developed in the 1920s by the brother of Juliette Gordon Low, the founder of the Girl Scouts, on property that was once part of the family farm. In some ways, it is like a miniature Ardsley Park. Similar to its bigger cousin, throughout the development you will find tree-lined streets filled with a variety of older homes on large properties with front yards and backyards. Home styles include bungalows, cottages, and large mansions, and they tend to be comparable to Ardsley Park.

Windsor Forest. When the city began suburban sprawl in earnest during the 1960s, south was the direction and Windsor Forest was the place. Windsor Forest is now a sprawl of neighborhoods between Savannah's malls that still reflect the look of the '60s, even after all these years. Here are classic American suburbs—ranch-style homes, split-levels, two-car garages, backyard barbecues, and so on. You can find virtually any price range here, even tony marshfront property, but it's a decidedly middle-class enclave gradually giving way to a larger rental presence. Here, you'll find your biggest, most elaborate grocery stores, your movie theaters, and on the nearby commercial arteries, the car dealerships and the fast-food franchises.

Georgetown. Although Georgetown debuted in 1974 on open land most Savannahians consider south of the Southside, you will still find homes going up there. More than 1,600 homes have been built throughout the development, located off the far southern reaches of Abercorn Street on King George Boulevard. There are nine subdivisions in total in the community offering a variety of home styles and prices. There's also a pool and amenities center. Don't buy here without checking out the afternoon commute from Savannah, as this is an infamously congested route—although a flyover now under construction should remedy the situation by 2016 or 2017.

Islands

The Islands area covers a lot of ground. Places such as Dutch Island and Skidaway Island, home of the Landings, are high end and exclusive (we mean that literally: They have gates). Islands such as Wilmington, Whitemarsh, and Talahi are more standard suburbia, and people who don't live there can't tell where one island ends and another begins. Tybee Island, the only one of the islands that actually feels like an island, covers a wide range of incomes and is sort of a world unto itself. (In fact, it has its own chapter in this book.)

Dutch Island. Dutch Island, an exclusive, gated enclave 20 minutes from downtown Savannah, is a popular choice for young professionals or those looking to move up to a larger home. The first neighborhoods on the island opened up in the early 1980s. Today it is home to about 300 families and expected to reach its maximum capacity of 500 homes within the next few years. Spacious homes with pristine lawns and traditional architecture can be found throughout Dutch Island. Home sizes range from 2,400 square feet up to 12,000 square feet, while prices go from $600,000 to "the sky's the limit."

Isle of Hope. This peninsula in southeast Chatham County was an early summer resort for tourists. Situated with the Herb River on the west and the Skidaway River on the east, the community is one of Savannah's most picturesque. Beautiful old cottages with white picket fences and massive oak trees in the front yards overlook the waterways, while newer, typically suburban, homes scatter throughout other neighborhoods. The very old and very new mix together nicely.

There is a small-town feel even though large developments and the hustle of Savannah are just 20 minutes away. Longtime residents live on Isle of Hope as well as young families and professionals. Home prices vary from modest, older two-bedroom bungalows around $200,000 to new three- and four-bedroom homes with all the amenities for $350,000 or more. The beautiful waterfront mansions on Bluff Drive are the stuff dreams are made of, and when one goes on the market, expect a multimillion-dollar price tag.

Long Point. More than 130 new homes have been built since 1992 at this popular Whitemarsh Island development. Conveniently located on Johnny Mercer Boulevard, it puts homeowners a short, 20-minute drive away from downtown or the Southside. Home prices start around $450,000 and climb to great heights for waterfront property and include many amenities like hardwood floors, cathedral ceilings, gourmet kitchens, and more. Styles differ throughout the development from sprawling single-story brick homes with circular drives to two-story stuccos with large front porches. Wide streets circulate through the community, and there is a staffed gate.

The Landings on Skidaway Island. Spend any time in Savannah and no doubt you will hear someone refer to "the Landings." This massive gated community takes up approximately 4,450 acres on Skidaway Island and is considered among Savannah's most prestigious developments. Started in 1972, the Landings is currently home to 6,500 residents from 45 states and 15 foreign countries. Since debuting more than 30 years ago, four phases have been built at the Landings, providing a diversity of architectural styles in a variety of prices ranging from the high $200s-plus to $1 million-plus.

All the homes are on nicely landscaped lots that are often filled with trees, giving the feeling that you're living in the country, not a development with thousands of homes. The Landings' other main selling points include 6 golf courses, designed by such golfing luminaries as Arnold Palmer and Tom Fazio; 34 tennis courts; 2 marinas; and a yacht club. At the Oakridge Fitness Center there is a pool, plus fitness and exercise rooms. At the Franklin Creek Activity Center, there is a pro shop, clubhouse, 25-meter pool with hydro spa, and a snack bar. Membership fees are required to use the various facilities.

Many interested people purchase a lot a few years before retirement in anticipation of eventually building a home. A more recent trend for a community made up so heavily of out-of-state retirees is the interest of affluent families already living in the area. All development at the Landings is closely monitored and must be approved by the Architectural Review Board. A number of restrictive covenants apply.

> **i** There are dozens of neighborhood associations in Savannah. To find out information about a neighborhood group you are interested in, call the city of Savannah's Community Services Department at (912) 651-6520.

West Chatham

Southbridge. Southbridge is a 1,100-acre planned community 8 miles west of the Historic District. Developed by Hall Development of Myrtle Beach, South Carolina, it is the first community of its size to open in West Chatham.

More than 500 families, including a mix of retired residents, young families, and professionals, have moved to Southbridge since its opening in 1987. As its literature explains, Southbridge is "a residential golf community blending Southern tradition with the amenities of a country club." Traditional Southern architecture is the development's hallmark. Drive around the neatly landscaped neighborhoods and you will see classic Georgian- and Federal-style wooden, brick, and stucco homes nestled among trees or along fairways on the golf course. Think comparable to the Landings' mid-range properties, minus the staffed gate. One of the latest additions to the development is Steeple Run, offering three-bedroom town houses of roughly 2,000 square feet.

Golf architect Rees Jones designed Southbridge's 18-hole course, which is rated one of Georgia's 25 best courses by *Golfweek* magazine. The semiprivate Southbridge Golf Club includes a 6,000-square-foot clubhouse with a pro shop, dining room, and lounge. Besides golf, there is the Southbridge Racquet and Swim Club, featuring 12 clay tennis courts, 2 hard courts, a swimming pool, and spa. Membership dues are required to use these facilities.

Godley Station. In the spring of 1999, construction began on the first homes in this planned unit, mixed-use development. It turned into an almost "instant community," with a growing population and adjacent "big-box" retail all well established by 2001. Today it's an example of geometric growth. Remember the old adage about "retail follows rooftops"? This massive tract is near the Savannah/Hilton Head International Airport and just off I-95. As predicted, this has been the major new direction for suburban expansion in Chatham County. The neighborhoods here are heavily pitched to families and have a strong sense of traditional community. The residential section, which lies partly in Savannah and partly in the West Chatham municipality of Pooler, has protective covenants, sidewalks, and community amenities such as a pool and clubhouse.

Westbrook. This new gated community in western Chatham County began home construction in mid-2001. It is part of a larger development known as Savannah Quarters. Westbrook, however, is clearly the upscale part of the new development. This community may be unique because it tore up one designer golf course and put in another. A Robert Cupp course went in first. Then, Medallist Developments assumed full ownership of the development. Golfer Greg Norman is behind Medallist, and it was decided to replace the existing two-year-old course with one of Norman's design.

Other Westside. New residential development is booming around the West Chatham municipalities of Pooler and Bloomingdale. These tend to be smaller subdivisions, not the massive planned developments like those outlined earlier—solid, middle-class homes for folks who are willing to drive a bit to get out of the city. Many of these include starter homes in the $150,000 range. It is here you'll find national homebuilders like Centex and D.R. Horton competing in what was previously pretty much a local-builders environment.

But don't get the idea that these municipalities began with these neighborhoods. These fiercely independent little communities have been around for years, housing the blue-collar workforce for the industries of Chatham County (which are clustered toward the west) and the remnants of the county's agricultural population. If you are looking to buy acreage, this is about your only remaining option in Chatham County, and you're probably too late.

Outside the County

Savannah has developed its own commuter culture as well, with people driving into Savannah from bedroom communities in adjacent Richmond Hill (Bryan County) to the south, and Rincon, Guyton, and Springfield to the west in neighboring Effingham County. Here, you'll find typical suburbia, with its typical advantages and disadvantages. A word of caution: Don't trust anyone's estimate of commuting time. Drive it yourself during peak morning and afternoon traffic times. Development has brought predictable rush-hour traffic problems.

Although Savannah doesn't approach the metropolitan gridlock of larger cities during commuting hours, it still takes time to cover distance. We've heard radio ads cheerfully tout these out-of-county addresses as "20 minutes from Savannah." Remember,

Savannah is a big place, and perhaps whoever timed that trip was in a helicopter. Still, many families find the open spaces, near rural quiet, and a lightning bug population that hasn't succumbed to mosquito spraying to be well worth a daily drive.

It's hard to leave this topic without at least mentioning the Ford Plantation in Bryan County. This literally was the Fords' plantation, as in Henry Ford. The land has been developed into ultraluxury homes designed as second or third homes for the jet set. There's a club, spa, marina, shooting, and other outdoor sports—you name it. Prices are predictably stratospheric.

Hilton Head

They're luxuriant and they're extravagant and many are recognized by stately gated entranceways, classic fountains, and striking landscaping. These are Hilton Head's 11 planned residential communities that cover 65 percent of the island. Some communities are more private than others: A few admit only residents and their guests; others are accessible to vacationers staying at hotels and villas within the communities and to golfers playing on courses that allow public participation.

HILTON HEAD PLANTATION. Hilton Head Plantation is the second-largest planned community on the island, covering 4,000 acres on the northern tip of Hilton Head between Port Royal Sound and Skull Creek, which is part of the Intracoastal Waterway. Within the plantation's borders are 4,400 residential lots, four 18-hole golf courses, a beach fronting on the sound, the Whooping Crane Pond and Cypress Nature Conservancies, the Seabrook Farm garden plots, and tennis courts and swimming pools.

On the Skull Creek side of the plantation are Skull Creek Marina, a deepwater facility with 180 boat slips, the Old Fort Pub restaurant, and Fort Mitchel, a historic site that was a Union gun battery during the Civil War.

INDIGO RUN. Most of the homesites at this 1,775-acre development on the northern portion of Hilton Head Island border one of two 18-hole golf courses: the Golf Club at Indigo Run, a members-only layout designed by Jack Nicklaus and his son, Jack Nicklaus II, and opened in 1996; and the Golden Bear Golf Club, which was designed by Nicklaus's company and can be played by the public (see listing in the Hilton Head chapter). All property owners at Indigo Run are entitled to join Golden Bear, and membership includes access to Sunningdale Park, which has six tennis courts, an Olympic-size pool, a kiddie pool, and a large playground for children. Membership in the golf club is open to owners of homesites and homes in Indigo Run.

LONG COVE CLUB. Established in the early 1980s, Long Cove Club on Hilton Head Island has been recognized as a friendly private community. Small by design, the natural beauty and casual elegance are a true reflection of this community's relaxed and unpretentious Lowcountry lifestyle. There's a championship tennis facility, state-of-the-art marina (with direct access to the Atlantic Ocean and the Intracoastal Waterway), a spacious dog park, community pool and complex, and a nationally acclaimed golf course designed by Pete Dye.

PALMETTO HALL PLANTATION. Palmetto Hall is a strictly residential, golf-oriented community covering 775 acres in the northern portion of the island. Most of the 500 homesites border the fairways of the plantation's two 18-hole golf courses—the Arthur Hills and Robert Cupp Courses—both of which are open to the public. Started by

Greenwood Development Corporation in 1991, Palmetto Hall is now a part of the Heritage Group and offers its residents a 14,000-square-foot clubhouse and an activities center with pools, tennis courts, and a children's playground. Palmetto Hall Plantation is one of the few plantations allowing its 550 members to own private carts for transportation.

The homes here, all of them single-family residences, reflect the style of the Lowcountry with their verandas, dormers, and colorful shutters.

PORT ROYAL PLANTATION. Living on the beach (or having easy access to it) is the main drawing card of this 1,000-acre community in the northeastern corner of the island. There are 2.5 miles of beach stretching along the plantation on the east and southeast—1.5 miles on the Atlantic Ocean and the rest on Port Royal Sound. The eastern side is the site of the actual Hilton Head, the bluff where English sea captain William Hilton looked out on the sound while exploring the region; it's the spot for which the entire island was eventually named. Port Royal was one of the island's first planned communities, and the 920 homes within its gates reflect a wide variety of sizes and styles.

THE SEA PINES RESORT. A Hilton Head architect once called Sea Pines the "daddy rabbit" of planned residential/resort communities. It's an apt description of the largest and oldest of the island's major developments—the first community of its kind in the nation. The Sea Pines Resort covers 5,200 acres on the south end of Hilton Head and was started in 1957. It's the site of the island's first golf course, the Ocean Course, one of three courses in the community, all of which can be played by the public. Sea Pines has nearly 3,500 single-family homes. A total of 530 villas and homes are available for rent by vacationers, and the Inn at Harbour Town provides luxurious accommodations for those seeking a hotel-type setting.

Within the borders of Sea Pines are a 605-acre nature preserve, 5 miles of beach, the ruins of the Stoney-Baynard Plantation, two swimming pools, the Lawton Stables equestrian center, and a beach club that has an open-air grill, an oceanfront bar, a gift shop, live entertainment and dinner nightly in season, and picnic tables. The Sea Pines Resort offers 10,000 square feet of meeting space at the Plantation Club Conference Center, the Harbour Town Clubhouse, and the Harbour Town Conference Center.

SHIPYARD PLANTATION. Shipyard has a mixture of single-family residences, condominiums, time-share units, and commercial developments within its 834 acres. The plantation, in the southeastern part of the island, is the site of more than 1,400 villas grouped in 22 different villa regimes. The Shipyard Golf Club consists of 27 holes on 3 courses open to the public: Brigantine, Clipper, and Galleon (see teh Hilton Head chapter). Residents and guests have other forms of recreation available, particularly tennis and the beach. The Van Der Meer Shipyard Racquet Club boasts 20 championship courts, and the eastern side of the plantation is on the Atlantic Ocean.

SPANISH WELLS. There are some 200 single-family lots at this 350-acre community on the western portion of the island; the houses at Spanish Wells are on lots of at least 1 acre. Spanish Wells is the most secluded of the island's communities; it's at the end of Spanish Wells Road, nearly 3 miles from William Hilton Parkway. The private golf club has a nine-hole course, two tennis courts, and a swimming pool. Many of the homes at Spanish Wells are on Calibogue Sound or Broad Creek, and those on Brahms Point, a narrow finger of land at the southwestern reaches of the community, have views of both bodies of water. The community derives its name from the wells from which Spanish explorers drew fresh water while visiting Hilton Head. Also of historical note is the fact that Spanish Wells is the site of Battery Holbrook, a Civil War gun emplacement.

WEXFORD PLANTATION. Wexford Plantation is one of the island's most glamorous private residential communities. The emphasis is on privacy at Wexford, where rentals are prohibited and admittance is open only to residents, their guests, and prospective home-buyers. This golf and yachting community covers 525 acres near the middle of the island. About a third of the homes are on the plantation's scenic 35.5-acre harbor, which winds through the center of the community and is lock controlled to keep the water calm and at a minimum of 8 feet deep. The harbor, with slips accommodating yachts up to 66 feet long, provides access to Broad Creek. Most of the other homes are on Wexford's 18-hole golf course, a layout by Willard Byrd that's reserved solely for members and their guests and was restored to its original design.

WINDMILL HARBOUR. Designed for boating enthusiasts, Windmill Harbour covers 172 acres in the northwestern portion of Hilton Head. Unlike the island's other planned communities, Windmill Harbour has no golf course, but it does have a 15.5-acre yacht basin with 260 boat slips. The harbor, the site of the South Carolina Yacht Club, has a lock system that keeps tides and currents to a minimum; the lack of movement of water also inhibits the growth of barnacles on the bottom of boats, allowing their owners to save on maintenance costs. The harbor lies on Calibogue Sound, which is part of the Intracoastal Waterway.

Tybee Island

Like the Historic District in Savannah, Tybee has been one of the most popular places to buy real estate in the last few years. The small-town atmosphere, along with its ideal climate and proximity to Savannah, has made this island community attractive as a year-round residence for many.

This interest has led to much development and a few growing pains. After a large hotel went up on the beach, a movement was started to restrict the height of all development on Tybee to avoid a resort full of high-rises. Many residents want to keep the beach community what it is—a small town by the sea.

It's difficult to identify distinct neighborhoods on Tybee. There's basically a mix of old and new all over the island. In some neighborhoods, you might find older beach houses next door to modest, one-story homes. A few doors down there could be two or three new homes or a set of two or three new town houses. Near Fort Screven or North Beach, you will find a few new housing developments that can offer large two- and sometimes three-story homes with ocean views and wraparound porches on fairly large lots. A few streets away there could be a modest home needing quite a lot of work. It's worth noting that streets often don't follow a particular pattern on Tybee; many are dirt roads that zigzag, and in some cases just stop.

Tybee's older beach homes are usually found along Butler Avenue, the city's main thoroughfare, which goes to the southern end of the island. Here the streets follow a grid pattern with the numbered streets increasing the closer you get to downtown. Again, in many blocks, there is a smattering of new homes followed by several older ones. During the last few years, many older homes have been torn down to make room for condos, townhomes, and the like.

Regardless of the area or price range you are considering, there are hundreds of local Realtors ready to help you with your real estate needs.

You might want to touch base with the Savannah Area Board of Realtors (912-354-1513; sav.interealty.com). They won't recommend one member over another, of course, but they can provide information about a member's credentials.

i Wonder why the new homes here (and some of the older ones) are built so high off the ground? It leaves ample room for an open parking area under the house, but the real reason is the building codes that require lifting the finished floor out of the reach of floods.

Apartments

Due to the highly competitive apartment market in Savannah, many of the franchise complexes reflect updated and contemporary settings with incentives like reduced rent to bring in new residents. Many will be found on the Islands and Southside/Midtown. They are clustered in the Islands area because of the local reputation of the schools there (and usually are priced higher there), and on the Southside, in large part, because that is where off-base housing for Hunter Army Airfield tends to concentrate, close to base. The complexes are listed in several free publications offered in racks at area grocery stores.

The Historic District also has a healthy market. Many residents have converted part of their private homes into apartments, and there are also a few apartment buildings to choose from. With the influx of students wanting to live downtown, finding an apartment in this area has become more of a challenge. One of the best ways to find apartments in the Historic District is to check in the *Savannah Morning News*. However, many owners don't bother advertising and simply post a "For Rent" sign on their apartment—a walk or drive around town is a good way to get leads.

You will also find houses for rent in several areas of Savannah, including Southside, Midtown, and the Islands. As the real estate slowdown has made it harder for relocating homeowners to sell their properties, they are putting them into use as rentals. The homes vary from area to area and can include everything from older bungalows to new homes in gated developments. Like apartment rentals, many of the owners simply post a "For Rent" sign or advertise in a local newspaper. Some list their homes with local Realtors.

EDUCATION & CHILD CARE

Savannah and Chatham County offer a wide spectrum of educational opportunities, from excellent public schools to satellite branches of many out-of-state schools and a top-rated technical school. In addition to the forward-looking public school system, there are a variety of private high schools, a technical school, two state universities, and one of the largest art schools in the US.

PUBLIC SCHOOLS

SAVANNAH-CHATHAM COUNTY PUBLIC SCHOOLS, 208 Bull St.; (912) 201-5600; savannah.chatham.k12.ga.us. One of the most attractive incentives in relocating to the state of Georgia and hence, Savannah, is the Hope Scholarship and Grant Program, one of the state's most successful education initiatives. Launched in 1993, the Georgia lottery program resulted in free college education for thousands of Georgia students, a voluntary prekindergarten program for four-year-olds, and new capital construction outlays that result in updated and contemporary new facilities, technical institutes, colleges, and universities. The Savannah-Chatham school system serves more than 34,000 students in prekindergarten through 12th grade. A special purpose local option sales tax has fueled a building and renovation boom in the school system, which offers elementary, middle, pre-K through eighth, high school, and alternative programs. Count in that number charter schools and schools with special focuses and missions. All area schools are accredited by the Southern Association of Colleges and Schools.

Two unique features of the local system are the Massie Heritage Interpretation Center and the Oatland Island Education Center (see our Attractions chapter). Massie, which is at 207 E. Gordon St., is the oldest standing school in Georgia (see the Close-up in this chapter). The school does not hold regular classes, but programs on the history of Georgia are offered. Teachers arrange for their classes to attend programs at Massie. Oatland, at 711 Sandtown Rd., covers 75 acres, and its 1.75-mile Discovery Trail takes visitors through woodlands, past marshes, and to specially constructed habitats of endangered and protected animals of the state—wolves, bison, panthers, and birds of prey among them. There's a re-creation of a colonial settlement and a barnyard where youngsters can get a feel for life on the farm, past and present. The Oatland staff holds several special events throughout the year.

PRIVATE SCHOOLS

Savannah's private high schools provide teenagers and their parents with alternatives to what's offered by the public school system. Many of the private schools are church-related, and most are focused on preparing their students for college.

BENEDICTINE MILITARY SCHOOL, 6502 Seawright Dr.; (912) 644-7000; bcsav .net. This Catholic high school for boys

Close-up

Massie School

Supporters of Massie School, the oldest operating public school in Georgia, celebrated the facility's 150th birthday in 2006. A public school from 1856 to 1974, Massie continues to serve as a focal point of education in its role as the Massie Heritage Center, a museum for teaching Savannah's history to students and adults. Housed in three Greek Revival–style buildings on Calhoun Square, Massie offers visitors a look at a 19th-century classroom and exhibits involving the history of the school, Savannah's city plan, the preservation of the city, its architectural treasures, American Indians in coastal Georgia, and the legacy of Savannahian W. W. Law, who was a civil rights leader, historian, and preservationist.

Massie began its long life as Massie Common School House in a single building designed by architect John S. Norris, who drew the plans for many of Savannah's important structures. A western annex was added in 1872, and the eastern annex was built 14 years later. The school was listed on the National Register of Historic Places in 1977, the year it began serving as an education and resource center under the aegis of the Savannah-Chatham County Public Schools.

From its location at 207 E. Gordon St., the center purports to offer local residents and visitors alike "the best orientation to Savannah's built environment." A highlight of this experience is a visit to the City Plan Room, which holds the only three-dimensional model of the city's Historic District. It's a huge layout that affords a bird's-eye view of the downtown. The room also contains maps and photographs describing the development and preservation of the city plan set forth in the 1700s by Savannah's founder, James Edward Oglethorpe. There's more to be learned about Savannah's buildings and efforts to preserve them via exhibits involving the city's classical architecture and the beginnings of the preservation movement—displays that make use of photos and artifacts.

Massie is open Mon through Sat 10 a.m. until 4 p.m. Admission starts at $7 for adults. Visit the website at massieschool.com.

dates back to 1902, when it was founded on Bull and 32nd streets as Benedictine College. Having sons become "BC boys" is a prestigious tradition in many Savannah families, a circumstance that has led this military school for 9th through 12th graders to have an extremely faithful and active group of alumni. Sixty percent of those who attend the school are Catholic, but the remainder of the student body is as diverse as the faculty, which is composed of Benedictine priests and monks, laymen and laywomen, and military retirees. Enrollment is about 400.

Benedictine is a college-prep school, and 95 percent of graduates attend college.

The school is housed in large, contemporary-style buildings on 100 acres in the Southside. Junior ROTC classes are mandatory only for freshmen and sophomores and optional for juniors and seniors.

BIBLE BAPTIST SCHOOL, 4700 Skidaway Rd.; (912) 352-3067; bbsav.org. The administration and faculty of Bible Baptist seek to educate the whole child while emphasizing the spiritual side of students' development. The Bible is taught in every class of this traditional Christian school, which has an enrollment of 380 students in prekindergarten through high school. The coed, college-prep school is a mission of Bible Baptist Church, and it's located on a 19-acre church-school complex that includes a football stadium, a lighted baseball field, and a gymnasium with two full basketball courts. Although the school is open to students of all faiths, the teaching of Christian values is stressed.

The school is a member of the Georgia Christian Athletic Association and Georgia Association of Christian Schools.

CALVARY DAY SCHOOL, 4625 Waters Ave.; (912) 351-2299; calvarydayschool .com. This coed school in Savannah's Midtown is a ministry of Calvary in Savannah and open to students of all faiths and creeds. The school and church occupy 22 acres at Waters Avenue and 63rd Street. Calvary, now provides Christian-based education to more than 900 students in prekindergarten through 12th grade.

According to school officials, academics are blended with a strong program of athletics and other activities to help students evolve into well-rounded citizens. The curriculum is college prep.

The school has its own football stadium and track, a complex named M. C. Anderson Field. Cavalry offers before- and after-school programs for students prekindergarten through sixth grades.

i Thinking about homeschooling your child? You must first register with the state. You can find support for your homeschooling efforts in Savannah by meeting with members of Family Education for Christ (fefonline.com), which can be reached by calling (912) 355-2722. This group schedules special activities for homeschooled students. Another organization, the Kingdom Builders Co-op (kingdombuilderscoop .com), offers small classes for homeschoolers in a variety of subjects.

MEMORIAL DAY SCHOOL, 6500 Habersham St.; (912) 352-4535; memorial dayschool.com. Established in 1971 by a Baptist congregation, this college preparatory school focuses on equipping each of its students for the diverse challenges and opportunities of higher education and for responsible citizenship. With a fully degreed faculty and a schoolwide pupil-teacher ratio of 12 to 1, Memorial provides more than 300 students with wireless laptop computer technology, software, and a variety of current media resources. Before- and after-school programs include remedial and enrichment activities for students through the age of 10, and there's a fully licensed day-care program for children 6 weeks to 4 years old. The school offers extracurricular activities that encourage participation in academic competitive events and athletic programs.

ST. ANDREW'S SCHOOL, 601 Penn Waller Rd.; (912) 897-4941; saintschool .com. St. Andrew's includes classes for prekindergarten through high school. About 500 students are enrolled at the coed, nonsectarian, college-prep school, which is on 28 tree-filled acres on Wilmington Island.

Virtually all graduates attend college. A series of seminars, multiple counseling sessions, and school-arranged tours of various colleges assist students in making their postsecondary decisions. Limited need-based financial aid is available for qualifying families. St. Andrew's offers a broad range of extracurricular activities, including participation in athletics, with St. Andrew's competing on the varsity level in the South Carolina Independent School Association because of its proximity to similar-size schools in the Palmetto State. The school's fine-arts programs are extensive.

ST. VINCENT'S ACADEMY, 207 E. Liberty St.; (912) 236-5508; svaga.net. St. Vincent's—a Catholic, college preparatory school for girls—has been owned by the Sisters of Mercy since 1845 and is the only private high school in the Historic District. The three main buildings of the school cover a city block on the south side of Liberty Street between Abercorn and Lincoln Streets, and St. Vincent's also includes the Walsh Hall gymnasium on Harris Street and the Peg F. Dressel Library at Liberty and Lincoln. Although the Sisters of Mercy still operate the school, the majority of the faculty consists of professional lay teachers.

St. Vincent's teaches grades 9 through 12. About two-thirds of the school's 350 students are Catholic, but St. Vincent's is open to all young women regardless of creed, race, or socioeconomic status. There is a long tradition of graduates sending their daughters and granddaughters to their alma mater, up to the fourth and fifth generations. St. Vincent's offers an extensive program in visual arts, and the school's chorus is known throughout Savannah. St. Vincent's competes in eight varsity sports: volleyball, softball, basketball, tennis, track, soccer, riflery, and swimming.

SAVANNAH CHRISTIAN PREPARATORY SCHOOL, 1599 Chatham Pkwy.; (912) 234-1653; savcps.com. Savannah Christian is an independent, nondenominational Christian school for students in prekindergarten through 12th grade. The school's staff says its college prep curriculum produces a college placement rate of 100 percent.

Savannah Christian maintains two campuses. The 254-acre Chatham Parkway campus hosts nearly 1,000 lower- and upper-school students and 160 day-care /preschool students. Facilities include 13 buildings with classrooms, labs, media centers, a gym, and a cafeteria; an outdoor pool;

a track; five athletic fields; three playgrounds; and E.D.E.N. (Ecological Diversity for Educational Networking), a 125-acre outdoor learning center. A 14-acre campus on eastern DeRenne Avenue is home to more than 500 lower- and middle-school students, and facilities there include four buildings with classrooms, labs, media centers, a cafeteria, and two gyms.

Chatham Academy

Chatham Academy, a private school for students in grades 1 through 12, offers a full-day program of instruction for children with specific learning disabilities and attention deficit disorders. The school, located at Royce Learning Center at 4 Oglethorpe Professional Blvd., serves children of at least average intelligence who have been unable to function successfully in a traditional classroom. Chatham Academy provides a low student-teacher ratio and addresses the academic, social, and emotional needs of its students in classes grouped according to age and academic functioning level. You can contact the school by calling (912) 354-4047.

SAVANNAH COUNTRY DAY SCHOOL, 824 Stillwood Dr.; (912) 925-8800; savcds .org. Savannah Country Day School is the most expensive of the county's private schools and has an exclusively college prep emphasis that begins well before the high school years. It offers preschool, lower, middle, and high school. Offerings at the high school level include an extensive Advanced Placement curriculum. A broad range of athletics and extracurricular activities is offered, with the middle and upper schools fielding more than 40 sports teams. The school has 2 libraries with more than 25,000 volumes and 85 online services, 4 computer labs with 350 networked computers, 4 music and art studios, a fine-arts center, 3 gymnasiums, and a football stadium.

The Country Day campus is on 65 wooded acres tucked away in the Windsor Forest subdivision on the Southside

TECHNICAL SCHOOLS

SAVANNAH TECHNICAL COLLEGE, 5717 White Bluff Rd.; (912) 443-5700; savannah tech.edu. Savannah Tech offers credit, non-credit, and specialized industry services and training. Credit offerings include technical certificates of credit, diploma programs, and associate's degree programs in allied health, business, and industrial technology. Articulated classes transfer to other Georgia public colleges and universities. The school has more than 50 different credit programs, ranging from one-quarter programs in areas such as automotive technology and surgical technology to marketing and computer information systems. Some 4,000 students attend Savannah Tech.

The school serves four counties—Chatham, Bryan, Effingham, and Liberty. With the opening of the Army Education Center on Fort Stewart, the college has a presence on-post to serve military families with the necessary skills and education. The Liberty Campus continues to serve the educational needs of the community with programs in nursing, early childhood education, computers, and technology. The Crossroads Technology Campus in West Chatham, a key element in the development of a high-tech corridor along I-95, is a catalyst for regional business development.

COLLEGES AND UNIVERSITIES

ARMSTRONG STATE UNIVERSITY, 11935 Abercorn St.; (912) 927-5277, (800) 633-2349; armstrong.edu. Armstrong provides more than 75 academic programs through its College of Arts and Sciences, College of Education, College of Health Professions, School of Computing, and School of Graduate Studies. The university's teacher education program has gained state and national recognition, and its economics, computer science, and chemistry programs are also particularly strong. The College of Health Professions is the regional health-professions education center for southeast Georgia. Among master's degrees are those offered in history, criminal justice, liberal and professional studies, nursing, education, public health, sports medicine, and physical therapy. Armstrong has an abundance of online, evening, and weekend classes.

More than 7,000 students, including 810 graduate students, attend the school. They are taught by almost 500 professors. Dormitories are available. The school is situated in the Southside on 268 acres in an arboretum setting.

The school fields NCAA Division II teams in men's basketball, baseball, tennis, and golf and in women's basketball, fast-pitch softball, volleyball, soccer, golf, and tennis.

SAVANNAH COLLEGE OF ART AND DESIGN (SCAD), 342 Bull St.; (912) 525-5100, (800) 869-7223; scad.edu. The Savannah College of Art and Design has grown tremendously since its founding in 1979 with one building and 71 students. Today SCAD is the largest art school in the country with its enrollment of more than 7,000 students. The college has almost 60 buildings (and seemingly constantly buying more) spread throughout the Historic and Victorian Districts, many of them of historic

Professional Schools

Savannah is home to a four-year medical school, Mercer University's School of Medicine, Savannah campus, with an enrollment of 160 students expected to expand to 240 within a few years. The medical school occupies quarters on the campus of Memorial University Medical Center (MUMC). MUMC also offers graduate medical education with residency programs in surgery, radiology, family medicine, internal medicine, OB/GYN, and pharmacy. Third- and fourth-year students from the GRU's Medical College of Georgia in Augusta also rotate through the facilities at St. Joseph's/Candler.

Savannah Law School opened in 2012 as a branch of Atlanta's John Marshall Law School. It anticipates graduating its first class in the spring of 2015. The school has gained the American Bar Association's recognition as an approved branch of the fully approved John Marshall Law School.

significance and beautifully renovated by the school.

The college offers bachelor's degrees in fine and performing arts and master's degrees in arts, urban design, fine arts, and architecture. Among its 30-plus fields of study are historic preservation, interior design, screenwriting, painting, photography, furniture design, and production design. Programs involving computer art and graphic design attract scads of students. Although founded and headquartered in Savannah, SCAD also has campus facilities in Atlanta, France, and Hong Kong.

SAVANNAH STATE UNIVERSITY, 3219 College St., Thunderbolt; (912) 356-2186; savannahstate.edu. Savannah State University is the oldest public historically African-American university in Georgia. The university enrolled 4,915 students in its fall semester in 2014. Those students were pursuing bachelor's or master's degrees in the university's three colleges (Sciences and Technology, Business Administration, and Liberal Arts and Social Sciences) and its newest entity, the School for Teacher Education. SSU's waterfront location makes it an ideal site for its marine sciences program,

complete with its own research vessel. Situated on some 200 acres of prime marshfront property by the small municipality of Thunderbolt (between Savannah and the beach at Tybee Island), the campus is a mix of historic and modern structures.

Savannah State has a full-scale athletic program and competes intercollegiately in football, baseball, men's and women's track and field, men's and women's basketball, and women's tennis, volleyball, and cross-country.

SOUTH UNIVERSITY, 709 Mall Blvd.; (912) 691-6000; southuniversity.edu. South University has grown from its humble beginnings as a two-year business college into a four-year institution offering degrees ranging from associate and bachelor's to master's and doctorates. Through its School of Business, School of Health Professions, School of Pharmacy, and a diverse offering of online programs, students can now pursue a wide variety of majors in the classroom, online, or through a combination of both.

The school dates from 1899, when it was founded as a practical business college. The university was formerly located in downtown Savannah but moved to its current location on Mall Boulevard to accommodate the significant growth in students. Today, the campus covers more than 10 acres and features complete wireless computer access, student lounges, state-of-the-art classrooms and labs, and a 47-foot-high clock and bell tower that marks the center of campus.

The Hope Scholarship Program

There's Hope for Georgia residents entering their first year at the state's colleges and universities. The Hope Scholarship pays tuition, some fees, and a textbook stipend to students attending a state school who have earned a B average in high school. B students attending eligible private colleges in Georgia can receive Hope tuition grants, too. Funding formulas can be complex, so learn more at gacollege411.org. Students can renew these scholarships in their sophomore, junior, and senior years by maintaining a 3.0 grade-point average. Hope is funded by the Georgia Lottery for Education. For more information on the Hope program, call (800) 546-HOPE.

CHILD CARE

The state of Georgia regulates the businesses of people who provide care for more than two children at a time. To comply with state law, a person who provides care for up to six children in his or her home—officially called a family day-care home—must be registered with Bright from the Start: Georgia Department of Early Care and Learning.

Persons operating businesses caring for more than six children must obtain licenses. Such businesses fall within two categories: group day-care homes, which provide supervision and care for 7 to 18 children either in a home or another location, and day-care centers, which provide care and supervision for 19 or more children. To be certified or licensed, the operator of a child-care business must be at least 21 years old, have a high school or general equivalency diploma, and pass criminal background and fingerprinting checks. They must have completed training in first aid and in infant and child cardiopulmonary resuscitation, and they must annually undergo 10 hours of continuing education in health and safety and child development.

When you're shopping for child care, make sure the provider you're dealing with is registered with or licensed by the state. Take a good look at the facility you're visiting: Ascertain that the inspection data on the fire extinguisher is current, that the smoke alarm and telephone operate properly, and that rooms are in good repair, well lit, and spacious. Check to see if instructions involving fire drills and other emergency procedures are posted. Ask about the program offered—it should provide age-appropriate toys and activities that encourage children to use their five senses.

HEALTH CARE

According to historians Preston Russell and Barbara Hines, the city's "first civic hero" was a physician, Dr. Samuel Nunes Ribeiro, who was among a boatload of Portuguese Jews who came to the town about five months after Savannah was settled. Georgia's founder, James Oglethorpe, credited Nunez, as he became known, with saving the colonists from the fevers that had killed several of them, including the only other doctor, William Cox.

The city was the site of Georgia's first hospital, a facility incorporated in 1808, and since the mid-1950s, Savannah has been served by three large hospitals, two of which merged into a single health-care system in the spring of 1997. The other hospital, Memorial University Medical Center, is the regional tertiary medical center, a circumstance that draws many medical specialists to the area.

HOSPITALS

MEMORIAL UNIVERSITY MEDICAL CENTER, 4700 Waters Ave.; (912) 350-8000; memorialhealth.com. This 654-bed academic medical center provides the region's only Level 1 trauma center and its only Love 3 neonatal intensive care nursery, the highest level of care available for the sickest and smallest newborns. It is home for The Children's Hospital, the Curtis and Elizabeth Anderson Cancer Institute, a newly expanded Heart & Vascular Institute, and an array of facilities to cover women's and obstetrics services, orthopedics, behavioral medicine, bariatrics, and general surgery and medical services. Memorial operates multiple graduate medical education programs and serves as the Savannah campus for Mercer University's School of Medicine.

Memorial opened in 1955 as a 300-bed general hospital. As a regional referral center, it now ranks in size among the top 5 percent of hospitals in the US.

St. Joseph's/Candler Health System

This faith-based (Catholic) health-care system was created in April 1997 as the result of the merger of Savannah's two oldest hospitals, St. Joseph's on the Southside and Candler in Midtown. Both facilities are general hospitals with a wide array of services, including emergency departments, but the health system divides the major specialties between the two campuses.

ST. JOSEPH'S HOSPITAL, 11705 Mercy Blvd.; (912) 819-4100; sjchs.org. This 330-bed hospital underwent a massive face-lift and renovation in 2014. This general acute-care hospital specializes in orthopedics, cardiovascular disease, and neurology. It dates from 1875 when the Sisters of Mercy of the Roman Catholic Church took over operation of the Forest City Marine Hospital, a facility in downtown Savannah that specialized in the treatment of sick seamen. A year later the operation was moved to more spacious facilities at Taylor and Habersham Streets and was renamed St. Joseph's Infirmary. It was named St. Joseph's Hospital in 1901 and expanded several times before a new facility was built on the Southside in 1970.

CANDLER HOSPITAL, 5353 Reynolds St.; (912) 692-6000; sjchs.org. The parent health system bases its women's and children's services, oncology, digestive, and pulmonary services at this 384-bed hospital. The Nancy N. and J.C. Lewis Cancer and Research Pavilion, St. Joseph's/Candler's oncology center, is adjacent to Candler's campus.

One of the longest continually operating hospitals in the US and the first in Georgia, Candler was founded in 1805 and chartered in 1808 as the Savannah Poor House and Hospital. It picked up the Candler name in honor of Warren A. Candler, a Methodist bishop, and went through a variety of other name changes over its history. Along the way, it absorbed the Telfair Hospital, retaining the Telfair name for its women's services and obstetrics unit.

WALK-IN CLINICS

Savannah has had a growth spurt of immediate care or urgent care facilities where you can get medical treatment for accidents and illnesses which need to be addressed but are short of life- and limb-threatening emergencies. You can also get many routine services, like immunizations and sports physicals, at these businesses. What follows is a partial list. Because the hours change as often as quarterly at these businesses, the list is addresses and phone numbers only. These facilities are in addition to the emergency rooms at the three local hospitals.

IMMEDIATE MED, 10410 Abercorn St.; (912) 927-6832

MEMORIAL HEALTH/APPLECARE URGENT CARE, Savannah Mall, 14089 Abercorn Street; (912) 350-2121

MEMORIAL HEALTH URGENT CARE, Pooler, 110 Medical Park; (912) 748-1515

SOUTHCOAST WEEKEND CARE CENTER, 1326 Eisenhower Dr., Bldg. 1; (912) 354-5543

SOUTHERN URGENT CARE (two locations), 4714 US 80 East, Ste. H-1, (912) 898-2227, and 10 Whitaker St., (912) 401-0682

ST. JOSEPH'S/CANDLER IMMEDIATE CARE (three Chatham County locations, plus outlying counties), 361 Commercial Dr. (at Eisenhower Drive), (912) 355-6221; 4704 August Rd., Garden City, (912) 966-2366; and 107 Canal Street, Pooler, (912) 450-1945

COMPLEMENTARY MEDICINE

Although it's nowhere near a hotbed of complementary medicine, Savannah shows signs of beginning to catch on to this style of healing. More than two decades ago, at least one physician in town was practicing nutritional medicine, but an awareness of and growth in complementary medicine took shape in the 1990s. Now there are a handful of full-fledged acupuncturists available and several medical doctors learning acupuncture techniques. You can avail yourself of the services of a slew of chiropractors, and there are also practitioners of herbal medicine, massage therapy, aromatherapy, and shiatsu (Japanese pressure-point massage).

If you're looking for practitioners of complementary medicine, a good place to start is the Brighter Day (1102 Bull St.; 912-236-4703) natural foods and organic produce store at Bull and Park Streets. Owners Peter and Janie Brodhead don't make recommendations pertaining to practitioners, but they do maintain a "community bulletin board" that might steer you in the right direction.

RETIREMENT

Savannah's a retiree's dream place to settle. Recreational opportunities for the active retiree abound, from the opportunity to play golf virtually year-round on a variety of courses to boating and sailing around the abundant islands that feed into the city, which are attractive, plentiful, and challenging enough to have landed the city Olympic venue status. Social opportunities are plentiful also, with a variety of organizations tailoring their offerings strictly to older members. Those who are eager to explore new educational horizons have the resources of area universities and their related programs.

Services for the changing needs of an elderly population are in place in Savannah, and they are growing in scope as the demand increases. Health-care options are first class, and there are two cancer centers in the middle of the city. If you have family members who are likely to need assistance with household chores or daily supervision because of Alzheimer's disease, programs are available to help both them and you. Expanded transportation, meal, and utility programs have been established to serve the elderly who need additional help.

SENIOR HOUSING OPTIONS

Savannah, like almost any other American city, has its full complement of nursing homes. As baby boomers and their parents age, however, the trend across the country includes residential options that provide a degree of support while stopping well short of the custodial/medical role of the classic nursing home. Some may be apartment complexes catering to older residents, while others offer a full "continuum of care" program where residents live independently in a complex's houses or apartments and, as their needs increase, move on to the complex's assisted-living quarters or on-site nursing home (usually marketed under more attractive terms, such as "skilled-nursing facility"). The personal-care home, which closely approaches the nursing home, is another in this new breed of senior housing options.

The broader spectrum of options began cropping up in Savannah about 20 years ago. This has been a real growth industry in the past few years here, but only recently did the upper end of the range—a full-scale continuing-care retirement community (CCRC) complete with capital investment requirements—launch here.

These types of housing options tend to fall at the extremes of the income range, with provisions for the lowest-income seniors in public-housing high-rises on one end and luxurious private quarters with amenities and prices to match on the other, with not much middle ground.

For the purposes of this book, we selected a few of the more luxurious and pricey options for further discussion: one because it is the newest and plushest of the lot, reflecting a concept familiar to people relocating here from larger population centers; another because it pioneered such options here and has proven to be a popular choice for middle-class and higher incomes; and one because it provides more affordable options while maintaining lots of amenities and resident choices.

MAGNOLIA MANOR ON THE COAST, 141 Timber Trail, Richmond Hill; (912) 756-4300; magnoliamanor.com. This apartment complex for seniors emphasizes independence. There are 120 apartments in the three-story complex, which opened in 1990. The dining room provides a mid-day meal that is designed to be the major meal of the day. Amenities include a full schedule of classes and activities, and the property includes a lakeside walking trail and other fitness options. A limited number of assisted-living units are available. It is affiliated with the Methodist church and offers a chapel and variety of spiritual activities, but it is nondenominational and sets no religious requirements for eligibility. (Richmond Hill is a bedroom community just outside Savannah's Chatham County.)

THE MARSHES OF SKIDAWAY, 50 Diamond Causeway; (912) 598-5030, (800) 889-6238; marshesofskidaway.com. This CCRC shares a socioeconomic rung with the Landings, Chatham County's first gated, golf course–oriented community, although there is no formal connection beyond the fact that the two developments are neighbors on Skidaway Island. Residents buy a residential agreement in various designs of free-standing homes, duplexes, or apartments. When residents die or relocate, the bulk of the investment (given certain conditions) is returned to the resident or estate. The facility offers assisted-living options and a nursing home. A set monthly fee buys residents a broad array of amenities, including

dining privileges in one of four dining rooms, maintenance, utilities, spa and pool access, scheduled activities, and more.

i Savannah's movie theaters offer discount ticket prices to senior citizens.

SAVANNAH SQUARE RETIREMENT COMMUNITY, 1 Savannah Square Dr.; (912) 927-7550; savannahsquare.net. This facility began offering independent-living, assisted-living, and skilled-nursing housing options in 1990. Amenities include communal dining, transportation, security, a library, a variety of community spaces, and other services. The facility covers a total of 15 acres and, between its apartments and cottages, incorporates 200 housing units.

SUMMER BREEZE, 351 Wilmington Island Rd.; (912) 228-4473; kapdev.com. This assisted living home offers private cottages and spacious studio-type housing for senior citizens, with an on-site beauty salon, transportation to medical visits and shopping, a full cafeteria with first-class meals, and a setting that is on the skirts of one of Savannah's most picturesque country clubs.

SENIOR SERVICES

RETIREMENT SERVICES OFFICE THIRD INFANTRY DIVISION (MECH.), 368 Hase Rd.; Fort Stewart; (912) 767-3326. We've found that military retirees are well versed on the benefits they carry into retirement. They probably don't need a reminder that they retain shopping privileges at post exchanges and commissaries, and that there are active posts in Savannah for all the various military organizations. But those moving into or passing through the area might be pleased to know the extent of services available in the region, thanks to the major military presence here.

Golden Age & Other Senior Centers

Golden Age Centers and Community Centers are daily gathering places that provide active senior citizens with an opportunity to participate in classes and other events. Lunches are served. The centers operated by the city of Savannah are known as Golden Age Centers. Senior Citizens, Inc. operates three additional centers in arrangements with the municipalities of Garden City, Port Wentworth, and Thunderbolt. Pooler has its own center. All offer very similar programs.

The following is an alphabetical listing of the **Golden Age Centers** (all of them are area code 912): **Cunningham Center,** 121 E. 36th St. (651-6779); **Cuyler Center,** 812 W. 36th St. (651-6780); **Frazier Center,** 805 May St. (233-4796); **Grant Center,** 1310 Richard St. (651-6785); **Savannah Gardens Center,** 2500 Elgin St. (651-6775); **Stillwell Towers Center,** 5100 Waters Ave. (351-3855); **Stubbs Towers Center,** 1301 Bee Rd. (651-6776); **Wimberly Center,** 121 W. 37th St. (651-6778); and **Windsor Forest Center,** 303 Briarcliff Circle (921-2104).

The three nearby community centers operated by **Senior Citizens, Inc.** include the **Garden City Center,** 100 Main St., Garden City (966-7791); the **Port Wentworth Center,** 100 Aberfeldy St., Port Wentworth (964-5411); and the **Thunderbolt Center,** 3236 Russell St., Thunderbolt (352-4846). The Pooler Center is at 100 W. Collins St., Pooler (964-5411).

Hunter Army Airfield in Savannah is a subinstallation of Fort Stewart, which is about 40 miles southeast of the city. Some 4,300 soldiers are assigned to Hunter, and 16,000 are based at 279,000-acre Fort Stewart, the largest military installation east of the Mississippi. With that many personnel, you've got recreation facilities, and retirees have access to the Morale, Welfare, and Recreation programs at these installations. Although it is unlikely that many retirees are interested in the concerts staged for young soldiers, they may well want to know about the golf courses, skeet shooting, movie theaters, and other activities and facilities at the two military reservations. Because it is far larger, many of these will be found at Fort Stewart in Hinesville, which is an accessible commute.

On the more serious side of things, Tuttle Army Health Clinic serves Hunter for primary and ambulatory care, and the larger, full-service Wynn Army Community Hospital is at Fort Stewart. The office listed at the head of this entry is largely concerned with such major tasks as straightening out retirement check problems or arranging veteran burials at sea, but personnel there can also provide information on other retiree services.

SENIOR CITIZENS, INC., 3025 Bull St.; (912) 236-0363; seniorcitizens-inc.org. Think of this nonprofit organization as a clearinghouse for senior services. Social and educational opportunities, as well as discounts provided by various merchants, are the primary benefits available to the younger segment of members. The range of services (some on a fee basis, others free or on sliding scales) runs all the way to home-delivered meals and utility assistance—whatever it takes to keep even frail and very low-income seniors independent as long as possible. The Meals on Wheels program, which delivers hot meals to housebound seniors, is excellent and affordable. Call the center for more information.

Senior Citizens derives much of its funding from federal grants, foundation donations, and personal bequests. It is also a participating member in the United Way of the Coastal Empire.

i **The Live Oak Public Library offers records and cassettes of print items to those with vision problems and can also arrange to deliver items to homebound patrons. Call (912) 652-3600 for more information.**

HOSPITAL-SPONSORED CLUBS

Both of Savannah's hospital systems offer special clubs to senior citizens (defined, for these purposes, as ages 55 and up), focusing not only on health-care and wellness activities but also on education and social opportunities. Each charges a nominal annual fee (currently $15).

GENERATIONONE, 1100 Eisenhower Dr.; (912) 350-7587. This club, sponsored by Memorial University Medical Center, offers health fairs and screenings, a member discount program, and visits to members hospitalized at Memorial. Classes in such areas as arts and crafts, line dancing, and bridge are scheduled, along with Senior Net computer classes and Internet access. Seminars are offered on health and retirement issues, healthy aging, and driver's safety. This group also has an active ongoing arrangement with a group-tour company.

SMARTSENIOR, No. 8 Medical Arts Center; (912) 352-4405. This program of St. Joseph's/Candler Health System provides health seminars, educational programs, medical screenings, and visits to members hospitalized at either St. Joseph's Hospital or Candler Hospital. That may sound a bit stodgy, but it isn't—much of this group's activity is geared toward active retirees. There's a travel club that has gone from the Bahamas to Canada and points in between, ranging from two-week excursions to overnighters to catch an Atlanta Braves game. Activities scheduled throughout the year include tours of local industry, arts and crafts classes, and line dance lessons, for example.

INDEX

INDEX